Sales
Promotion
Management

Sales Promotion Management

Don E. Schultz

William A. Robinson

NTC Business Books
a division of National Textbook Company • Lincolnwood Illinois U.S.A.

1986 Printing

Published by NTC Business Books, an imprint of
National Textbook Company, 4255 West Touhy Avenue,
Lincolnwood, Illinois 60646-1975.
Manufactured in the United States of America.
Library of Congress Catalog Card Number: 82-70974

67890 RD 987654321

Contents

Figures

Tables

PART I

UNDERSTANDING SALES PROMOTION

1

Just What Is Sales Promotion?

If you are a sales promotion veteran, you undoubtedly will recognize the question, "I know you are in sales promotion, but what exactly do you do?" If you are new to the industry and haven't been asked that question, you probably will. It offers a clue to the problems the industry faces. Many people realize that there is a specific, distinct activity called sales promotion, but they don't know exactly what it is or they confuse it with other marketing activities. Because of this, we'll start with a look at the entire field of sales promotion. We'll see how it fits into the marketing scheme, outline the definitions used in this text, describe how the sales promotion business is organized, and take a look at how various types of sales promotion departments and service groups operate. Later on, we will look at the different types of sales promotion and their applications. We will examine in detail just what sales promotion can—and can't—do to generate sales and profits.

The Growth of the Sales Promotion Industry

Because sales promotion is growing and changing so rapidly and embraces so many different activities, it's not surprising that today U.S. manufacturers and marketers invest as much or more in sales promotion as they do in measurable advertising. Unfortunately, there is no official, recognized source of information on sales promotion investments in the U.S. However, by using figures developed by Russell D. Bowman,[1] we

1. Russell D. Bowman, "Creativity in Couponing," *Marketing Communications*, Sept., 1981, p. 63.

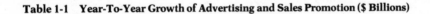

Table 1-1   Year-To-Year Growth of Advertising and Sales Promotion ($ Billions)

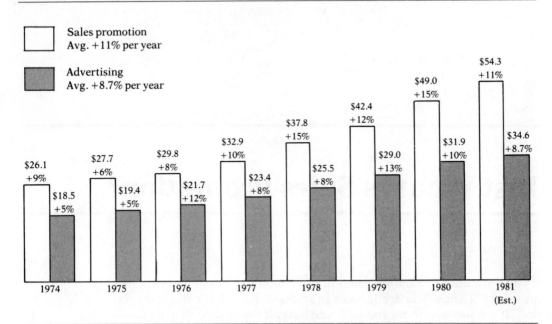

Source: Russell D. Bowman, "MC's 2nd Annual Report on Advertising and Promotion Expenditures," *Marketing Communications*, August 1981, p. 43.

Note: Most sources place advertising expenditures higher than sales promotion. The ANA chart above is for national advertising only.

estimate that 1980 U.S. sales promotion expenditures were more than $49 billion. Measurable advertising for 1980 was estimated by *Advertising Age* to be $31.9 billion dollars. More important, sales promotion is estimated to be growing at a faster rate than advertising. This fact is illustrated in Table 1-1, which compares the recent growth of advertising and sales promotion investment. (Note: Many sources place total advertising expenditures higher than sales promotion expenditures. The chart in Table 1-1 is for national advertising only.)

Perhaps the rapid growth of sales promotion is surprising to many simply because media advertising is so much more visible. Most people are familiar with consumer radio and television commercials, magazine ads, billboards, and newspaper advertisements. Many sales promotion activities, however, are not as well known or recognized because the manufacturer directs them to the trade, i.e., retailers, wholesalers, and salespeople. Thus, while many sales promotion activities may be effective, they aren't very apparent to the average person. While sales promotion growth is obvious to those who work in the field, it isn't as clear to most of the general public.

Perhaps as important as the growth of sales promotion investment is the increase in consumer acceptance and use of sales promotion offers. As prices have increased over the past few years, consumers seem to have become much more interested in sales promotion offers, such as coupons, refunds, and price reductions, which can save them money. Using their Nielsen Retail Index Field Representatives and information from the Nielsen Clearing House, the A. C. Nielsen Company conducted a study of sales promotion activity in 1977 that clearly shows manufacturers are making more use of consumer sales promotion offers and consumers are responding to those offers more than ever before.

Table 1-2 illustrates the trend in the distribution of coupons by manufacturers from 1977 to 1981. As you can see, the number of coupons distributed just about doubled during that five-year period. And while manufacturers were distributing more coupons, more and more consumers were making use of them. Table 1-3 shows that more than 20 percent more families were using coupons in 1980 than in 1971. Today, a whopping 76 percent of all U.S. families use coupons at one time or another.

Table 1-4 shows the percentage of consumers in a Nielsen study who

Table 1-2 Trend in Coupon Distributions (billions of coupons)

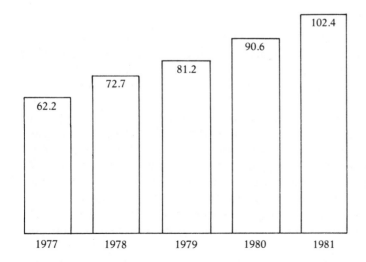

1977	1978	1979	1980	1981
62.2	72.7	81.2	90.6	102.4

Source: A. C. Nielsen Company, *NCH Reporter*, No. 1, 1982, p. 2

Table 1-3 Percent of Households Using Coupons

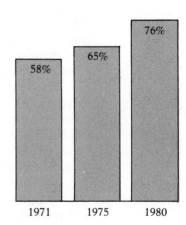

1971	1975	1980
58%	65%	76%

Source: A. C. Nielsen Company, *NCH Reporter*, No. 1, 1981, p. 3.

Table 1-4   Participation in Refund Offers

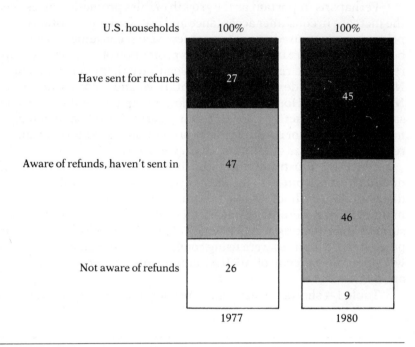

	1977	1980
U.S. households	100%	100%
Have sent for refunds	27	45
Aware of refunds, haven't sent in	47	46
Not aware of refunds	26	9

Source: A. C. Nielsen Company, *NCH Reporter*, No. 1, 1981, p. 11.

have reported participating in refund offers. (In a refund offer the manu-facturer offers to refund all or part of the purchase price of his product on receipt of a proof-of-purchase.) It is apparent from this chart that more and more consumers are not only aware of refunds but are using them in their shopping.

The upward trend in sales promotion usage is not confined just to marketers, however. Retailers too are increasing their use of sales promotion programs. The use of sales promotion is increasing among all types of marketers. During the past couple of years there have been sales promotion programs for many products and services that never used them before. Figure 1-1 illustrates the techniques that were used by two such companies: Craig Corporation and Waterford Crystal. These promotions are about as far from the traditional coupon or cents-off offer as you can get. Yet, both of them worked successfully. Clearly, sales promotion is growing. And it will grow even more as sales promotion people learn how to use the available techniques innova-tively and expertly.

Figure 1-1   Sales Promotion for New Product Areas

Craig Corporation (a)   Waterford Crystal (b)

Source: (a) William A. Robinson, *100 Best Sales Promotions* (Chicago: Crain Books, 1980), p. 40. (b) Robinson, *100 Best Sales Promotions*, p. 53.

Some Useful Definitions

It may have been obvious from the preceding paragraphs that the term *sales promotion* can have many meanings. Indeed, the careless use of categories and titles plagues the entire field of marketing. While some companies call their staff "brand managers," others call them "product managers." What might be a "sales promotion manager" in one organization is called a "merchandising specialist" in another. Therefore, to make sure that we are all speaking the same language, here are the definitions of some of the major terms that will be used in this text. Others will be added as we go along.

Marketing is considered all those activities used in satisfying the needs and wants of consumers. For our purposes, however, we'll confine our definition of marketing to all those activities, except for production or manufacturing, used by a company to provide for the needs and wants of the consumer. In other words, marketing begins after a product or service has been developed and is ready for sale.

Advertising is the paid-for communication of sales messages through any media. In most instances, we will consider advertising's primary purpose to be to convey a positive idea about or a favorable image of the brand or product to the consumer. Thus, to be successful, advertising need not necessarily create an actual or immediate sale. It need only communicate the sales message of the advertiser to the consumer.

Sales promotion is the direct inducement or incentive to the sales force, the distributor, or the consumer, with the primary objective of creating an immediate sale. Therefore, we can contrast advertising and sales promotion by saying that advertising is designed to create an image of, or to carry a sales message about, the product or service to the consumer. Sales promotion, on the other hand, is an activity used to generate an immediate sale of the product or service.

Publicity is the non-paid-for communication of information about the company or product. Whereas advertising is information that the company pays someone to convey, publicity is any information that is disseminated at no media cost to the company.

Media are communication vehicles used by companies and organizations to carry advertising and publicity. Media can take many forms, from interpersonal communication between two people to the use of network television time. To simplify our use of the term, we'll confine our definition to any method by which a message is disseminated through formal print or broadcast systems. While the distribution of plastic rulers with the name and slogan of a company could be considered a media activity, we'll limit the term to such recognized media forms as newspapers, magazines, radio or television broadcasts, direct mail, outdoor, and transit.

Distribution or trade channels are those suppliers or systems that allow the product to move from the manufacturer to the final consumer. The trade or distribution system may include wholesalers or distributors, who act as middlemen between the manufacturer and the retailer. Channels may vary in length and number of intermediaries involved, depending on the type of product being distributed.

Using these definitions, we now move into a more concrete discussion of exactly how sales promotion fits into the sales and marketing plans of an organization.

The Two Major Types of Sales Promotion

Now that we have defined sales promotion, we need to determine exactly what it is and what it isn't. There are probably as many forms of sales

Table 1-5   Estimated Division of a U.S. Marketing Budget

Packaged food or household product sold through supermarkets

	100%	
Media advertising	15%	Moving goods *out of* the stores
Consumer promotions (couponing, sampling, premiums, price-off packaging)	18%	
Trade allowances and trade deals, etc.	23%	Moving goods *into* the stores
Personal selling (sales force, brokerage, etc.)	44%	

Source: J. O. Peckham, Sr., *The Wheel of Marketing* (Scarsdale, NY: privately printed, 1978), p. 2.

promotion as there are companies that use it. Yet, sales promotion can be divided into two basic types. The first, used to move the product from the manufacturer to the distributor or retailer, is called "internal" sales promotion. Manufacturers using this type of sales promotion attempt to "push" goods through the distribution channels to the customer. Those activities used to promote the product from the manufacturer or distributor through the retailer to the ultimate consumer are termed "external" sales promotion. Manufacturers using this type of sales promotion try to create demand by the end consumer, thus "pulling" the product through distribution channels. As you might not suspect, much more sales promotion investment is made in moving the goods into the store than out of it; i.e., more is spent in sales promotion directed to the trade than to the consumer. This is illustrated in Table 1-5. We'll discuss both types of sales promotion briefly here and deal with them in greater detail in later sections.

Internal Sales Promotion

Generally, sales promotion to the distributor or retailer or simply "to the

Figure 1-2   Internal Promotion: Norelco Lightbulbs

Source: Courtesy of North American Philips Lighting Corporation.

trade" is designed to do one major thing: move the product from the manufacturer's plant into or through the trade channels and make it available to the consumer—a push strategy. As the first step in any marketing effort, the manufacturer must have distribution of the product through wholesalers and retailers. Unless the wholesalers purchase or distribute the product to the retailers and unless the retailers have an adequate supply of the product on their shelves, all other forms of promotion used by the manufacturer in his mix will probably fail. Thus, the goal of sales promotion to the trade is to provide an incentive for the wholesaler to distribute the product and for the retailer to stock it.

Most sales promotion directed to the trade revolves around some sort of reduced product price, either for a certain volume of purchase or for a limited period of time. These offers are called "trade deals" and involve such sales promotion programs as allowances, free goods, buyback arrangements, display allowances, and merchandising offers. Other forms of sales promotion activities used with the trade are point-of-purchase materials, cooperative advertising, and dealer contests. All of them will be discussed in detail in later chapters. Often, these sales promotion offers are used with the trade to get special attention from the wholesaler or retailer and to encourage him to promote a product rather than some competitive brands or another product in stock.

Trade promotions may range from the very simplest to the most complex. For example, the Norelco offer to the trade in Figure 1-2 is quite simple, consisting of a special display to be used in retail stores to call attention to and help increase the sale of Norelco light bulbs.

The American Express promotion in Figure 1-3 on the other hand, is a very complex trade promotion, involving the owner/manager and restaurant staff of restaurants that accept the American Express card. Built around a "Winning Menu Sweepstakes" idea, the promotion offers over 1,000 prizes worth more than $235,000.

External Sales Promotion

The more common and familiar forms of sales promotion are those intended to influence the ultimate consumer and, thus, pull goods through the sales pipeline. These techniques include the use of cents-off coupons, price packs, premiums, sweepstakes and contests, free offers, and cash refunds. These types of promotional offers are usually directed to the ultimate consumer by the manufacturer and/or retailer through mass media, by in-store displays, or on/in the product itself. Much more attention will be given to each of these techniques in later chapters.

The objective of all these sales promotion activities is to influence the ultimate consumer into making a buying decision in favor of the promoted brand. For example, a floor display of a bar soap in a super-

Figure 1-3   Internal Promotion: American Express Cards

Source: Robinson, *100 Best Sales Promotions, 1980,* p. 47.

market is designed to provide additional incentive to shoppers to purchase that particular brand at that particular time. The offer may be made more enticing by use of a reduced price, a combination offer of several bars at one price, an offer of a free premium with the purchase for a limited time only, or any other of a number of sales promotion techniques. Figure 1-4 illustrates examples of various consumer sales promotion offers by manufacturers or producers.

Sales promotion to the ultimate consumer is not limited to the activities of the manufacturer. Retailers and distributors either join with the manufacturer or develop the sales promotion offer themselves. In these cases, the retailer is attempting to influence the consumer to shop in his store or to maintain consumer loyalty rather than just to move a

Figure 1-4   Sales Promotions Come in Many Forms

(b)

(c)

(a)

(d)

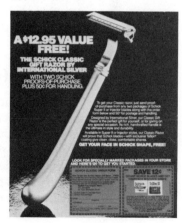

Source: (a) William A. Robinson, *100 Best Sales Promotions* (Chicago: Crain Books, 1977), p. 14. (b) Robinson, *100 Best Sales Promotions*, p. 120. (c) Robinson, *100 Best Sales Promotions* (Chicago: Crain Books, 1980), p. 35. (d) Robinson, *100 Best Sales Promotions* (Chicago: Crain Books, 1977), p. 25. (e) Robinson, *100 Best Sales Promotions* (Chicago: Crain Books, 1980), p. 18.

single product or item. While there is no way of even estimating the value of retailer-originated sales promotion programs, they no doubt exceed the manufacturer-originated programs both in terms of dollar value and number.

Retailer-originated promotions can range from annual "Back-to-School" promotions to full-fledged long-term events, such as the famous Nieman-Marcus "Fortnight" or the Macy's "Thanksgiving Day" parade and sale. In many instances, particularly in the food field, retail promotions are built around private label products or feature controlled brands. As we explore the field of sales promotion in later chapters, we'll see more illustrations of these types of sales promotion activities.

The external sales promotion mix. While the mix of sales promotion activities may vary widely from company to company, depending on the type of product the company manufactures, the general allocation of the sales promotion budget for consumer packaged-goods companies might look something like that in Table 1-6. Note that this allocation is only for external, or consumer, promotion. It does not include the larger area of internal, or trade, promotion.

The Structure of the Sales Promotion Business

The next step in our overview is a brief look at the structure of the sales promotion business. The entire field of sales promotion is so broad that it is sometimes difficult to get a clear idea of how the field is organized. It is possible, however, to distinguish five specific types of organizations involved in the development or implementation of a sales promotion program.

The Manufacturer, Marketer, or Retailer

These are the organizations that generate most sales promotion programs and activities. While we use the terms *manufacturer, marketer,* or *retailer,* it should be clear that we include all types of companies that seek to market a product or service to the trade or the ultimate consumer, including wholesalers. The primary point is that these organizations initiate sales promotion programs as a part of their marketing mix.

In terms of internal and external sales promotion, it is generally the manufacturer, or marketer, who develops internal programs, since he directly controls the price and promotion mix for the product.

Advertising Agencies

Advertising agencies assist the manufacturer, marketer, or retailer in developing a promotional plan. As a result, they are often involved in the

Table 1-6   Selected Elements of the Promotion Mix

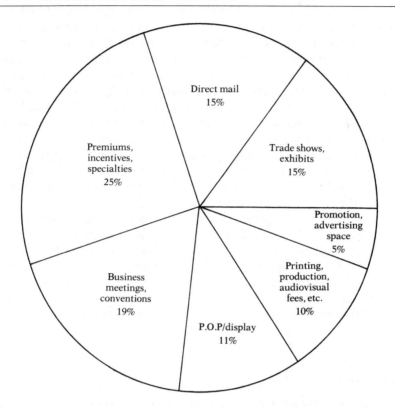

development and implementation of sales promotion plans and programs. For the most part, since they are usually only concerned with the preparation of advertising for the media, advertising agencies limit their involvement in sales promotion to the development of external sales promotion programs. In some instances, however, particularly for industrial or specialized marketers, they may provide guidance and assistance in the development of internal sales promotion programs as well.

Advertising agencies are usually thought of as providing the ideas or suggestions for specific sales promotion programs, including the design of the various promotional materials, the development of advertisements and commercials for use in the media, and the art and copywriting needed to implement the program.

Sales Promotion Agencies

A relatively new development in the sales promotion field is the rise of the sales promotion, or, as it is sometimes called, marketing, agency. This is usually an organization that operates much like an advertising agency in that it gives advice, counsel, and direction to clients and also provides them with a creative product. The primary difference between advertising and sales promotion agencies is that the latter specialize in the field of sales promotion. Advertising agencies usually specialize in the development of media advertising and use sales promotion as a supplementary activity.

Sales promotion agencies are often retained by manufacturers and/ or marketers in addition to advertising agencies. Their primary job is to develop the sales promotion program for the company and coordinate it with the other activities in the marketing mix.

The duties of a sales promotion agency might include making recommendations on both internal and external sales promotion programs, estimating or calculating costs, working with suppliers and vendors to implement the program, and, finally, setting up evaluation systems to determine the success of the promotion. As opposed to advertising agencies, sales promotion or marketing agencies are usually involved in all phases of the promotional program and do many tasks usually reserved for the manufacturers or marketers.

Suppliers or Vendors

Suppliers and *vendors* are very broad terms describing an even wider range of companies, groups, and organizations, including groups that supply the material or provide the direct services for the implementation of sales promotion activities. Vendors or suppliers could mean printers involved in the production of sales promotion literature; point-of-sale designers; manufacturers of promotional materials, such as pencils, rulers, and key chains; or premium designers and manufacturers. Sales promotion vendors and suppliers are usually experts in some specific field, such as printing, design, implementation, or manufacturing. They are often used as consultants by both the manufacturers and the marketers and the advertising and sales promotion agencies. Most suppliers and vendors provide their services to the manufacturer or agency on a contract basis.

Support Organizations

Support organizations are very specialized groups that provide services or facilities necessary for the completion of the sales promotion program.

These would include coupon clearing houses (organizations that collect redeemed coupons from retailers, count the coupons, calculate the value, and then reimburse the retailer while billing the manufacturer for the costs), contest-judging organizations, sweepstakes developers, and organizations providing legal advice. As with suppliers and vendors, support organizations may work directly with the manufacturer or marketer in a sales promotion program or with the advertising or sales promotion agency. Like most vendors or suppliers, support organizations usually work on some sort of contractual basis with the marketer.

How Sales Promotion Fits into Marketing

The actual activity of marketing can be carried on by the simplest as well as the most complex of organizational systems. The newspaper boy on the corner is practicing marketing, just as are giant corporations, such as Procter & Gamble, General Foods, and General Motors. In each case, the marketer is seeking to fill consumer needs and wants at a profit to himself. The way that marketers go about organizing their activities to satisfy consumer needs and wants is called the marketing mix.

The Marketing Mix

Both the newspaper boy and General Motors use a combination of products, services, and activities when they market a product. In simplified form, this "marketing mix" always consists of four basic items: a product, a price, a place, and a promotion necessary to inform consumers of the offer.

The newspaper boy's marketing mix is quite simple. He has a product for sale (a newspaper) at a price (25¢) and at a certain location (a street corner). His promotion consists of his shouts to call attention to his product or, perhaps, a few crude signs.

General Motors, on the other hand, has a very complex marketing mix. First, the company has multiple products ranging from the lowest priced Chevrolet to the most expensive Cadillac. The prices of these products vary widely and are complicated even more by the opportunity for the consumer to add additional items or extras to the basic product, such as air conditioning, radio, and electric windows. The place factor in the automobile example is also quite complex, for it consists of a dealer network in which some dealers have only one brand of automobile while others offer several. To complicate the distribution system even more, there are often several dealers selling the same brand of automobile in the same market. Finally, the promotional plan of General Motors con-

Table 1-7   The Elements of the Marketing Mix I

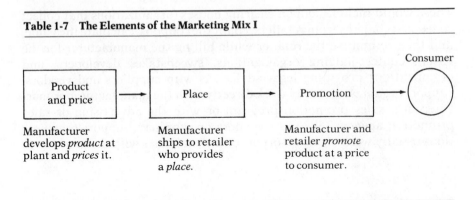

Manufacturer
develops *product* at
plant and *prices* it.

Manufacturer
ships to retailer
who provides
a *place.*

Manufacturer and
retailer *promote*
product at a price
to consumer.

sists of a wide variety of activities, including advertising, sales promotion, publicity, and personal selling.

Table 1-7 illustrates the various portions of the marketing mix and
how they flow from one to the other in successfully moving the product
from the manufacturer to the ultimate consumer.

As you can see from our General Motors and newspaper boy illustrations, the overall term *marketing* refers to different activities for different
types of businesses or organizations. In addition, the marketing mix
varies with the company's attitude or approach to selling its products—
the organization's philosophy. Every company that seeks to sell a product or service to a consumer at a profit uses one of three primary philosophies.

Organizational Philosophies

There are three basic organizational philosophies: the "product concept," the "selling concept," and the "marketing concept." The first two
have been widely used for many years, although the product concept is
by far the oldest. In this approach, the product is considered the most
important factor. The people who produce the product believe that if
they produce a good product and price it reasonably, consumers will seek
it out and purchase it from them. They consider marketing to include
only the product and the price and pay relatively little attention to place
or promotion.

The second concept is that of selling. In this instance, the company
produces a good product, prices it well, and then relies on personal
selling to move it to the customer. The company that practices the selling
concept believes that it must convince the consumer that the product is
needed and wanted. Without aggressive selling, a company practicing
this concept may not be successful.

Contrasted with the previous two, the marketing concept assumes that consumer needs and wants come first in the development of any product or service. Rather than concentrating on producing products it believes to be best, the marketing-oriented company determines what consumers need and want and then fills that need and want with the best possible product. Inherent in the marketing concept is the need for all types of promotion to let consumers know that the products or services are available.

The major difference among many companies is the philosophy they use. Their choice has a great impact not only on the development of products and services but also on the need for promotional activities to support the distribution of products. Those companies following the product or selling concept have less need for promotion than those following the marketing concept. This need for promotion results in what is called the company's promotional mix.

The Promotional Mix

While product-oriented and sales-oriented organizations use promotion in some form, even if only in the most superficial way, it is the marketing-oriented company that relies extensively on promotional efforts. Promotion is the method used to help move products from the plant through the distribution channels to the ultimate consumer. Because of the importance of promotion to the marketing-oriented company, we will use this type of organization as an example throughout the book. It will better illustrate the actual potentially superior ability of sales promotion to move products from the manufacturer to the consumer than either the product or the selling concept.

In the description of the marketing mix, we identified the four primary elements in any company as product, price, place, and promotion. It is within this overall term *promotion* that we find what is called *sales promotion*. Take a look at the four elements of the marketing mix in Table 1-8. You can see that sales promotion is but one of the four types of promotion activities the marketer can use.

As you'll recall, we defined advertising as the communication of a sales message that may or may not result in an actual sale. We defined sales promotion as a direct inducement to the sales force, the distributor, or the consumer to create an immediate sale. *Personal selling* is direct, face-to-face contact between the buyer or prospect and the seller. *Public relations* is that form of promotion that seeks to make use of publicity and other non-paid forms of communication to influence the feelings, opinions, or beliefs about the company that manufactures the product, about the product itself, or about the value of the product to the consumer. A marketing organization can and often does make use of each of these

Table 1-8   The Elements of the Marketing Mix II

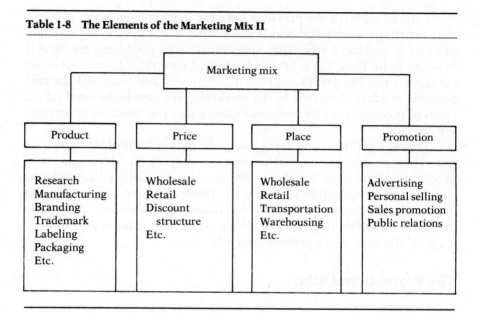

Product	Price	Place	Promotion
Research	Wholesale	Wholesale	Advertising
Manufacturing	Retail	Retail	Personal selling
Branding	Discount	Transportation	Sales promotion
Trademark	structure	Warehousing	Public relations
Labeling	Etc.	Etc.	
Packaging			
Etc.			

promotional techniques singly or in combination to promote its products or services.

Some companies use only advertising in the promotion of their product. An example is a company that sells directly to the consumer through the form of media called "direct response." This includes any number of mail-order companies or the newest form of direct-response selling, that being done on television. One excellent example is the K-Tel Company, which advertises its popular music records and tapes for sale through television commercials. The viewer hears part of the music, is shown pictures of the records or tapes and musical artists, and is then asked to order directly either by calling a toll-free 800 telephone number or writing for the record or tape. In this example, the entire K-Tel sales effort is in direct-response television advertising. The product may not even be available in retail outlets. K-Tel makes limited use of sales promotion, personal selling, and public relations in its promotional mix.

Avon Cosmetics is an entirely different type of organization. It relies primarily on personal selling to move its products. Avon has about 350,000 people, primarily women, who act as sales representatives and are involved in door-to-door selling of Avon products or have a list of customers on whom they call. While Avon relies almost entirely on these sales people to make the final sale, it supports its sales force with a strong media campaign in print and broadcast, plus sales promotion programs and publicity to help "presell" the Avon line. An important ingredient in the final sale, along with personal selling and advertising, is the sales promotion program Avon conducts. This usually consists of special features, such as combination offers of two products at one lower price, reduced-price specials, and new product introductions. The sales people use these sales promotion offers extensively in regular calls. The promotions give them something new to talk about and a reason to contact their customers on a regular basis.

In contrast to these direct response organizations is General Electric, which manufactures a line of home appliances. Let's use a G.E. washing machine as an example, since all types of promotional tools are used in marketing this product. G.E. uses media advertising in newspapers and magazines and on radio and television to get its sales message to the consumer. It also uses sales promotion, including such devices as dealer incentives to sell certain models and sales contests to reward outstanding sales efforts. G.E. uses personal selling with the retailer to convince him to stock and sell G.E. washers. And that technique is transferred to the ultimate consumer through the salesperson on the appliance store floor. Finally, G.E. sends publicity and news releases about the product to the national and local media. Thus, rather than relying on only one promotional tool, G.E. uses all of the promotional methods in its promotional mix. It is usually such a mix of the four elements that most effectively moves the product from the manufacturer to the consumer.

The Sales Promotion Function

We can now investigate the sales promotion function at the marketer and manufacturer level. First, we'll look at how the business is managed; i.e., who has the responsibility for the sales promotion function in the two basic types of marketing organizations, the traditional sales organization and the brand management system.

The Sales Organization

The sales organization type of management is typical of the company that is relatively small or that has only a limited line of products. It is also quite popular in the industrial field. The typical organization chart is illustrated in Table 1-9.

The sales promotion director in this instance reports directly to the president of the company. It is his responsibility to work with the sales director and the advertising director to develop and implement sales promotion programs. In this case, sales promotion would be considered as important as advertising.

Table 1-9   Sales Organization Chart

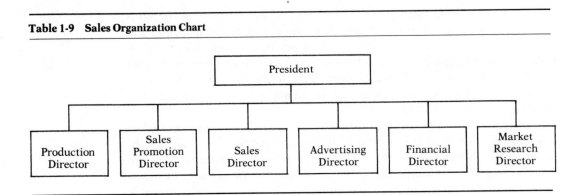

In some cases, particularly where the promotion budget is quite small, we often find an organization like the one shown in Table 1-10. In this case, the sales promotion manager would report directly to the sales director rather than the president. This is more typically the case in industrial organizations or in companies in which personal selling is the most important promotional method or in which the selling concept is practiced. In very small companies, the sales director often serves as the advertising manager and the sales promotion manager as well.

The Marketing Organization

A form of management organization that has become quite popular with many large package-goods companies is called the "product" or "brand

Table 1-10   Personal Selling Organization Chart

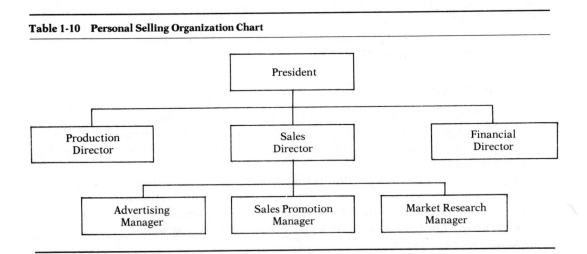

Table 1-11   Brand Management System Chart

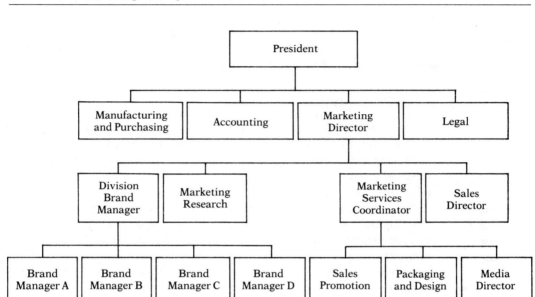

management" system. This management idea evolved as companies entered more and more separate business areas. For example, suppose that a company that originally manufactured soap and soap products expanded its business by entering the toothpaste field, the peanut butter market, the toilet tissue business, and so on. Obviously, a single sales manager or even a group of sales managers could not keep up with events in such diverse businesses. The brand management system was developed to give control of all the management functions to the person directly responsible for the profit and loss on the business.The organization chart shown in Table 1-11 is common in this type of organization.

In the brand management system, the brand manager has primary responsibility for all sales and marketing efforts on his brand, including all sales promotion activities. The brand manager reports directly through his division brand manager to the marketing director, who is responsible to the president of the organization for all efforts on behalf of all brands. In some small organizations, the division brand manager position may not exist, but the flow is generally the same.

The important point in this organizational structure is that the sales promotion manager is now a member of a service team. Since the brand manager makes all the sales promotion decisions with regard to the brand for which he is responsible, the sales promotion manager is now more of a consultant to the brand manager than head of the programs. The sales promotion manager consults with the brand manager in the development of the sales promotion program and then carries out many of the responsibilities to implement the plan. This is particularly true for most external sales promotion programs directed to the consumer.

Sales Promotion—the Bridge

In any of the organizational models described above, sales promotion can be thought of as the bridge between the various elements in the marketing mix. Usually, the sales director is responsible for all the personal selling efforts on behalf of the product or service. The advertising director is responsible for all the communications and mass media advertising for the product. The sales promotion manager is responsible for bridging the gap between the two. For example, sales promotion can provide promotional efforts to assist the sales manager in motivating sales personnel or in developing tools the sales force can use in calling on customers. For media advertising, sales promotion may be called on to bridge the gap between a media plan and the retailer by explaining how the advertising the company is doing will help sell the ultimate consumer. Sales promotion may also be used to help develop a point-of-purchase display featuring the same selling message as that being used on television. In both instances, sales promotion has served as the middleman between the actual activities of the personal selling function and the sales force or the distributor. In other instances, it serves as the bridge between advertising and the ultimate consumer of the product. Because of the mediating function of sales promotion, it is sometimes difficult to state exactly what sales promotion is and isn't or where sales promotion activities begin and end. The fact remains, however, that within almost any type of marketing organization, sales promotion is the one function that helps bring all the promotional activities of the organization together. It is truly the bridge in the promotional mix.

How Sales Promotion Departments Operate

Sales promotion departments vary in size, scope, and method of operation. We'll review how several sales promotion departments operate to give an indication of the various approaches.

For example, Table 1-12 illustrates how a major brewer has organized its marketing services department within which the sales promotion function is contained. As you can see, six department heads report to the director of beer brands marketing services. These include

Table 1-12 Functional System

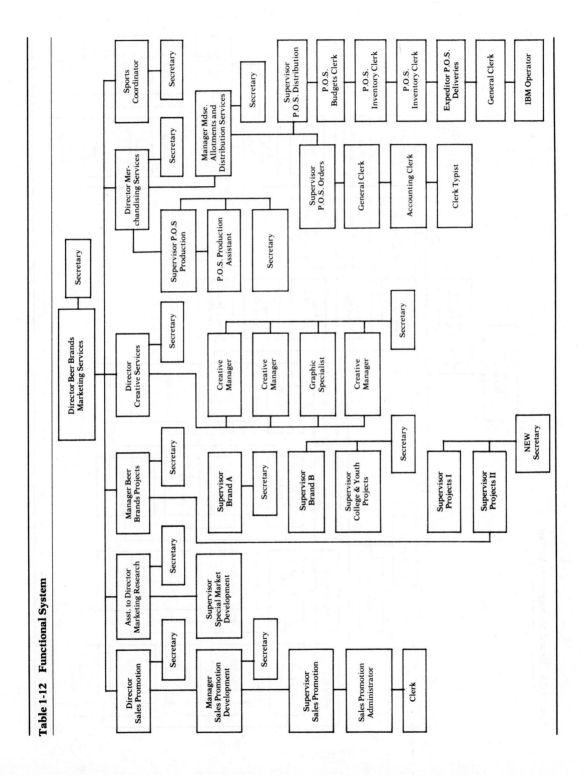

Table 1-13   Brand Management System

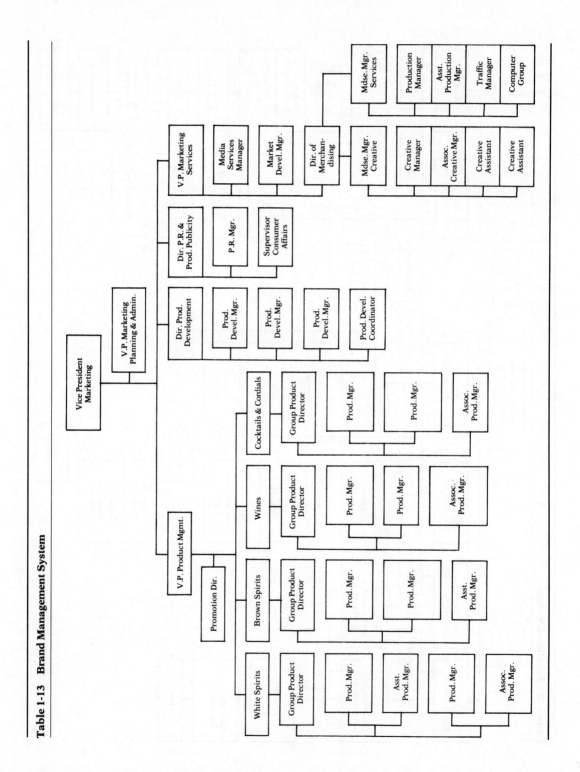

the director of sales promotion, the assistant to the director of marketing research, the manager of beer brands projects, the director of creative services, the director of merchandising services, and the sports coordinator. In this case, sales promotion is actually divided into several responsibilities, such as the development, creation, and distribution of the sales promotional programs.

Alternatively, a major liquor company has organized the sales promotion function along the traditional lines of a brand management system, as illustrated in Table 1-13. Here, sales promotion, which in this company is called "merchandising," reports to a vice-president-marketing services, who in turn reports to the vice-president-marketing. All the sales promotion functions are contained within the marketing services area, with the specific responsibilities split between creative and services and both reporting to the director of merchandising.

Finally, to give total flexibility, a major recreation equipment manufacturer organizes its sales promotion department within a marketing services department with a regional organization, as shown in Table 1-14.

Regardless of which form the sales promotion department takes, it is—and should be—integrated with the other marketing functions of the organization.

Table 1-14   Regional System

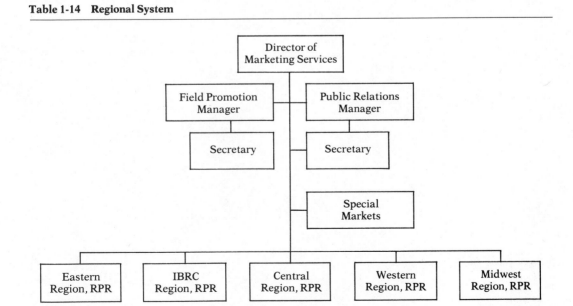

Summary

To understand the rapidly growing, increasingly important sales promotion industry, you need to know its parts and how they fit together. Sales promotion consists of two major types—internal sales promotion, directed to the trade; and external sales promotion, directed to the consumer. The proportion of each type to the other in any company varies according to the requirements of the product to be promoted.

The industry can also be thought of in terms of its operating components: the manufacturers, marketers, and retailers; the advertising and sales promotion agencies; and the suppliers, vendors, and support organizations.

Sales promotion is only a part of a larger whole called marketing. It is part of any company's "marketing mix." As such, its relative importance becomes a function of the company's organizational philosophy. Within a marketing organization, sales promotion must relate to the sales organization and the marketing organization. It does so in various ways within various corporate constraints.

2

The 12 Sales Promotion Techniques

It is vital to understand the 12 basic sales promotion techniques and how they work. Each of them is outlined on the following pages, with their strong and weak points. This overview will establish a common language and perspective for later discussions of sales promotion management.

The 12 Sales Promotion Techniques

All great sales promotion ideas can be reduced to 12 basic techniques. They are:

1. Sampling
2. Coupons
3. Trade coupons
4. Trade allowances
5. Price-offs
6. In-, on-, and near-packs (and reusable containers)
7. Free-in-the-mail premiums
8. Self-liquidating premiums
9. Contests and sweepstakes
10. Refund offers
11. Bonus packs
12. Stamp plans and continuity premiums

These techniques can be used singly or in combination. In fact, you can combine these 12 techniques into more than 8,000,000 different combinations. And that doesn't count the almost infinite variety of headlines, copy, and layouts that can be employed.

The many combinations of these 12 techniques are what really make the job of sales promotion management so exciting and interesting and, at the same time, so difficult. It is the job of selecting, combining, and budgeting the techniques that quickly separates the novice from the pro. The experienced sales promotion manager has learned that each of the 12 techniques has its own specific strengths and weaknesses. It is the ability to combine the strengths and compensate for the weaknesses that shows a manager's true expertise.

An example will help illustrate the point. Assume you are the sales promotion manager for a regional brand of margarine. In this tough, competitive business, sales promotion is a key factor in success, but, as a regional brand, you have a limited budget and really can't compete head-on with the national brands. What to do?

If you were planning a couponing program with a rather modest cents-off offer alone, your ad might get lost in the blizzard of food-day coupons in the local newspapers for other products and competitive margarines. By reviewing the strengths and weaknesses of the various techniques, however, you remember that a sweepstakes can help build ad readership. And, if you combine the coupon offer with a sweepstakes, you will likely build ad readership and thus higher redemption rates for your coupon, as well as more real proof-of-purchase with your sweepstakes entries *and* more trade cooperation. That's synergism in sales promotion, and that's what separates the winners from the losers.

With the possibility of near-infinite combinations in mind, we'll review the twelve promotion techniques and discuss the strong and weak points of each.[1]

Sampling

This is the one you must consider when you want to reach new users in the introduction of a new product, the improvement of an old product, or the opening of new markets for an established product. Generally, sampling is more effective than other techniques when your product's feature or benefit can't be fully conveyed in advertising—for example, a unique new flavor or aroma.

On the other hand, sampling can lack precision in reaching the best prospects, and it's expensive, in any form. It is said to be less efficient than couponing in converting triers to regular users.

Obviously, Lipton had these limitations in mind when it offered

---

1. See Don Schultz and William Robinson, *Sales Promotion Essentials* (Chicago: Crain Books, 1982).

Figure 2-1   Sample: Lipton Tea

Source: Courtesy of Thomas J. Lipton Co.

free-in-the-mail samples of five new flavored teas. (See Figure 2-1.) With unique new flavors, sampling was definitely called for. Door-to-door sampling would have been expensive and wasteful, and not everyone drinks tea, much less flavored tea. By making the consumer write in for samples, Lipton was able to focus on serious prospects.

Coupons

The incredible growth of couponing over the years (over 90 billion in 1980, according to A. C. Nielsen Clearing House, up nearly 10 billion in just one year) makes this look like the magic elixir of sales promotion techniques. It also means there is more and more competition as all types of brands and products compete for the consumer's limited dollars. So, with all this competition out there, to be a successful couponer, you must know the advantages and disadvantages.

You can use coupons to produce trial, to convert triers to regular users, to reach large numbers of prospects more economically than sampling, to load regular users or trade them up to larger sizes, to increase usage by present users, to hold current users against competitive activity, and to increase trade buy-ins. In today's inflation-troubled economy, it is the cheapest and simplest method for delivering a price-off to the consumer.

The biggest problem with couponing is proliferation. With probably 100 billion coupons distributed in 1982, it will be more and more difficult to get attention for your offer or to get a leg up on your competitor. The best way to counter this without going into bankruptcy is by combining coupon offers with overlays—refunds, sweepstakes, and so on. The method of distribution is another problem. It limits the response. In-pack coupons, for example, get few new triers, but their purpose, of course, is to load and hold present users.

Strangely enough, coupons work better with older, more affluent, better-educated, urban, married consumers than with consumers who need the savings more—the less affluent, young, single, and less educated.

Misredemption is another big problem (especially with the trade), but redemption houses are taking a tougher stand to curb it. Or brands are budgeting for it. The great number of variables—face value, competition, timing, brand share, distribution systems, design, etc.—also make results and redemption liabilities hard to predict.

An example of the coupon with overlay technique is shown in Figure 2-2. Quaker took a rather modest coupon, 10¢ on Instant Quaker oatmeal, and turned it into a sound promotional program. In this case, Quaker provided the ad and 10¢ coupon redemption, and Sears absorbed the redemption on the jeans.

Trade Coupons

These are offered by retailers, usually in cooperation with the manufacturer, in their own ads or flyers. This technique should be considered when your goal is trial on a geographic basis or when you want to gain

Figure 2-2   Coupon: Instant Quaker Oatmeal

Source: William A. Robinson, *100 Best Sales Promotions* (Chicago: Crain Books, 1980), p. 60.

Figure 2-3   Trade Coupon: Dominick's Finer Foods

Source: Courtesy of Dominick's Finer Foods.

trade cooperation in getting some off-shelf display and price features. Other uses of trade coupons are to help build distribution, to reduce trade inventories on a market-by-market basis, and to increase redemptions (trade coupons usually do much better than those offered by manufacturers). Another advantage is that a price reduction is offered by a third party, the store, rather than the brand, which is important if the brand image might be impaired by price-offs. And trade coupons don't have to go through a clearing house.

Trade coupons can be very expensive when the retailers want pre-redeemed allowances or ad allowances to cover expenses. This is why some brands settle for smaller redemption figures and run their own coupons. For example, Figure 2-3 shows a sheet of coupons that Dominick's Finer Foods makes available each week in its stores. As you can see, a number of manufacturers are represented with trade coupons.

Trade Allowances

You don't read much about trade allowances in the text or the trade press. But trade allowances are essential when you're thinking about gaining distribution, getting off-shelf display, encouraging price features, and building up inventories. It's almost impossible to get a new product into distribution without a special introductory allowance.

Trade allowances can be abused. The trade frequently doesn't want to hear about performance standards. And there is a lot of laxity about passing on savings to consumers. Also, there is a lack of direct consumer involvement—unless you accept the fact that the most desirable involvement centers around displays and advertising features. Trade allowances truly fit the vicious circle category: You'd like to get along without them, but you can't.

Price-Offs

Here's another technique that doesn't always grab the creative limelight. But you must think about price-offs, especially if you propose to reward and load present users, head off competition by taking consumers out of the market, establish purchase patterns after initial trial, enforce pass-through of savings to the consumer, create on-shelf attention (with a package flag), get off-shelf display (when combined with trade allowances), accelerate upward sales trends and, finally, merely give the sales force some extra ammunition to load the trade.

Don't expect miracles with price-offs. They can give sales a bump, but they will not reverse a downward sales trend. They will not produce loyal new users. (Price-conscious buyers go right back to private labels when price-offs aren't available.) Price-offs produce only a temporary increase in market share, and repeated use tends to degrade the perceived value of the product while giving progressively smaller "bumps" in the market share. What are the other limitations? To have any real effect, prices must be cut 15 to 20 percent. And the smaller the brand's share, the larger the price break must be. Also, if it's trial you're after, don't opt for price-offs; they give you less trial than on-pack premiums, couponing, or sampling. Finally, price-offs based on a trade allowance don't always reach the consumer. The retailer may keep part or all of the discount.

To introduce new, improved, advanced formula Crest toothpaste, Procter & Gamble offered consumers a price-off, shown in Figure 2-4, of 30¢ on the 8.2-ounce size. That's a saving the consumer can see quickly and it's banded right on the package. No chance of its getting lost in trade channels.

In-, On-, and Near-Packs (and Reusable Containers)

The most consistent users of in-packs are the ready-to-eat cereal manufacturers. Among other notable users of on-packs are the cigarette companies (e.g., Virginia Slims' "Book of Days" and Winston's free beer stein holding five packs). What's good about the category? Pack premiums can help increase product usage if the premium is directly related to the way the product is used (coffee cups for coffee, lighters for cigarettes, etc.). On-packs that don't fit easily on the shelf can be used to force off-shelf display—but it's a dangerous way to go for weak brands that just might get thrown off the shelf and out of the store.

Pack premiums tend to give consumers greater perceived value for the same amount spent than you can give them with price-offs or coupons. Properly used, the pack premium technique can produce premiums that extend the advertising and the image of the brand to point-of-sale.

But watch out: A bad one can actually reduce sales, and the trade resists premiums that compete with products they can sell for a profit. (Give some thought to custom on-packs if your budget can take it.) Also, pilferage can be a problem, but it's not as bad a problem as it's painted.

Figure 2-5 is an example of an in-pack and an on-pack from the same company. Personal Touch shavers were on-packs to Agree creme rinse and conditioner. The shaver was free with purchase. This is an appropriate, desirable premium because it is practical and has universal appeal for Agree's target market.

Free-in-the-Mail Premiums

It seems you see fewer and fewer of these offers, at least in the pure form,

Figure 2-4   Price-Off: Crest Toothpaste

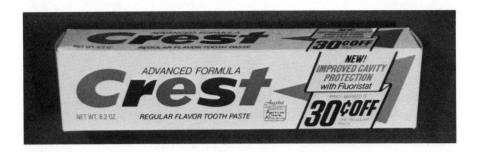

Source: Courtesy of the Procter & Gamble Company.

Figure 2-5   In-/On-Pack: Agree Creme Rinse and Personal Touch Razors

Source: Courtesy of S. C. Johnson & Son, Inc.

probably because it is so difficult to find anything attractive at a reasonable price. Usually, consumers send in proofs-of-purchase to get their free premiums. The technique is often used to load and reward consumers by requiring multiple purchases.

However, sales increases are seldom measurable, and offers are seldom picked up by more than 1 percent of the media circulation. Also, offers that require multiple purchase proofs will not attract triers or prospective new users. To get around this, brands sometimes make a "sliding scale" offer. For one proof-of-purchase, the premium is a self-liquidator; for three proofs, the deal gets better; for six proofs, it's free.

Using a point system, Cat Chow offered a free calendar. For six points (one 20-lb. bag or six boxes), the buyer got a calendar with 12 irresistible cat pictures and some Cat Chow advertising. And to get the buyer started, Cat Chow threw in a 15¢ coupon. It was a good way to load cat lovers and keep the brand name in front of them all year long.

Anacin and Kleenex teamed up to offer a free fever detector that was sure to appeal to mothers: the detector is used on the forehead, not in the mouth. Consumers could get the fever detector for 25¢ and the Universal Product Code from Kleenex tissues and Anacin tablets. (See Figure 2-6.) That's the kind of directly related free-in-the-mail premium that usually works.

Self-Liquidating Premiums

Self-liquidators once were used when a manufacturer couldn't think of anything else to do. Today, liquidators seem better understood, and marketers seem to be using the technique more sensibly. Self-liquidating premiums can extend brand image, reinforce advertising, and increase ad readership by as much as 50 percent. They also give you something to talk about to the trade. And the self-liquidator can serve as a not-too-disguised dealer loader.

Lets face it—they're no good for building trial. Less than 10 percent of households have ever sent for a premium. And redemption is less than 1 percent of circulation.

Not too long ago, self-liquidators were priced under $5. But now anything seems possible; for example, Kool's $699 catamaran or J&B Scotch's $30 book, *Gold of Tutankhamen*. Both of these were very powerful reinforcements of the brand's image. We also see more "collections," such as Marlboro's Country Store, which offer a range of items priced from $3.50 to $250, all image reinforcing, for broader appeal.

The promotion shown in Figure 2-7 supported Mitchum's summer advertising campaign theme, "I can skip a day." And what ties in better with jogging than an antiperspirant? When you combine the $15 jogging suit at half price (and one proof-of-purchase) with a 25¢ coupon, it looks

Figure 2-6   Free-in-the-Mail Premium: Anacin Tablets and Kleenex Tissues

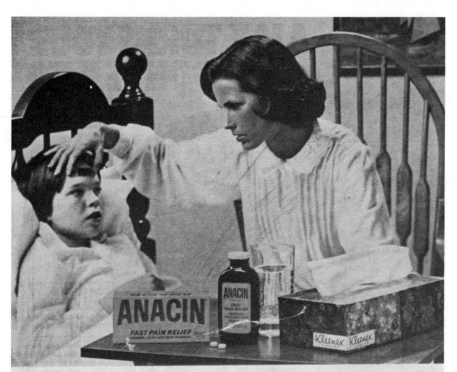

Free! Revolutionary Fever Detector from Anacin® and Kleenex.®

$1.95 retail value FREE with proof of purchase from Kleenex tissues & Anacin. SAVINGS BONUS: 15¢ Anacin coupon on specially marked packages of Kleenex 200's. Total retail value: $2.10
(You must include 25¢ for postage and handling.)

Kleenex tissues and Anacin—a great combination for colds and flu season comfort.

There's nothing more comforting than a soft Kleenex tissue and Kleenex offers more colors, shapes and sizes tha any other brand. Kleenex is the only real choice.

For medicine, Anacin contains the pain reliever doctors recommend most for relieving the aches, pain and fever of colds and flu. Compared with regular headache tablets, Anacin has 23% more pain reliever . . . plus an extra ingredient.

And now Anacin and Kleenex have combined to give you more—a revolutionary new way to check for fever. The new Fever Detector is specially recommended for children who often find it hard to hold thermometers in their mouths. Check the certificate for details on how you can get your FREE Fever Detector. Get your 15¢-Off Anacin coupon when you buy one specially marked box of Kleenex 200's tissues. Do it now.

Only the Universal Product Code from one package of Kleenex tissues 200's and one package of Anacin tablets (any size except 12's) will be accepted as valid proof of purchase.

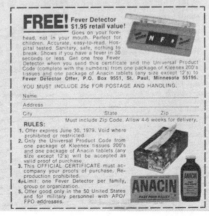

FREE! Fever Detector $1.95 retail value!
Goes on your forehead, not in your mouth. Perfect for children. Accurate, easy-to-read. Hospital tested. Sanitary, safe, nothing to break. Shows if you have a fever in 30 seconds or less. Get one free Fever Detector when you send this certificate and the Universal Product Code (complete with the numbers) from one package of Kleenex 200's tissues and one package of Anacin tablets (any size except 12's) to **Fever Detector Offer, P.O. Box 9551, St. Paul, Minnesota 55195.**

YOU MUST INCLUDE 25¢ FOR POSTAGE AND HANDLING.

Name _____
Address _____
City _____ State _____ Zip _____
Must include Zip Code. Allow 4-6 weeks for delivery.

RULES:
1. Offer expires June 30, 1979. Void where prohibited or restricted.
2. Only the Universal Product Code from one package of Kleenex tissues 200's and one package of Anacin tablets (any size except 12's) will be accepted as valid proof of purchase.
3. This OFFICIAL CERTIFICATE must accompany your proofs of purchase. Reproduction prohibited.
4. Limit: one Fever Detector per family, group or organization.
5. Offer good only in the 50 United States and for military personnel with APO/FPO addresses.

Source: Robinson, *100 Best Sales Promotions*, p. 130.

Figure 2-7   Self-liquidating Premium: Mitchum Products

Source: Robinson, *100 Best Sales Promotions*, p. 68.

like the kind of self-liquidating premium promotion that can really pay off at the cash register.

Contests and Sweepstakes

If you're looking for something that will get your advertising read, extend and reinforce your product's image, provide a reason (when combined with others) for getting off-the-shelf and on-the-floor display space; if you want a change of pace in your advertising, plus a chance to lure new triers through a unique method of entering a contest or sweeps; and if you can afford to give it the support it deserves; then this technique is for you.

But remember these things when you budget your dollars: Contests and sweeps won't produce mass trial (barely 20 percent of the population has ever sent in an entry); over 75 percent of entries are accompanied by facsimiles—not proofs-of-purchase; and you'll always be entertaining a lot of professional entrants with your program.

One of the recent trends in sweepstakes is illustrated by Land O Lakes in Figure 2-8. This is the multiple sweepstakes approach. It's not just one contest; it's seven, with prizes ranging from a Dodge Omni to a motor home to $10,000 worth of airline travel. This sort of sweepstakes is a good bet to build ad readership for a product that has practically nothing new or exciting to say in its advertising.

Refund Offers

This is one of the basics—like trade allowances and price-offs. Refunds create excitement at fairly modest cost. They provide the sales force with something to talk about and give you a chance to flag your package. And the ploy is a good one for reinforcing brand loyalty—especially when multiple purchase is required.

Don't look for a lot of consumer interest with refunds. They don't generate trial; they're slow, and results are hard to measure. The trade would usually rather see store coupons.

At one time most refunds were straight cash. In the past few years, there has been an upswing in refund payments in the form of coupons good only for repurchase of the brand or restricted certificates redeemable only at a specific type of retailer. Refunds have been growing at a fantastic rate. An A. C. Nielsen Clearing House study found that 74 percent of all U.S. households are aware of refund offers and that one in four has actually sent in for a refund of some sort. Refunds appeal to all ages but seem to be most popular with younger housewives.[2]

---

2. Richard H. Aycrigg, *NCH Reporter*, No. 3, 1979, pp. 2-4.

Figure 2-8   Sweepstakes: Land O Lakes Products

Source: Robinson, *100 Best Sales Promotions*, p. 91.

Figure 2-9   Refund: Johnson & Johnson Products

Source: Robinson, *100 Best Sales Promotions*, p. 71.

An example of a growing trend in refunds is the "varying refund," based on the number of proofs returned, or the "earn-a-refund," which is constructed by combining brands and products. Johnson & Johnson combined 12 different products and offered three different levels of refund in the promotion shown in Figure 2-9. The kicker was a requirement to include a mail-in request form from a store display. That helped involve the trade.

Stamp Plans, Continuity Premiums

These come in a variety of shapes and sizes. Campbell has had a successful "Labels for Education" program going for some time; Post has followed up with a similar "Fun 'n Fitness" equipment program for schools; Imperial sugar has always had a teaspoon offer going; some companies have subscribed to co-op (bonus gift) stamp programs originated and administered by outside promotion firms; and Raleigh, Bel Air, and Alpine are probably the last cigarette brands basing their marketing on on-pack coupons. This strategy can be used to get steady users and create differences in parity products. Perhaps it can best be thought of as a small part of a larger program or a low-cost substitute for higher-budget brand-image building.

Such plans appeal only to small segments of buyers; they don't motivate the retailer to do anything to boost sales to the trade; and they won't get you off-shelf display (although one of the co-op stamp plans did try a joint point-of-sale effort). If you overemphasize them in your programming, you'll find you're advertising premiums in place of your brand's features and image.

One of the top users of continuity premiums are fast food outlets. For example, Figure 2-10 shows the program Arby's developed for Norman Rockwell's *Post* covers glasses. The offer: each week for six weeks, purchase a different glass filled with a soft drink. This, like other continuity programs, is designed to attract traffic, generate repeat business, and stimulate sales.

Bonus Packs

Bonus packs are useful in converting triers into users. They are a good technique for making something happen at the shelf. Offered on the right display (sometimes a pre-pack), bonus packs can get you off the shelf. All this, and they give you an advertisable event, too.

However, bonus packs don't get trial, they do nothing for brand image, and they can be abused by the trade. Banded packs, for example, can be ripped apart for a separate sale. Also, when a larger package is

Figure 2-10   Continuity Premium: Arby's Restaurants

Source: Robinson, *100 Best Sales Promotions,* p. 79.

Figure 2-11   Bonus Pack: Keebler Cookies

Source: Courtesy of Keebler Company.

used—say for offering a bonus four ounces for free—packaging changes can be expensive.

Keebler used a typical bonus pack with its "Free, 1 Dozen Cookies" on its special Elfwich cookie pack. The actual offer was 18 ounces of cookies at the price of 14 ounces, but that translates into a dozen cookies, a value the consumer can easily see and understand. See Figure 2-11.

Summary

There are twelve basic sales promotion techniques. They are: sampling, coupons, trade coupons, trade allowances, price-offs, on-, in-, and near-packs, free-in-the-mail premiums, self-liquidating premiums, contests and sweepstakes, refund offers, stamp plans and continuity premiums, and bonus packs. Each has general advantages and disadvantages. Each may be particularly well suited to solve certain sales promotion problems. In addition, these twelve techniques can be joined in various combinations to produce innovative, effective sales promotion programs.

3

What Sales Promotion
Can and Can't Do

One of the major hazards in marketing is the temptation to attribute more power or potential to a particular technique, method, or strategy than it deserves. Too often, people in public relations or advertising, for example, suggest that only P.R. or TV commercials can solve marketing problems. Unfortunately, those of us involved in sales promotion are often guilty of the same blindness. When a marketing problem arises, our first thought is to pick out a sales promotion tool and apply it, thinking that it will automatically solve the problem. But the solution to any marketing problem requires a thorough investigation of the problem and a careful consideration of *all* the possible solutions before a recommendation can be made. In this chapter, we'll look at which marketing problems can best be solved with sales promotion and which problems are usually best answered with other marketing tools.

Growth in Sales Promotion Clouds the Issue

One of the factors causing people to believe that sales promotion can solve any type of marketing problem is the rapid growth of the industry. In Chapter 1, we discussed the dollar growth of sales promotion over the past few years. But we didn't investigate the cause of that spectacular growth. Unfortunately, not everyone agrees on the cause. Clarence Eldridge, a recognized marketing expert, believes that sales promotion has grown for three reasons:

47

1. Franchise-building advertising (sometimes called "image build-ing") is a slow process. And many marketers don't believe they can wait for advertising to have its long-term effect in the market place. They want more direct-action-oriented approaches and thus have turned to sales promotion.
2. There is an increasing lack of discernible differences between many brands in most product categories. With no competitive advantage for the product, advertising's ability to move the public to buy is reduced. Sales promotion, however, offers an important differentiat-ing factor in the market place.
3. The "cult of creativity" is increasing in advertising. Much of the advertising we now see is designed to entertain, not to sell the product. Sales promotion is designed to achieve a sale and an im-mediate sale, at that.[1]

While some may argue with Eldridge's position, the immediacy of action that sales promotion activities can provide is no doubt appealing to many marketers. Sales promotion seems to appeal particularly to con-sumer-product manufacturers, who are constantly faced with increasing competition and the need to obtain satisfactory sales shares in an in-creasingly fragmented market.

Roger A. Strang, basing his comments on research with 54 execu-tives from 17 leading consumer-goods manufacturers and advertising agencies, attributes the growth of sales promotion to "internal and external reasons." Among the "internal developments" Strang cites are: (1) Promotion has become more acceptable as a "marketing activity"; (2) more executives are better qualified to develop and administer sales promotion programs. With the increased emphasis on sales promotion, new staff positions have been created in sales promotion and new, highly trained people have filled those positions; (3) more and more companies are implementing the product management system in which product managers are rewarded on the basis of prompt returns. Since sales promotion programs often give faster returns than do advertising or public relations programs, the product manager relies on them to satisfy the expectations of management. Also, since sales promotion programs are short term, they are often easier to get approved than are longer-term advertising campaigns.

External changes in the business environment have also had an effect on the growth of sales promotion. Strang says: (1) there are more brands in almost every product category. Since consumer goods com-panies rely heavily on sales promotion to introduce new products and

---

1. Clarence E. Eldridge, *Marketing for Profit* (New York: Macmillan, 1970), pp. 125-138.

since the number of new products has grown dramatically, the resulting increase in sales promotion investments is only natural. Also, (2) competitors are increasing their spending on sales promotion. And as more competitors make use of sales promotion activities, the obvious choice of the marketer is to increase his own sales promotion spending. Thus, investment in the category has a spiraling effect; (3) economic conditions have been unstable. Since the end of the Vietnam war, the U.S. economy has been undergoing dramatic changes. Energy and product shortages, inflation, and increased governmental restraints in all phases of business have had their effect. Also, as was discussed in Chapter 1, consumer response to sales promotion activities, due in many instances to rapidly increasing prices, has grown dramatically in the past few years. Consumers are taking advantage of sales promotion offers more frequently as they seek to make their dollars go further. Finally, (4) trade pressure on manufacturers and marketers has increased as well. The increasing consolidation of food and drug chains, discount houses, and other retailers, along with their increased marketing sophistication, has brought greater pressure on manufacturers to provide broader and wider sales promotion support and allowances. Retailers expect a totally integrated marketing plan to help support the products they stock. This naturally means an increase in sales promotion dollars. Strang predicts no decline in the importance of sales promotion in the future. In fact, he predicts even more rapid future growth.[2]

Finally, the growth of sales promotion can probably be attributed to the growth of marketing activity in all fields. J. O. Peckham, Sr., using A. C. Nielsen Retail Index information, found there is a direct correlation between the share of market achieved by an individual brand and the brand's share of the total investment in marketing by all brands in the category. For example, if a brand holds a 25 percent share of sales in a retail category such as razor blades, it can hold that share only by investing approximately 25 percent of all branded marketing dollars in the razor blade category.

On the other hand, to break through the competitive activities, a new brand in a category must invest one and one-half to two (or even more) times the share of market it expects to achieve in marketing dollars. This relationship, which is a helpful rule of thumb for marketers, is another reason why sales promotion activities are probably increasing overall. As established brands invest more and more dollars in marketing to achieve a greater share of the overall category, sales promotion, used simply as a

---

2. Reprinted by permission of the *Harvard Business Review*. Excerpt adapted from "Sales Promotion—Fast Growth, Faulty Management," by Roger A. Strang (July-August, 1976); Copyright © 1976 by the President and Fellows of Harvard College. All rights reserved.

marketing tool, must increase. And this amounts to a constantly increasing spending spiral in every category. Additionally, as product categories become more crowded with new brands seeking a share of the market, more direct marketing activities, such as sales promotion, are usually favored over other, less direct means, such as advertising or public relations.

Whatever the cause, sales promotion is increasing both in terms of the percentage of dollars of the marketing budget and in total investment as well. However, because this growth may seem to suggest that sales promotion can solve any marketing problem, it is important to understand exactly what sales promotion can and can't do.

First, the Product or Service Must Be Good

Before launching into a discussion of the "can's and can't's of sales promotion," we must make one thing clear. The product or service making use of sales promotion must offer a sound consumer benefit or solve a consumer problem. If the product is not worthwhile, no marketing activity can ever produce more than a one-time sale.

For example, let's assume consumers believe and react to the advertising they see for a brand or that they are motivated by the sales promotion program. In either case, they are influenced to purchase the product. If the product does not provide the value or the benefit the consumer seeks or has been promised, it is unlikely that he or she will buy the product again. In fact, it has often been said that a good sales promotion program, which encourages trial and usage, will do more to purge the market of a poor product than any other single activity. This occurs simply because the greater the number of consumers who purchase the product, the greater the number the product will displease, and, thus, fewer and fewer prospects will remain in the market to repurchase. Eventually, no new users will try and no old users will buy, and the product will disappear.

So, in the following discussion of sales promotion, remember that the product or service must be a sound one: it must provide a benefit to the purchaser or solve some consumer problem. If it doesn't, all the promotional activity in the world won't guarantee success.

Another important point to remember is the value of the marketing concept to the sales promotion manager. You'll recall from Chapter 1 that the marketing concept involves providing products or services that the consumer wants or needs. That simply means looking at the product from the consumer's viewpoint, not the manufacturer's. A good way to do that is to say, "If I were the consumer and I bought my product, what benefit would it provide or what problem would it solve for me as the user?" If you can't think of any, then it's time to take a good, hard look at what you plan to promote. Remember, you might sell someone your product the first time with advertising, sales promotion, or some other marketing method; but it's the repeat sale that will make or break you as a marketer.

What Sales Promotion Can Do

We'll look at two kinds of sales promotion capabilities: those directed externally, or toward the consumer, and those directed internally, or toward the trade. Since each kind has a different goal and objective, we'll discuss them separately.

With the Consumer

There are eight basic goals that external or consumer-oriented sales promotion can accomplish. Each is treated generally here and will be dealt with later in more detail in connection with the various sales promotion techniques available to sales promotion managers.

Sales promotion can obtain trial of a product. Because sales promotion techniques are usually designed to provide a short-term incentive to the consumer, they can generate trial of a new product, trial of a reformulation of an existing product, or trial within a previously unused product category. Trial based on sales promotion activities is usually most successful with products having a low initial selling cost or in which the use risk by the purchaser is quite low. Sampling is an excellent sales promotion tool to achieve trial. For example, S. C. Johnson & Son, Inc. invested over $6,000,000 in sampling its new Agree creme rinse and conditioner. (See Figure 3-1.) More than 31,000,000 free samples were distributed. And the sampling worked. Agree gained an 18 percent share of the category in the first year.

In spite of the ability of sales promotion to gain successful trial of the product or service, it should always be remembered that this is initial trial only. If the product or service doesn't provide the benefits the consumer is seeking or solve the problem the consumer has, long-term repeat sales will probably not result.

Sales promotion can encourage repeat usage of a product. Through various sales promotion techniques, such as premiums, continuity programs, or savings plans, consumer purchasing habits can sometimes be influenced or product purchase patterns established. That is, if the consumer is initially satisfied with the product or service, sales promotion

Figure 3-1   Getting Trial: Agree Products

Source: *Advertising Age*, May 8, 1978, p. 54.

can often be used to encourage repeat purchase or repeat usage. A prime example of this sales promotion technique is the "Collect the Spirit of America in Glass" promotion developed by General Foods for its Log Cabin brand syrup to tie in with the Bicentennial celebration in 1976. The promotion itself was quite simple. Log Cabin developed a set of five replicas of authentic Early American flasks and used them as packages for the Log Cabin product. To obtain the complete set, a consumer had to

Figure 3-2   Getting Repeat Usage: Log Cabin Syrup

Source: William A. Robinson, *100 Best Sales Promotions of 1976/7* (Chicago: Crain Books, 1977), p. 33.

purchase the product at least five times. An example of the material used with this promotion is shown in Figure 3-2. This and similar sales promotion techniques can keep consumers coming back to the same brand, building repeat purchases and repeat usage at fairly low cost.

Figure 3-3   Increasing Product Usage: Sun Maid Raisins

Generation...
Once upon a time a little girl helped her mother bake a spicy gingerbread boy; then give him black beady eyes of tart 'n' tangy Sun Maid Zante Currants. Sun Maid is still her own sweet self, but...

...after generation...
...another little girl helps her mother stuff the bird. Her job, to toss in a handful of Sun Maid Golden Seedless Raisins, just right for the traditional sage dressing Sun Maid lives on, but...

SUN-MAID
ZANTE
CURRANTS

SUN-MAID
GOLDEN SEEDLESS
RAISINS

...after generation...
...another little girl helps bake a birthday cake. It's a mix, so it's easy to add a special touch. A cupful of plump, chewy Sun Maid Muscat Raisins. Also adds natural fruit sugar energy. Kids grow up, but...

...making life a little sweeter for all of us.
...some things never change. Like Sun Maid Raisins in the familiar red box. Nothing's been added. No preservatives. Still dried in the sun the natural way. Still the number one raisin, outselling all other brands combined. America's favorite for 3 generations.

SUN-MAID
NATURAL CALIFORNIA
RAISINS

Write for our free SWEET MEMORY COLLECTION... 3 generations of famous recipes. Write Sun Maid Recipe Offer, P.O. Box 2268...

SUN-MAID
SEEDLESS
RAISINS

Source: William A. Robinson, *100 Best Sales Promotions of 1975/6* (Chicago: Crain Books, 1976), p. 101.

Sales promotion can help build more frequent or multiple purchases. Sales promotion can be used to increase either the amount of product purchased at one time or the frequency with which consumers purchase it. By identifying new uses for an old product, consumers can be encouraged to buy more of the product or to consume more than they normally would. A very common sales promotion technique to encourage usage is the recipe book. An example is given in Figure 3-3 for Sun Maid raisins. Obviously, if consumers can be encouraged to use the

Figure 3-4   Increasing Product Usage: Imperial Sugar

Television storyboard

Magazine and newspaper ad

Back of 5# sugar bag

Dealer mat

Source: Courtesy of Imperial Sugar Company, Sugarland, Texas.

recipes Sun Maid has developed, they will likely increase their use of Sun Maid raisins.

An even more creative sales promotion idea is the Imperial Sugar home canning program. Ordinary sugar is a common household item whose use has declined over the years. To increase usage, Imperial appealed to the desire for economy and better food taste by showing consumers how to do their own home canning, which requires a great deal of sugar. Of course, Imperial tried to make sure that its brand of sugar was used through the sales promotion program. Some of the promotional materials are illustrated in Figure 3-4.

Another sales promotion technique to increase product usage is to develop a combination program for two products, such as the Bacardi

Figure 3-5   Increasing Product Usage: Bacardi Rum and Coca-Cola Soft Drink

Source: Robinson, *100 Best Sales Promotions of 1975/6*, p. 12.

rum and Coca-Cola event illustrated in Figure 3-5. This tie-in plan increased the purchase and consumption of both products.

Sales promotion can introduce a new or improved product. Established products are constantly being improved, either to keep up with
competition or as new scientific developments occur. Usually, a combination of advertising and sales promotion is used to acquaint the
consumer with these changes or improvements. Since the product is well

Figure 3-6   Introducing a Product Improvement: Glade Air Freshener

Source: Photo courtesy of Johnson Wax.

known and has been used by some consumers, a sales promotion incentive is very often enough to generate trial of the new or improved product. The Sunday newspaper supplement advertisement and coupon shown in Figure 3-6 were designed to do the job for "new" Glade Rainshower Fresh.

Sales promotion can introduce new packaging or different size packages. Often, the change to be announced isn't in the product but in

---

Figure 3-7   Introducing New Packaging: Sanka Brand Coffee

Beautiful things can happen when you save on Sanka.

For a limited time, you can get the Sunburst Jars and Cameo Tin free when you buy the Sanka inside.

Save 40¢ on Sanka

Source: Courtesy of General Foods Corp.

---

the package. This might be a new, larger size, an easier-to-use container, or a more convenient method of dispensing the product. In such cases, sales promotion is a widely used and often successful method of promoting the package change. Like product improvements, most successful package changes are made on well-known or established products. Since consumers are familiar with the product's benefits, the marketer's goal is to generate additional purchase or trial of the product right now.

Over the years Sanka brand coffee has introduced several new jars and cans as a special promotional item to consumers. In one such promotion, instead of the traditional Sanka brand package, the consumer got the new "Sunburst Jar" or "Cameo Tin" free with the purchase of the product. (See Figure 3-7.)

Sales promotion can be used to neutralize competitive advertising or sales promotion. Sales promotion techniques are often used to help

Figure 3-8   Neutralizing Competitive Activities: Schick Razor Blades

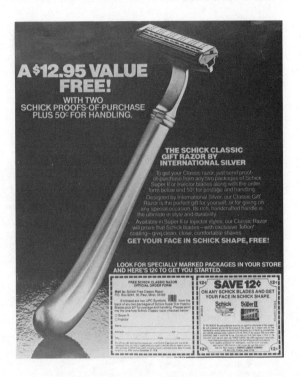

Source: Courtesy of Warner-Lambert.

offset activities by competition, either in the form of media advertising or sales promotion. For example, when a competitor launches a strong media advertising campaign for a product, consumer interest is naturally heightened in the product and the category. An aggressive marketer can blunt the competitive effort either through strong sales promotion at the point-of-sale or through some form of media program. His objective is to exploit the competitor's promotional program and turn it to his own advantage. Sometimes, he may actually build sales for the product, and, sometimes, he may only neutralize the effects of the competitive program. At the very least, the goal of the marketer is to hold his own customers in the face of this increased competition.

An example of a plan designed to neutralize a competitive sales promotion program is illustrated in Figure 3-8. Schick was faced with a massive advertising and sales promotion program by Gillette during the introduction of the Atra Shaving System. Schick wasn't able to match

Figure 3-9   Capitalizing on Special Events: Kleenex Tissues and Florida Orange Juice

Source: Robinson, *100 Best Sales Promotions of 1976/7*, p. 128.

dollars with Gillette, so they tried to offset the Gillette introduction with a sales promotion program of their own. In this case, they offered a free Schick Classic razor simply for proof-of-purchase of two packages of Schick Super II or injector blades. The idea was to offer a razor at the same time as the Gillette introduction and thus take advantage of the heightened consumer interest in the razor category. And it worked.

Sales promotion can capitalize on seasonal, geographic, or special events. There are numerous opportunities to use sales promotion for

Figure 3-10   Capitalizing on Special Events: Coca-Cola Soft Drink

Source: William A. Robinson, *Best Sales Promotions of 1977/78* (Chicago: Crain Books, 1979), p. 78.

special events that occur during the year. For example, Kleenex tissues and Florida orange juice developed a combination offer of a "cold fighters'" thermometer to tie in with the rise of colds and flu in the winter season. (See Figure 3-9.) Coca-Cola and its bottlers developed a sales promotion program on all types of balls used during the summer outdoor season to help build soft drink sales. (See Figure 3-10.) Other special events, such as the Olympics or the presidential elections, occur regularly. Perhaps the biggest special event in many years was the U.S. Bicentennial in 1976. Marketers of all types of products developed

Figure 3-11   Stemming a Seasonal Decline: Country Time Drink Mix

SONG: Country Time's for summer time, Country Time's for fall,

We love that good old-fashioned taste anytime at all.

Seasons come and seasons go, Changing all the time,

But Winter, Summer, Spring or Fall,

It's always Country Time.

CHORUS: Country Time. . .Anytime!

Tastes like that good old-fashioned lemonade.

ANNCR: Country Time Lemonade Flavor Drink. . .tastes great anytime!

SONG: Tastes like that good old-fashioned lemonade.

Source: Courtesy of General Foods Corp. and Ogilvy & Mather.

special sales promotion programs to take advantage of this "once-in-a-lifetime" promotional opportunity.

Similarly, sales promotion can be used to help stem a normal seasonal decline in sales or to help overcome a traditional change in buying patterns. For example, Country Time lemonade-flavor drink mix has used advertising and sales promotion to try and overcome the traditional decline in soft drink mix sales after Labor Day. The idea is to extend the soft drink mix season by promoting the product in an off-season, such as fall. (See Figure 3-11.)

Sales promotion can encourage consumers to "trade up" to a larger size, a more profitable line, or another product in the line. Often, sales promotion techniques are used to encourage the consumer to purchase a more expensive product in the line (trade up), purchase a larger size, or combine the purchase of one item in the line with another. Usually, this is accomplished by either a price promotion of some sort or a combination offer of two products. In most instances, the success of this type of promotion depends on the quality and image of the product being "traded up." In other words, this idea relies heavily on the image or acceptance of the product by the consumer. If this is high, then sales promotion can help.

To encourage the sale of the larger, half-gallon bottle of Chivas Regal scotch, the company promoted a personalized cradle to hold the bottle. Since it works only with the half-gallon bottle, consumers were encouraged to purchase that size rather than the more traditional fifth or quart. (See Figure 3-12.)

With the Trade

Sales promotion can be just as effective with the trade (internal sales promotion) as it is with the consumer. While the objectives and goals of promotional programs aimed at the trade are different from those directed to the consumer, the results can be just as impressive. Unfortunately, sales promotion to the trade is often not as well understood as is consumer promotion. This is because it normally receives little exposure outside the group to whom it is directed. Further, the use of sales promotion to the trade is often misunderstood by those who use it. Here, we take only a general look at what sales promotion can do with the trade.

Sales promotion can obtain feature pricing, displays, and other dealer in-store support. Probably the single greatest objective of sales promotion directed to retailers or distributors is to obtain some sort of visible support for the product at the retail level. Even the most well-

Figure 3-12   Encouraging Trade-Up: Chivas Regal Scotch

Source: Robinson, *100 Best Sales Promotions of 1976/7*, p. 77.

planned and well-executed consumer sales promotion program will usually fail if there isn't sufficient retail support. Sales promotion plans are
developed to cover all the necessary channels of distribution. The retailer, therefore, is an integral part of any sales promotion program mix.
The marketer may plan and execute the advertising and consumer promotions, but he is still dependent on the retailer to complete the chain by
making the product available.

A common method of obtaining trade support for a price promotion

---

Figure 3-13 Getting In-Store Support: Seven Crown Whiskey and Ocean Spray Cranberry Juice

---

Source: Robinson, *100 Best Sales Promotions of 1976/7*, p. 15.

---

is through a prepriced combination package or "price-pack." Another way of getting retailer pricing support is through "deals" in which the price of the product is reduced by the manufacturer, and the retailer is encouraged to pass this savings along to the consumer. Several other types of pricing concessions are also used. They will be discussed in later chapters.

Perhaps the most common sales promotion activity aimed at the trade is manufacturer-developed-and-supplied retail sales promotion and point-of-purchase materials. An example of an integrated retail program that offered the dealer a wide choice of merchandising and in-store promotional materials is illustrated in Figure 3-13. The program was developed by Seagrams for its Seven Crown whiskey and by Ocean Spray cranberry juice cocktail. They completed the promotion by scheduling it during the summer selling season and calling it "The Firecracker."

Sales promotion can help increase or reduce trade inventories. One of the major uses of sales promotion is to help build up or deplete the inventory of the manufacturer's product in the hands of distributors or retailers. Normally, this is done through some sort of trade deal that involves a price reduction, such as an off-invoice allowance, a stocking allowance, or a count-and-recount deal.

Normally, sales promotion programs designed to build trade inventories are used when the manufacturer is planning a major advertising or consumer sales promotion program. The objective is to be sure that there are sufficient stocks of the product available at the retail level to support the planned consumer campaign. An example of a totally integrated trade inventory-building sales promotion program, developed by Valvoline, is shown in Figure 3-14. The idea was to get the trade to stock up on Valvoline motor oil to take advantage of the upcoming consumer promotion.

Often, manufacturers have just the opposite objective—they would like to reduce the stock of product held by distributors or retailers rather than build it up. This may happen when a new or improved product is about to be introduced or a package changed. At that time, the manufacturer wants as few of the old products in the market place as possible. Programs are therefore designed to encourage the distributors or retailers to move out the old stock as quickly as possible. This type of sales promotion program is usually conducted through some sort of trade promotion, such as a count-and-recount offer, or through the use of advertising or merchandising allowances.

Sales promotion can help expand or improve product distribution. Sales promotion can be used to expand distribution of the product either geographically or through new trade channels. The usual approach for a manufacturer who wants to expand his geographic distribution is to offer prospective distributors and retailers some form of sales promotion program as an incentive to stock the product—a buying allowance, reduced price, or free goods. Once the product is on the shelves, the consumer advertising and sales promotion program can then be started.

Another objective is to get the product into other types of retail stores. For example, the sale of automotive accessories and parts is now quite common in supermarkets. In many cases, that additional distribution was gained through some type of sales promotion program that was attractive enough to encourage supermarkets to stock the products (plus, of course, the opportunity for the supermarkets to increase sales and profits with little or no additional costs).

Finally, sales promotion can be used to help break the exclusivity hold some manufacturers have with distributors or retailers. This exclu-

Figure 3-14   Increasing Trade Inventory: Valvoline Motor Oil

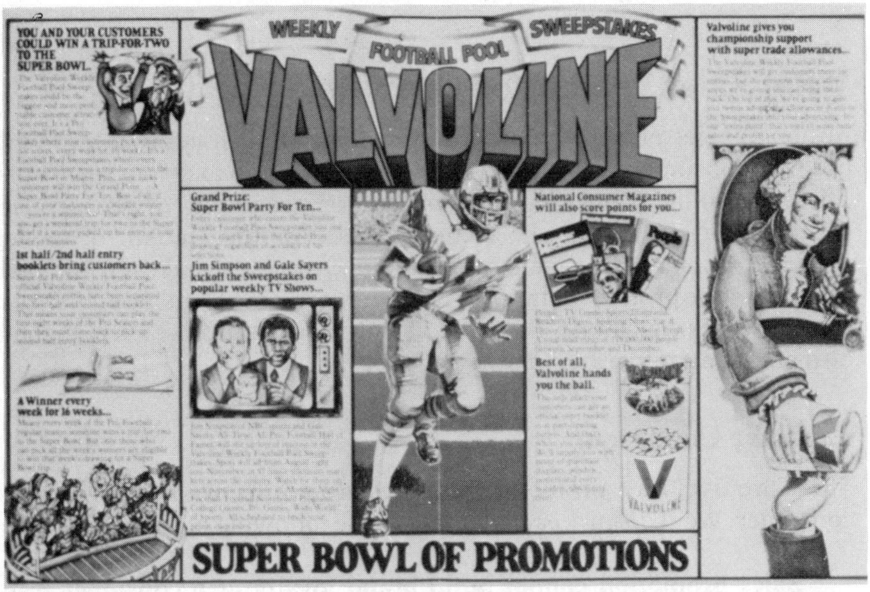

Source: William A. Robinson, *100 Best Sales Promotions* (Chicago: Crain Books, 1980), p. 37.

sive distribution phenomenon is particularly prevalent in the department store field and in such traditional single brand retailers as clothing stores, jewelers, and small appliance dealers. But attractive sales promotion programs can be developed that encourage dealers to stock more than one brand in a product category.

Sales promotion can be used to motivate the sales force, dealers, brokers, or wholesalers. A very common use of sales promotion by a manufacturer or marketer is to motivate the employees, sales force, distributors, or retailers who are responsible for the sale of the product or service. This is done through many types of programs, ranging from sales contests with expensive prizes for employees, such as trips to Hawaii or Europe, to small,free items for the store manager included with the purchase of a certain amount of the product. In either case, the objective is simple: get the people who are selling the product to either the trade or the consumer more enthusiastic about that task. Often, the sales promotion program is built around some sort of award or bonus for performance or activity on behalf of the brand. Figure 3-15 illustrates a program developed by Valvoline motor oil, offering their dealers a chance to win a trip to the Super Bowl for promoting Valvoline at retail.

What Sales Promotion Can't Do

Although sales promotion programs can accomplish many things with both the consumer and the trade, they are no cure-all for a marketer's ills. There are some things that sales promotion programs simply can't accomplish, regardless of the technique used or the amount of money invested. For example, sales promotion can never make up for deficiencies in the product or failures in other marketing areas. In addition, it seldom works well alone. To be successful, the sales promotion plan must be a part of an integrated marketing program.

With the Consumer

There are five basic problems that sales promotion can't solve with the consumer. We'll discuss each of these in the following pages.

Sales promotion cannot build brand loyalty or a consumer franchise. While sales promotion can help obtain trial of a product or service, it is still just a short-term incentive to purchase. The only thing that can really build brand loyalty or establish a consumer franchise is the satisfaction the consumer receives from the use of the product. Promotion may keep consumers purchasing in the short term, but once the promotion stops, consumers may well switch to another brand, unless the product fills a real need. The old saying "business bought with sales promotion can be lost to sales promotion" is often true. If the product does fill a consumer need or solve a consumer problem, then trial of the product may be sufficient to gain a repeat purchase. As a general rule, however, sales promotion by itself cannot build brand loyalty or establish a consumer franchise.

A great concern of many sales promotion managers is that, instead of building a consumer franchise or brand loyalty, sales promotion may, in fact, work in the opposite direction. That is, when sales promotion techniques, such as reduced prices, special features, or price-packs, are used on a regular, ongoing basis, the brand itself may be weakened. This comes about because consumers become accustomed to seeing the product at a featured price or at a reduction below normal retail. They assume that the product is always "on sale." The product may thus become a price brand rather than establishing a strong brand identity based on product benefits. In addition, with a brand that is "always on special," it

Figure 3-15   Motivating Resellers: Valvoline Motor Oil

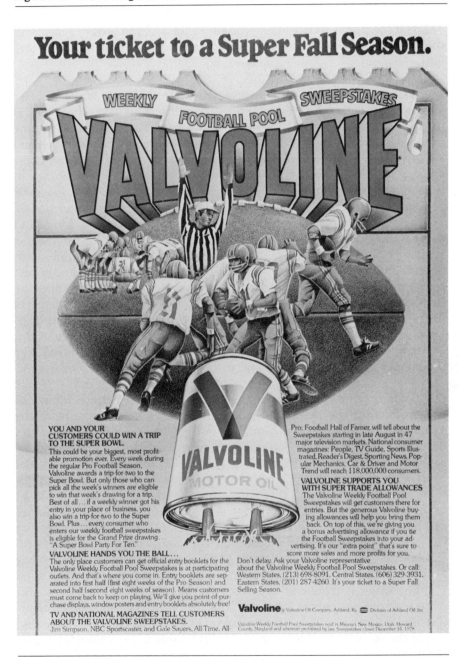

becomes difficult for the consumer to determine the regular price. Thus, when a return to normal pricing is attempted, consumers may refuse to purchase the product, thinking it is overpriced.

The continual use of sales promotion for a brand is very risky, and the line between "just enough" sales promotion and "too much" is fine indeed.

Sales promotion cannot reverse a declining sales trend. No matter what its advantages, sales promotion is still a short-term incentive. It does not have the strength or power to reverse a long-term sales decline by a brand or product. While sales promotion techniques can be used effectively to offset sales losses temporarily, they usually cannot overcome a basic marketing weakness in the product or service, a lack of repeat sales because the product or service doesn't live up to its promise, or a long-term sales decline brought on by changes in consumer image. For example, regardless of the size of the sales promotion investment and the brilliance with which the plan is conceived and conducted, it is unlikely that any technique can reverse the long-term sales decline of hot cereal. Changes in consumer living patterns and product usage are just too great. Few hot breakfasts are served in homes today because the emphasis is on "eat and run." Thus, the demand for hot cereal has declined and will probably continue to do so in the future. While short-term sales promotion techniques can be used to help offset this sales decline, little can be done to build consumer demand for hot cereal over the long term. It is simply not a product many people want or use today.

Sales promotion cannot change basic consumer nonacceptance of the product. If the consumer doesn't believe the product to be of the same quality as the competition, it is unlikely that sales promotion can correct that impression. For example, American Motors has conceived and executed many brilliant sales promotion programs, such as the "Buyer Protection Plan," making certain accessories standard equipment, and rebates, yet all these programs apparently have not made up for the consumer's lack of interest or desire for the American Motors product. If given a choice between an American Motors car and one from General Motors or Ford, the consumer will usually buy from GM or Ford. While sales promotion has brought AMC products much attention, it has failed to improve the basic acceptance of the product itself.

The same is true of many other products, such as cigarettes, soft drinks, and even yogurt. For example, in the early 1960s when fruit-flavored yogurt was first being introduced into this country, sampling, one of the staples of sales promotion, was unable to increase trial or sale of the product significantly. Research showed that the consumer was convinced that yogurt did not taste good. Many consumers would not even accept a free sample of the product. Until the taste misconception was overcome, no amount of sales promotion could convince them otherwise. Only a combination of advertising, publicity, public relations, and sales promotion was able to do the job, and that took several years.

Sales promotion cannot compensate for inadequate levels of consumer advertising. For most consumer products, advertising is a key ingredient in the marketing mix. The use of sales promotion cannot make up for a lack of consumer advertising any more than advertising can make up for a lack of sales promotion. In most instances, advertising and sales promotion seem to work synergistically; i.e., the effect of the combination of the two is greater than either used alone. Studies have shown that a combination of media advertising and a strong sales promotion program is much more effective than investing the same amount in either technique individually.

Because of pressure to increase sales, marketing neophytes often attempt to use sales promotion as a temporary replacement for a well-planned, totally integrated marketing program. In many cases, this reliance on sales promotion alone just doesn't work. In an article in the *Harvard Business Review*, Strang described a "promotion war" that illustrates this point clearly. (See Table 3-1.) As the evidence shows, no one wins a sales promotion war. The best solution to the problem is to use sales promotion in combination with other marketing activities, most particularly media advertising.

Sales promotion cannot overcome product problems in pricing, packaging, quality, or performance. The use of sales promotion assumes a good product at a reasonable price in a convenient package. If those ingredients aren't present, no amount of sales promotion, advertising, or other marketing activity can make the product successful over the long term. Repeat purchase and long-term growth depend entirely upon the consumer's satisfaction with the performance of the product. Without that, sales promotion can be of little help in increasing sales.

With the Trade

While sales promotion is widely used with the trade, there are certain objectives it can't achieve. By knowing these limitations in advance, you can avoid major problems. We'll look only at the general limitations here. Each will be dealt with in more detail in later chapters.

Sales promotion cannot compensate for a poorly trained sales force. Too often, it seems, marketing management believes that if you make the sales promotion program strong enough, anyone who walks

Table 3-1a   Net Results of Promotion War

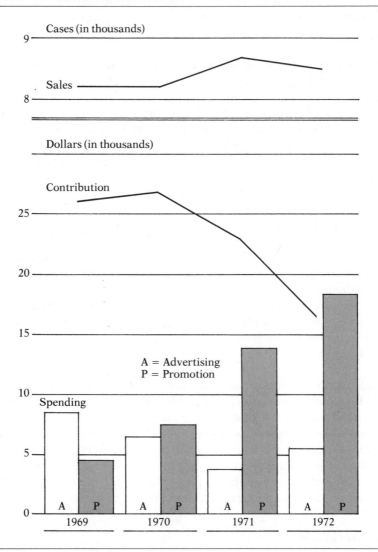

Note: Richard J. Weber, an experienced marketing executive, has documented the history of a trade promotion war that cut profits for the major competitors. He did not identify the market, but it appears to be that of a frequently purchased consumer good.

In 1969 the market was growing at twice the population rate and three brands accounted for 55.5% of total sales. In the following year, a new brand manager for the smallest

Table 3-1b   Brand Comparison

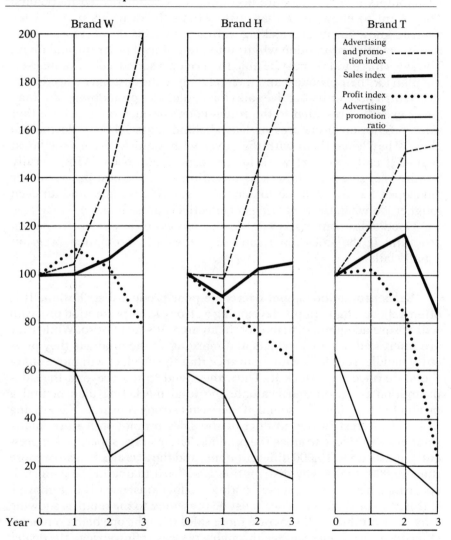

of these brands decided to try to increase sales by reducing advertising and offering higher trade allowances. This tactic led to an initial increase in sales, but it also let to a response from ompetitors.

Over the next two years, cycles of response and counter response saw promotion increase by 450 percent and advertising decrease by 38 percent [Table 3-1a]. The net result for all three brands together was: a 3 percent increase in total sales, a 1.4 percent drop in market share, and a 35 percent decline in profits.

Table 3-1b shows that all three leading brands were affected, although it appears that the greater reliance placed on advertising, the less severe the impact was.

and talks can sell the program to the trade. That just isn't so anymore. Distributors and retailers are becoming very sophisticated marketers. They want to know more than just "what's the deal this time?" They want to know turnover, stocking, estimated effects of consumer advertising, how this promotion will fit into their overall program, and more. The sales force today must be able to develop a sound, cohesive marketing plan for their products and then relate it to the customer's needs.

With a poor or ineffective sales force, the sales promotion plans may never even be presented to the trade. Poor salesmen often believe that sales promotion brochures or leave-behind materials can do the job alone. They leave them with the buyer with a quick "Here's the latest deal—I'll call you next week for the order" approach. With literally hundreds of sales people seeking attention, even the best program ever developed has a tough job under the best circumstances and an even tougher job when the program isn't effectively presented.

Good sales training is vital to the success of any sales promotion program. If the sales force can't sell, the sales promotion program usually fails.

Sales promotion cannot overcome poor product distribution. It is often believed that simply developing a strong sales promotion program will ensure adequate distribution in an area. It's just not so. While they are interested in new products and margins on the products they presently handle, retailers want assurance that the product will move out of the store once they stock it. Thus, they tend to look beyond the sales promotion program and evaluate the total marketing plan behind a product. If the plan isn't sound, if there isn't strong consumer advertising to build interest in the product or the sales promotion feature, many retailers will refuse to stock the product. The average supermarket presently stocks up to 10,000 different items and the average drugstore more than 15,000; that's why distribution is so hard to obtain. To gain shelf space for a new product, some existing product must usually be removed. If this is to be done, evidence must be presented to the retailer, showing why your product will generate more sales than the one being replaced. Offering a certain percentage through a per-case allowance to the dealer means nothing if the product doesn't move. A dealer margin of 100 percent profit on zero sales is still zero profit.

To gain distribution, sales promotion must be combined with the other elements of the marketing mix. It seldom works well alone.

Sales promotion cannot compensate for a lack of consumer advertising. This limitation is very closely related to limitations discussed in preceding sections. While it can be extremely effective in moving products, sales promotion relies in most cases on a strong media advertising plan to make consumers aware of the product benefits. If the consumer isn't aware of the product or the sales promotion offer or doesn't know about the feature price, chances of success are greatly reduced. In addition, media advertising is usually required to establish the value of the product or service, so that the sales promotion offer will have appeal. A large discount or combination offer on two unknown products usually doesn't fare too well with consumers these days.

All of these advantages and disadvantages have been proven in the market place over the years. Sales promotion can be an exciting and effective tool for increasing the sales of most types of products and services, but you must know what sales promotion can and can't do to use it effectively.

Consumer Sales Promotion Effectiveness

The next natural question is, "When is sales promotion most effective?" J. O. Peckham, Sr., working with years of A. C. Nielsen Company store audit data, developed the following list. Peckham says that sales promotion is most effective in building a franchise for consumer products under the following conditions.

1. On *new* brands or established brands with a major product *improvement*
2. On brands already enjoying an improving competitive trend
3. In conjunction with a sales drive to increase store distribution
4. When used only occasionally
5. In addition to—rather than as a replacement of—brand advertising[3]

As further explanation, Peckham has found that to be most effective the new brand or the major product improvement must be readily apparent to the consumer. Small or inconsequential changes in the product or changes that are not readily discernible do not have the same effect. Peckham also found that sales promotion programs work best when used on an occasional or infrequent basis. In addition they are more successful if they are confined to a campaign in which rigidly limited quantities of the product are used and at intervals no closer together than 8 to 10 months.

Using the same data, Peckham also discovered when sales promotion programs were found to be least effective.

3. J. O. Peckham, Sr., *The Wheel of Marketing* (Scarsdale, NY: privately printed, 1978), p. 46.

1. On established brands with no product change
2. On established brands with a declining market share
3. As a replacement for intelligent media advertising support
4. On brands where consumer promotions are already a "way of life"
5. In product classifications subjected to intensive consumer promotion by competition[4]

If the product has gone unchanged or remained essentially the same for the past two years, sales promotion is not as effective. For those brands with a declining share of market, most gains will be temporary and will often cost more than the income from the additional business gained through sales promotion. Finally, Peckham found that manufacturers are often forced to adopt consumer promotions to offset competitive activities. When this occurs, sales promotion should be used only as a defensive measure and not as a means of increasing the share of market over the long term.

A Word of Caution

One of the hazards in using sales promotion is its very effectiveness. Marketers have often overlooked or misunderstood major product or marketing problems simply because they were blinded by the success of a strong sales promotion program. In the long run, for example, sales promotion cannot compensate for the lack of a sound, effective, and coordinated marketing program. And the same is true for other product problems. Sales promotion can often disguise the need for a strong media advertising campaign. Because sales are achieved with sales promotion, the assumption is often made that advertising is unnecessary. But nothing could be further from the truth, particularly for consumer products. A sales promotion success might also hide a product defect. In this instance, sales promotion might achieve trial, but it might be only a one-time trial. And while sales figures might be level overall, sales to regular customers might be declining.

A common mistake made by marketers when introducing a new product is to assume that the product will sell at the same rate as the first-time trial. But it is only after consumers try the product and go into the repeat-purchase cycle that the actual share of market can be estimated. Forecasting sales on the basis of initial trial usually greatly overstates what sales will be achieved on an ongoing basis.

Finally, one should be hesitant about crediting success to the product when very unusual or extreme sales promotion tactics are used. It is

---

4. Peckham, *The Wheel of Marketing*, p. 46.

easy to give a product away. It is more difficult to sell it. The major objective of most sales promotion programs is to obtain trial or usage under special conditions that will lead to regular purchase of the product at the normal price. If that cannot be done, then sales promotion has not really achieved its goal. Therefore, with any sales promotion program, one must be sure the results achieved will eventually lead to "regular price" sales over the long term.

Summary

Because of the great growth of the industry, some think of sales promotion as a cure-all for marketing problems. It is not. It can do nothing at all, really, without a good product or service to promote. Sales promotion has strengths and weaknesses, and it is equally important for a sales promotion manager to know what it can't do as to know what it can do—both with consumers and the trade. Some examples: with the consumer, sales promotion can obtain trial and repeat usage, but it can't build brand loyalty or reverse a declining sales trend. With the trade, it can obtain dealer in-store support and increase or reduce trade inventory, but sales promotion can't compensate for a poor sales force or poor distribution.

4

How Sales Promotion
Works: Types

Up to this point we have dealt with the general topic of sales promotion and identified some of the areas in which sales promotion might assist in the sale of the product. We haven't looked specifically at how sales promotion actually works. This is a difficult task for three reasons. First, all the data on sales promotion is brand- and situation-specific. Although there is a good deal of data on individual sales promotion events, the information applies only to specific brands in specific situations—to particular times and places. Therefore, the success of one sales promotion event in no way guarantees the success of another, even for the same brand using the same technique. There are just too many variables, such as economic conditions, competitive activities, and consumer attitudes, to permit broad generalizations and absolute projections.

Second, sales promotion is only a part (though often a major part) of the marketing mix. The success or failure of any sales promotion technique is therefore always at least partly dependent on other marketing factors, such as advertising, packaging, retailer cooperation, and sales force motivation. One weak link in the marketing chain can ruin any sales promotion program, regardless of investments made and skills applied. And when a particular program does succeed, it is impossible to determine precisely how much any of these marketing factors actually contributed. Furthermore, sales promotion techniques are often used in combination—coupons with refunds, price-offs with trade allowances, and it is always hard to tell which partner in the temporary marriage did what.

Third, while sales promotion has been growing and almost every

79

consumer product manufacturer has used at least one promotion technique (and most have used many), companies tend to be very secretive
about plans, performances, and results. Marketing people are usually
willing to release information on advertising expenditures, for example,
but are unwilling to discuss sales promotion data. Thus, although there
are no doubt large quantities of information on all aspects of sales
promotion locked away in the files of manufacturers and marketers,
much of it has yet to be released for public use. Until this attitude
changes, we will be much less informed about this important area of
marketing than we are about advertising, public relations, and retail
sales.

All this does not mean that we know absolutely nothing about sales
promotion. But generalization and extrapolation must proceed cautiously and tentatively. Though the facts are narrow, limited, and sometimes inaccessible, at least they exist. And some reliable guidelines,
based on the available data—used judiciously—can be developed. We
can say with reasonable confidence, for example, that coupons help
induce repurchase and that free-in-the-mail premiums help load customers. In addition, the job of sales promotion analysis has been greatly
aided by the recent advent of AFE (automated front end) scanners and
data-gathering equipment using the Universal Product Code. They have
enabled us to trace specific sales results from specific sales promotions
with extraordinary precision and comprehensiveness for the 15,000
brands and products sold by supermarkets and drug stores. The quantity
of data allows us to generalize more confidently. The frequency with
which data are analyzed (weekly for most products) and the length of
time over which they can be collected (a year or more, if necessary)
allows us to determine the effects and aftereffects of particular marketing activities more precisely. And the availability of the data (limited
only by accidental erasures) allows us to study various brands, products,
and product categories more thoroughly.

In this chapter we will use some of the guidelines developed from the
more or less limited data gathered over the past few years and refine
them with the help of the scanner data now available. Although the
generalizations that follow may not hold for every product in every
competitive situation, they can be used to provide some fairly accurate
and reliable indications of what can and can't be expected from sales
promotion.

What We Know: Some Basics

Despite the obstacles, we know that sales promotion works. And we also
know something about *how* it works. Table 4-1 shows the results of
marketing activities, including sales promotion, for a new product intro-

Table 4-1 Marketing Results for a New Product Introduction (market share %)

Source: Courtesy of *Chain Store Age/Supermarkets* magazine.

duction over a period of 16 weeks. (This material is based on scan data from TRIM, Inc..) As the table indicates, during the first three weeks the product got shelf space in stores and achieved a modest share of the market. In Week 4, television advertising began. In Week 6, the manufacturer distributed a coupon, which pushed sales up immediately. In Week 7, a coupon was distributed by a competitor, and sales declined. The brand increased sales again in Week 9 when a trade coupon was used for support. During the 11th and 12th weeks competition offered price reductions and set up some special displays. In the 13th week the manufacturer began a heavy advertising campaign for the brand, and sales began to rise again.

For this one product and in this one instance, we can see several effects of sales promotion:

1. Sales promotion can generate product sales immediately. (See effects of promotion in Weeks 6 and 9.)
2. Competitive promotions can have an adverse effect on sales of a brand. (Note how sales declined as a result of competitive actions in Weeks 7, 11, and 12.)

**Table 4-2   Effect of Sampling/Couponing on New Product Introduction
(% share of market)**

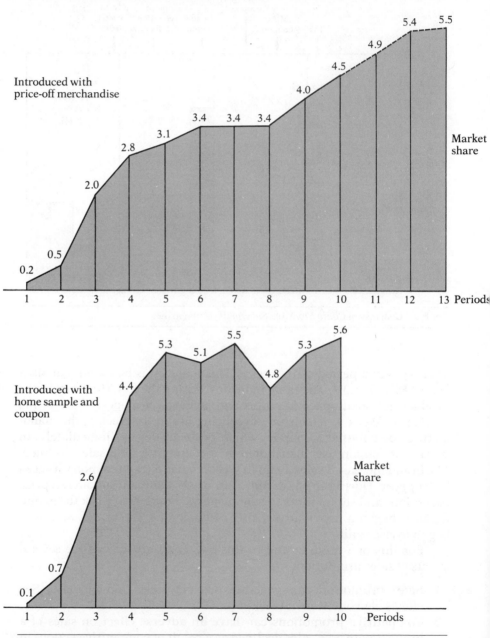

Source: A. C. Nielsen Company, *The Nielsen Researcher*, No. 3, 1980, pp. 14-15.

3. Sales promotion can build sales more rapidly than can advertising. (Note the difference in immediate sales gains with sales promotion in Weeks 6 and 9 compared to sales gains with advertising in Weeks 4 and 13 through 16.)

In addition to knowing that sales promotion works, we also know that different types of sales promotion techniques have differing effects in the market place. This is illustrated in Table 4-2. In this example, a new brand was introduced in half the country with price-off merchandise (illustrated in the upper half of the chart). In the other half of the country, the sales promotion support was a 10¢ coupon and a home sample (shown in the lower half of the chart). At the end of Period 5 (10 months), the brand had reached a market share of 5.3 percent in the sample/coupon areas, while that level was not achieved in the price-off areas until Period 12 (about 14 months later). From this example, it appears that sampling/couponing affects consumers more quickly than price-off promotions.[1] From experience, we also know that sales promotion techniques work synergistically; i.e., when combined, the total effect of the two elements is greater than the sum of the parts. This has been proven over and over in almost all product categories. Unfortunately, in most instances, there has not been sufficient information on experiments with the parts (sales promotion techniques) to say which one or ones are more effective than the others. But we are gradually learning.

Where Do Customers Come from?

Before attempting to understand how sales promotion works, it is first necessary to have an understanding of just how the market place works. This means, of course, an understanding of where customers come from, how they operate, and how a marketer might attract more of them. Unfortunately, customers don't just spring full-grown from the ground. There are some very specific rules that apply. Our first step is to look at the total market place.

Generally, we can say that all customers or prospects for any type of brand, product, or service can be located in one of the three market groups illustrated in Table 4-3. This particular concept applies to all products, all brands, and all situations. It's one of the few marketing concepts that is not dependent on conditions.

The illustration shows that there are three types of customers or prospects. Group N includes all those people who are not presently buying any product or brand within the selected category. If we were in the automatic washing machine detergent business, these would be

---

1. A. C. Nielsen Company, *The Nielsen Researcher*, No. 3, 1980, pp. 14-15.

Table 4-3   The Market Place

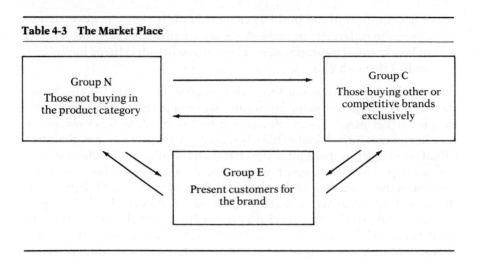

people who don't buy at all. This may be because they don't own a washer, do not use a detergent, or perhaps never wash their clothes. There could, of course, be other reasons for nonusage of the product category, but the main point is that Group N simply doesn't buy an automatic washing machine detergent under most conditions.

Group C includes those people who are buying competitive brands of automatic washing machine detergent exclusively. They use a detergent, but they use a brand other than the one we market. Notice that we said nothing about the amount of detergent they use, only that they use it and that they use a brand different from the one we are promoting.

Finally, Group E includes the customers for our brand. These people presently buy our brand of automatic washing machine detergent either exclusively or on some sort of regular basis. Notice, again, we don't discriminate as to how much of the product they use or whether or not they use other brands. We are interested only in the fact that they use our brand sometimes. We can count them as customers.

These three segments make up the entire market for automatic washing machine detergents. Note, however, that the market is not stagnant. People move from one group to another, based on their needs for the product or as they are influenced by the promotional activities of the various brands in the category. This influence can come about in many ways—from media advertising to sales promotion activities to simple word-of-mouth from a friend. The important point is simply that the people within the various categories move from one to the other, and they do so constantly. If they didn't or couldn't move among these categories, there would be no need for any type of market activity, and our discussion of sales promotion would be quite simple.

The major question, of course, is: Why do the people move from one group to another in this type of market place? First, persons in Group N can start using an automatic washing machine detergent. They may buy an automatic washer, start using a laundromat, or just start washing their clothes. When they do begin their product usage, they have two choices. They can purchase either a competitive brand or our brand. If they start purchasing a competitive brand exclusively, they become part of Group C. If they start using our brand, even if they purchase another brand, too, they become part of Group E, or our existing customers. The same sort of movement can occur among our present customers. Should they become unhappy with our brand or decide for some reason to stop using our product, they can do one of two things. (1) They can either stop using the product category altogether—by selling their automatic washing machine, ceasing to wash their clothes, or simply finding another method of cleaning their clothes, such as sending them to a commercial laundry; (2) they can continue using a product in the category but switch to a competitive brand. The same thing can happen in Group C. A person may move out of that segment because he or she has stopped using any product in the category or started using our brand. There simply aren't any other choices.

When we look at the market place in this manner, the role of all promotional activities becomes quite clear. There are really only three tasks that promotion can accomplish: (1) bring a nonuser into the product category, i.e., convert a previous nonuser to a product category user, regardless of brand; (2) switch a competitive product user to our brand; or, (3) keep our present brand users as customers and offset competitive appeals. From this example, it should also be clear that various sales promotion techniques may have a very limited effect on certain persons, based on the particular market segment in which they are located. For example, no matter how many samples of the product we give persons in Group N, there is little likelihood they will start buying our product if they don't own an automatic washing machine. They simply don't have any need for the product. But a technique such as sampling might be very effective with persons in Group C. If we could demonstrate to them, through a sample, the advantages of our product over the one they are presently using, we stand a good chance of getting trial for our product.

This concept is supported with some material recently released by A. C. Nielsen Company, based on scanner data. Nielsen traced a new product introduced into the edible food category and carried in the dairy section of food stores. Table 4-4 shows how the introduction of the product built sales in the entire category. (Note: the product was introduced in Week 4.) Of more interest to us, however, are the results of a trial and repeat study of the same product. Table 4-5 shows that by the end of the introductory period (after Weeks 5 through 8, when feature adver-

Table 4-4   Volume Sales of Category (All ScanTrack Stores)

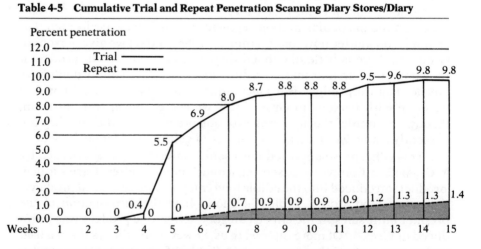

Ounce volume (hundreds)   ——— Total category

Source: A. C. Nielsen Company, *The Nielsen Researcher*, No. 1, 1981, p. 8.

tising, displays, and reduced price were used to support the brand), 8.7
percent of the households had purchased the new brand.

   In addition, a source-of-volume study was also conducted on the
brand (Brand B in the example). It showed that 71 percent of the volume
gained by the new brand came from households that had not purchased
any product in the category in the base period, that about 13 percent

Table 4-5   Cumulative Trial and Repeat Penetration Scanning Diary Stores/Diary

Percent penetration

Source: A. C. Nielsen Company, *The Nielsen Researcher*, No. 1, 1981, p. 8.

Table 4-6   Brand B Source of Volume

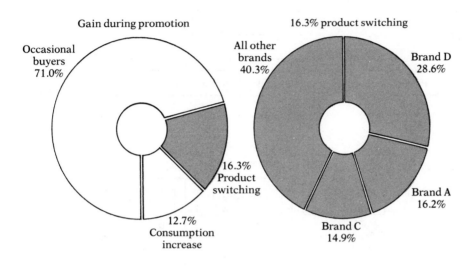

Source: A. C. Nielsen Company, *The Nielsen Researcher*, No. 1, 1981, p. 9.

came from increased consumer consumption, and that 16 percent came from product switching. This is illustrated in Table 4-6. In addition, on the right-hand side of Table 4-6, you can see that Brand B gained 28.6 percent from Brand D and 40.3 percent from the All Others category, which included primarily price brands. Brand A, which was the category leader and sold at a premium price, was hardly affected by the introduction.[2]

Thus, when this scanner data is related back to the idea of the three groups in the market place, present users, competitive users, and non-users, it is evident that the concept works in the real world, too.

It becomes apparent that no product can appeal to everyone. No matter how widely the product is used, there are some people who simply will never be users or even prospects for some products. Thus, one of the keys to successful sales promotion is targeting the sales promotion activity to the most logical prospect groups. This is called selecting a "target market." It is usually done by identifying various segments within these brand groups as the ones most likely to buy.

From Table 4-7, it should be obvious that in addition to the general segment categories, there are numerous subsegments in each group. For

2. A. C. Nielsen Company, *The Nielsen Researcher*, No. 1, 1981, pp. 8-9.

Table 4-7   Subsegments of Group E

Group E			
Product usage	**Loyalty to brand**	**With additives**	**Water temperature**
Heavy	Exclusive	None	Hot
Medium	Majority of use	Bleach	Warm
Light	Regular	Pre-soak	Cold
	Occasional	Brightener	

Type of machine	**Ownership of machine**	**Washing frequency**
Top loading	Own	Daily
Front loading	Borrow neighbor's	2 per week
Other	Coin-operated (apt.)	Weekly
	Laundromat	

Type of wash	**Size of pkg. purchased**
Work clothes	Family size
Normal wash	Large size
Permanent press	Smallest size
Fragile fabrics	

example, just in Group E, our existing customers, we might find the following types of users for an automatic washing machine detergent. There are many, many ways to segment, differentiate, or identify just the present users of our brand. And, this doesn't include persons in the other two groups.

Clearly, the market place can be a very complex arena for the sales promotion manager. And that complexity is one reason why we can't be certain of what sales promotion can and can't do. There are simply too many variables to contend with. We can't point to any one model as the definitive indication of how the market place works or how sales promotion functions within it. We do, however, have a general understanding of the kinds of situations the sales promotion manager often faces. We'll look at them now.

Trade Promotion

The general objective of a sales promotion program to the trade is to accomplish one or both of the following goals:

1. To increase the sale of the product to existing wholesalers, distributors, brokers, retailers, etc., so that they will either promote increased sales to the ultimate consumer or carry a larger inventory of the product.
2. To increase the distribution of the product to include new geographic areas, new types of distributors and retailers, or new retail categories.

Most manufacturers or marketers consider sales promotion to the trade to be a method of increasing short-term sales. It can also increase long-term sales if the promotion can broaden the distribution of the product. For example, a manufacturer might develop a trade promotion designed to get distribution of a new size of the product. If existing trade channels accept the new size, while maintaining present sizes, the total trade market for the product will be expanded. If new distributors decide to stock the product because of the promotion, additional sales will result. In both instances, these will be net gains for the marketer. If, however, the existing distributors simply exchange one size for another—for example, stock the smaller size and drop the larger one, total sales could actually decline. Thus, the success of the sales promotion program depends not only on moving additional product but also on the net gains achieved from the sales promotion program. We'll look at this in more detail later in this chapter.

Types of Trade Promotions

J. O. Peckham, Sr., has divided the general category of trade promotions into two types.

1. Payment for services rendered by the trade. This is a discount to the trade at the wholesale or direct buyer level of so much per case, for featuring, displaying, or advertising the brand for a specified, limited period of time. The wholesaler must agree to pass this discount along to the retailer, who, in turn, must agree to cooperate. Basically, this is meant to be a payment for services rendered the manufacturer by the retailer, rather than a means of lowering prices to the consumer.
2. Buying allowance or trade deal. Again, this is a discount to the trade at the wholesale or direct buying level, in order to increase trade

purchases and, hopefully, to bring about a reduction of the retail price to the consumer and in this way stimulate sales at the store level.[3]

The first type of sales promotion program (payment for services rendered) is simply an attempt by the manufacturer or the marketer to bring his promotional activities down to the local level. While national advertising may be effective for many products, unless the product is featured at the local retail store, so the consumer knows where to purchase it, the promotion may go unnoticed. Thus, the manufacturer pays the organizations in the distribution channel to localize his product, his offer, or his sales promotion event.

In the second type (buying allowance), the direct offer is made through the distribution channels in an attempt to obtain a lower retail shelf price. If the retailer will feature the product at a reduced price (and often the retailer reduces the price below the amount the manufacturer allows for competitive reasons), the product will usually receive the attention of the consumer.

How a Trade Promotion Works

Regardless of the type used, trade promotions can succeed only if some incentive is ultimately offered to the consumer—whether it be a lower price, a store display, a premium, or a refund. The assumption is that the consumer will recognize the value of the incentive and purchase the product, favoring it over competition for as long as the promotion lasts.

Ideally, a trade promotion in the form of a trade discount is designed to lower the shelf price of the product during the period of the promotion. This price reduction is intended to appeal to all three market groups. That is, the lower price would reward present customers (Group E) and keep them purchasing; should influence Group C, who use another brand, to try the product because of the lower cost; and might influence those in Group N who don't use the product at all, but might if the price were lower. Thus, the lower retail price is used to increase sales to all three consumer groups, either at the expense of other brands or by bringing new customers into the market for the product. This is illustrated in Table 4-8.

The simplified chart in Table 4-8 shows the planned effects of a reduced price sales promotion event based on a trade discount. During Month 1, when regular prices existed at retail for Brand XYZ, the product held a 10 percent share of the total market. During Month 2, a reduced price sales promotion program was instituted through a trade promo-

---

3. J. O. Peckham, Sr., *The Wheel of Marketing* (Scarsdale, NY: privately printed, 1978), p. 29.

Table 4-8   Planned Effects of a Reduced-Price Sales Promotion Program through Trade Promotion Brand XYZ

Source: Adapted from Peckham, *The Wheel of Marketing*, p. 33.

tion. This reduced price was passed along by the wholesaler to the retailer, and the retailer passed it along to the final consumer. As a result of the reduced price, the share of the market (SOM) for Brand XYZ increased 5 percent to 15 percent during Month 2. This increase was made up of a 2 percent gain in additional product used by existing consumers (Group E), a 2 percent gain from competitive product users (Group C), and a 1 percent increase from people who previously had not used any product in the category (Group N). (Technically, the share of market would not have increased at the same rate as the increased usage by people entering the market, which would have been distributed over the entire product category. It is used here for illustrative purposes only.)

The promotion was discontinued at the end of Month 2. However, Brand XYZ maintained a 13 percent share of market. It did this by holding half of the increased usage among existing customers, or 1 percent. It also held half of the original 2 percent from competitive brands and all of the new users of the product. This increased share of market becomes apparent in Month 3. By the end of Month 4, all these

SOM gains were consolidated, so that Brand XYZ considered all its customers to be existing, even though they had been gained over the past two months. This SOM, of course, includes the increased usage by the brand's regular customers, as a result of the sales promotion program. It thus had a new base of 13 percent SOM as a result of its sales promotion program.

This is what happens ideally with the reduced price sales trade promotion program. Unfortunately, it doesn't always work that way. Often, competitive users who purchase during the promotion do so only that one time. They don't remain customers of Brand XYZ after the promotion. Existing customers may only take advantage of the reduced price to stock up on the brand and not truly increase their usage. Sometimes, no new customers come into the market, regardless of the price incentive offered through the promotion. In spite of these potential problems, however, this is the way a sales promotion program is designed to work. If all three consumer groups react to the event at once, which is rare, the sales promotion program is a great success. More often, though, the share of market for a brand ebbs and flows because other marketers are developing and implementing their own sales promotion programs that affect the market place. They too are trying to increase sales and attract new customers.

Through research we are able to verify that various sales promotion tactics achieve certain results. For example, A. C. Nielsen reported the results of a study of the effects of a bonus pack offered the trade by a manufacturer in the health care field. The bonus pack was made available by the manufacturer in a package that contained as much as 40 percent more of the product at no increase in price. Illustrated in Table 4-9 are the sales results achieved by retail stores under four conditions: (1) stores handling the promotion in 1979 and again in 1980, (2) stores handling the bonus pack in 1979 but not in 1980, (3) stores not handling the bonus pack in either year, and (4) stores not handling the bonus pack in 1979 but handling it in 1980. It is clear that drugstores handling the bonus pack did much better than those that didn't. The same is true for the food stores. Thus, we have further evidence that sales promotions do work and an indication that trade deals or promotional packs can help build sales for retailers if they accept and use the promotion.

With this general idea in mind, we can now look at the economics of a trade promotion and see what effect a reduced price or other promotional tool might have on the sales and profits of an organization.

The Economics of a Trade Promotion

No matter what type of sales promotion program a manufacturer or marketer might use, there is a direct relationship between the sales

Table 4-9   Sales Trend of Stores Handling Factory Pack vs. Stores Not Handling

	Drugstores Total Client Sales			Food Stores Total Client Sales		
	1979	1980	% Chg.	1979	1980	% Chg.
Total unified stores	591.2	658.5	+11%	637.1	656.1	+3%
Condition 1: Stores *handling* any Client Brand bonus packs in 1980 *and handling* in 1979.	424.5	473.5	+11	415.8	409.7	−1
Condition 2: Stores *handling* any Client Brand bonus packs in 1979 *but not handling* in 1980.	14.3	12.4	−14	20.9	14.2	−32
Condition 3: Stores *not handling* any Client Brand bonus packs in 1980 *and not handling* in 1979.	39.0	31.9	−18	34.7	31.7	−9
Condition 4: Stores *not handling* any Client Brand bonus packs in 1979 *but handling* in 1980.	113.4	140.7	+24	165.7	200.5	+21

Source: A. C. Nielsen, *The Nielsen Researcher*, No. 4, 1980, p. 7.

promotion program and the profitability of the product being promoted. J. O. Peckham, Sr., has calculated the economics of a 10 percent trade deal in terms of a break-even return. This is illustrated in Table 4-10.

While it is almost impossible to determine exactly what the effects of a 10 percent trade deal might be, an idea can be obtained by contrasting the Gross Trading Profit (GTP) on the additional consumer sales resulting from the trade deal with the trade deal itself. Peckham says:

What increase in *consumer* sales would be necessary just to break even—to balance promotion costs? [This can be answered] by analyzing the economics of a 10% trade deal on a branded item normally selling to the trade at $20 per case.

Assume that the manufacturer normally averages sales to the trade of 5,000 cases per month—$100M at the normal trade price of $20 per case. If he cuts this price 10% to $18 for, say a 30-day period, obviously he must sell through, *at the consumer level,* 11.1% more than this or a total of 5,556 cases merely to break even on a manufacturer's revenue basis.

Further assume that he operates on a 50% gross trading profit margin or $10 per case; the $2 per case trade discount must come out of the gross trading profit since it will still require $10 per case to pay for the cost of goods sold. Thus the GTP on the deal goods is not $10 but $8, and the number of cases he must sell through at the consumer level to break even on a GTP basis must be 6,250 cases—an increase of 25% for the 30-day period the deal is in effect and normal sales thereafter.

If the trade buyer decides to really take advantage of the deal, and many

**Table 4-10   Economics of a 10% Trade Deal on Branded Item
Normally Selling to Trade at $20 Per Case**

Consumer sales required to produce equivalent revenues (break even)

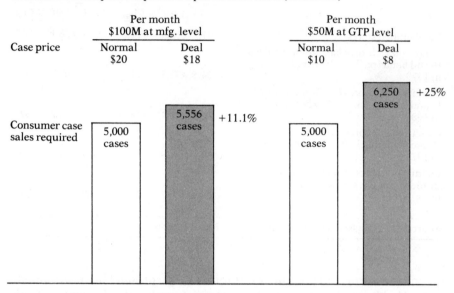

Source: Peckham, *The Wheel of Marketing*, p. 33.

of them customarily act in this fashion even to the extent of buying only on deals when they know that the manufacturer has a consistent deal policy, he may buy ahead an additional month or two (at the expense of future purchases, of course), in which event sales to the consumer will have to increase 25% for each extra month of deal purchases as well.[4]

As you can see from Peckham's calculations, unless they are extremely successful at the retail level, trade deals can actually end up as a loss instead of a gain to the manufacturer. Therefore, unless a trade (or any) sales promotion program is carefully developed and controlled, a major expense may result. Further, major Gross Trading Margin losses can also quickly result.

As we demonstrated earlier, the objective of most trade promotions is to increase total sales of the product. Unfortunately, that isn't always the result. Using several years of A. C. Nielsen Company data, Peckham found that, in many cases, instead of increasing sales to the trade, trade

---

4. Peckham, *The Wheel of Marketing*, p. 34.

Table 4-11 Effect of Cents-Off Promotion on Well-Established Major Advertised Brand "A"

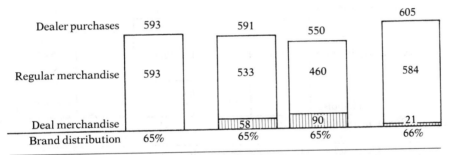

	Pre-deal	Peak-deal		Post-deal
Consumer sales	601	600	559	592
Regular merchandise	601	561	468	558
Deal merchandise		39	91	34
Brand share	10.2%	9.9%	9.3%	9.6%
Dealer purchases	593	591	550	605
Regular merchandise	593	533	460	584
Deal merchandise		58	90	21
Brand distribution	65%	65%	65%	66%

Source: Peckham, *Wheel of Marketing*, p. 45, opposite.

deals really only replaced sales of regularly priced merchandise. The two charts in Tables 4-11 and 4-12 illustrate that point.

As these two examples show, neither sales promotion program was really successful in producing more profit, although large sales occurred. In both cases, the dealer simply sold deal merchandise at regular prices. Peckham contends, and we agree, that no trade promotion can really be considered successful unless it

1. Sells more merchandise to the trade than normal (including the customary postpromotion fall-off in sales to the trade)
2. Increases distribution in the retail outlets.[5]

Consumer Promotion

As is the case with trade promotion, there are some areas in which there

---

5. Peckham, *The Wheel of Marketing*, p. 45.

**Table 4-12   Effect of Cents-Off Promotion on
Well-Established Major Advertised Brand "B"**

	Pre-deal	Peak-deal	Post-deal
Consumer sales	29.5	30.0	29.6
Regular merchandise	29.5	18.8	27.0
Deal merchandise		11.2	2.6
Brand share	13.7%	14.7%	12.7%
Dealer purchases	29.4	29.7	29.2
Regular merchandise	29.4	18.5	25.5
Deal merchandise		11.2	3.7
Brand distribution	92%	92%	92%

Source: Peckham, *Wheel of Marketing*, p. 45, opposite.

is fairly detailed data on how consumer promotion works, while in other areas we lack the solid information we'd like to have. In spite of these problems, we'll deal with the subject as thoroughly as possible.

Types of Consumer Promotions

A consumer sales promotion may be any type of price or premium that furnishes a special incentive to the consumer to purchase a specific brand. Generally, a consumer sales promotion technique requires the use of some form of mass communication, but not always. In addition, for most consumer sales promotions to work, the product must be available to the consumer; i.e., the consumer must have a fairly wide range of stores at which he or she can take advantage of the sales promotion offer.

How a Consumer Promotion Works

Using A. C. Nielsen Company data, J. O. Peckham, Sr., suggests that

Table 4-13   Consumer Promotions Are Supposed To Work Like This

Source: Peckham, *The Wheel of Marketing*, p. 37, opposite.

consumer sales promotions are supposed to work as illustrated in Table 4-13. That is, a consumer promotion is supposed to build sales and share, as shown. From the prepromotion level of 10 percent, sales promotion should generate additional brand sales, raising them to the 12 percent level. Since some of the purchasers will only be triers or will buy only when the price is reduced, some of these triers will be lost. It is hoped, however, that the promotion will provide a net gain in the form of an increased market share—in this instance, about 1 percent or a total SOM of 11 percent as a result of the promotion.

The data reveal, however, that the sales promotion gain isn't always that successful. Often the results are more like those given in Table 4-14. The promotion succeeds only in attracting one-time new users (left-hand side of chart). Or it provides the product at a lower price to some regular customers, fails to attract new users, and then loses some regular customers when they refuse to pay the normal price for the product after the promotion is over (right-hand side of chart). Thus, sales promotion may not only cost the marketer income in the short term but may even result in a long-term loss.

The Economics of a Consumer Promotion

While the goal of sales promotion is to increase market share, this is often hard to do, simply because there are numerous other manufacturers flooding the market with their own promotional programs. The consumer is, it seems, constantly bombarded by sales promotion offers. As a result, many consumers apparently simply swing from brand to brand,

Table 4-14   But Only Too Frequently They Work:

Like This . . .

| Pre-promotion market share | Promotion period market share | Post-promotion market share |

Or Even Like This!

| Pre-promotion market share | Promotion period market share | Post-promotion market share |

Regular merchandise

Source: Peckham, *The Wheel of Marketing*, p. 38, opposite.

taking advantage of various offers, without developing any brand loyalty.

While this switching is disconcerting, a sales promotion program can be successful even though it does not provide long-term results. That depends, of course, on the cost of the promotion. If it is not too high, the manufacturer can profit even in the short term. Peckham illustrates this with the "10-Cents Off" offer in Table 4-15.

Peckham goes on to say:

Now, of course, there is nothing wrong with a sales gain even if it occurs only during the promotion itself and does not carry over into subsequent periods—*providing* it does not cost too much! [Table 4-15] examines the economics of a "10-cents off" promotion on a $1.00 item—a 10% reduction in price at the consumer level. The chart assumes that the manufacturer merely wants to break even by producing the same number of dollars and examines the situation from three levels—the consumer level, the manufacturer's sales level, and the manufacturer's gross profit level.

Table 4-15   Economics of "10-Cents Off" on a $1.00 Item

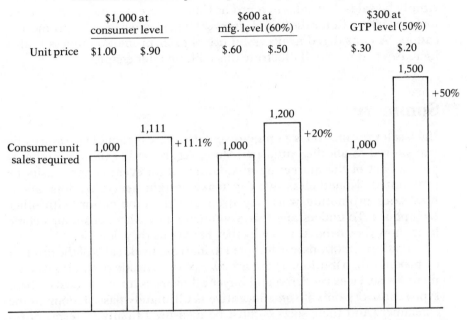

Consumer unit sales required to produce equivalent revenues of:

	$1,000 at consumer level		$600 at mfg. level (60%)		$300 at GTP level (50%)	
Unit price	$1.00	$.90	$.60	$.50	$.30	$.20

Consumer unit sales required:
1,000   1,111   +11.1%   1,000   1,200   +20%   1,000   1,500   +50%

Source: Peckham, *The Wheel of Marketing*, p. 39, opposite.
Note: Assumes same number of cents per unit trade profit.

Assume that the manufacturer wants to take in $1,000 at the consumer level. At the standard price of $1.00 per unit he'll obviously have to sell 1,000 units; at ninety cents, however, he will have to sell 1,111 units or 11.1% more to produce the same consumer revenue.

What does this situation look like at the manufacturer's revenue level, as shown in the central section? Deducting trade discounts and allowances from the $1,000 consumer sales leaves, say $600 at the manufacturer's revenue level or sixty cents each of the 1,000 units. But, since he is cutting his revenue by 10 cents per unit, he only nets fifty cents which means he must sell 1,200 units or 20% more in order to break even.

However, the manufacturer cannot stop his analysis here, because out of his revenue of sixty cents per unit he still has to pay the factory for the goods. Assuming that he's working on a 50% gross trading profit level and that the increased sales generated by the promotion will not materially lower his unit GTP. To generate the required $300 GTP, therefore, he will have to sell 1,500 units or 50% more than the 1,000 units required by the normal thirty-cent per unit GTP. Since sales gains of this size rarely occur, one must conclude that these temporary gains frequently cost more than the gross trading profit that they bring in.[6]

The primary interest of the sales promotion manager must not simply be sales, but sales at a profit. Unless there is some short-term or long-term benefit for the brand, gross sales generated by sales promotion cannot be considered a successful use of sales promotion unless it also increases profits. We'll illustrate this point in later chapters.

Summary

Each sales promotion is a unique event. Its success cannot necessarily be transferred to another situation. Moreover, because sales promotion is only a part of the marketing mix, failure of an event cannot easily be pinpointed. Nonetheless, we can make certain generalizations about how sales promotion works by itself and in combination with other techniques. To understand this, you must know where customers come from, how they behave, and why they behave as they do.

Trade promotions are designed to increase trade sales of the product or product distribution. There are two types of trade promotions: payment for services rendered and buyer allowances, or trade deals. These types can work only if some incentive is ultimately passed along to the consumer. And their success must be measured finally in terms of increased profit to the manufacturing company.

Consumer sales promotions include any type of price or premium promotion providing consumer incentive to purchase. They do not always work, and their costs should be measured against the return in increased sales and profits.

---

6. Peckham, *The Wheel of Marketing*, p. 39.

5

How Sales Promotion
Works: Examples

With this general background, we turn now to illustrations of how some
specific sales promotion techniques work. Most of the illustrations are
limited examples that have been made possible by the use of UPC and
scanning equipment. While they do not indicate how sales promotion
works for all products in all situations, they will serve to illustrate what
generally happens.

The chief advantage of this newly available scanner data is that for
the first time we can follow the effects of a sales promotion program over
a long period of time, such as a year, rather than being limited to just the
three to five weeks that many promotions run. That gives us the luxury of
seeing the longer-range effects of sales promotion on the brand, instead of
forcing us to evaluate the event on the basis of increased sales for a
certain period or even on the basis of an increased share of market
immediately following the promotional activity.

The General Effects of Sales Promotion

Using its ScanTrack service, which reports weekly sales data in several
stores in Rochester, New York, and Seattle, Washington, A. C. Nielsen
Company prepared the following illustration of how various sales promotion techniques affected two major household product brands
through a local supermarket chain. While this is only an example, it does
illustrate the effect that sales promotion can have over a period of time
and the resulting impact on the gross trading profit (GTP).

Table 5-1   Weekly Consumer Case Sales for Two Major Household Product Brands through Local Supermarket Chain

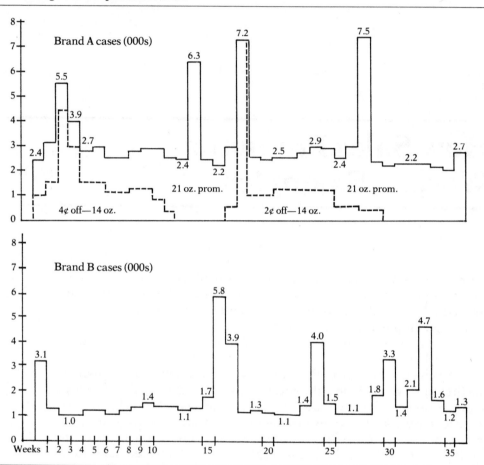

Source: A. C. Nielsen Company, *The Nielsen Researcher*, No. 1, 1979, p. 11.

[Table 5-1] presents the situation in a household product category in which sales are split between two brands. Over a 36-week period, both brands offered a number of short-term promotions. Brand A mixed cents-off label merchandise with in-store specials, while Brand B relied strictly on in-store specials.

As can be seen in the exhibit, each offer performed very much as one might expect. Brand A's 4¢-off label offer peaked at 550 cases/week movement, with an even higher response to its later 2¢-off label. Brand B's promotions produced similar peaks in sales.

An interesting point to note, however, is that the peaks in one brand's

Table 5-2 Competitive Division between Sales at Normal Rate and Added Sales during Promotional Weeks

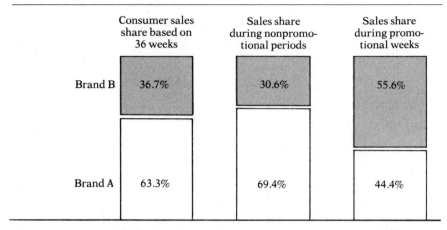

	Consumer sales share based on 36 weeks	Sales share during nonpromotional periods	Sales share during promotional weeks
Brand B	36.7%	30.6%	55.6%
Brand A	63.3%	69.4%	44.4%

Source: A. C. Nielsen Company, *The Nielsen Researcher*, No. 1, 1979, p. 12.

sales did not produce a corresponding dip in the competition's sales. In many situations this would indicate that regular customers were taking advantage of the deal to load home stocks. In this case, however, sales for both brands following the deals did not drop [significantly] below previously established averages (240 cases/week for Brand A and 110 cases/week for Brand B), suggesting that a number of consumers bought *only* on deal.

It is clear, however, that both brands were initiating successful promotions. The question that might be asked, though, is which brand was most successful?

[Table 5-2] provides an answer to this question. During the entire 36-week period, Brand B was responsible for an average of nearly one-third of case sales. When only non-promotional periods are examined, Brand B's share is even smaller (the middle bar on the exhibit). During those weeks when promotions were in effect, however, Brand B's share of sales exceeded 50 percent, indicating that the type of promotion used by Brand B outperformed that of Brand A.

In addition to these competitive comparisons, a brand manager can also make profitability evaluations. For example, Brand A's 4¢-off label produced an increase in product movement of nearly 35 percent [Table 5-3a]. It can be seen, however, that over half of the movement derived from the off-label merchandise, which carried only $4.92 in gross trading profit (GTP) per 1,000 ounces. The net result was gross trading profit of $21,147 or 1.2 percent less than what would probably have occurred without the promotion.

An examination of the 2¢-off label deal turned out somewhat differently [Table 5-3b]. With a similar increase in case sales, the gross trading profit was reduced by only $1.43 for deal merchandise. The result was $24,155 in gross

Table 5-3   Impact of Cents-Off Promotions on Consumer Sales and Manufacturer's Gross Trading Profit (GTP) 11-Weeks Duration

Sales (oz. 000)		A	Mfg $ gross trading profit (50%)		Sales (oz. 000)		B	Mfg $ gross trading profit (50%)	
Normal rate	4-cents off		4-cents off (3,374 cases)	Normal rate (2,750 cases)	Normal rate	2-cents off		2-cents off (3,382 cases)	Normal rate (2,750 cases)

→ +22.7%   −1.2% ←   → +23%   +13% ←

A:
- Normal rate: 2,750
- 4-cents off: 3,374 (1,784 / 1,590)
- 4¢ off × $4.92 GTP/1,000 ozs.
- Regular mdse. × $7.78 GTP/1,000 ozs.
- 4-cents off profit: $21,147 ($8,777 / $12,370)
- Normal rate profit: $21,395

B:
- Normal rate: 2,750
- 2-cents off: 3,382 (1,508 / 1,874)
- 2¢ off × $6.35 GTP/1,000 ozs.
- Regular mdse. × $7.78 GTP/1,000 ozs.
- 2-cents off profit: $24,155 ($9,575 / $14,580)
- Normal rate profit: $21,395

Source: A. C. Nielsen Company, *The Nielsen Researcher*, No. 1, 1979, p. 13

trading profit, or 13 percent above what might have occurred without the promotion.

Obviously, the 2¢-off label presented the most viable promotional option. It generated as much movement as did the 4¢-off label and did so profitably.[1]

As you can see from these illustrations, most sales promotion activities simply can't be evaluated strictly on the number of units sold, the amount of sales generated, or the short-run change in market share. An evaluation must go much deeper. Fortunately, the type of data now being provided by the UPC and AFE scanners are providing a great deal of the needed information.

Scanner data developed by A. C. Nielsen are illustrated in Table 5-4. They demonstrate the effects sales promotions have in the market and also the effects that competitive promotions may have on a brand. In the example there were no promotions in the first two weeks of the study period. However, there was promotion activity during 11 of the next 12 weeks. As an illustration of how sales promotions influence the sale of various brands, consider the following observations made by Nielsen personnel in regard to this example.

1. A. C. Nielsen Company, *The Nielsen Researcher*, No. 1, 1979, pp. 10-13.

Table 5-4a Promotion/Feature Price Analysis: Sales—Equivalent Ounce Basis

Week	Total market Sales—Ounces	Equivalent (ounce) sales shares					Causal data
		Brand A	Brand B	Generic	Cont. Br.	Rem. Brands	
1	131.1	57.5	8.1	13.8	16.5	4.2	
2	174.6	45.2	12.2	12.3	24.9	5.4	
3	144.9	29.7	26.0	14.2	12.7	17.4	Brand B - 24 oz. LAD - 53¢
4	341.1	30.3	57.4	5.1	3.7	3.6	Brand B - 14 oz. MAD - 3/$1.00 - save 41¢
5	239.9	35.1	48.0	7.4	5.3	4.1	Brand B - 14 oz. MAD - 3/$1.00 - save 41¢ Generic - 1 qt. LAD - 77¢ - save 32¢
6	215.2	31.8	48.5	9.7	5.9	4.1	Brand B - 14 oz. MAD - 3/$1.00 - save 41¢
7	186.2	38.5	36.7	9.1	13.7	2.1	Brand B - 14 oz. MAD - 3/$1.00 - save 41¢
8	193.3	40.5	7.8	7.2	42.7	1.9	CTL Brand - 1 qt. MAD - 69¢ - save 20¢
9	186.3	50.4	6.9	7.8	33.9	1.1	CTL Brand - 1 qt. MAD - 69¢ - save 20¢ Brand A - 1 qt. LAD - 99¢
10	188.9	50.2	12.0	8.3	27.8	1.7	CTL Brand - 1 qt. LAD - 69¢
11	225.0	42.3	29.5	8.3	18.4	1.5	CTL Brand - 1 qt. LAD - 69¢ Brand B - 14 oz. MAD - 3/$1.00 - save 17¢
12	218.0	74.0	8.9	7.3	7.7	2.0	Brand A - 14 oz. CAD - with coupon price 39¢ - coupon value 10¢
13	147.6	45.6	30.1	12.1	9.1	3.0	
14	254.9	23.2	66.9	5.4	3.9	0.5	Brand B - 44 oz. MAD - 99¢ - save 30¢

MAD = Major ad
LAD = Line ad
CAD = In-ad coupon

Source: A. C. Nielsen Company, *The Nielsen Researcher*, No. 1, 1979, p. 13.

Brand A was the share leader by a wide margin during base Weeks 1 and 2 but lost that leadership as Brand B was promoted heavily during Weeks 3 thru 7. In Weeks 4 and 5 when the market reached its highest level (2-3 times the base week volumes), Brand A, which was not being promoted, enjoyed modest share increases *and significant* volume increases in the expanded market. Brand A regained market leadership in Weeks 7 and 8, after Brand B promotions had run their course and were replaced with controlled brand promotions. It wasn't until Week 9 that Brand A promoted with the quart size at a price (99¢) 30¢ higher than the controlled brand quart at 69¢. Brand A gained 10 points in share that week, while controlled brands declined 9 points in a stable market. The second Brand A promotion occurred in Week 12 on the 14-oz. size—no competitive promotion present. The brand commanded 74.0 percent of equivalent and 79.9 percent of unit sales, the highest on record for the 14 weeks. Not only were the Brand A promotions effective when they occurred, but the strength of the brand was evident during Brand B promotion weeks when Brand A sales were "assisted" by the Brand B promotions which attracted consumers to the product category.

Brand B was promoted with feature prices during 7 of the 14 weeks, with a string of 5 consecutive weeks of promotion at one point. Consumer response

Table 5-4b Promotion/Feature Price Analysis: Sales—Unit Basis

Week	Total market Sales—Units	Brand A	Brand B	Generic	Cont. br.	Rem. brands	Causal data
				Unit sales shares			
1	4,906	59.2	7.5	11.2	18.5	3.6	
2	6,227	43.5	12.6	10.1	29.0	4.8	
3	6,458	28.3	34.5	11.3	13.6	12.4	Brand B - 24 oz. LAD - 53¢
4	18,689	19.5	72.4	2.9	3.1	2.0	Brand B - 14 oz. MAD - 3/$1.00 - save 41¢
5	12,380	25.7	63.0	4.5	4.3	2.5	Brand B - 14 oz. MAD - 3/$1.00 - save 41¢
							Generic - 1 qt. LAD - 77¢ - save 32¢
6	11,255	25.1	62.0	6.2	4.2	2.5	Brand B - 14 oz. MAD - 3/$1.00 - save 41¢
7	8,868	31.6	50.4	6.7	9.9	1.5	Brand B - 14 oz. MAD - 3/$1.00 - save 41¢
8	6,824	42.4	9.8	7.0	39.0	1.7	CTL Brand - 1 qt. MAD - 69¢ - save 20¢
9	6,673	49.9	8.4	7.2	33.4	1.0	CTL Brand - 1 qt. MAD - 69¢ - save 20¢
							Brand A - 1 qt. LAD - 99¢
10	6,924	48.8	17.2	7.7	24.6	1.6	CTL Brand - 1 qt. LAD - 69¢
11	10,076	36.2	42.8	6.4	13.5	1.1	CTL Brand - 1 qt. LAD - 69¢
							Brand B - 14 oz. MAD - 3/$1.00 - save 17¢
12	11,586	79.9	8.5	4.6	5.8	1.3	Brand A - 14 oz. CAD - with coupon
							price 39¢ - coupon value 10¢
13	5,669	52.2	24.6	10.7	10.1	2.5	
14	7,730	33.4	54.8	6.0	5.2	0.5	Brand B - 44 oz. MAD - 99¢ - save 30¢

MAD = Major ad
LAD = Line ad
CAD = In-ad coupon

Source: A. C. Nielsen Company, *The Nielsen Researcher*, No. 1, 1979, pp. 10-13.

to these promotions was substantial, not only for Brand B but also for total product category sales. When Brand B was not on promotion, its share decreased significantly (in three weeks to the 7-9 percent range). The brand's peak equivalent [ounce] share was in Week 14 when the 44-oz. size was promoted at a price (99¢) which was the same price as Brand A's 32-oz. promotion 5 weeks earlier. During the 14-oz. promotion weeks, unit share reached 72.4 percent, although the equivalent ounce share was at a lower, but still significant 57.4 percent. You'll note during Week 11, Brand B's 14-oz. promotion (3/$1.00) indicated a savings of only 17¢ versus previous indicated savings of 41¢. The ad incorrectly stated the savings in Week 11 and coincidentally Brand B's share increase and level was less than in previous weeks when the 3/$1.00 promotion was in effect.

Controlled Brands were promoted during weeks when Brand B was not on promotion. As all 14 weeks are evaluated, the major interplay in the market was between Brand B and the Controlled Brands with share progress evident for Brand B in Week 13 (no promotions) and a significant share loss for the Controlled Brand segment versus the first 2 base weeks.

Generic Brands had the most stable trend throughout the 14-week span

Table 5-5   The Side Effect of Sales Promotion

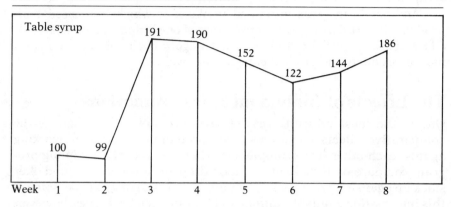

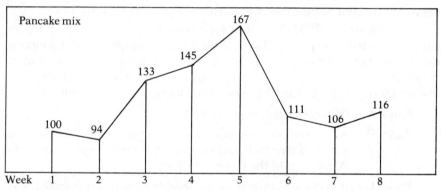

Source: A. C. Nielsen Company, *Nielsen National ScanTrack Service: Applications*, Sept. 1980, p. 11.

with a share range of only 4-5 points during the intense promotions in Weeks 4 thru 12. The only generic promotion in Week 5 yielded little response against a strong Brand B promotion that same week.[2]

An interesting side effect of sales promotion for a product is the impact it often has on companion products; i.e., hot dogs on hot dog buns, lettuce on salad dressings, dips on potato chips. In Table 5-5, some data from A. C. Nielsen illustrate this. This example illustrates the effect that a major promotion by a brand in the table syrup category had on the entire pancake mix product class. Both categories are indexed at 100 in Week 1. While there were no major promotions in the pancake mix product class, the trends of both product categories were similar. And the

---

2. A. C. Nielsen Company, *Nielsen National ScanTrack Service: Applications*, Sept., 1980, p. 3.

big gain in pancake mix could be traced to a major promotion by a table syrup brand in Weeks 3 through 8.

Another brand was promoted in Week 8, which influenced both product classes. Clearly, sales promotion of one brand can often have an effect not only on the brand and the category but apparently on companion products and product categories as well.

The Effects of Individual Sales Promotions

One of the most difficult areas of sales promotion to explain is the comparative effects of various sales promotion techniques working against each other. For example, how do the effects of a sampling program compare with those of a coupon drop, or how does a refund offer stack up against a price-pack? Scanning data is starting to make some of this information available, although it is quite sketchy. It does, however, serve to give us a better idea of how various promotion activities work.

For example, TRIM (Tele-Research Item Movement, Inc.) set up an experiment to compare the effects of direct mail samples and/or coupons on the introduction of a new product. The new product was stocked in retail stores, and no special activity was carried out on the product for the first four weeks. In the fifth week, the following activity took place:

Panel A: Control stores; no activity.

Panel B: A cents-off coupon was mailed to homemakers who lived within a two-mile radius of the test stores (approximately 90 percent of the stores' shoppers).

Panel C: A cents-off coupon plus a free sample of the product was mailed to homemakers who lived within a two-mile radius of the test stores (approximately 90 percent of the stores' shoppers).

The results of the test are shown in Table 5-6. The example shows the week-by-week purchases of the product per 1,000 shoppers for a period of 16 weeks. Stores using the cents-off coupon (Panel B) produced sales 250 percent better than stores with no promotion. The stores in areas that received a cents-off coupon plus the free sample did more than 300 percent better than the control stores. From this analysis, by determining the cost of the free sample, the sales promotion manager could easily determine whether or not the increased sales resulting from the free sample were worth the cost.[3]

TRIM has provided much of the information on how various sales promotion techniques work in the market. Thomas L. Mindrum reported the following to the Association of National Advertisers' "Trends in

3. TRIM, Inc., *Tele/Scope*, vol. 1, no. 1, p. 1.

Table 5-6   Effects of a Coupon vs. Coupon Plus Sample

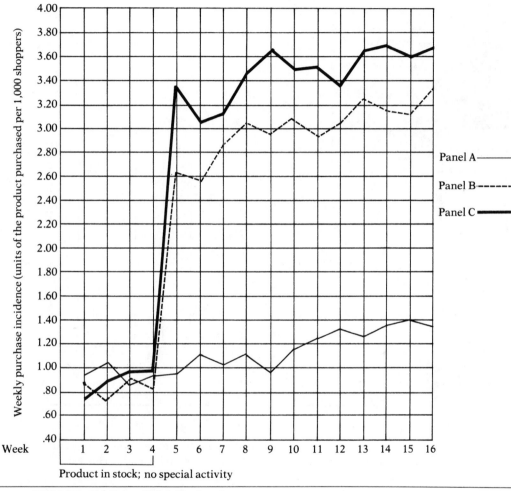

Source: TRIM, Inc., *Tele/Scope*, Vol. 1, No. 1, p. 1.

Promotion Workshop." (All data is based on a study from January through August, 1978, for two supermarket chains: Ralph's Grocery Company, Los Angeles, with 12 stores reporting data, and Wegman's Food Markets in Rochester, New York, with 18 stores equipped with scanners. All data refers to one or both of these chains.)

Retailer couponing effects

[In this example] we have a retailer coupon. The example is an in-ad coupon that ran in Rochester on Mennen's 2½-oz. stick. (For each of the case his-

Table 5-7   Retailer Coupon: Mennen Antiperspirant

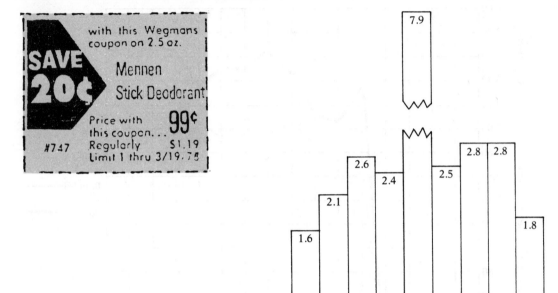

Source: Thomas L. Mindrum, Speech given at the "Trends in Promotion Workshop—Update '78," Association of National Advertisers, New York, 1978, p. 5.

tories . . . we have attempted to provide a unit share on a four-week pre-promotion basis prior to the promotion taking place. This was followed by a one-week period, or however long the promotion lasted. Finally, there was a post-promotion period.)

You can see [Table 5-7] that we trended these unit sales on a weekly basis for nine weeks. In the four weeks prior to this retailer coupon, Mennen had an average share ranging between 1.6 and 2.6 of the deodorant category. When the retailer ran his coupon, the price of Mennen went from $1.19 to 99¢. You can see the immediate short-term effect of that activity on the sales and market share, actually increasing their share four times, from a level of 2 to a level of 8.

We also tracked a retailer coupon ad in Rochester on Ultra Ban 1½-oz. roll-on. The product had an average share of about 2.5 to 3 in the four weeks prior to the promotion. When it received the retailer coupon, it actually went off the graph. We had to cut it off to get it on the page, but it went all the way to 22.3 percent of the category.

Table 5-8   Retailer Coupon: Right Guard Antiperspirant

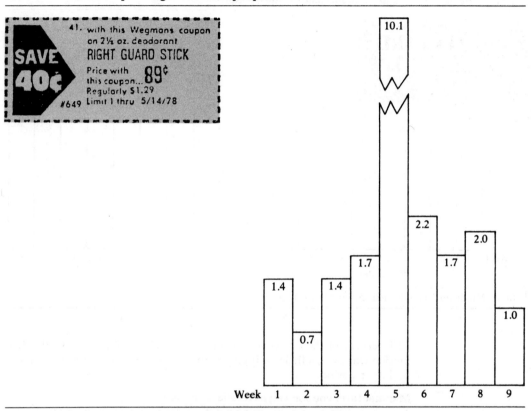

Source: Mindrum, "Trends in Promotion Workshop," p. 7.

. . . Almost without exception in the deodorant/antiperspirant category, however, we did find this immediate, very drastic increase in the sales and market share.

Measuring mortgaged sales
Another point about using scanner data to evaluate promotions like this is that we can look week by week into the post-promotional period and see the degree, if any, that the promotion was mortgaging future sales. Of course, a full analysis would have to take into account the purchase cycle for the brand. This would differ by category, but we can see that the shares in the four-week post-period are somewhat lower than they were in the pre-period. It is possible, therefore, to analyze the degree to which promotions mortgage future sales.

In [Table 5-8], which shows the effect of a 40¢ coupon on Right Guard stick, we can see an improvement from an average share of about 1-1.5 up to

Table 5-9   Manufacturer Coupon: Right Guard Antiperspirant

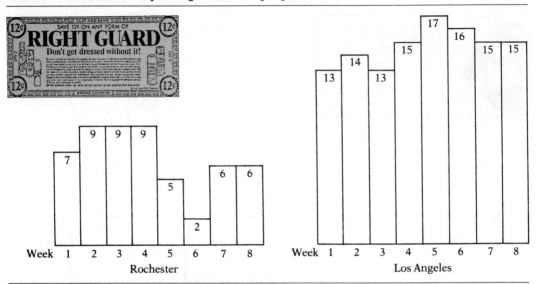

Source: Mindrum, "Trends in Promotion Workshop," p. 3.

10.1 percent of the category. It came right back down as soon as the promotion was over, a little bit higher in the post-promotion period than it was in the pre-period.

Manufacturer coupon versus retailer coupon

There is a difference between a manufacturer coupon's effect on retail sales as opposed to a retailer coupon. A 12¢ coupon for Right Guard happened to run at about the same time in both Rochester and Los Angeles. [See Table 5-9.]

In Rochester, a kind of disturbing thing happened. In the week that the coupon dropped, the share actually declined. I can assure you that this is not normally what we see in a product category. Couponing does not make your sales and share go down. Here is what actually happened: The same week that the manufacturer coupon for Right Guard hit the newspaper, a retailer coupon for Arrid also appeared. It was a 60¢ coupon. In that battle of the antiperspirants, you can understand which one was the winner.

The more typical response to a manufacturer's coupon is represented by the figures for Los Angeles. During the week that the coupon appeared for the item, we saw a very moderate increase in the market share. It went from an average of approximately 14 to 15 percent of the category up to 17 percent the one week that the manufacturer's coupon appeared. After that it fell back down to 16 percent and then down to about its original level. In the deodorant/antiperspirant category, this is generally what we have seen with regard to the two kinds of coupons.

Table 5-10   Manufacturer Coupon: Secret Antiperspirant

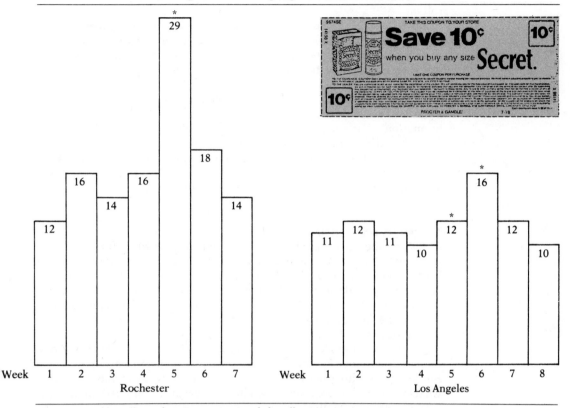

Source: Mindrum, "Trends in Promotion Workshop," p. 10.

A manufacturer's coupon has nowhere near the same effect as a retailer's coupon. Often a manufacturer's coupon will increase sales only from one to three share points. About 90 percent of the increase over its base period share will be reflected for the one week that the coupon appears in the newspaper. After that time, there is virtually no measurable effect of these coupons on retail sales.

The effect of an overlay
In a promotion for Secret, we noticed that the week the manufacturer coupon appeared, there was an increase in share almost comparable to that of a retailer coupon in Rochester. You can see by the asterisks in the Los Angeles graph that the coupons were seen almost simultaneously—in successive weeks. [See Table 5-10.]

Perhaps it was coincidence, but the week that the Secret coupon was in the Rochester paper, the Wegman chain happened to have an advertised feature on two different forms of the deodorant. A customer could save 30¢ on the 4-ounce or 5-ounce Secret spray and save 40¢ on the 1½-ounce Secret roll-on.

In Los Angeles when the Secret coupon appeared in the paper, Ralph's Grocery chain was also running an ad for the deodorant which they called their 1½ coupon. Any consumer who brought in a coupon with a value of 30¢ would receive a 15¢ "gift" from Ralph's. This would then give the consumer a total of 45¢ off the item.

We feel, therefore, that the reason the share of Secret did increase so much in that one particular week was a result of its really being concurrent promotion.

When the Secret coupon ran alone, in the first week the increase was more typical. During the second week the ad was in the Los Angeles paper, the share was up to 16 percent. It is our contention that this was due to the additional promotion from Ralph's Grocery store chain.

Temporary retail price reduction

At Ralph's they introduced a four-week temporary retail price reduction on four different items. One of these was Dial 2-ounce stick, which was reduced from $1.49 to $1.19 for the four-week promotion. What we saw over this eight-week period was the typical response of a product's market share to a temporary retail price reduction that is not featured in the chain's ad. It is measurable, but it is minimal.

In the case of Tickle 2-ounce roll-on, with a retail price reduction of 20¢ (from $1.69 to $1.49) for one week of the promotion, there did appear to be a measurable change in market share. It went from an average of 1.3 up to 2. But in the last three weeks of the promotion there was virtually no change whatsoever. And interestingly enough, after the price went back up to regular retail, the share fell.

Lastly, I have a 25¢-off label that ran in Rochester on Sure 2½-ounce roll-on. In the graph here [Table 5-11], the white represents the non-deal pack; the striped portion of the graph indicates the share for the 25¢-off label, and they have been combined together to show you the total share for the two items during the first part of the promotion.

In the first two weeks, you can see it was all non-deal pack, with a share of about 1 percent of the category. In the third week, we see a little bit of the cents-off label beginning to come into some of the stores. By the fourth week it's virtually all cents-off labels.

We studied cents-off labels across a number of different product categories, such as health and beauty aids, and this illustration is really indicative of what we have seen in an enormous number of cases. For the first couple of weeks that the cents-off label is really on the shelf, there's often a drop in market share from its previous levels.

We have investigated a few of these and found two potential reasons for the decline. One is out-of-stocks. Retailers know that a deal pack is coming in. They don't want to have both non-deal pack and deal pack on the shelf, so they cut their order of the non-deal pack, but they can't time it precisely with

---

Table 5-11   Cents-Off Label: Sure Antiperspirant

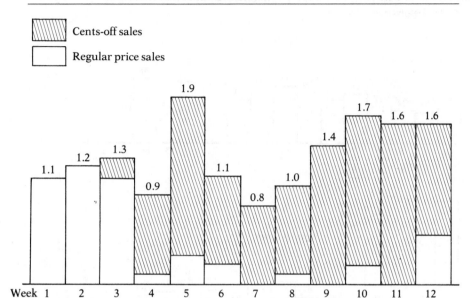

Cents-off sales

Regular price sales

Source: Mindrum, "Trends in Promotion Workshop," p. 12.

---

the arrival of the deal pack, and therefore they are out of stock for a period of time.

The other thing that sometimes happens is that the deal pack is on the shelf, but the retailer hasn't priced it at the price reduction. Therefore, there is consumer confusion and dissatisfaction with the promotion that's taking place.[4]

Perhaps the best way to summarize what we know about how sales promotion works is through a case history developed by A. C. Nielsen Company.

The first example [Table 5-12] follows a new product introduction (Brand B) in a growth household product class against Brand A—the leader in the category. As we pick up the analysis in Week 1, we find that Brand B had achieved an initial volume of 1,900 cases, which represents 25.3 percent of the two brand sales. In Week 3, Brand A decided to promote heavily against the new entry and while achieving a significant volume increase by almost tripling sales, Brand B volume held steady. Both brands remained at relatively constant levels through Weeks 4, 5, and 6. In Week 7, Brand A decided to strike a second time to combat the new entry. Once again, sales almost

---

4. Mindrum, "Trends in Promotion Workshop," pp. 5-13.

Table 5-12   Weekly Consumer Case Sales for Two Major Brands in Growth Product Category through Local Supermarket Chain

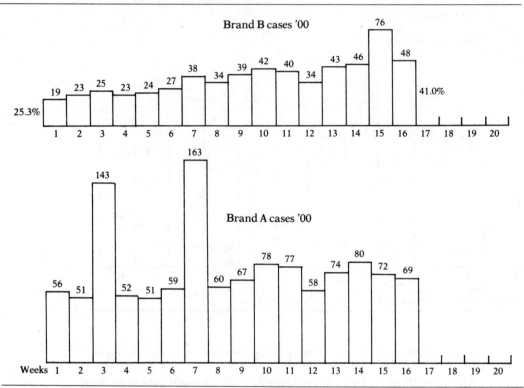

Source: A. C. Nielsen Co., 1981.

tripled, but this time Brand B also enjoyed a sales increase at the same time. Throughout the next seven weeks Brand B continued to gain volume, while Brand A volume steadied at a level slightly higher than the pre-promotion weeks. During Week 15, the new product was promoted and it reduced Brand A to a sales level slightly below its own promotion peak. The following week Brand B settled back to its previous sales level. Weekly data allows for a much earlier evaluation of the new product introduction with the option of altering the marketing program at an early stage of development. We might conclude that promotions do result in significant volume gains short-term, with sales returning to the pre-promotion levels afterwards. We might also conclude that a new viable brand entry can't be deterred from becoming successful by competitive promotions. We haven't attempted to bring in the total product class picture, or the effect of non-scanning store activity, which would be essential for a full evaluation of the market where this new product was introduced.

The second example [Table 5-13] is a year-long study on the margarine product class looking at activity of the four leading brands. Here you are looking at the first 18 weeks of the 52-week analyses—Brand A is on the top grid, with Brands B, C, and D following down the chart. The weeks go across, beginning with the week ending April 1, 1978, and running through the end of July. Sales are shown for each brand, each week, in the scaled portion of the chart, with the retail price in effect for each week below the base line for each brand. Let's look at Brand A. Feature price cuts from 58¢ to 38¢ occurred on four occasions, and each time the volume increased by 26 to 32 times the pre-promotional level—quite a significant increase! These price reductions of 20¢ each time were 35 percent below the normal 58¢ sell-price. We wonder how profitable the promotion was to the manufacturer, considering cost of goods. We are certain it was profitable to the retailers. It is interesting to note that following the feature price promotions in each case, volume returned to the previous non-promotion sales level.

Brand B promotions were more modest, with 5¢ to 8¢ reductions, or about 15 percent, which you will observe throughout this analysis is the norm for most of the price promotions. Sales increases were also more modest at 3-8 times the normal sales level.

Brand C had a 38¢ feature also in the first week of the study. Subsequent weeks revealed feature price cuts of 5¢ to 9¢, with sales response in a range of 5-8 times normal volume. Brand D followed the same pattern.

Three other observations before we leave this chart: first, the data represents activity in one chain organization, and you will note that during the first three weeks one of the brands was featured at either 38¢ or 44¢. Of the 18 weeks shown on this chart there were only four weeks during which a feature price promotion was not in effect for one of the four brands. Second, all brands returned to sales levels established before the promotion and didn't appear on the surface to borrow from their future sales, which leads one to a possible conclusion—that there are a group of loyal brand buyers and a group of price buyers who buy only what's on sale. Third, scanner data was used to evaluate an increase in regular shelf price. Note on Brand B that after the 49¢ feature during the week ending May 27, the normal price was increased by 4¢ from 54¢ to 58¢. Sales declined from previous non-promotion levels.

This next chart [Table 5-14] extends the analysis another four months. Let us point out that Brand A discontinued the deep 20¢ price cuts, used more normal 8¢ reductions, with somewhat less but yet significant sales increases, and reduced the frequency of promotions. In those cases where a question mark is shown for the price, it indicates an in-ad coupon promotion by the retailer, with the scanning price being the normal price and the in-ad coupon value being taken off at the end of each consumer transaction at the check-out. Brands B, C, and D appear to have obtained greater sales gains from their promotions during this interval, as the effect of Brand A's 38¢ features disappeared. Note the week ending October 28 (shown as NA) where no data appears. The retailer erased the data from his files before copying it. This is one of the pitfalls of scanning and there is no way to retrieve the data.

Table 5-13   Sales-Price Promotion Relationships I—Margarine

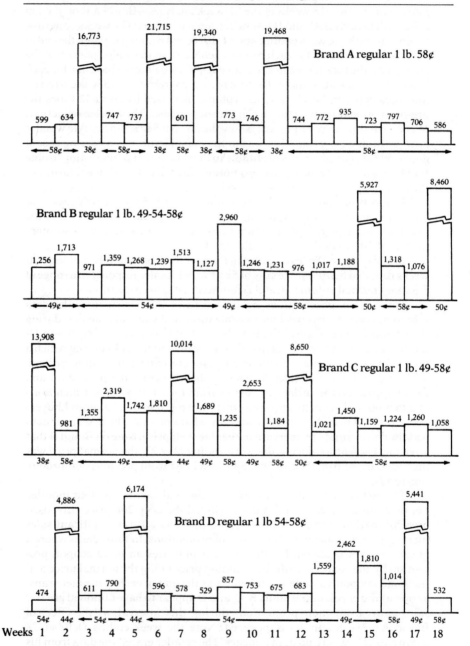

Source: A. C. Nielsen Co., 1981.

Table 5-14   Sales-Price Promotion Relationships II—Margarine

Brand A regular 1 lb. 58¢

10,967   11,204   13,627   10,737
683   854   771   881   883   951   639   644
1,013   861   921   1,131   855
NA

50¢   58¢   50¢   ◄——58¢——►   ?   ◄—58¢—►   50¢   ◄———58¢———►

Brand B regular 1 lb. 49-54-58¢

10,394   13,383   14,412   12,859
1,131   1,103   1,016   1,208   1,222   1,273   1,277   1,283   1,480   1,173   1,335   2,086   1,470
NA

◄———58¢———►   50¢   ◄—59¢—►   ?   ◄—58¢—►   50¢   59¢   50¢   ◄—59¢—►

Brand C regular 1 lb. 49-58¢

13,270   18,069   15,041   15,377   19,573
1,313   1,097   1,168   1,847   1,736   1,638   1,484   1,627   1,578   1,754   1,700   2,305
NA

58¢   50¢   ◄—58¢—►   ?   ◄———58¢———►   50¢   58¢   58¢   50¢   ◄—58¢—►   50¢

Brand D regular 1 lb. 54-58¢

12,648   9,425
753   629   646   747   762   957   770   798   916   828   719   1,361   775   821   832
NA

◄———58¢———►   ?   ◄———58¢———►   ◄—58¢—►   ?   58¢

Weeks	19	20	21	22	23	24	25	26	27	28	29	30	31	32	33	34	35	36

Source: A. C. Nielsen Co., 1981.

Table 5-15 Sales-Price Promotion Relationships III—Margarine

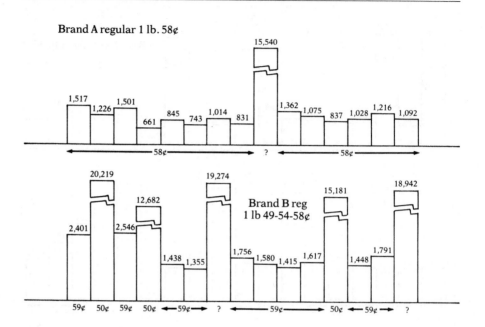

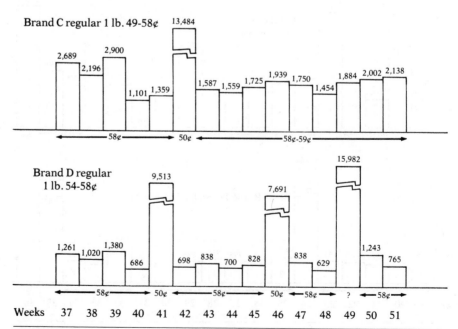

Source: A. C. Nielsen Co., 1981.

The last chart in the series [Table 5-15] completes the year. You will note similar sales response to 15 percent price cut features by each of the brands. Note that Brand A had only one feature during this four-month period, while Brand B picked up its activity.

Let's summarize. On [Table 5-16] we have attempted to evaluate each brand's market share, including all promotion merchandise. We can look at weeks when the brands were not on promotion. We have divided the year into two 6-month intervals; on the left grids you'll note that Brand A had a share of 38.9 percent of total sales during the first six months, when the 38¢ features were in effect. During the next six months, without the benefit of the 38¢ feature prices and less feature price activity, Brand A's share dipped to 13.2 percent, as sales were down 63 percent. Brand B enjoyed a share increase from 16.9 percent to 42.4 percent, with sales up 171 percent. As you

---

Table 5-16   Impact of Store Price Promotions on Basic Brand Franchise—Margarine

	Market share based on total sales including promotional merchandise			Market share based on average weekly sales nonpromotional weeks	
	331,357 lbs.	357,883 lbs.	+8%	4,007 lbs.	5,482 lbs.
Brand A	38.9%	13.2 / 7	−63.1	18.9%	19.3
Deal	34%*	42.4 / 35	+171		
Brand B	16.9 / 8			30.4	30.3
Brand C	29.3 / 13	27.6 / 18	+2.5	33.1	33.9
Brand D	14.9 / 11	16.8 / 12	+22	17.6	16.5
	1st 6 mos.	2nd 6 mos.		1st 6 mos.	2nd 6 mos.

*Brand A deal merchandise as a percent to total sales.
Source: A. C. Nielsen Co., 1981.

can see, promotion week sales for Brand B during the first 6 months represented only 8 percent of total sales for the four brands. During the second 6 months, with increased promotional activity, Brand B's promotional merchandise accounted for 35 percent of total sales—just the reverse of what happened to Brand A between the two six month intervals. Brands C & D have less fluctuation in their share due to a more consistent promotion pattern. On the right two grids, we have taken all of the non-promotion weeks for each brand separately, and computed average weekly sales for each brand. These are different weeks for each of the brands. You'll note, the non-promotion shares are virtually unchanged for the two 6-month intervals, which supports the loyal brand/price brand shopper conclusions mentioned earlier. It is interesting to note that sales were up 37 percent for the non-promotion averages, while total sales, including all the promotion merchandise for all weeks, were up only 8 percent.[5]

The Limits of Sales Promotion

The effects of sales promotion techniques vary widely and seem particularly dependent on the type of product, the price, the offer, the competitive situation, and, of course, the frequency of promotion. In line with this, the question, Can you use too much sales promotion? naturally arises. Can various techniques be overused so that they no longer have any effect? The answer is a definite yes, as illustrated by J. O. Peckham, Sr. Table 5-17 illustrates the two-year competitive sales records of four brands in a Nielsen Food Index product group that Peckham studied. The dark portion in each bar represents the volume of consumer sales in consumer price promotions. Peckham's comments follow.

[Table 5-17] shows the two-year competitive sales records of four brands in one of the Nielsen Food Index product groups. The crosshatched portion in each bar represents the volume of consumer sales in consumer price promotions. Observe that while these deal goods were increased from 35 percent to 60 percent of Brand A's volume between Year 1 and Year 2, the share of market represented by Brand A remained stationary at 40 percent, nor were there any appreciable changes in the competitive standings of the remaining three brands.

What are the conditions which could have led to Brand A marketing as much as 60 percent of its annual sales in consumer price promotions? It all started when the raw material price dropped substantially; rather than reflect this as a cut in the brand's wholesale list, the manufacturer chose to use his added margin in cents-off-the-label pack, and competition followed. This, of course, stimulated trade buying well in excess of current consumer demand and thus provided a substantial boost to manufacturer's factory shipments during the initial year of consumer price promotion.

These inflated factory shipments posed a real problem for the manu-

5. Nielsen Scanning Services, *National ScanTrack* [brochure] (Northbrook, Ill.: A. C. Nielsen Co., 1981).

**Table 5-17   Continuous Consumer Dealing Doesn't Promote—
It's Really a Price Adjustment in Another Form**

*Share of market—case basis.
Source: Peckham, *The Wheel of Marketing*, p. 41, opposite.

facturer during the second year. Since substantial quantities had not moved through to the consumer and were still in trade channels, virtually the only way the manufacturer could produce a satisfactory increase in his *second year factory shipments* was to have an even larger price promotion, thus adding further to trade inventories. The solution was to eliminate all consumer price promotions, cut the wholesale list to reflect normal manufacturer's gross trading profit margins, thus stabilizing consumer price at about the level it had been when price promotions were in effect.

This situation also illustrates the dilemma faced by marketing men all over the world when confronted with the need to produce a substantial increase in factory sales in a limited time frame. This need can be a management directive or perhaps just the fact that brand sales are below budget through the first three quarters of the fiscal year and something must be done quickly. Under these circumstances, the temptation is to borrow from next year's factory shipments by having a substantial trade deal during the last quarter, perhaps with a consumer price promotion thrown in for good measure. When the next year comes around, a bigger and better deal is required just to equal the previous year's factory shipments, etc.

This illustrates one of the points made earlier; namely, that while an established brand *might* find it necessary to promote as a defensive measure consistent with its competitive position, the aggressive use of promotions as a means of increasing share of market on an *established* brand is not an effective device. In my opinion, such marketing tactics should not be considered "promotions" at all; they constitute merely another form of price reduction.[6]

Conclusions

From the foregoing information, it is possible to draw some general conclusions about how sales promotion works.

1. First, sales promotion does work. It moves products through trade channels to the consumer and results in final sales.
2. The sign of a successful sales promotion program is not sales made during the promotion period, but the increase in volume or share of market after the promotion has ended.
3. Unless trade promotions increase the sale of the product enough to cover the costs of the promotion as well as increased share or product distribution after the promotion, they should not be considered successful.
4. Consumer promotions may be necessary for consumers who purchase the product only when it is involved in some form of promotion activity. Sales promotion may be the only way to bring them into the market.
5. Combinations of various sales promotion techniques are usually more successful than individual sales promotion techniques used alone.
6. You *can* use sales promotion too often.

Balancing Advertising and Sales Promotion

With this general understanding of how sales promotion works, we can now look at how to allocate the promotion budget between advertising and sales promotion. We will deal with the actual budgeting activity in Chapter 16. Our interest here is in the general theory to be used.

There is little question that advertising and sales promotion work hand in hand to provide the most effective combination for moving products to the consumer. The major question, however, is how much

---

6. J. O. Peckham, Sr., *The Wheel of Marketing* (Scarsdale, NY: privately printed, 1978), p. 41.

emphasis to put on advertising and how much on sales promotion in order to provide the most effective return.

While this allocation question has long been debated, it is only recently that any sort of definitive answer has been proposed. That came about as the result of a major study released in 1975 by Professor Roger A. Strang for the Marketing Service Institute. In general, Strang found: "It appears that advertising and promotion interact, at least in the sense that money spent on a combination of advertising and promotion produces higher sales and profits than does the same amount spent on either alone."[7]

We have reprinted Strang's analysis of five experimental studies in Appendix II. In brief, these studies suggest that

1. Increasing promotion at the expense of advertising does not result in long-term sales or profit increases.
2. Long-term sales begin to decline when the A/P (advertising/promotion) ratio falls below a certain "threshold"—probably 60/40.
3. Advertising more strongly influences brand image and consumer attitudes than does sales promotion.
4. Brand image and brand loyalty can be adversely affected by sales promotion, irrespective of advertising expenditures.

Thus, as Strang's analysis shows, there seems to be a limit on the amount of money that should be spent on sales promotion. That conclusion may be difficult to accept, particularly for people in sales promotion. In our opinion, however, there is little doubt that you can, in the case of sales promotion, have "too much of a good thing."

In summary, sales promotion works. And it works best in combination with advertising. But there is apparently a limit to the amount that should be invested in sales promotion relative to advertising. If we accept Strang's findings, that relationship is in the area of 60 percent for advertising and 40 percent for sales promotion, although there may be variations in that relationship based on many marketing, product, and company variables.

Summary

By examining studies of specific situations, the effects of sales promotion and the interplay of different sales promotions by different brands in the same product category can be seen. The results of sales promotion in specific situations are often surprising and not always profitable. It is clear that sales promotion is a tool that can be overused.

---

7. Roger A. Strang, with contributions by Robert M. Prentice and Alden G. Clayton, *The Relationship Between Advertising and Promotion in Brand Strategy* (Cambridge, Mass.: Marketing Service Institute, 1975), p. 62.

6

Identifying Sales Promotion Problems and Opportunities

What makes marketing problems so difficult is simply that they almost always involve people. In spite of the great strides we've made in research, our understanding of how and why people think and act is still quite limited. We simply don't know what makes people do what they do, particularly in the market place. As a result, marketing is still an inexact science at best, and, generally speaking, advertising and sales promotion are the least certain and precise of all marketing areas.

To compound the problem, because the various marketing elements are so interrelated, finding a particular cause for a particular effect is usually quite difficult. For example, if a company is suffering a sales decline, the cause could be a poor product, a weak advertising program, insufficient distribution, poor follow-through on the part of the distributor or retailer, losses to an aggressive competitor, or insufficient sales promotion. Often, we can identify the problem—say, declining sales— but have a hard time determining what caused it. That's one of the reasons there are no standard answers or common solutions to marketing problems.

Yet, you've no doubt heard the old saying, "When you identify the problem, you've found half the solution." That's often true in marketing and usually true in promotion, especially sales promotion. Thus, if the sales promotion manager can define the problem and can identify the *possible* causes, then selecting the proper sales promotion technique for solving the problem can be a simple matter of weighing the various costs of each technique against its potential benefits. With this approach, there is little likelihood that sales promotion or a particular sales promotion technique will be used where it isn't applicable or where it can't possibly work. And that's the sign of a good manager: being able to define the problem, determine the cause, and then select the proper tools to solve the problem.

However, finding the cause of a promotion problem is not easy. And the remaining chapters in this book are intended to help you learn to identify sales promotion problems and their causes more easily and to describe the various solutions available to you.

Identifying the Problem

The basic difficulty in defining marketing problems in general and sales promotion problems in particular is that what causes a problem in one situation doesn't necessarily cause the same problem in another. Marketing is dynamic. Every product or service is different, just as every customer for each product and service is different. Every selling situation is unique. For that reason, we can develop some general rules for solving marketing problems, but the key ingredient is to dig for information. Nothing can substitute for information, and it comes simply from gathering and evaluating data, asking questions, and following every lead.

On the following pages, you'll find a step-by-step procedure for identifying and dealing with marketing and sales promotion problems. One of the major errors that occurs in developing solutions to problems is failing to properly identify the problem initially. In sales promotion, this simply means that you must be sure the problem you are trying to solve can be answered with sales promotion. That is, the problem must first be identified as a marketing problem, then as a promotion problem, and, finally, as a sales promotion problem. Thus, we start with a very broad first question: "Is it a marketing problem?" The following example will explain what we mean.

Is It a Marketing Problem?

Top management of XYZ Company has identified the problem in their organization as the failure of Able Division to meet its profit goal for the first quarter of the year. Able Division management identifies the problem as the failure of Product R to meet its sales goals for that period. Marketing management of Able Division then identifies the problem more precisely as declining sales of Product R based on distribution losses. That is, the real problem in this example is not specifically profit or profit margins at the marketing level. It is a distribution loss by Product R. The key question to be answered then is not why the divisional profit loss occurred but why the product distribution loss occurred. Is it because of a failure in the marketing system or is it because of something else?

Let's assume further that marketing management makes a thorough investigation of Product R's problem. Indeed, distribution has been lost but that loss is a result of declining product quality over the past few months. Finding that Product R has fallen in quality and no longer meets their expectations, consumers have stopped purchasing it. As a result of these reduced purchases, many retailers have stopped stocking the product. Thus, distribution has declined dramatically, overall sales have gone down, and profits have disappeared.

While the problem technically is a marketing one—that is, sales and profits are declining—there is little marketing management can actually do at this point with typical promotion tools. Until the product is returned to its previous quality level or the price is adjusted to accommodate the decline in quality, distribution probably cannot be regained or sales and profits improved. From this example, you can see how the initial step in solving any marketing problem is first to be sure that it is a marketing problem or at least a problem for which marketing activities can provide a solution.

Is It a Promotion Problem?

The second step is to determine whether or not the problem to be solved is related specifically to the promotional area of marketing. In other words, is advertising, sales promotion, personal selling, or public relations the area in which the problem exists and in which, therefore, the solution can be found? In the example cited above, a decline in product quality was found to be the cause of declining sales. Suppose, instead, it had been determined that the loss in distribution was the result of very rapid increases in the price of Product R, price increases that were far above those of competition. Further, it was learned that one of the primary ingredients of Product R was grown in South America and that a crop failure there had caused the price of the ingredient to skyrocket. Competition used raw materials from Africa where no such crop failure had occurred. Thus there was a substantial difference in the prices of Product R and its competition. Since Product R and its competitors were seen by the consumer to be similar in quality and use, the higher price could not be justified. Consumers stopped buying, retailers stopped stocking, and distribution losses resulted.

This particular situation could well be a marketing problem. If we could substitute the African for the South American ingredient in Product R until the South American supply recovered, we might be able to reduce the price of the product to competitive levels. Distribution could then be regained and consumers might once again start purchasing. We could say, then, that the problem is in the marketing system and could be solved with marketing elements, such as pricing. It is not a promotion problem. No matter how much advertising, sales promotion, personal selling, or public relations are used by Able Division for Product R, it is unlikely that retailers would stock the product or consumers would buy it until the price was once again competitive.

If we had learned consumer dissatisfaction and the resulting distribution were caused by a problem in the advertising, sales promotion, personal selling, or public relations areas rather than by a change in pricing, then we could then evaluate the potential of sales promotion as a solution to the problem.

Is It an Advertising, Sales Promotion, Personal Selling, or Public Relations Problem?

Once we've determined that the problem is the result of marketing and promotion difficulties, the third step is to determine whether the problem can be solved with advertising, sales promotion, personal selling, or public relations. Again, assume the problem Company XYZ faces is loss of distribution of Product R at retail. In our investigation, we learn that the sales responsibility for Product R has been shifted from a company sales force to a group of independent distributors. These distributors, while enthusiastic, are not familiar with Product R and how it is sold. Because of the changeover, the distributors have not had time to call on many of the retailers. Competition has taken advantage of the situation by mounting a strong personal selling effort with their sales force and supporting it with an aggressive advertising and sales promotion program. As a result, retailers are now featuring a competitive product, and many have discontinued Product R.

In this example, the problem and the apparent solution are in the personal selling area of the promotional program for Product R. Even if we acted immediately, it is doubtful that an aggressive advertising and sales promotion program directed to consumers or the trade could overcome the personal selling advantage competition has in this situation. Thus, while we can identify the distribution loss of Product R as a promotional problem, it is primarily a personal selling problem requiring a personal selling solution—although other promotional solutions might also be used.

Is It a Sales Promotion Problem?

The final step in the process is to determine whether or not the problem is one of sales promotion or one that a sales promotion technique can solve. Again, returning to Company XYZ and the distribution loss of Product R, let's now assume that competition has developed a sales promotion program featuring rather dramatic off-invoice discounts to retailers as an inducement to stock their product. Our promotional approach for Product R has been to rely primarily on personal selling by our sales force, supported with a minimum of consumer advertising and almost no reduced-price offers to the trade. As a result of the off-invoice deals, retailers have stocked the competitive product and dropped ours. Therefore, we've lost distribution to competition and, as a direct result, sales and profits of Product R have declined.

In this example, the profit loss is a marketing problem. It is the result of a promotional error, and it can be corrected by a sales promotion solution. There is a good chance that if Company XYZ develops its own sales promotion program with lucrative discounts, gives it to the sales force, and has them aggressively sell it, the product could recapture its previous distribution.

From these examples, you can see that the key to the successful use of sales promotion revolves around a four-step process:

1. Identifying the problem.
2. Tracing the problem to its cause and determining whether it is a marketing responsibility.
3. Determining whether promotion is a viable general solution.
4. If promotion is a viable solution, determining whether sales promotion is a viable specific solution.

Inherent in this process is a knowledge of what sales promotion can and can't do in the marketplace, which was discussed in Chapter 3. That knowledge is vital. The capabilities and limitations of sales promotion play an integral part in determining whether or not it can or should be used to solve the identified problem.

When to Use Sales Promotion

Generally, the identification of promotion problems is fairly clear-cut. One can usually determine which problems can be solved by advertising, sales promotion, and public relations and which can be solved through personal selling. A choice between whether a face-to-face contact with customers is needed or whether some form of media promotion would be effective can usually be made fairly quickly. Deciding whether to use advertising, sales promotion, or public relations is usually the greatest problem for the marketing manager. Our general view is that public relations, while powerful in many situations, works best to provide long-term solutions to rather general problems. For example, few marketers would expect public relations to offer a fast and effective solution

Table 6-1   How 57 Companies Choose between Advertising and Promotion

| | Impact on allocation | |
Brand factor	Increase advertising	Increase sales promotion
Stage in brand life cycle		
Introduction	X	
Growth	X	
Maturity		X
Decline		X
Favorable profit performance	X	
Market dominance	X	
Regional brand		X
Promotion-oriented competitor		X
Advertising-oriented competitor	X	
High differentiation	X	
High quality	X	
High purchase frequency	X	
Distribution vulnerability		X

Source: Roger Strang, "Marketing and Sales Promotions," Special Report from *Sales and Marketing Management* magazine, n.d.

to a declining sales problem or to being out-advertised by competition. The usual response in these cases would be either advertising or sales promotion or both. This is because, unlike public relations, advertising and sales promotion can be used to solve immediate, short-term problems.

Because the decision to use advertising or sales promotion is complex, and to help develop some general guidelines, Roger A. Strang, Professor of Marketing at the University of Southern California, conducted a study among 57 major consumer goods companies. His purpose was to get a more definitive view of the role of sales promotion in achieving company objectives. The results, showing how the surveyed companies decided between advertising and sales promotion, are shown in Table 6-1.

To understand the data in Table 6-1, some additional explanation of marketing and marketing terminology may be needed. If you are familiar with the terminology used in the chart, skip to page 134. If you are not, the following definitions should help.

1. Strang's first category is the stage of the brand in "the product life cycle." The product life cycle is a marketing concept that suggests that all product categories, all products, and even all brands go though a "life cycle" similar to that of a human being. That is, the product is developed and introduced to the market as at birth. In this

Table 6-2   The Product Life Cycle Concept

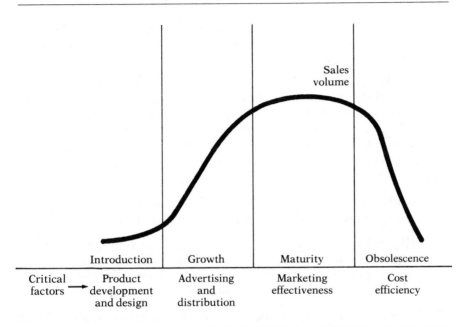

Source: Donald K. Clifford, Jr., "Managing the Product Life Cycle," *The McKinsey Quarterly*, Spring, 1965.

introductory stage, the brand has few sales. As consumers learn about it from promotion or usage, the brand passes from the low-volume introductory stage to that of rapid growth. At some point, growth stabilizes as the brand reaches its maximum usage and share of market. Finally, in the obsolescence stage, sales decline and eventually the brand disappears from the market. The concept is illustrated in Table 6-2. In explaining the product life cycle, Donald K. Clifford, Jr., says that most products reach the obsolescence stage because of three factors.

First, the need may disappear. This is what happened to the orange juice squeezer when frozen juice caught on. Second, a better, cheaper, or more convenient product may be developed to suit the same need. Oil-based paint lost its position in the home to water-based paint; plastics have replaced wood, metal, and paper in product categories ranging from dry-cleaning bags to aircraft parts. Third, a competitive product may, through superior marketing strategy, suddenly gain a decisive advantage. This happened to competing products . . . when Procter and Gamble secured the American

Dental Association's endorsement of its decay-prevention claims for Crest toothpaste.[1]

2. "Favorable profit performance" simply means that the product provides adequate profit to the company or meets management objectives.

3. "Market dominance" means that the product or brand has a major share of the total sales within that category. In the case of ready-to-eat cereal this might be a 7 to 8 percent share of the total market, while in a category such as unsweetened powdered soft drink mix, the brand leader might have an 80 to 85 percent share of total sales. Dominance can mean many things in marketing and depends to a great extent on the specific product or category involved.

4. "Regional brand," "promotion-oriented competitor," and "advertising-oriented competitor" are all self-explanatory.

5. "High differentiation" means that a brand has something that distinguishes it from competition. It could be the size, the price, the construction, or any number of other characteristics. The key point is that it can be differentiated from competitive products.

6. The final three—"high quality," "high purchase frequency," and "distribution vulnerability"—are self-explanatory.

Returning to Strang's chart, you can see that the choices between advertising and sales promotion as evidenced by these 57 companies suggest something of a "good news-bad news" approach. In other words, it appears that when the brand is growing and other factors are favorable, companies tend to favor advertising. When sales level off, start to decline, or face stiff competition, sales promotion is preferred. It appears that sales promotion is generally favored as a "fighter" or a problem-solver by the companies surveyed. However, the fact that these companies used sales promotion in the particular situations described in Table 6-1 doesn't necessarily mean that they are the best or the only situations for using sales promotion. The survey shows only that sales promotion is viewed in this way by many large companies. Whether or not this view is correct depends, of course, on the individual company and its general view of sales promotion. While we obviously don't argue with the results of Strang's survey, we believe a somewhat broader view of the uses and capabilities of sales promotion should be taken. We'll demonstrate that in later chapters.

---

1. Donald K. Clifford, Jr., "Managing the Product Life Cycle," *The McKinsey Quarterly*, Spring, 1965, pp. 49-50.

Problems and Opportunities

In the following sections, we have identified seven kinds of marketing problems that can best be solved with sales promotion. While each may be of more or less importance to you and your particular organization, as a group they encompass most problem areas for all types of marketers. We have also identified some of the more specific problems a company might face within each of these general problem areas.

These seven problem areas form the basis for our approach to sales promotion management. As we said earlier in this chapter, the primary challenge facing any marketer is to accurately identify the problems facing his product or service. Having done that, he can then evaluate and select the proper sales promotion tool to overcome the problem.

In Chapters 8 to 14 we will deal with each of the problem/opportunity areas in more detail. We will suggest specific sales promotion techniques that might be used to deal with the specific problem, and (where practical) we will give specific examples.

The seven problem/opportunity areas are:

1. Economic problems
2. Consumer problems
3. Product and product-related problems
4. Competitive problems
5. Reseller/reselling problems
6. Internal selling problems
7. New product problems

A brief overview of each of these areas follows.

Economic

Economic problems and opportunities normally affect all marketers, regardless of product or service. This is because the category includes many factors beyond the control of manufacturers and marketers in a given product category. And these factors may affect any aspect of business activity—the acquisition of raw materials (international events, the weather, U.S. foreign policy); the production process (technological advances, labor-management relations, energy supplies); or marketing decisions (economic conditions, price changes, or distribution channels). Of special importance are economic factors that directly affect consumer behavior. Economic conditions—inflation, recession, high interest rates, unemployment—influence consumer buying habits. And technological advances—the invention of the microcomputer chip and the jet airplane, the control of diseases (such as TB and diabetes), and the development of frozen foods and cable TV—affect consumer lifestyles.

In this area, of course, our interest is in how marketing generally and sales promotion specifically can help solve major economic problems when they arise. In Chapter 8 we'll review in more detail the specific economic problems a sales promotion manager might face and suggest sales promotion techniques that can be and have been used successfully.

Consumer

Consumer problems are those that relate specifically to changes in consumer lifestyles—pervasive modifications and alterations in the way consumers live, especially as these changes affect tastes, alter buying habits, and generally influence behavior. In recent years the most important changes have been (1) the movement from North and East to South and West, (2) the aging of the population, (3) the entry of large numbers of women into the labor force, (4) the increase in leisure time, and (5) the growing availability of convenient credit. Like economic problems, consumer problems cannot be solved. They can only be coped with because widespread changes in consumer lifestyles cannot be significantly affected by the marketing decisions of a single company or even a single industry.

Unlike economic problems, however, consumer problems offer as many opportunities as obstacles—that is, if the manufacturer or marketer is able to see them clearly and act on them quickly. As we will show in Chapter 9, the sales promotion manager can meet some of today's consumer challenges by regionalizing sales promotions, revising target markets, and generally paying close attention to changes in fashion, work habits, leisure activities, and so on.

Product and Product Related

Product and product-related problems are simply those in which the product or service under consideration isn't living up to sales or profit expectations or projections—excluding product or service defects or problems in quality control.

Some of the problems we have identified in this area are:

1. An overall decline in sales of the product category.
2. A declining share for the brand in the total category.
3. Static sales for the brand in a growing market.
4. A declining margin for the brand in spite of steady or growing sales in the category.

You'll note that in each of these areas the primary emphasis is on sales, share of sales, or profits for the brand. In Chapter 10 we'll look at these problems in more detail and suggest specific sales promotion techniques that can be used to help overcome these problems or take advantage of the opportunities they may present.

Competitive

Many of the problems in this category are related to those in the product problem area because sales, share of market, and profits are often directly affected by competitive activities. We separate them here, however, since the problems that we have identified can be traced directly to specific competitive actions that can be overcome with sales promotion techniques. Some of the problems in this area are:

- Pricing changes in competitive products.
- Competitive product line extensions or new product introductions.
- Competitive product reformulations, repackaging, or ingredient changes.
- Disruptive competitive activities in distribution, such as pressure on present dealers to add the competitive line and/or drop our line or an invasion of the brand's marketing areas by new brands or products.
- New, revised, or increased levels of competitive advertising.
- New, revised, or increased competitive sales promotion.
- Increased or improved trade deals offered by competition to the trade at either the wholesale or retail level.

As you can see, in each of these areas we have been able to trace the problem to specific activities by competition. This is the reason we have emphasized the importance of being able to properly identify the marketing problem that you face. Only in that way can you select the proper sales promotion tool to deal with it.

In Chapter 11 we'll discuss these problems in more detail and suggest specific sales promotion tactics to deal with them. Where appropriate, we will also give examples of successful sales promotion programs.

Reseller or Reselling

Again, some of the problems in this area may be indirectly related to those in other categories such as product or competition. We identify these problems, however, as being directly related to the reseller system, including the wholesaler, the distributor, and the retailer. Regardless of the method of moving the product from the manufacturer to the ultimate consumer, the following are typical reseller problems.

1. A loss of distribution at the retail level brought on by any number of causes. The specific problem here is that the ultimate consumer has

fewer opportunities to obtain the product or service because it is being offered at fewer locations.

2. In-store or display problems. This includes improper in-store location, lack of shelf space, misuse or nonuse of displays, out-of-stock conditions, and the like.

3. Entering new geographic areas with the product or brand. For example, regional products moving into national distribution or expanding their geographic market area need new, expanded, or additional retail outlets.

4. Entering new trade categories. This requires finding new types of distributors for the product; e.g., selling motor oil in supermarkets in addition to traditional automotive outlets.

5. Timing and frequency of sales promotion activities.

The above problems arise with resellers in both existing markets and new or expanded markets. Again, it is vital to specifically identify the problem or opportunity you face. For example, a sales promotion technique that might be quite effective in an existing market might be totally ineffective in a new market. The same is true of the method of distribution. What might work with a wholesaler might be totally ineffective with a retailer. In Chapter 12 we'll deal with these reseller and reselling problems in more detail.

Internal Selling

Most of the problems we have described up to this point are external; that is, they are normally caused by outside forces. Internal selling problems, however, can be just as serious. By internal selling problems, we mean those involving the sales or selling force who call on or sell to resellers. In addition, we divide the sales force into that which is controlled (the company's own sales employees) and that which is uncontrolled, including wholesalers, brokers, distributors, and vendors who are not direct employees. We have identified the following as the most common problems with both types of sales organization.

- Improving or changing the attitude of the sales force toward the product or service.
- Obtaining a sufficient amount of the sales force's time to properly promote or sell the product or service.
- Creating reward or incentive programs for all levels of the sales force.
- Changing or reallocating duties of the sales force in the selling effort for the product or service.
- Obtaining the support of the sales force for changes in the marketing and/or promotional program for the product or service.

As you can see, most of the problems in this category deal with motivation of the sales force. Certain sales promotion tactics, if used properly, can be tremendously helpful in overcoming some of these types of problems. In Chapter 13 we'll look at specific methods of using sales promotion to overcome problems or increase the effectiveness of the sales force.

New Products

There are several excellent books and articles dealing exclusively with the area of new products. We have, therefore, confined our discussion of new products to the sales promotion activities related to the introduction of a new product to the market. Further, we believe that the sales promotion function in new product work should be split into two areas.

1. The actual introduction of the product into the market.
2. Follow-up activities that ensure the survival of the product in the market.

While most sales promotion programs are designed to obtain initial trial of the product, too often insufficient attention is given to the all-important follow-up or supporting activities. For this reason, in Chapter 14 we'll review the problems and opportunities inherent in the introduction of all types of consumer products and the specific sales promotion techniques that have been most successful. In addition, we'll discuss the more demanding area of follow-up to the introduction to ensure product success after trial.

A Step-by-Step Approach

With this outline of typical problems (and opportunities) that might be faced by a sales promotion manager for a consumer product, we move to the next logical step: how to solve the problems that have been identified. We've found the best approach is a step-by-step method. Each step is discussed in some detail.

Identify the Problem

As we have continually stressed, the identification of the problem is vital to the determination of a successful solution. One point must be emphasized: The successful sales promotion manager must be able to dig beneath the surface of most marketing problems to be sure he is dealing with the source and not just a result of the problem. Often, problem identification can be difficult because of the interrelationship of the many marketing variables. Sales promotion managers who don't dig deep enough can often be misled.

Isolate the Cause

You must know the exact cause of the problem to be able to choose and implement the proper sales promotion technique. Misidentifying the cause of the problem, which then results in choosing the wrong remedy, can create additional problems.

Set Objectives

We cannot stress this step in the process too much. It is vital. Until you know what you want to accomplish, it is impossible to decide on a correct course of action. Here, too, your objectives must be quite specific and, if possible, measurable. This step is so important that we'll devote the entire following chapter to it.

Identify Potential Solutions

In the following chapters, in which we discuss various sales promotion problems, we'll suggest specific sales promotion techniques for solving those problems. In most cases, a variety of alternatives are available. The job of the sales promotion manager at this point is to identify the alternatives or the potential solutions that might be used. This leads to the next step.

Evaluate the Alternative Solutions

Each of the alternative solutions will have strengths and weaknesses. By knowing the potential of each technique and its capability, you can determine which one might be most effective in solving the specific problem. In most cases, the evaluation of alternatives is essentially a cost-benefit trade-off. In other words, one tactic might provide a much faster solution to the problem than another, but it could be a great deal more expensive. In this case, the choice of the manager is whether to trade speed of results for increased costs or to trade slower results for lower costs. A simple way to evaluate alternatives is to list each of the sales promotion techniques being evaluated, then jot down their advantages and disadvantages. One can then easily see the trade-offs of the various sales promotion techniques and make a more thorough evaluation.

Inherent in this step is the selection of the sales promotion technique that offers the best possible solution. Based on this choice, you can move to the next step.

Develop a Budget and Control System

Too often, it seems, sales promotion programs fail to accomplish their objectives because of a laxity in budgeting and control. For that reason, this step is crucial for a good sales promotion manager. Chapter 16 is devoted to a complete discussion of how to establish sales promotion budgets and develop control systems that will keep the programs within the established bounds.

Implement the Sales Promotion Program

With the necessary preplanning done, budgets established, and controls in place, the next step is to implement the program. While it might seem that we have overloaded the process leading up to this step, we can assure you we have not. Implementation is actually the natural flow from a well-planned and well-developed sales promotion plan. If the proper planning has been done in advance, the implementation of the sales promotion program is actually very simple.

Measure the Results

The final, but most important, step in the process is to establish some method for measuring results. Unless you know what you have achieved, you have no way of knowing whether or not the cost of the promotion was worthwhile. In Chapter 17 you'll find additional details on how to set up measurement procedures and use them to evaluate your results.

To put our suggestions into a more usable form, we have prepared an outline in Table 6-3 for setting up a problem-solving program. If you will follow the step-by-step outline, you will find it can work for almost any type of organization, company, or group and for any type of product or service. As an example of how sales promotion planning is done in large corporations, you might be interested in Table 6-4. This is a sales promotion planning flow chart developed by Grayson Associates for use in the cosmetics, fragrance, toiletry, and proprietary-goods industries. As you can see, this flow chart deals more with how sales promotion fits into the overall marketing plan and approval process of the organization than our more simplified model does. However, you will also note that not as much emphasis is given to the identification or isolation of the initial problem. This approach assumes that the problem has been identified as one that can be solved with sales promotion techniques. Quite logically, this model could be initiated at the "Evaluation of Alternative Solutions" stage of our model, and followed from there.

With this look at identifying problems and opportunities in sales promotion, we move to the next step, that of setting sales promotion objectives. That's the subject of Chapter 7.

Table 6-3   Outline of Problem-Solving Program

Sales, profits, margins, etc.	→ Identify problem	
	↓	
Product, distribution, price, promotion	→ Isolate cause of problem	
	↓	
Increase sales, expand distribution, enlarge profits, etc.	→ Set objectives →	Clear, measurable, specific
	↓	
Advertising, sales promotion, personal selling, public relations	→ Identify potential solutions	
	↓	
Couponing, sampling contests, trade deals, etc.	→ Evaluate alternative solutions →	Advantages, disadvantages
	↓	
Costs, scheduling, delivery, etc.	→ Develop budget and control system	
	↓	
Consumer, trade, sales force, etc.	→ Implement sales promotion program	
	↓	
Reverse sales decline, coupon redemption, contest entries, etc.	→ Measure results	

Source: Grayson Associates

Table 6-4   Sales Promotion Planning Flow Chart

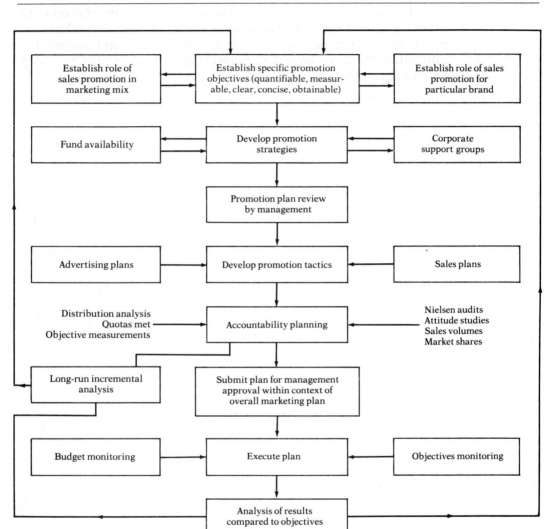

Establish role of sales promotion in marketing mix	Establish specific promotion objectives (quantifiable, measurable, clear, concise, obtainable)	Establish role of sales promotion for particular brand
Fund availability	Develop promotion strategies	Corporate support groups
	Promotion plan review by management	
Advertising plans	Develop promotion tactics	Sales plans
Distribution analysis / Quotas met / Objective measurements	Accountability planning	Nielsen audits / Attitude studies / Sales volumes / Market shares
Long-run incremental analysis	Submit plan for management approval within context of overall marketing plan	
Budget monitoring	Execute plan	Objectives monitoring
	Analysis of results compared to objectives	

Source: Grayson Associates, Inc.

Summary

Problems mean opportunity. The sales promotion manager, faced with a sales problem, must first make sure that the problem is, in fact, a sales promotion problem by eliminating other possible causes, such as advertising or personal selling. That tells you whether sales promotion should be used to attack the problem.

There are seven common problem areas that may provide opportunities for sales promotion. These are economic, consumer, and product problems, and competitive, reseller, internal selling, and new product difficulties. Once you have determined your particular problem, a step-by-step approach to solution is best.

7

Setting Sales Promotion Objectives

What method should a company use to set sales promotion objectives? Sales promotion programs are often started without specific goals in mind. And, many times, the objectives that are established tend to be so vague and broad as to be useless. The question naturally arises, How can this happen in a $49-billion industry? How can companies launch sales promotion programs costing thousands or even millions of dollars without knowing exactly what they hope to accomplish?

Unfortunately, the sales promotion field lags far behind other areas of marketing in developing an objective measurement system for determining results. No manufacturer would think of starting up a plant to manufacture television sets without having a firm idea of how many sets were to be manufactured, how many workers would be employed, where the parts would come from, and what the cost of each set would be. However, we sometimes find marketers implementing sales promotion programs with only a general idea of costs simply because "we've always had a promotion at this time of the year" or "reducing the price of the product for a while will boost sales." Starting a sales promotion program with these vague objectives is somewhat akin to starting a cross-country automobile trip without a map, a supply of gasoline, or a definite destination. You may well end up on the other side of the country, but it will take longer than you thought and cost much more than you anticipated, and you might not end up where you wanted to go.

Part of the reason for the prevalence of this problem in the sales promotion field may well be the traditional casual method of evaluating sales promotion results. And part of it may simply be the failure to collect sufficient data for accurate judgment. As we demonstrated in Chapter 4, you can have a very successful promotion in terms of sales and yet lose money because of the sales promotion costs. When we also understand that it is possible to have so much sales promotion that sales actually decline, we see why it might be difficult for some marketers to measure the results of their sales promotion efforts objectively. Because of these problems, we believe that sales promotion, if it is to be a useful marketing tool and not just a gimmick, must have clear, measurable goals and objectives and accurate methods of evaluating the results.

What Is a Sales Promotion Objective?

In some cases, the reason for the absence of sales promotion objectives is simply that the sales promotion manager doesn't have a clear understanding of what objectives are or should be. Much of this confusion seems to come about because of a lack of clear-cut terminology. To make sure we're all speaking the same language, we'll use the following terms in setting sales promotion objectives.

Objectives vs. Strategies and Executions

Initially, like Webster, we define an "objective" as "an aim or end of action, a point to be hit or reached." A sales promotion objective is something to be attained. To know if we have attained the objective, our results must be measurable. One part of the problem with setting a sales promotion objective is that many sales promotion people confuse objectives with strategies and executions. In this context, these definitions should be useful.

Sales promotion objective. A sales promotion "objective" or "goal"—we consider the terms interchangeable—is the clearly measurable end result of the sales promotion program. For example, a measurable sales promotion objective might be "to have 50,000 prospective new customers try the product within the next year." Notice that the objective is specific and measurable. If only 40,000 prospects try the product in the next 12 months, the sales promotion manager will not have achieved his or her sales promotion objective. The objective states clearly, and in measurable terms, what the manager expects the sales promotion program to achieve.

Sales promotion strategy. A sales promotion "strategy" is the plan for accomplishing the sales promotion objective of having 50,000 new customers try the product within the year. To do this, a manager might select a sales promotion strategy involving sampling the product. Or he might use a coupon offer, a reduced price, or any other of a multitude of sales promotion activities. The sales promotion strategy simply specifies how the sales promotion manager intends to achieve his sales promotion objective. It does not include the specific details of the offer.

Sales promotion execution. The final step in the implementation of a sales promotion program is the "execution," or the actual physical form the sales promotion program takes. For example, let's assume that with the objective of having 50,000 new customers try the product within the next year, a sampling strategy is selected. Based on this strategy, the execution would be how the program was actually carried out—in this case, how the samples were to be put into the hands of consumers. This could be done in any number of ways: by distributing samples on street corners to passers-by, hand-delivering samples to a very finely defined group of prospects, or giving out sample packages in retail stores. Further, one of the decisions in the execution would be whether a full size, a trial size, or some size in-between would be used as the actual sample.

By using these definitions, a sales promotion manager can make his objective quite clear. Again, it is what he or she expects the sales promotion program to achieve, in measurable terms. Thus, a sales promotion objective of "increasing sales" or "making people aware of the brand" is simply too broad to be useful. There is no way to quantify the results.

The use of this terminology also has another advantage. By understanding the differences between an objective and a strategy and between a strategy and an execution, and by using these terms clearly and consistently, the sales promotion manager should be able to minimize confusion and thereby establish objectives, strategies, and executions much more easily.

Marketing, Advertising, and Sales Promotion Objectives

Another problem that arises in establishing sales promotion objectives is the confusion between marketing objectives, advertising objectives, and sales promotion objectives. To help clarify this problem, we'll discuss each separately.

Marketing objectives. Generally, marketing objectives are specific goals to be achieved by the product in such broad areas as sales or profits. For example, a marketing objective might be to increase the brand's market share from 8 to 10 percent in one year. Or, it might be to improve the profit margin from 7 to 9 percent in the next six months. Notice, with marketing objectives such as these, several specific marketing functions may be involved. To increase the market share from 8 to 10 percent might involve the use of increased distribution, different pricing, and several forms of promotion, such as advertising, personal selling, and sales promotion.

Advertising objectives. Unlike marketing objectives, advertising objectives generally have to do with the communication effects to be achieved with advertising messages. Since advertising is usually considered to be the communication of a sales message through the mass media, an advertising objective would involve measures of awareness or comprehension of the sales message being communicated. A typical advertising objective might be within a three-month period to "make 50 percent of the target audience aware that the product now has 30 percent more magic ingredient J than before." Notice, the advertising objective says nothing about generating a sale or changing the behavior of the consumer. It deals only with the communication of a sales message and the effects of that communication on consumer knowledge. Since advertising is only one part of the promotion mix (see Chapter 2), it is difficult to set more specific objectives in most cases.

Sales promotion objectives. Unlike advertising, sales promotion is immediate. It's action oriented. When a sales promotion program is initiated, it is expected that some change will occur in the market place. Thus, sales promotion objectives are usually defined in terms of something happening; i.e., getting new users to try, increasing product usage, holding current users, or gaining new or additional distribution with the trade. The major difference between sales promotion objectives and marketing and advertising objectives is that the former can be accomplished by using recognized sales promotion techniques, such as sampling, couponing, price-packs, and off-invoice allowances. They are not specifically dependent on other marketing activities to be successful, although often advertising and sales promotion objectives are used in combination since there is a synergistic effect between the two.

These explanations of the differences among objectives, strategies, and executions and among marketing, advertising, and sales promotion objectives should make it easier for you to develop sound objectives for your own brands. We move now to the more specific area of setting sales promotion objectives.

General Guidelines for Sales Promotion Objectives

While it is true that every product and every sales promotion plan has different objectives, there are some general guidelines that apply to the setting of objectives under any circumstances. They are quite simple, but they are so often overlooked that we list them here as a reminder.

We suggest that, regardless of the situation, sales promotion objectives must be:

- *Specific.* You can have no generalities. What is the program supposed to achieve and within what time frame?
- *Measurable.* If the objectives are to be specific, they must be measurable. There must be a starting point, an ending point, and a way to measure the difference between the two.
- *Clear and concise.* Objectives should be easy to understand. To make them confusing or complicated is to reduce the likelihood that they will be achieved.
- *Practical and realistic.* Setting objectives that obviously can't be carried out by the organization either because of lack of ability or lack of facilities is pointless.
- *Affordable.* While setting an objective of having every person in the country try a sample of the product within the next six months might be a lofty ambition, it is probably beyond the financial reach of almost any marketer. Objectives must be within the financial capabilities of the organization.
- *Attainable.* High sales promotion goals must be tempered with knowledge of the marketer and the market, the organization, its financial resources, and the capabilities of the sales promotion program to achieve the objectives.

We strongly urge you to use this checklist when developing sales promotion objectives. If your objectives fail on any of these points, either adjust your objectives or reevaluate your plan.

Typical Objectives for Sales Promotion Plans

While we reiterate that all sales promotion plans are brand- and situation-specific, there are some general objectives that can be achieved with sales promotion programs. Here, it is not possible for us to be as specific as we would like, although we have included examples of each program, but these general objectives should indicate the various goals which a sales promotion program can typically achieve. We have separated them into consumer or external sales promotion objectives and internal or trade promotion objectives.

Consumer Sales Promotion Objectives

Generally, sales promotion programs can achieve seven objectives with consumers. In no particular order, they can:

Figure 7-1   Getting New Users: Jockey Underwear   **Figure 7-2   Holding Present Users: Post Cereals**

Source: William A. Robinson, *100 Best Sales Promotions of 1976/7* (Chicago: Crain Books, 1977), p. 112 and p. 26.

1. *Reach new users.* One of the major strengths of sales promotion is its ability to obtain trial of a product by new users. Figure 7-1 illustrates the Jockey underwear sales promotion program designed to achieve this objective.
2. *Hold current users.* Current users can be encouraged to continue using the product rather than switching to a competitor through several sales promotion techniques. The obvious objective of the Post cereals continuity program in Figure 7-2 is to hold present customers by encouraging them to save box tops to aid schools in obtaining needed sports equipment.
3. *Load current users.* Often the objective of a sales promotion program is to encourage present users to stock up on the product. In effect, this

Figure 7-3   Loading Present Users: Snow Crop Orange Juice

Figure 7-4   Increasing Usage: Chicken of the Sea Tuna

Source: Robinson, *100 Best Sales Promotions of 1976/7*, p. 113 and p. 109.

prevents them from being persuaded to try a competitive product. The objective of Snow Crop orange juice (Figure 7-3) is clearly to attempt to get the consumer to purchase a large supply of the product in order to obtain the larger refund. A purchase of 12 cans of Snow Crop would "load" most consumers for a reasonable length of time.

4. *Increase product usage.* An objective of many sales promotion programs is to increase product usage either through increased regular use by consumers or through suggested new uses. Recipe books have proven to be a very successful strategy for achieving this objective. The *Chicken of the Sea Tuna Cookbook* offer in Figure 7-4 is an excellent example of an execution of this sales promotion strategy.

Figure 7-5   Getting Trade-Up: Audi Cars

Source: Robinson, *100 Best Sales Promotions of 1976/7*, p. 134.

5. *Trade consumers up.* Often the objective of a sales promotion plan is to encourage consumers to use a better quality or higher profit margin product in the line. The sales promotion offer of $1,000 off on a new Audi in Figure 7-5 is an example of a strategy designed to achieve that objective. The Audi is an expensive car. This special price reduction was an attempt to encourage those who thought they couldn't afford an Audi to move up because of the $1000-off offer.

6. *Reinforce brand advertising.* Often, the objective of the sales promotion program is simply to reinforce the message, the image, or the idea being conveyed in media advertising. Since there is actually

Figure 7-6   Supporting Advertising: Marlboro Cigarettes

Source: Robinson, *100 Best Sales Promotions of 1976/7*, p. 30.

little that can be said about cigarettes, the Marlboro sales promotion program, supporting the western theme used in media advertising, fits this objective beautifully. Figure 7-6 illustrates the products available at the "Marlboro Country Store."

7. *Introduce a new product.* Probably one of the more widely used objectives for a sales promotion program is to help introduce a new product. While there are many strategies that can be used to accomplish this objective (and literally hundreds of executions), the free package offer for Nestlé cookie mix in Figure 7-7 was an outstanding success.

Figure 7-7   Introducing a New Product: Nestlé Cookie Mix

Source: Robinson, *100 Best Sales Promotions of 1976/7*, p. 22.

Trade Sales Promotion Objectives

Like the consumer sales promotion objectives just described, there are several general objectives that can be achieved in sales promotion programs directed to the trade. Again, in no specific order but with some specific examples, trade promotions can achieve the following results.

1. *Gain new distribution.* One of the primary objectives of many trade promotions or deals is to gain new distribution for the product. Some of the typical strategies for achieving this objective are free goods, profitable trade allowances, and introductory or stocking allowances. An example of this objective and strategy is illustrated in Figure 7-8. Norelco put together several ideas to encourage re-

Figure 7-8   Gaining New Distribution: Norelco Light Bulbs

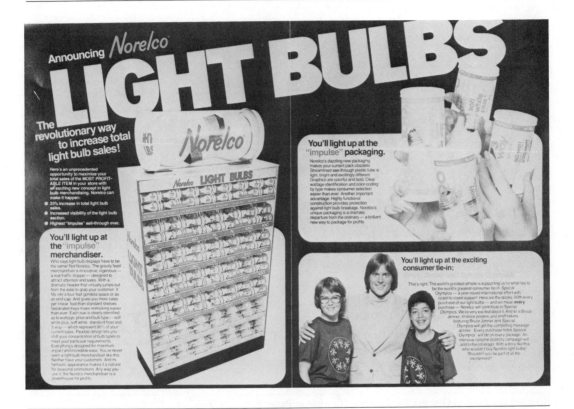

Source: Courtesy of North American Philips Lighting Corporation.

tailers to stock its particular brand of light bulbs. These included an "impulse" merchandiser, a special consumer promotion involving a contribution to the Olympic fund, and in-store promotional display materials. All were designed to encourage retailers to stock and sell Norelco light bulbs.

2. *Obtain trade support for a consumer sales promotion program.* Often the trade promotion objective is to build interest in and work in harmony with a consumer promotion, i.e., to encourage the trade to feature the product, develop special displays in their stores, or take advantage of the event in some other way. While typical sales promotion programs, such as retail display allowances, contests or sweepstakes for retailers, and theme promotion display materials, are the most common strategies employed, others can be used also.

Figure 7-9   Getting Trade Support: Coronet Paper

Source: Courtesy of Georgia-Pacific Corp., Consumer Paper Products Division.

In Figure 7-9, Coronet paper introduced the "2nd Annual $100,000 Sweepstakes" promotion to its retailers. As you can see, the consumer portion of the sweepstakes is featured inside the folder. This showed the retailer the size and scope of the consumer event. On the back, the retailer's portion of the program was illustrated with 156 prizes for winning participants.

3. *Build or reduce trade inventories.* Often the trade objective is to build or reduce trade inventories. Such sales promotion strategies as higher trade allowances, impending price increases, or count-and-recount offers are often used. In Figure 7-10 you'll find an example of a contest developed by the Florida Citrus Commission designed to encourage retailers to stock up and display Florida orange and grapefruit juices. The promotion requirement was the construction of a retail display, with prizes to go to the best. Of course, to build the

Figure 7-10   Increasing Inventories: Florida Citrus Commission

Source: William A. Robinson, *100 Best Sales Promotions* (Chicago: Crain Books, 1980), p. 43.

display, the retailer would have to order and stock more Florida orange and grapefruit juice than normal, thus building trade inventories.

4. *Improve trade relations.* Sometimes, the marketer simply believes he needs to improve his relations with the trade. He then sets this as the objective of his sales promotion program. This need to improve trade relations may be brought about by increases in prices to the trade or reduced margins, or it may simply be a method of warding off competition. Many strategies can be used to achieve these sales promotion objectives. Where it is legal, the marketer may plan dealer contests or sweepstakes or may offer gifts or prizes for selling certain amounts of product. In other instances, the marketer may be limited in what can be done due to legal or other restrictions. In these cases, such strategies as merchandising the consumer advertising

Figure 7-11   Building Dealer Good Will: Seagram's 7 Crown

Source: Courtesy of Seagram Distillers Company, Seagram's 7 Crown.

program through trade advertising, making dealer aids available, or simply reminding the trade of the marketer's interest in their good will are often used.

In Figure 7-11 you'll see how Seagram's 7 Crown used its consumer advertising program to build dealer good will and improve its trade relations. The theme of the promotion shows what and how Seagram's is doing to help the retailer sell more of its products at a profit to both. That should appeal to any retailer since it costs him nothing and can improve his sales and profits.

A Sample Sales Promotion Planning Form

Table 7-1 is a sales promotion planning form. It has been used success-fully by many organizations and we recommend its use. Notice that it is quite specific; it is almost impossible to set sales promotion objectives unless you have all the information required to complete the form. An explanation of the various parts of the form should help you use it more quickly and easily.

1. *Market situation.* Briefly describe in general terms what is happen-ing in the market place. For example, is the product category in-creasing or decreasing? What is the economic situation as it affects the product? Is the category heavily promoted at this time? Any new product entires or competitive developments? As you can see from these suggestions, this is a thumbnail sketch of the market designed to help you get the overall picture.

2. *Problem to be solved.* This point is more specific. Exactly what is happening and what effect is it having on your brand? Dig beneath the surface to get the answer. As we suggested in Chapter 5, it is vital that you identify the problem exactly and then trace the cause to the source. In our opinion, this is the key element in the entire planning program.

3. *Competition.* Identify the major competition. If possible, list their current promotional theme or offers to the consumer and the trade. Be sure to list their advertising, personal selling, public relations, and, of course, their current sales promotion programs. The more you know about competition, the better your chances of finding a successful solution to the problem.

4. *Sales promotion objective.* You'll note that we ask that you define your objectives to the consumer and the trade. Sometimes only a consumer program will be involved, and sometimes only a trade program. In either case, be sure to list the objectives your sales promotion plan is intended to achieve. Here, you must be very specific. How many new customers do you want to sample? How many dealers will your new point-of-sale material be directed to? How many cases of your product will you pack with the special reduced price label? If you aren't specific, you won't have measur-able objectives. Then you'll have no method of evaluation.

5. *Area of promotion.* Here, describe exactly the area of the country and the number of dealers—the territory and the scope of the sales promotion plan. Often, you'll find that describing exactly where and in what area the program will take place will help you later with cost estimates.

6. *Sales promotion strategy to be used.* We've been moving from the general to the specific. Now you need to identify the strategy you

---

Table 7-1   Sales Promotion Planning Form

---

1. Market situation:

2. Problem to be solved:

3. Competition:

4. Sales promotion objective:

   Consumer:

   Trade:

5. Area of promotion:

6. Sales promotion strategy to be used:

   Timing:

   Budget:

7. Method of measurement to be used:

---

plan to use or the general sales promotion technique to be employed. For example, will you use an off-invoice allowance to the dealer or will you offer a display allowance? Do you plan to sample the product or will you build the program around a refund offer? You'll want to review the various alternatives available to you and select the one most appropriate for accomplishing your objectives.

Table 7-2 Sales Promotion Planning Form

1. *Market situation:* Shampoo is a highly competitive category. $730,000,000 retail market with 193 major brands. Increasing at 12-15 percent rate annually. Trend toward more cleansing products or products that give hair body. Seven new brands introduced last year have captured 20 percent share, i.e., Agree, Farrah Fawcett, Clairol conditioner, Wheat Germ 'n Honey, and Ultra Max.

   [Our Brand] down from 2.4 percent to 1 percent share in last year. Concern over loss of distribution in addition to sales. Heavily outadvertised by new brands. Our budget only 10 percent of estimated $6,000,000 Agree introduction.

2. *Problem to be solved:* Develop a consumer and trade sales promotion package that will generate maximum awareness and sales for a short period of time with a minimal budget on a national scale. Help hold line until initial new product thrust is over.

3. *Competition:* Present established brands, plus new brands being introduced, particularly new cleansing shampoos and after-shampoo products. Particular emphasis against Agree, Farrah Fawcett, Clairol, Wheat Germ 'n Honey, and Ultra Max. Primary competition is Agree, with massive sampling program plus couponing. Theme is "Stops the Greasies." Farrah Fawcett uses heavy TV expenditures with star presenter. Little promo activity with consumer. More against trade. Others are standard new product introductions.

4. *Sales promotion objective:*

   Consumer: Stop sales decline and hold present 1 percent share, plus start to rebuild.

   Trade: Hold present distribution at 70 percent with average of four [Our Brand] varieties stocked. Increase pull-through by consumer at trade level. Revitalize awareness of brand with trade.

5. *Area of promotion:* National but with special emphasis on coastal and resort areas where usage is higher. Major push in California, Florida, Texas, and Chicago.

6. *Sales promotion strategy to be used:* Promotion to be aimed at teenage girls 12 to 17 to bring them to retail stores for immediate purchase. Recommend the use of a full-color 22″ × 37″ poster featuring John Travolta of movie *Grease* free in exchange for one proof-of-purchase from [Our Brand] shampoo or conditioner plus 50¢ for handling. Tie in promotion with movie *Grease* nationally. Promote in media, primarily through target-market oriented magazines. Support with TV commercials. Free-standing floor displays packed with three dozen 8-ounce bottles plus poster dealer loader. Include headers, shelf talkers, and take-one order pads in package. Put hang-tags on bottles.

   Develop trade contest through sweepstakes. Retailer to answer three questions from sales presentation. All entries pooled. Prize is appearance in Paramount movie or TV show. Other prizes of smaller nature to tie in. Also use books and movie tickets in promotion.

   Deals: $2-per-dozen off-invoice shampoo allowance. $2.87-per-dozen off-invoice allowance on conditioner. 50¢-per-dozen ad allowance with proof-of-performance. $6 off-invoice allowance on floor-stand display and $1 display allowance rebate.

   Timing: Schedule promotion to break in each market with introduction of movie *Grease.*

   Budget: $600,000 for consumer media and trade and sales promotion. All discounts, allowances for deals to be handled separately.

7. *Method of measurement to be used:*

   Consumer: Share of market measurement pre-post promotion to determine if decline has stopped.

   Trade: Measure of trade distribution through regular sources. Measure displays and promotions by retailers vs. previous promotional programs in same budget range.

A. *Timing.* Specify the timing of the program. What is the starting date in the field and in your own organization? How long will the sales promotion program last? What will be the final date of the offer? When do you expect to have the total results? This element is the key to your success. You must allow sufficient time not only to develop the program but to implement it too.

B. *Budget.* Establish an anticipated budget. This can be developed either from the ground up (determining what you want to do and then costing it out) or from an estimated availability (we have so many dollars available and want to maximize our program within that amount). Be sure that you include all costs here. Too often there is a surprise item in the billing for a change that had been either overlooked or forgotten. In either case, it creates real havoc to discover additional costs after the program has already been completed.

7. *Method of measurement to be used.* The final step is to identify the method that will be used to evaluate the sales promotion program. Will you use consumer surveys? Total sales? Measured sales over a previous period? Number of displays built? What? Obviously, this evaluation must be keyed to your sales promotion objectives. For example, it makes little sense to say that the objective of the program is to trade consumers up to a higher-priced product and then count the number of entries in a sweepstakes. One doesn't necessarily measure the other. Be sure the measurement fits the task. And don't forget to include the cost of the evaluation in the total budget for the promotion. Someone has to pay for it.

A Completed Sales Promotion Planning Form

In Table 7-2 you'll find a completed sales promotion planning form. While we've masked the figures and changed some of the names, it should give you a good idea of exactly how the form is used in practice.

Summary

Sales promotion objectives, strategies, and executions are different things. So are marketing objectives, advertising objectives, and sales promotion objectives. Once you have made the appropriate distinctions, follow the guidelines for setting your sales promotion objectives.

Those objectives, whether for trade or consumer sales promotions, should be specific, measurable, clear and concise, practical and realistic, affordable, and attainable. A detailed planning form for your sales promotion programs is necessary.

PART II

SOLVING PROBLEMS WITH SALES PROMOTION

8

Economic Problems and Opportunities

Throughout Part II we will use a problem-solution format. First we will identify various problems that can be either partially or totally solved with sales promotion. Then we will suggest specific strategies that can be used to solve those particular problems. In Chapter 6 we identified seven specific marketing problem areas. In this chapter we will be dealing with the first of those areas, economic problems, and we'll deal with each of the others in succeeding chapters.

What Are Economic Problems?

Economic problems are those deriving from the economic system and economic conditions nationally and internationally. What makes economic problems unique among all marketing problems is that they cannot be solved. There is little if anything an individual company can do to change our economic system or to control the economic situation. Yet, the individual organization must nevertheless cope with problems caused by the economy in order to be successful. The problems arising from the economy cannot be ignored—they have too much of an impact to permit that. So, in spite of the difficulty, it is necessary for the individual company to understand the economy and to develop marketing and sales promotion strategies in light of economic conditions—if not to solve economic problems, at least to diminish their effect.

In the following pages we'll look briefly at different economic problems in order to provide a better understanding of them. Then we'll suggest some sales promotion strategies and show what other companies have done. Unfortunately, our suggestions cannot be as specific as we would like since economic problems affect each organization differently. In spite of that, our recommendations are applicable to most types of consumer products and brands. Because economic problems are usually so broad, general marketing strategies are often more successful in deal-ing with them than individual sales promotion programs are. There are, however, situations in which sales promotion can play a major role in a program intended to offset or reduce the effect of economic problems.

Solving Economic Problems

The general economic problems that impinge most on marketing activ-ities are inflation and recession and a relatively new problem in this country—shortages. Historically, we have lived in a land of abundance, and the major marketing task has been to encourage consumption. Now, however, we are faced with dwindling supplies of many natural re-sources, and this has brought about a new concept and a new term: "demarketing." *Demarketing* simply means that rather than stressing consumption, we should try to reduce it and use available resources more efficiently. From this point of view, marketing can be used to reduce demand or to switch it to more abundant supplies. As shortages increase, there will probably be a greater need for demarketing many products and services. In spite of shortages, however, the market economy of the United States, with its general emphasis on consumption, is likely to continue in the foreseeable future.

Since the 1940s, the general trend in this country has been infla-tionary. While there have been recessions and adjustments over the years, they have been relatively minor. Thus, most of our modern mar-keting experience in the U.S. has occurred in an inflationary setting. Since sales promotion has literally grown up and matured during this time, many of our general guidelines for the use of sales promotion must be applied cautiously in a recessionary period. Because we haven't had a deep recession in more than 40 years, many currently popular sales promotion plans have never been tried in that economic climate. We believe that the theories are correct, but they might not perform as well as we might expect in all economic situations.

Sales Promotion: Limitations

While dramatic results have often been achieved with sales promotion, none of the techniques are powerful enough to overcome major economic problems such as inflation and recession. Sales promotion programs simply can't offset either rising or declining prices or make up for re-source shortages. Much broader marketing strategies are usually needed, and even they may not be strong enough. While we'll suggest some sales promotion strategies and give examples that have been used to combat economic problems, keep in mind they are not likely to solve the entire problem, although they may help. Sales promotion is usually most effective in dealing with a product category, product-related, or brand-related problem.

Building Demand: Primary or Selective?

In a period of inflation, recession, or shortage, the first consideration of the marketer should be whether to use promotion to build primary or selective demand for the product. Building primary demand means that the marketer of a product or service attempts to persuade consumers to purchase a product in the general category rather than the specific brand. In other words, automakers attempt to get consumers to purchase cars rather than boats, houses, or gold, regardless of the brand purchased. Building selective demand means that marketers attempt to persuade consumers to purchase their specific brand in a category, assuming they will purchase some brand initially. The decision of whether to build primary or selective demand is basic for all marketers, regardless of the economic situation. In many instances, though, the economic climate influences the decision.

In a period of inflation, the usual choice has been to develop a selective demand program and attempt to get consumers to purchase a specific brand. Inflation usually means more money is available and consumers expect higher prices in the future. The choice of a brand seems more important than whether or not to buy, since most consumers are buying anyway. Conversely, in a period of recession, when there is less available money in the market and consumers are reducing their purchases, the use of a primary demand appeal is more important. For example, in the mid 1970s, when inflation was reasonable, the sales of home swimming pools were fairly high. Since many consumers had discretionary income and wanted a pool, marketers stressed the differences in the brands and the superiority of one over the others. In a period of recession, however, consumer demand for swimming pools usually declines dramatically. Swimming pool marketers then choose to sell the idea of a swimming pool per se to consumers. Their marketing task is to convince the consumer to buy a pool rather than an automobile, a snowmobile, or even a vacation.

An excellent example of the use of sales promotion to attempt to offset economic conditions occurred in 1974 in the automobile industry. Late that year the U.S. had suffered its first oil shortage and was moving toward recession. As a direct result, the sale of automobiles declined significantly. In an effort to offset the downturn in the economy brought on by the oil shortage, Chrysler announced the first automobile rebates. (See Figure 8-1.) This was an attempt to generate both primary and selective demand. Other automobile manufacturers soon followed Chrysler's lead, and, as all offered some form of rebate, the appeal changed from primary to selective demand. The great automobile rebate battle of 1974-75 illustrates how marketers attempted to overcome economic conditions with promotional action. Since that first rebate offer, this sales promotion technique has become a fairly standard merchandising program for all auto manufacturers.

Pricing Strategies

One of the most effective marketing tactics for overcoming adverse economic conditions is new or revised pricing strategies. In developing a pricing strategy, a marketer determines how important the price of the product is in relation to sales. Traditionally, lower prices tend to increase sales, while higher prices reduce them. The problem is that lower prices usually mean lower profits. Thus, if a marketer reduces prices in order to increase sales, he must recognize that he may also reduce his margin. He must therefore gain a sufficient amount of sales simply to maintain his previous profit.

An example of how pricing strategy is used and misused is the case of Sears, Roebuck & Company. At one time, Sears had an excellent low-price image: good quality at a reasonable price. As inflation increased and the price of all products rose, Sears raised its prices at the same or a higher rate. At the same time, it apparently believed that it could also improve the quality of its goods and change its pricing strategy. Thus, rather than maintaining its traditional low-price image, Sears moved into the middle- and sometimes even the high-price areas with its merchandise. At the same time, discount merchandisers, such as Kmart and Woolco, were moving into the low-price field, the area previously held by Sears. Because of its change in pricing strategy, Sears found itself in a strange marketing situation. It apparently lost some of its low-price image with consumers (many of whom had switched to Kmart); yet its quality image was not high enough to enable Sears to compete directly with the higher-price, higher-quality department stores that sell nationally advertised products. There apparently wasn't sufficient volume in the higher-price area to make up for the lost sales in the low-price category. As a result, Sears was forced to reevaluate its entire marketing strategy in an attempt to find a niche for itself in the retail field.

Another example of pricing strategy change, which had a dramatic effect on the market, occurred in the electronic calculator field. In the

Figure 8-1   Combatting Inflation: Chrysler Cars

Source: William A. Robinson, *100 Best Sales Promotions of 1975/6* (Chicago: Crain Books, 1976), p. 110.

late 1960s, hand-held electronic calculators were a novelty. In fact, one of the great concerns of calculator marketers was to justify the need for the product, particularly to consumers who really didn't understand electronics in general and calculators in particular.

At that time, a simple four-function calculator sold at retail in the $125-$150 range. With the development of the microchip, however, the cost of the product fell dramatically. While the initial promotional effort of marketers was to explain the product and to obtain trial, the lower product cost made a new marketing strategy necessary. In a period of inflation, marketers significantly lowered the price of calculators in order to expand the sale of the product as rapidly as possible. This penetration strategy worked. Now, electronic calculators, which perform the same functions as those of the late 1960s, cost only about a tenth of what they did then. Some brands have even become sales promotion premiums.

Figure 8-2 illustrates part of the Texas Instruments' sales promotion program for its calculator line in 1973. Figure 8-3 illustrates how calculators, now such a common item, have been used as a premium, in this case by Hunt-Wesson Foods, Inc.

A major consideration in any pricing strategy change is the long-term effect such a change might have on the brand. For example, if the price of a brand is reduced through sales promotion on a regular basis, the technique may lose its power and the quality image of the product may suffer as well. The consumer might come to believe that the product is always "on sale" and buy only when the price is reduced. Or the reduced price might be perceived as the "regular price." In this case, it becomes impossible to move the product price up when it is required. As a very sensitive aspect of marketing, pricing must be handled with great care.

Product and Package Modifications

Another method of dealing with economic problems is through product or package modifications. An example of trying to deal with inflation with this technique is the Hershey chocolate bar promotion. For many years, the Hershey bar sold at retail for 5¢. With increased ingredient prices, Hershey attempted to maintain a profitable margin by reducing the size and weight of the product. Thus, while it was able to maintain the price at 5¢ for a while, the product became smaller and smaller. At some point, however, the product simply couldn't be physically reduced any more. Hershey was then forced to make a pricing change. In an attempt to solve an economic problem (rising prices), Hershey used a product modification as long as it could, then switched to a pricing strategy.

Product modifications occur all the time. Because of rising ingre-

Figure 8-2   Lowering Prices: Texas Instruments

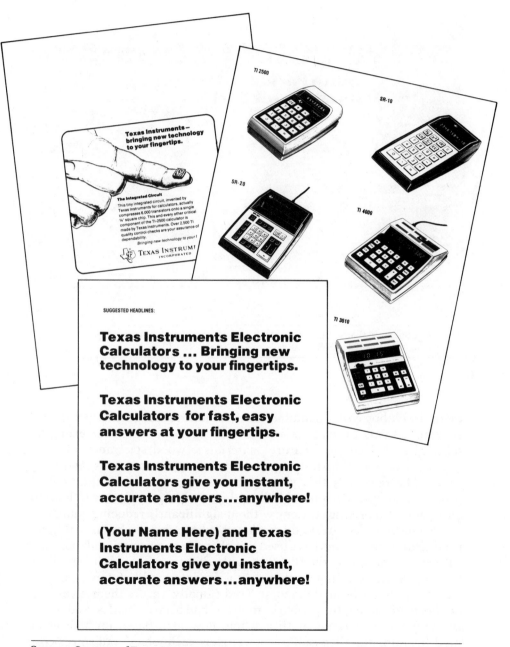

Figure 8-3 Using Premiums: Hunt Products

Source: Eugene Mahany, "Examine the 'Grocer Gestalt' to See What Turns Them on," *Advertising Age*, Nov. 22, 1976, p. 60.

dient and labor costs, manufacturers sometimes substitute less expensive ingredients or materials for more expensive ones. For example, plastic has replaced such natural materials as wood, steel, and leather in the construction of furniture, automobiles, appliances, toys, and even shoes. The reason is that plastic often serves as well as the natural product and costs considerably less, thus enabling marketers to hold to an established pricing strategy without significantly reducing quality.

Some manufacturers and marketers who have switched to synthetic products or ingredients have used this change as a promotional tool. One successful example is the Bic disposable shaver—although it is really a product category change rather than a product modification (since Bic had not previously made razors). Traditionally, razors themselves had not been promoted; the primary emphasis had been on blades. Suddenly, Bic entered the market with a whole new idea based on a product modification, the disposable shaver. New technology and lower-cost ingredients made the whole idea possible. And Bic introduced its new

Figure 8-4   Modifying the Product: Bic Disposable Shavers

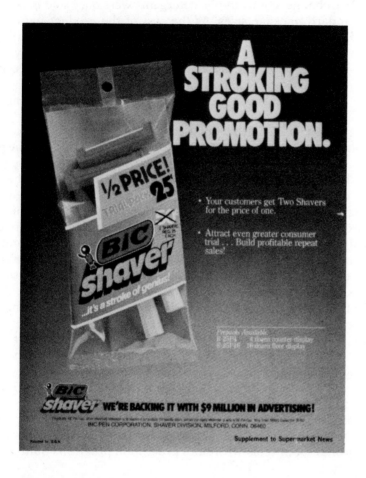

Source: William A. Robinson, "Five More 'Best Promotions' Shave the Facts and Shed Light on Marketing Success," *Advertising Age,* April 3, 1978, p. 52.

idea with a sales promotion technique: a Bic shaver at half price. (See Figure 8-4.) That was an impressive offer when you could obtain the entire shaver for about 12¢ and when many individual blades were retailing for 25¢ or more at the same time. The Bic approach combined not only a product change but also a packaging modification. And it worked very well.

A typical promotional strategy for dealing with inflationary problems is to offer an unusual size package as a lead into a product or
package size change. For example, detergents were once sold in only one
or two standard package sizes. As the cost of the product ingredients
increased, the number of package sizes more than tripled. This allowed
detergent manufacturers to develop volume pricing based on the various
package sizes. The larger the package, the lower the cost per ounce of the
product. These packaging modifications enabled detergent manufacturers to deal with the rising cost of the product and still maintain
consumer satisfaction.

One good example of turning a packaging modification into a promotional plus is the introduction of plastic soft drink bottles. In the place
of returnable glass bottles or cans, large-size plastic bottles were introduced. While the plastic bottles usually cost the consumer more because
they are nonreturnable, the bottlers have successfully promoted their
convenience and weight advantage over the traditional containers. An
example of how this was done by Pepsi-Cola is illustrated in Figure 8-5.

Finally, another method of dealing with inflation in the promotion
area is illustrated by the changes made by Cracker Jack. The "prize" or
in-pack premium that has been included in the package for more than 60
years has changed dramatically because of changing economic conditions. In the 1940s, the premium was usually a metal toy of some sort.
Today, because of rising costs (and a concern for safety), most premiums
are made of paper. Because the prize was such an integral part of the
product, it would have been impossible to drop it. Therefore, the company sought and found alternative ways to meet the economic conditions. In spite of these changes, Cracker Jack has managed to develop
over 600 different toy surprises as in-pack premiums.[1]

As you can see from these examples, the product or package can be
modified to meet changing economic conditions, and the changes can be
used as promotional tools with sales promotion programs built around
them.

Product Positioning or Repositioning

A favored way to offset economic problems is through the positioning or,
in many instances, repositioning of the product or service. While the
term "positioning" has been bandied about in marketing circles for some
time, the idea is really quite simple. Positioning simply means establishing a place the product can occupy in the consumer's mind. Thus,
Cadillac has been positioned as a luxury car because of its size, price,

1. Roger Strang, "Marketing and Sales Promotion," Special Section *Sales &*
Marketing Management magazine, no date.

Figure 8-5   Modifying the Package: Pepsi-Cola Soft Drink

design, decor, and special features, while the Chevette has been positioned as an economy car with fewer "extras" at a lower cost. The consumer thinks of the Cadillac as the ultimate in motor car luxury and the Chevette as an inexpensive means of transportation. This "positioning" has been achieved primarily through advertising by the manufacturer.

In terms of positioning or repositioning a product, the most common approach is to seek an unfilled niche in the product category matrix that exists in the consumer's mind. A very successful example of positioning was Avis's claim to be "only #2" in the automobile rental category. The Avis positioning approach was quite simple. Everyone knew that Hertz was first in car rentals—first in number of cars, first in number of locations, and first in number of cars rented. But no one knew exactly where Avis belonged. It really had no "position." Since everyone knew that Hertz was "number one," Avis decided to be "number two." With that idea, Avis built a promotional program stressing that it had to try harder to please the customer—to provide better service, cleaner cars, and better facilities—than Hertz. Avis positioned itself as the underdog *and* as the company worth trying because it provided more than the leader did. And the strategy worked. Avis is the solid #2 auto-rental company and has held that position for some time.

In periods of economic change, it is sometimes possible to position a product to take advantage of the existing situation. And it is sometimes possible to reposition a product to fit a different price or quality category. An example of positioning to exploit economic change is the promotional program developed by Paine, Webber, Jackson and Curtis, the stock brokerage firm. The New York Stock Exchange lost over 100 members between 1973 and 1978 as the bigger firms devoured the small. To survive in a shrinking industry, Paine Webber made great strides in improving efficiency and diversifying into related businesses, such as commodities. But there was a giant battle going on for market share among all brokerage firms, particularly such giants as E. F. Hutton and Merrill Lynch. And the struggle was complicated by the fact that there were many legal restrictions on what could and couldn't be said in brokerage promotional programs.

Paine Webber's traditional market had been among the larger investors, those with a portfolio of $25,000 or more. Through research, Paine Webber found that its promotional program in the 1970s just wasn't doing the job against competition. Its advertising awareness was less than 15 percent of that of Hutton or Merrill Lynch, its top competitors.

To combat this problem, Paine Webber made some internal changes and revised its market position through a promotional program. The

Figure 8-6   Positioning: Paine Webber

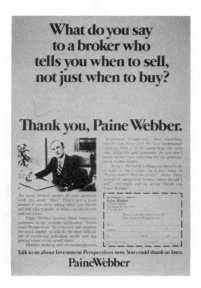

Source: Richard Christian and William A. Robinson, from a speech given at the "*Advertising Age* Workshop," Chicago, August, 1978.

implicit promise of all messages about choosing a stockbroker has something to do with making money. But Paine Webber changed the emphasis of its message from increasing wealth to conserving it. In a period of rapidly increasing prices, as was the case in the late 1970s, investors got the message that Paine Webber could help them hold onto what they had, in spite of the fact that inflation was continuing to eat away at their capital base. Paine Webber "positioned" itself as the one brokerage house able to meet the changing economic climate and did so successfully. Whereas once Paine Webber was considered by the consumer to be "just another brokerage house" with little to distinguish it from the multitude of other competitors, the promotional program it developed helped it to establish its organization in the mind of the consumer as the brokerage house which not only helps increase capital but helps to conserve it as well. That's the true task of positioning, establishing a solid sales message in the mind of the consumer. And it worked for Paine Webber. Advertisements such as the one shown in Figure 8-6 helped Paine Webber increase consumer awareness 63 percent and awareness of its advertising 157 percent in just nine months.

Figure 8-7   Repositioning: Renault Cars

Source: Christian and Robinson, "*Advertising Age* Workshop," 1978.

At the other end of the spectrum was Renault. Rather than establish a "position," Renault had to "reposition" or change the image or slot it had in the mind of the consumer. In 1976, when the energy crunch hit the U.S. market, subcompact car sales rose to 20 percent of total volume. But it wasn't enough to save the Renault R5 from a dismal first-year introduction. Too many people apparently remembered the poor product quality of the Renault Dauphine of some years before. And that wasn't the only problem. Renault had poor distribution and aggressive competition from Honda, Datsun, Toyota, and such American products as Ford, Plymouth, and Chevrolet. To further complicate matters, Renault had to charge more for its cars in order to make a profit. The solution: repositioning. The idea: Le Car. The concept was unique because it required only minor modifications in the product and relied heavily on promotion. The objective was to present the new model as totally different from competitive brands, primarily in terms of image. Le Car was classy, French, and fun. It had, according to its advertising, the quality of American subcompacts, the economy of Japanese cars, and something else as well. An example of the type of advertising Renault used with the introduction of Le Car is shown in Figure 8-7. And the repositioning worked. Sales of Le Car went up 144 percent; the number of dealers increased by 10 percent the first year. Le Car was a success built around a repositioning strategy that was actually aided by an economic problem.

Many other examples of the successful use of positioning or repositioning to fit the economic situation or to offset economic problems could be cited. The major point to remember, however, is that first you must determine your position in the market place or the position you wish to take. This usually can be done only through extensive consumer research. The next step is to make sure the new position you plan to occupy is a viable one. Then, and only then, should plans be made for a promotion program to gain that position. Since positioning or repositioning is such a major undertaking for a marketer, sales promotion is usually only a part of the overall program. It is the support rather than the major thrust. However, sales promotion can be a key ingredient in ensuring that the proper positioning or repositioning of the product or service is achieved.

New or Revised Distribution

Often, marketers must make distribution changes or revise their distribution patterns to fit economic changes. A prime example is the retail distribution change that small appliance manufacturers have made over the years. Initially, small appliances, such as coffeemakers, irons, and toasters, were stocked and sold by appliance dealers or department stores. As discount stores grew in popularity, manufacturers shifted their distribution emphasis to include them. Then, as supermarkets and drugstores grew in popularity, they were added. (See Figure 8-8.) The current distribution emphasis is on catalog stores—and no doubt there will be other changes in the future. Similar changes occurred in the wristwatch category. Distribution shifted from jewelry stores to discount stores, and now mail order is a major sales outlet for many types of watches.

While sales promotion is not the primary force in dealing with distribution changes or new distribution outlets, it can be a helpful tool in the overall program. An example of the development of a new or revised distribution channel to meet changing economic needs is illustrated in Figure 8-9 for Safeway Stores. In the 1970s, Safeway, a supermarket chain, started stocking and promoting automotive accessories. That's a distribution switch for the automotive supply manufacturers and the supermarkets as well, but it's one that seems to have worked for both of them.

Added Users or Uses

The final strategy that seems to work well in changing economic conditions is to find new uses or new users for the product. This is one area in

Figure 8-8   Changing Distribution: Norelco Products

Source: William A. Robinson, "Auto Parts Market Becomes More Confusing with Entry of New Style Retailers," *Advertising Age*, Jan. 2, 1978, p. 20.

which sales promotion can be a big help. The classic example of expanded product uses is the promotional campaign developed by Church & Dwight Company for its Arm & Hammer baking soda. Baking soda sales had been declining for years. Changing consumer economic conditions and lifestyles had reduced sales of what had been a household

Figure 8-9   Revising Distribution: Safeway Stores

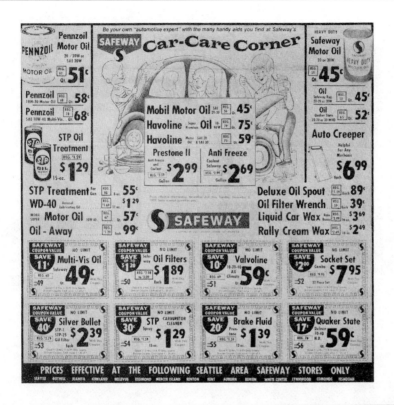

Source: Robinson, "Auto Parts Market Becomes More Confusing with Entry of New Style Retailers," p. 20.

staple to the "occasional, if ever" usage category. Arm & Hammer was faced with the choice of watching usage—and therefore sales—continue to decline or taking some positive action.

It decided that since pricing, product changes, repackaging, repositioning, and even changes in distribution would be of little help, finding new uses and new users for the product was the best approach. One of the first steps was the suggestion of an additional use for the product: as a deodorant in the refrigerator. The advertising for this new use is illustrated in Figure 8-10. The idea worked. It got millions of boxes of Arm & Hammer baking soda into refrigerators. The next step was to get the product used over and over. The result was a program suggesting that the Arm & Hammer box be replaced every few months in all those refrigerators. The TV commercial is shown in Figure 8-11.

Figure 8-10   Finding New Uses: Arm & Hammer Baking Soda

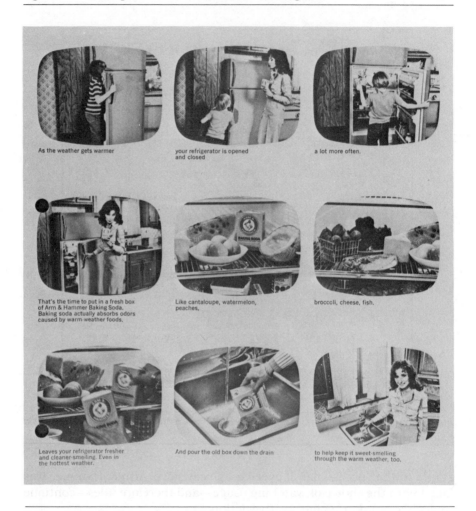

Source: Printed with permission of Church & Dwight Co., Inc.

Following that, Arm & Hammer developed a number of other products based on the baking soda product—including a washing powder and an oven cleaner. The final step in the sales promotion program to rescue this once-dying product was the contest shown in Figure 8-12. The idea was to ask consumers to come up with new ways to use Arm & Hammer baking soda. Prizes were awarded for the most novel uses.

Arm & Hammer has maximized the idea of added users and added

Figure 8-11   Getting Increased Usage: Arm & Hammer Baking Soda

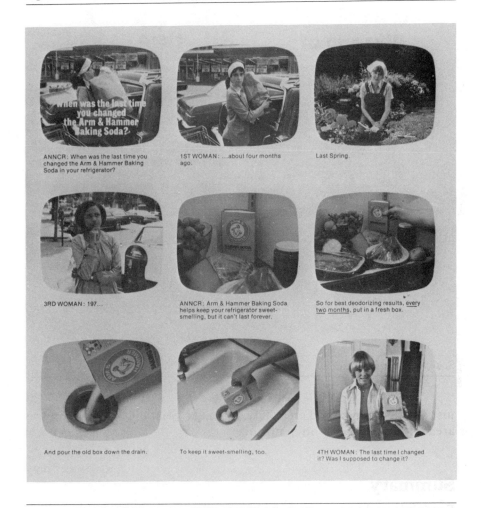

ANNCR: When was the last time you changed the Arm & Hammer Baking Soda in your refrigerator?

1ST WOMAN: ...about four months ago.

Last Spring.

3RD WOMAN: 197...

ANNCR: Arm & Hammer Baking Soda helps keep your refrigerator sweet-smelling, but it can't last forever.

So for best deodorizing results, every two months, put in a fresh box.

And pour the old box down the drain.

To keep it sweet-smelling, too.

4TH WOMAN: The last time I changed it? Was I supposed to change it?

Source: Printed with permission of Church & Dwight Co., Inc.

uses to build sales and profits for its product. It has apparently overcome what was considered a poor environment for its product with a sound promotional strategy.

To repeat, sales promotion is usually not a cure-all for economic problems, changes in the economic situation, and their effect on products, services, or brands. Usually, sales promotion is used in combination with other marketing strategies and promotional techniques. But with

Figure 8-12   Finding More New Uses: Arm & Hammer Baking Soda

Source: Printed with permission of Church & Dwight Co., Inc.

just a little thought and creativity, there are great opportunities in this area for the sales promotion manager.

Summary

Economic problems are unsolvable from the sales promotion manager's point of view. Nevertheless, they can be dealt with and sometimes turned to advantage. Specific examples of sales promotion approaches to economic problems illustrate how the creative use of sales promotion techniques can help. Pricing strategies, product and package modifications, product positioning, and new uses are among the possibilities.

9

Consumer Problems and Opportunities

Another marketing problem area that is more or less beyond the control of individual companies is the behavior of the consumer in the market place. We call the problems that arise in this area "life style" problems because they reflect the major changes in how consumers live and in what they want or need. In our opinion, the most important changes in life style, as they relate to sales promotion, are:

- Shifting geographical markets. The move from the Midwestern and Northeastern states to the Sun Belt has dramatically changed the marketing and promotional programs of many manufacturers.
- The increasing age of the population. While the "youth cult" still exists in the U.S., the average age of the population is increasing. The older population is therefore growing in number, and the need for products and services to serve them is increasing rapidly.
- Working women. Over 50 percent of the women in the U.S. are now employed in some type of job outside the home. That means new markets for many types of products and additional opportunities for others. There is a major emphasis on convenience and time saving to meet the needs of this growing market.
- Increased leisure time. Americans have more leisure time than ever before and it is growing every year. Promotion of leisure-time activities and equipment is now a major marketing thrust and will grow rapidly in the future.
- Convenient credit. The change in our economy and our market place

from cash to credit has been phenomenal. With this change has come increasing interest in higher-quality products and the decreasing postponement of major purchases.

Solving Consumer Problems

While these changes are very broad, some sales promotion techniques seem particularly appropriate for either exploiting or offsetting them. In general, as with the economic problems discussed in Chapter 8, sales promotion programs alone are not usually powerful enough to deal with these major shifts. However, used in combination with broader marketing strategies and other promotional techniques, such as advertising and personal selling, they can be effective. We've found five general approaches that can be used with "life style" problems or opportunities.

1. Localizing or regionalizing sales promotion activities.
2. Expanding or revising target markets.
3. Appealing to changing life styles.
4. Promoting leisure-time activities.
5. Setting or offsetting trends in the market.

We'll discuss each of these in detail and give examples of the methods some marketers have used.

Localizing or Regionalizing Sales Promotion Programs

More and more we're learning what we've always known: There really isn't any such thing as a "national" market for a product. The "national" market is just a series of smaller, local markets, all of which are interconnected. Each of these markets is different. What might work well in one market or what has been successful with one type of product might not be successful with another. While there are economies in so-called "national" sales promotion programs, localized promotions can be more effective in coping with consumer (and particularly life style) problems.

A major factor that encourages the use of local or regional promotions is the changing population pattern. Many of our heavily populated areas have stopped growing. Some, such as the major cities in the Northeast and Midwest, have even declined in population. Meanwhile, traditionally less populated areas, such as the West and Southwest, continue to grow. And the shifts aren't all confined to large regional moves. A major change in metropolitan population patterns is occurring as the flight to the suburbs from the cities seems to be slowing. In fact, younger, higher-income people are actually starting to move back to the cities in many areas.

In addition to population shifts, most marketers also have strong and weak sales areas for their individual products. This may be caused by historical situations, uneven patterns of distribution, regional product preferences, or geographic usage. For these reasons, marketers must now be prepared to deal with local or regional problems quickly and on an individual basis. An excellent method is with a local sales promotion program. Newport cigarettes built an attractive offer limited to the New York City area with its "Box Seat" sales promotion program, illustrated in Figure 9-1.

Promotions need not be limited just to cities either. For example, Kool-Aid developed a statewide promotion involving the Illinois State Fair. It's illustrated in Figure 9-2.

The potential for local or regional sales promotion programs is limited only by the imagination of the sales promotion manager and market needs of the brand. Programs of the type illustrated can often be fairly low in cost and easy to implement. A primary danger is in not investing enough in the event to ensure its success.

Expanding or Revising Target Markets

Traditionally, marketers have attempted to concentrate their promotional efforts on the people in the market who are the largest users or the best prospects for their products. This is called "target marketing" and the group of prospects is called the "target market." (See Chapter 4.) Most marketers believe the more precisely they can identify this target market group, the better they can aim their media advertising and sales promotion and the better their chances of success.

With the continually changing and shifting makeup of the population, however, today's marketers often find that they need to revise their target markets from time to time in order to reach the largest number of prospects for their product. Some of the factors that are involved in such change are age, sex, income, ethnic background, and location of the population. For example, as our general population grows older, marketers will have to revise not only their product but their promotional programs as well. The older segment of the population simply has different needs and interests than younger people. And since this older segment often has the purchasing capacity to satisfy its needs, it becomes a very lucrative target market. Likewise, ethnic groups, e.g., Blacks and Hispanics, are becoming increasingly important to marketers, especially as their proportion of the total population increases dramatically. And there is increasing interest in marketing products and services to both the husband and the wife in a family. Since in over 50 percent of the households the wife is employed outside the home, her opinion is vital in the purchase of many products that once had been considered only the province of the husband.

Figure 9-1   Localizing Sales Promotion: Newport Cigarettes

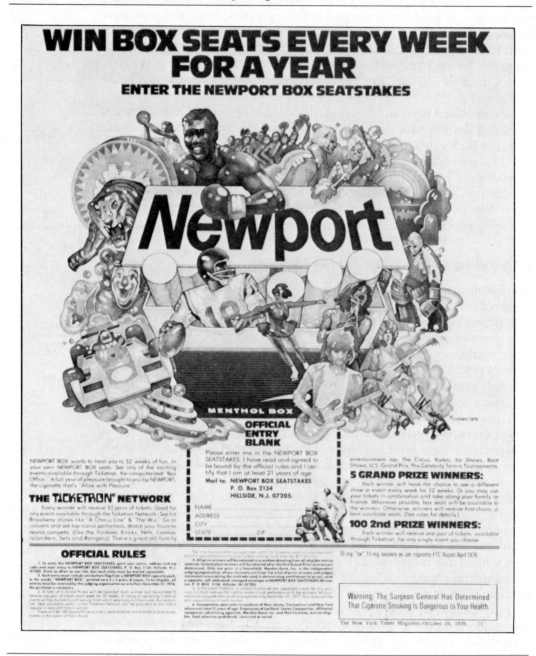

Source: William A. Robinson, *100 Best Sales Promotions of 1976/7* (Chicago: Crain Books, 1977), p. 51.

Figure 9-2   Regionalizing Sales Promotion: Kool-Aid Drink Mix

Source: Courtesy of KOOL-AID and General Foods Corporation.

Figure 9-3   Expanding the Target Market: M&M/Mars Candy

Source: Robinson, *100 Best Sales Promotions of 1976/7*, p. 71.

Marketing, and particularly sales promotion, managers should recognize these important new and changing target markets for their products. Often, new advertising and sales promotion campaigns are required. For example, although younger children have always been the target market for candy bars, M&M/Mars developed a sales promotion program aimed at an older segment of the market—high school and junior high school students. Its problem: keeping children in the market as long as possible. Its solution: having a contest in which the prize was a rock concert at the winners' school. (See Figure 9-3.)

Canadian Mist whiskey attempted to improve its penetration of the Black market with a sales promotion strategy directed specifically to that group. Traditionally, Blacks have not been major users of Canadian whisky, and this approach (Figure 9-4) is a clear attempt to expand the target market for the product with a sales promotion offer.

The preceding examples illustrate several marketers' attempts to expand or revise the target market for a product or service. Further, we have illustrated how various sales promotion techniques can be used to help make that transition. The only caution with this type of strategy is that unless the marketer is very familiar with the needs of the group, it is often easy to make major sales promotional errors. For example, ethnic promotions can easily backfire unless they are well researched and the needs of the market well understood. The same is true of the older market and the youth market. Some of these groups speak what amounts to a different language. If the sales promotion manager isn't familiar with the special vocabulary or uses it incorrectly, the promotional program will quickly fail. The best rule: Know your market and know the language of your market before you speak.

Appealing to Changing Life Styles

Some of the greatest changes in the marketing environment of the U.S. have been in the life style of the consumer, especially since World War II. Since then, we've seen women move into the work force and become leaders in industry, politics, and society. We've seen massive changes in the power and importance of ethnic groups. The U.S. has changed from a nation of small towns to a nation of cities. With increased mobility, both geographic and social, the population has been on the move, horizontally and vertically. We've changed our working habits and gone from a blue-collar to a white-collar society. Single-person households have increased rapidly, and the so-called sexual revolution has arrived. And these are just a few of the changes that have occurred since the 1940s. All have had a major impact on the way consumers live and the things they consider important.

With these changes in life style have come major changes in products

Figure 9-4   Expanding the Target Market: Canadian Mist Whisky

Source: Robinson, *100 Best Sales Promotions of 1975/76* (Chicago: Crain Books, 1976), p. 80.

and services. Many possessions that we now consider necessities are inventions of the past 50 years, such as television, jet airplanes, automatic washers, refrigerators, air conditioners, communications satellites, and computers. All have had an impact on consumers and the way they live and think. As these environmental changes have occurred, marketers have changed and adjusted their promotional programs and appeals, too. For example, the change in women's life styles has created major new markets for convenience items, such as labor-saving appliances, fast foods, more efficient cleaning aids, and more varied personal care products. Whole new industries have sprung up to cater to the working woman's needs.

Marketers have also developed new sales promotion techniques to cater to these consumer life style changes. One of the better-known advertising campaigns has come from a cigarette—Virginia Slims—and was developed to appeal to the "new woman." To take advantage of the theme, Virginia Slims also developed a number of sales promotion programs to appeal to this "new woman." Figure 9-5 shows the "Book of Days." This is designed to reach the woman with a life style dramatically different from that of her mother.

Swift Premium franks took yet another approach to women with its Levi's denim bag offer. (See Figure 9-6.) A few short years ago, this type of offer directed toward women would have had practically no takers. But it was a success, primarily due to changing life styles.

While the examples we've shown here illustrate women's changing life styles, that certainly isn't the only market that has changed or is changing. Just look at what has happened to young people, Hispanics, the elderly, and so on. These examples show the dramatic changes that can occur in a few short years and the speed with which sales promotion programs can be developed to appeal to new markets. The imaginative sales promotion manager must always be on the lookout for changing life styles, for they offer tremendous opportunities.

Promoting Leisure-Time Activities

An important result of the change in the American economy from an agricultural to an industrial and service base and from a blue-collar to a white-collar work force is the amount of leisure time now available to most workers. For many, the work week has gone from 60 hours or more, less than 50 years ago, to less than 40 today. Vacation time has more than tripled, and the number of paid holidays increases every year. As a result, Americans have more leisure time than anyone has had in the history of the world.

Many marketers have developed specific sales promotion programs to take advantage of this phenomenon. For example, in Figure 9-7

Figure 9-5   Appealing to New Life Styles: Virginia Slims Cigarettes

Source: Robinson, *100 Best Sales Promotions of 1976/7*, p. 36.

Figure 9-6   Appealing to New Life Styles: Swift Premium Franks

Source: William A. Robinson, "Build Up Marketing Strength, Preserve Image, Prepare for Better Times," *Advertising Age*, Feb. 10, 1975, p. 42.

Wheaties features a "Getaway Giveaway Sweepstakes," with all types of sporting goods and camping equipment as the prizes.

The leisure-time approach can work for all types of products or services, and Figure 9-8 shows how Thermos and General Electric developed sales promotion program using this theme. These sales promotion programs are just samplings of what can be done to take

Figure 9-7   Promoting Leisure-Time Activities: Wheaties Cereal

Source: Robinson, *100 Best Sales Promotions of 1976/7*, p. 67.

Figure 9-8   Promoting Leisure-Time Activities: General Electric Products and Thermos

Source: William A. Robinson, "Sponsors Find that Travel and Vacation Sweepstakes Are Strong Product Tie-Ins," *Advertising Age*, Feb. 6, 1978, p. 41.

advantage of the dramatic environmental changes that have occurred in the U.S. market place.

Setting or Offsetting Market Trends

Perhaps the most difficult consumer situation a sales promotion manager faces is a market trend. By a market trend, we mean a long-term change in the market place—not the fads, such as hoola-hoops, roller skates, or Nehru jackets, that may be here today and gone tomorrow, but major changes that evolve over time: the growth of television as an entertainment medium, the increasing number of smaller cars to replace "gas-hogs," and the growing popularity of eating away from home. These are all long-term trends that the alert sales promotion manager can spot and take advantage of with his plans and promotions.

The key element in trying to set or offset market trends is the sales promotion manager's ability to estimate the length and strength of a trend. For example, the growth of shopping centers, the use of credit cards, the popularity of more casual clothing for men and women, and the interest in do-it-yourself and self-expression crafts—such as needlecraft, painting, and woodworking—have all been long-term trends. All of these have caused dramatic changes in the market place. Marketers who recognized such trends early and adjusted their products or promotional programs for them have been extremely successful.

Possibly the most successful trend-setter has been McDonalds. Ray Kroc saw the need for more convenience, mobility, and standardization in eating out. And his company almost singlehandedly developed the fast-food industry. Other fast-food restaurateurs have spent the past 25 years trying to catch up. And the same has been true in other product categories, such as home music centers and stereo systems, radial tires, and vending machines. The important point is that you can either be the trendsetter or the one who is bucking the trend. The important point is to know which you are and what you should do.

Shell Oil saw a trend in the growth of do-it-yourself automotive activities. It developed a promotion around its "Answer Man" books. The one illustrated in Figure 9-9, *The On-the-Spot Repair Book,* was the 29th in the series. Shell recognized the increasing consumer interest in how automobiles work, especially with the increasing complexity of the machines and the high cost of labor. The result was the "Answer Man" books. Not only did Shell tie in with the do-it-yourself interest, it also helped build a great promotion for its dealers and itself.

Rather than trying to set a trend, the example in Figure 9-10 is a case of a marketer attempting to reverse a trend or at least to stem it a bit. The situation faced by Rath Packing was simply that more and more meals were being eaten away from home. More than one-third of all meals in the United States are now being eaten out, according to recent estimates. That's a serious trend if you are in the food business, particularly foods meant to be cooked and served at home. It really means you don't have a chance to sell your brand at least one-third of the time. Rath developed the sales promotion program called the "Home Cooking Contest" in an attempt to offset this trend.

A primary rule to remember in designing sales promotion programs to meet changing life styles is to make sure they appeal to a sufficiently large segment of the population. The United States is noted for fads and rapid but short-lived changes. Unless you carefully research the idea, you might develop a promotion that will be out of date before you get it started. Promotions designed to meet changing life styles can work, but only if they are well planned.

Figure 9-9   Setting a Market Trend: Shell Oil

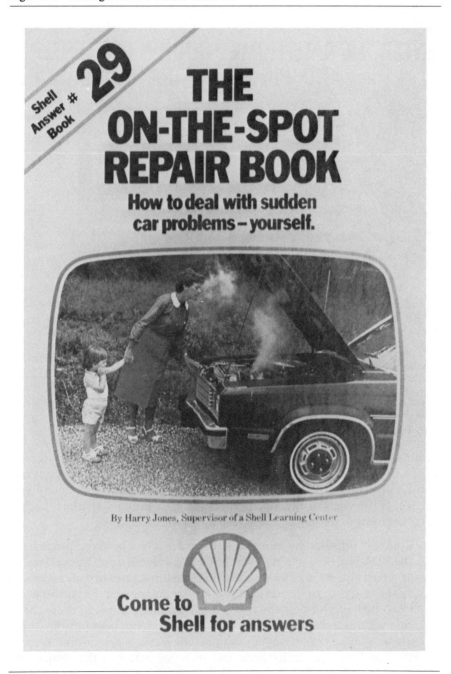

Figure 9-10 Offsetting a Trend: Rath Packing

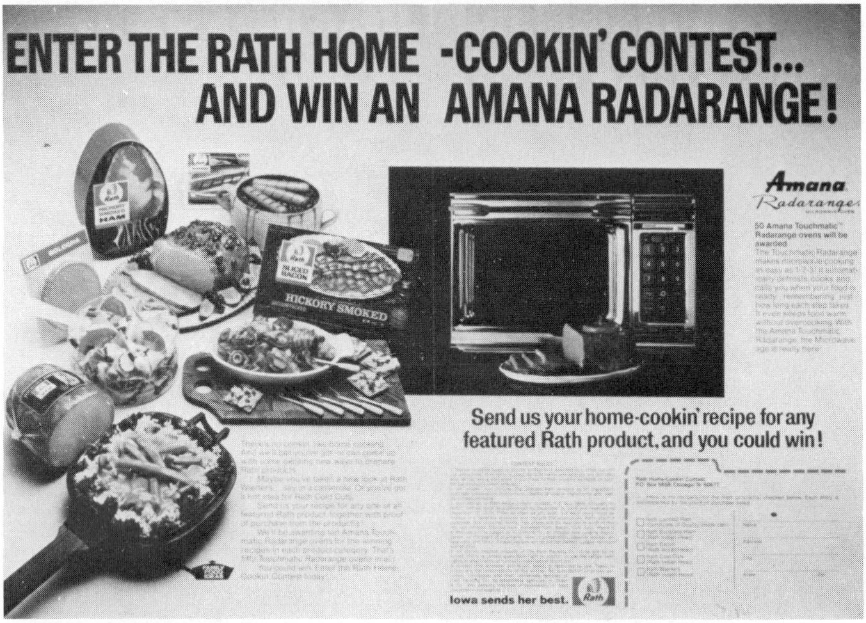
ENTER THE RATH HOME -COOKIN' CONTEST...
AND WIN AN AMANA RADARANGE!
Amana
Radarange
HICKORY SMOKED
Send us your home-cookin' recipe for any featured Rath product, and you could win!
Iowa sends her best.

Source: Robinson, *100 Best Sales Promotions of 1976/7*, p. 40.

Changes in Control: Government, Consumer, and Voluntary

Another important area that impacts on marketers is the system of controls on business. These controls may be instituted by the government, consumer groups, and, in some instances, the marketer himself. Whatever the basis, they can create major problems, particularly for the sales promotion manager. The two major types are:

1. Controls imposed by government at all levels. These can range from the FDA ban on certain products or ingredients, such as cyclamates and Red Dye #2, to the congressional prohibition of broadcast media advertising for cigarettes, to the FTC requirement that advertisers must provide support for various advertising claims. In these cases, restrictions are a form of law and not subject to negotiation. There are also some very stringent regulations on sales promotion. We will discuss them generally here and in more detail in the chapter on legal requirements (Chapter 14).

2. Consumer controls. Since the early 1950s, the consumer movement has grown dramatically in the United States. While many of the changes demanded by consumers have been beneficial to almost everyone, some have created major problems for marketers. For example, consumer pressure has forced many changes in the food industry. Objections to sugar and high sugar content in some foods have forced reformulation. Complaints about high fat levels have forced manufacturers to find substitute ingredients. Even labels have had to be changed to accommodate the consumer's desire for more information about ingredients and nutritional benefits of food products.

One of the difficulties in meeting consumer objections or complying with requests is in communicating what the company has done to solve the problem. This is usually accomplished by advertising or public relations programs. There are, however, some sales promotion programs that can be used. We'll illustrate examples later in this chapter.

The major difficulty in using sales promotion programs to deal with problems arising from government regulations or consumerism is the risk that they will backfire. In some instances, marketers have found that programs designed to meet consumer demands or federal laws created more problems than they solved. For example, in the automobile industry, consumer complaints resulted in the addition of many items to automobiles designed to reduce the amount of emissions to aid in cleaning up the air. These additional emission controls sharply reduced the mileage obtained by drivers. Thus, some drivers disconnect the emission controls or by-pass them in their automobiles to improve gasoline efficiency. As a result, a sales promotion program designed to encourage further reduction of emissions will find a hostile audience among those whose concern is improved gasoline mileage.

While there is risk in offending certain parties with any activity, it seems greater in these areas, since the issues are so sensitive. We highly recommend that pretesting be done with any sales promotion program intended to offset controls, to ensure that it has every chance of success.

Public Relations

Over the years, public relations has proven to be a far more practical tool than promotion for dealing with or offsetting controls. Sales promotion, by its very nature, is action-oriented. In many cases, action can't or shouldn't be taken. Additionally, most problems caused by controls can be solved only through long-term programs, often requiring that laws be changed or that consumers reverse their opinions. For example, it is highly unlikely that power companies will be able to convince consumers that nuclear power is a desirable alternative to fossil fuels with some sort of sales promotion program. That's something that must be explained in detail through a long-term educational program. Therefore, in this instance, the power companies will probably be better off using a public relations approach than a sales promotion tactic.

In the following discussions, public relations, rather than sales promotion, was the most effective way to deal with public policy problems.

Self-Policing

While not a sales promotion strategy, one of the best methods of dealing with proposed governmental controls or demands by consumers is a strong program of industry self-policing. The broadcasting industry has managed to avoid much actual legislation simply by developing and defining a set of rules or "codes" by which to govern itself. Thus, it has avoided many government and consumer problems by correcting questionable situations in advance. Many product groups, such as liquor and firearms, do the same. There may be opportunities for the use of sales promotion in combination with these self-regulatory activities, but public relations and advertising are usually considered the best tools.

Compliance

Closely akin to self-regulation is compliance. Often, marketers have been able to take advantage of restrictions and regulations and turn them to their advantage. Sales promotion has been used effectively in this area, especially with product bans. A few years ago, for example, the federal government imposed a ban on freon, the gas used as a propellant in many aerosol products. Since the ban was a legal restriction, there was nothing marketers could do except comply. Based on this ban, however, three different marketing strategies developed, each with a sound sales promotion program. Right Guard and Soft & Dri deodorants developed alternative propellants. As you can see in Figure 9-11, rather than look at the situation as a problem, they turned it to a sales promotion advantage by promoting the new product as "just like the good old sprays—only better." That's an effective way to solve a problem.

Other marketers developed pump sprays for their products. Again, rather than apologize for the new method of application, they turned it to an advantage, as Ban Basic's advertising approach in Figure 9-12 demonstrates.

And still other marketers developed a roll-on dispenser. Dry Idea promoted its roll-on product by selling the advantages of the product, not by presenting it as a solution to a restriction. (See Figure 9-13.)

Figure 9-11   Complying with the Law: Right Guard/Soft & Dri Antiperspirants

Figure 9-12   Complying with the Law: Ban Antiperspirant

Source: Courtesy of Bristol-Myers Products.

Figure 9-13   Complying with the Law: Dry Idea Antiperspirant

Source: Courtesy of The Gillette Company.

As you can see, a strong advertising and sales promotion program supporting the type of dispenser was developed for each product. These marketers actually turned a governmental control to their advantage.

Another example of turning a federal regulation or a consumer concern into a promotional advantage is illustrated by the approach detergent manufacturers took a few years ago when phosphates were subjected to consumer criticism. Procter & Gamble met the challenge head-on with advertisements directed to citizens in individual states and even to people in metropolitan areas (Figure 9-14).

In 1970 a ruling went into effect that prohibited cigarette manufacturers from advertising on radio or television. Since most cigarette mar-

Figure 9-14   Complying with the Law: Procter & Gamble Products

A Message to the People of Dade County and Neighboring Areas from Procter & Gamble

Procter & Gamble laundry products—Tide, Cheer, Bold, Dash, Gain, Oxydol, Duz Detergent, Bonus, and Dreft—will soon be back on the shelves of Dade County stores. We believe you will find that each of these newly formulated products will give you better washing results than any other zero phosphate product now available. Each brand, of course, will continue to provide the distinctive individual characteristics which have special appeal to its own users.

Procter & Gamble detergents sold in Dade County will represent a different formulation from that available in other parts of the country. But we will also begin a program of major change in our detergent formulations in the rest of the country. In recognition that detergents are products used by virtually every household in America, the following is a report on the progress Procter & Gamble has made to produce household laundry detergents with significantly lower phosphate content but that are still safe and fully as effective as present phosphate detergents.

DETERGENTS WITH HALF AS MUCH PHOSPHATE—THAT CLEAN JUST AS WELL

In most of the country, including areas covered by this newspaper outside of Dade County, new developments should enable us to cut the phosphate content of our laundry detergents in half. In other areas of the country, where local laws have already forced a reduction in phosphate levels, we should be able to make a further reduction of approximately one-third. Once all our plants are converted to these new formulas, we expect that our granulated laundry detergents will have a phosphorus content of approximately 6%.

We will be able to make such products because our Procter & Gamble scientists, as a result of years of intensive research efforts, have now developed in the laboratory a new type of surfactant system which permits the use of lower levels of phosphate than previously thought possible. This new surfactant system is more "calcium insensitive" than the ones in present use and allows the cleaning agents in the detergents to work more effectively despite the presence of minerals in the water. Tying up these minerals has been one of the many important functions of phosphates in detergents.

We are now hard at work trying to convert this laboratory development into a mass production effort. We expect the first fully equipped plant can go on stream eight or nine months from now. Once that plant is operating smoothly—and barring any unforeseen development—it is our intention to move to these lower phosphate products on a plant-by-plant basis just as rapidly as we can.

WORK WILL CONTINUE

In the United States this is as far and as fast as present knowledge will permit us to move in a sound and orderly manner. In Canada even lower phosphate levels will be achieved by the use of NTA which is permitted by the Canadian Government and which we are convinced is safe but which cannot yet be used in the United States.

We will, of course, continue to work intensively to find ways of lowering the phosphate content of laundry detergents even further while continuing to provide safe and effective products for use in the homes of America.

HERE IN DADE COUNTY

As part of our experimental efforts in this direction, we will be starting to sell zero phosphate products on a test basis in Dade County where by law we are prohibited from selling anything else. Our new surfactant system will enable us to make laundry detergents for Dade County which will be safe for use in the home and which we think will provide better laundry performance than other zero phosphate products now available to the consumer. However, in the present state of the art these products will still fall short of providing housewives with what we feel is the proper level of cleaning effectiveness. These zero phosphate products must evolve further before they can satisfactorily serve the consumer. Until they do, we continue to believe that laws which force the complete elimination of phosphates from detergents are unsound.

PROGRESS THROUGH RESEARCH

Procter & Gamble has so far spent more than $85,000,000 in its efforts to bring consumers lower phosphate detergents that are both safe and effective. We think our scientists know as much about detergency and water chemistry and home washing problems as any in the world, and they have devoted thousands and thousands of man-hours to this task. They will continue their efforts, of course, because it is clearly our job to respond to the public and political pressures against phosphates.

ADEQUATE WASTE TREATMENT IS THE REAL ANSWER

Nevertheless, the Company feels it must once again point out, based on all the scientific evidence it has seen, that the elimination of phosphates in detergents alone will not solve the problem of eutrophication in those limited areas of the country where this problem exists. Adequate sewage treatment plants still represent the most meaningful route to a significant improvement in the water quality of the nation's lakes. This need would exist even if phosphates were to be completely eliminated from all detergents. Procter & Gamble hopes, therefore, that the announcement of these planned reductions in the phosphate content of its detergents will not divert attention from the necessity of improvements in sewage disposal plants.

One further point. Some stores in areas near Dade County may also begin carrying Procter & Gamble non-phosphate formulations. This may occur because some stores outside Dade County are supplied by warehouses located inside Dade County which carry only the non-phosphate formula of these brands. Should you question which formula your store carries, you will find the phosphate content of each of these brands is clearly marked on the side panel of the package.

The Procter & Gamble Company
Box 599, Cincinnati, Ohio 45201

Source: Courtesy of The Procter & Gamble Company.

Figure 9-15   Complying with the Law: Decade Cigarettes

Source: William A. Robinson, *4th Annual 100 Best Sales Promotions* (Chicago: Crain Books, 1980), p. 151.

keters had invested the majority of their advertising dollars in broadcast, the problem was serious. But creative sales promotion people developed noncommercial advertising programs that got the name of the product on radio and television. The answer: sponsorship of sporting and other newsworthy events. For example, the Virginia Slims tennis tournament has received widespread broadcast coverage since its inception. Because it was newsworthy, it was covered on both radio and television as editorial material. Usually this coverage included the use of the name, illustrations, and other materials that were specifically prohibited as advertising.

When Virginia Slims and Philip Morris halted their tennis promotion, Decade and Liggett & Myers started one with a slightly different twist. The Virginia Slims tournament had been restricted to professionals. The Decade tournament invited only amateurs to participate, but under some very tough restrictions. Yet it accomplished the same result, promotion of the brand. (See Figure 9-15.)

Figure 9-16   Consumer Response Program: Mobil Oil

Let's look at the record

Too many people have been asking us, "Why did the oil industry let us get into this mess?" And some of our critics have suggested that the industry somehow contrived—or connived—to make the United States increasingly and dangerously dependent upon foreign oil. So we've been thumbing through the record, looking back at our messages over the past 10 years. And we ask again: Is anybody listening?

Heaven knows, we've tried to get the peril across. For example:

· **On the dangers of dependency,** we warned on May 11, 1972, long before the 1973 oil embargo, about the danger in becoming "dependent on sources that can be shut off as the result of foreign political or economic pressures." Again and again we repeated this theme, noting in November 1972: "Unless we assure ourselves of the energy required to sustain the well-being of the American people, no arms or armament can assure the nation's security...." We sounded the same note again two months later, with a warning that "fast-rising imports of oil and gas..." would "pose balance-of-payments and security problems to which we are not giving enough attention."

· **On the need for domestic petroleum development,** we repeatedly urged a step-up in domestic exploration and production, more sensible policies on offshore leasing, a realistic timetable for phasing in synthetic fuels. "Mobil is convinced the nation must start planning now to find rational solutions...," we said back in May 1972. We also noted in September 1972 that federal policy had definitely impeded the search for domestic natural gas; called on the government to "proceed with outer continental shelf lease sales" and "overhaul a system of price regulation that has boomeranged spectacularly."

· **On the necessity for conservation,** we stated in March 1972 that oil was growing scarcer and more costly, and we urged every American to: "1. Keep your car properly tuned, so it will run most efficiently. 2. Drive in ways that economize on gasoline and oil. 3. See that your home is properly insulated, as a way to save heating oil. 4. Campaign for mass transit legislation."

· **On the need for more mass transit,** Mobil called as early as October 1970 for a national mass transit plan "consistent with the wisest use of our energy resources." To this day, none exists (although we have hopes that the President's recent call for more funds for mass transit means one is coming).

· **On the crucial importance of a national energy policy,** we pointed out in November 1972 that excessive regulation was hindering "the expansion of energy production and distribution systems." Seven years later, it still is. We called for a national energy policy that would "match our energy potential to foreseeable energy needs." America still doesn't have it.

· **On striking a realistic environmental balance,** we discussed in January 1973 the urgent need for the nation to "strike a socially acceptable balance between environmental considerations and the need for additional energy supplies." This echoed an earlier plea, made in May 1972, for the nation to place "the national interest in energy matters above any regional or other special interest...." The balance required has yet to be struck.

The political leaders of the United States —despite frequent and specific warnings from the U.S. oil industry—walked into the nation's present energy situation with both eyes open. It remains to be seen whether they have the vision to struggle out of it.

M⦿bil

©1979 Mobil Corporation

Source: Courtesy of Mobil Oil, © Mobil Corporation, 1980.

Consumer Response Methods

A final way of dealing with governmental and consumer problems is through consumer response mechanisms, such as consumer departments, "hot lines" that answer consumer requests, and booklets and materials developed about specific problems facing the company or organization. While these programs are usually administered through the public relations or public affairs department, the sales promotion manager is often deeply involved. For example, a consumer "hot line" is of little value if no consumers know about it. The same is true for programs or materials the company might develop to support its point of view or its products. If they aren't distributed, nothing happens.

Often, marketers will design specific consumer response programs on major issues undergoing public debate. For example, during the oil and energy crisis of 1979, Mobil Corporation developed a complete package of materials on how the company was dealing with the problem and what it thought the consumer could do. (See Figure 9-16.)

Public utilities, such as power, electric, and telephone companies, have often used sales promotion materials to encourage additional regulation or deregulation by legislative groups. Usually, in addition to their lobbying activities, these utilities distribute special materials to consumers along with their regular statements for service. While not technically sales promotion as we have defined it, these programs do serve to promote sales by the company and to improve its profit margins. In these cases, the line between sales promotion and public relations is fine indeed.

For over 10 years, Whirlpool has maintained what it calls its "CoolLine" service: a telephone number consumers can call to ask questions about their appliances or to inquire about repairs. Figure 9-17 illustrates how Whirlpool promotes this service.

The primary job of most consumer response mechanisms is either to directly change negative consumer attitudes toward a particular product or simply to explain the company viewpoint. While these are not technically sales promotion programs, they can be viewed that way. If consumer resentment becomes so great that sales are affected, then preventing that problem in advance is technically sales promotion. The same is true if additional government or self-imposed regulation is avoided. Here again, sales are improved or promoted (or will be in the future); it is sometimes quite difficult to see the difference. That is why we suggest that the sales promotion manager take a broad view of the company marketing program. Only by doing this can the sales promotion function deal with broad consumer problems.

We wish we could say that consumer problems will decline. Unfortunately, they won't. The key to controlling these problems is usually

Figure 9-17   Consumer Response Program: Whirlpool Products

Source: Courtesy of Whirlpool Corporation.

advance planning. For the most part, the programs that fail are those designed as "firefighters" and not as offensive weapons. The key to a good sales promotion program is to generate sales rather than try to prevent their loss. In the next chapter, we will deal with problems that are more specifically related to the sales promotion function.

Summary

Changes in consumer behavior are not easily controlled by individual companies. They reflect the major social changes of the times—such as shifting geographical concentrations, increasing age of the population, and the advances of working women. There are a number of approaches to these vast social movements. These include localizing sales promotion activities, revising target markets, appealing to new life styles, and setting or offsetting market trends.

There is another related area that affects sales promotion—the complex system of legal, unofficial, and voluntary controls placed on business. Sales promotion managers must take into account legal changes, consumer pressures, and industry self-policing. Not all of these can be dealt with solely by sales promotion. Public relations, for example, will play an important role in many situations. Nonetheless, sales promotion can be a valuable support.

10

Product and Product-Related Problems and Opportunities

Product and product-related problems are the third major area in which sales promotion can be used. Again, when we say "product problems" we do not mean those created by poor product quality or defect. We simply mean that the product or service isn't living up to its sales or profit expectations, projections, or goals. There can be a number of reasons for this.

First, we define product problems. Then we suggest specific sales promotion programs for offsetting these problems. When and where possible, we have illustrated our suggestions with examples of sales promotion programs others have used in combating these problems. This step-by-step procedure provides you with both the questions and the answers.

What Are Product and Product-Related Problems?

We believe these are the major problems in the product and product-related category:

- An overall sales decline in the product or service category.
- A declining share for the particular brand in the total category.
- Static sales for the brand in a growing category.
- A declining margin for the brand in spite of steady or growing sales in the category.

Each of these problems should be relatively easy for the sales promotion

213

manager to identify on the basis of sales records. Determining the appropriate solution, however, is quite another matter.

As you'll recall, in Chapters 6 and 7 we stressed the importance of tracing the problem to its source. That's most important here. We can usually see that our sales have declined. We also probably know from industry sources whether or not category sales are declining too. Knowing whether or not our sales are declining as rapidly as those of the category, however, can make a major difference in the selection of the appropriate sales promotion technique to be used. This is also true for a product with a declining share or margin.

There's another caution here. Often, product problems, as we have defined them, are related to other types of marketing problems. For example, a declining share in the total category may be the result of a product problem, a competitive situation, weak effort on the part of the sales force, or even environmental factors. And it could be a combination of all four. For that reason, we again stress the importance of tracing the problem to its source. Only by knowing what caused or is causing the problem can you develop the right sales promotion plan to help overcome it.

Declining Category

Declining sales in an entire category is probably the most difficult of the four product problem areas to attack. The reason: declining category sales may indicate that the product is nearing the end of its product life cycle. You'll recall that in Chapter 6 we said products usually reach the obsolescence stage for one of three reasons:

1. The need disappears.
2. A better, cheaper, or more convenient product is developed to fill the same need.
3. A competitive product, through superior marketing strategy, gains a decisive advantage.

Usually, when the entire category is declining, it is because of the first or second reasons. These are indeed hard to combat, but many marketers have managed to keep products and services profitable for several years even when the entire category was declining. Possibly you can do the same.

We've found five specific sales promotion responses to problems caused by declining sales in the entire category. They are to: (1) establish industry-wide programs; (2) develop new markets; (3) find new uses; (4) create product publicity; and (5) change the size, shape, or design of the package.

Figure 10-1   Establishing an Industry-Wide Program: American Dairy Association

Source: Courtesy of American Dairy Association.

Establish Industry-Wide Programs

Often, a category-wide sales decline can be reversed by an industry-wide, cooperative promotional program. Since all products and services in the category stand to lose, competitive marketers can often be convinced that some sort of cooperative sales promotion program should be developed with proportionately shared costs.

An example of this type of cooperative sales promotion program for a declining category is the one developed by the American Dairy Association. Sales of milk and milk-based products have been declining in the U.S. for more than 20 years. Yet the ADA program has managed to keep that decline from becoming a headlong rush away from the product. Typical of the ADA promotions is the national "June is Dairy Month" program, which is now past its 20th year. A part of the program developed by the ADA and offered to cooperating manufacturers and retailers is shown in Figure 10-1.

Figure 10-2   Establishing a Program with Related Products: American Dairy Association and Oscar Mayer Products

Source: Eugene Mahany, "The 'Snip-Snip' of Coupon Clipping: Sounds of Buyers Saving and Sellers Selling," *Advertising Age*, Oct. 31, 1977, p. 64.

In addition to this very broad promotion, ADA has developed specific individual sales promotion programs with manufacturers of other products that go well with dairy foods. For example, Figure 10-2 illustrates a cheese program, with Oscar Mayer meats. The American Dairy Association pays for such programs from contributions by dairy farmers and processors to an overall promotional fund.

Another industry-wide promotional program designed to stem a decline in category sales was developed by the American Wool Council. This is the marketing arm of the American Sheep Producers Council. Its primary goal was to convince consumers and retailers that wool makes

Figure 10-3   Establishing an Industry-Wide Program: American Wool Council

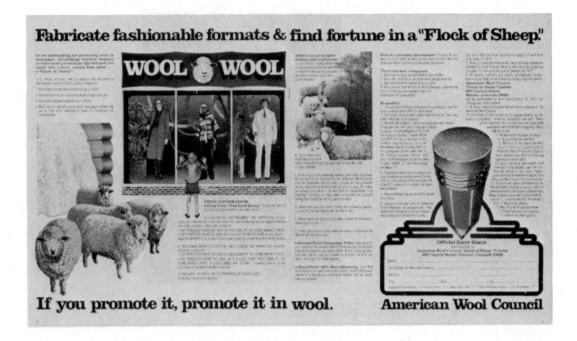

Source: William A. Robinson, "The World's Oldest Profession Comes of Age: Agribusiness Is a New Promo Area," *Advertising Age*, Nov. 14, 1977, p. 57.

better clothing than synthetic fabrics do. Illustrated in Figure 10-3 is the promotion developed by the American Wool Council and directed to manufacturers, retailers, and the media. As you can see, the idea was a sales incentive contest directed to the trade to encourage development, display, and promotion of wool and wool products.

As you might imagine, one of the most difficult situations in an industry-wide program is to get competitors to agree on a common sales promotion goal. When the program is designed to help offset declining category sales, however, agreement among competitors can sometimes be achieved. If done well, sales promotion programs can help everyone.

Develop New Markets

Declining sales in a declining category can sometimes be offset by devel-

---

Figure 10-4   Developing New Markets: The Potato Board

Source: Courtesy of The Potato Board.

---

oping new or additional markets for the product or service. In Chapter 8 we illustrated how Arm & Hammer baking soda overcame this problem by developing new uses for its product. It moved beyond the traditional cooking and baking categories into the deodorant and washing compound areas. This was a simple case of finding a new market for the product among consumers who might not have used it before.

The Potato Board used a similar tactic to find new markets for its products. Traditionally, the potato has been thought of as fattening, or at least as a product that should be restricted for dieters. In a reverse twist, the Potato Board chose to promote the potato as a dietary product. (See Figure 10-4.) In fact, the potato is claimed to be 99.9 percent fat free. So, rather than just hope to hold their own in a declining category, potato growers developed an aggressive strategy. That's a real switch and one that the Potato Board hoped would generate new product uses.

Johnson & Johnson faced a similar problem. The number of babies born in the United States has been declining since the 1950s. The demand for baby products has also fallen. To offset this category decline, Johnson & Johnson developed a totally new market for its baby shampoo—people who wash their hair often (Figure 10-5). Because heavy shampoo users

Figure 10-5   Developing a New Market: Johnson & Johnson Baby Shampoo

Source: Courtesy of Johnson & Johnson Baby Products Co.

Figure 10-6   Finding New Uses: Vaseline Petroleum Jelly

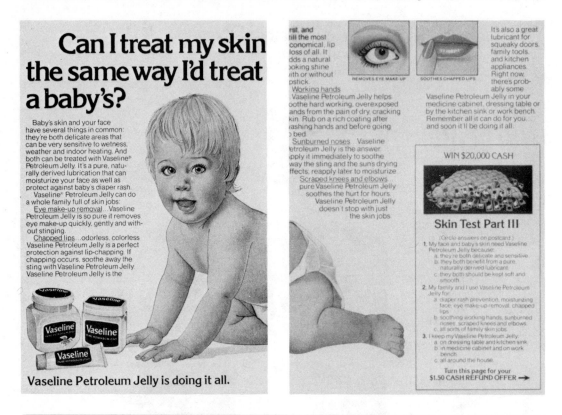

Source: William A. Robinson, *100 Best Sales Promotions of 1976/7* (Chicago: Crain Books, 1977), p. 61.

want a product that is mild, Johnson & Johnson's baby shampoo fills that need. Thus J & J found a new market for a product in a declining category by promoting in a new category. It also found new sales.

New markets aren't always that easy to find, however. Often, they are the result of additional uses consumers as well as marketers find for the product. Such was the case with Johnson & Johnson baby lotion, which is now being promoted as a product for women. That's another example of finding a new market for a product in a declining category. The creative sales promotion manager should always be looking for new markets and new uses for the product, whether or not the category is declining.

Find New Uses

A very effective way to increase sales for a product or service in a declining category is through ideas for new or increased usage. The primary goal is to expand the product usage among present users rather than trying to develop totally new markets. Sales promotion is often used in this way through such techniques as recipe books, additional usage ideas on the package, or in combination with other products.

Vaseline petroleum jelly is an old product that has been around many homes for years. When they thought of petroleum jelly at all, consumers often had limited uses for it in mind. Therefore, an effective way to increase sales of Vaseline was to suggest new or additional uses. The "Soft-to-Touch Skin Test and Sweepstakes" was a method of showing new ways of using Vaseline petroleum jelly as part of the total Vaseline product line. (See Figure 10-6.) Expanded uses for any product usually results in extra sales.

A story similar to Vaseline's might be told about fresh lemons. People simply don't think about lemons as much as the growers would like. As a result, fresh lemon sales have been declining because of the increased use of synthetics, concentrates, and substitutes, particularly those that can be easily stored and used later. To increase usage and thus sales, Sunkist lemons developed the "Great Food Sweepstakes." Not only was the winner awarded a 30-day gourmet tour of Europe, he or she also received an additional $1,000 for submitting a "use" suggestion or a recipe using fresh lemons. (See Figure 10-7.) This is an excellent example of how a sales promotion plan can increase product usage and also develop new usage ideas.

New usage ideas can help build sales, but they don't seem to be as effective as developing new markets. Recipes usually appeal only to current users. While this may increase sales for a period of time, unless new users are brought into the market, the category will likely continue to decline.

Create Product Publicity and Other Attention-Getting Devices

Another way to attempt to reverse sales in a declining category is through product publicity. This is usually done through events, features, or activities that help to build the brand or call attention to the category. An excellent example of a publicity event that has been successful for many years is the Pillsbury "Bake-Off" competition. This idea is now over 30 years old and still going strong. While the sale of flour has been declining for years, the "Bake-Off" has done several things for the brand and the category. It has built awareness for the Pillsbury name as the sponsor and

Figure 10-7 Finding New Uses: Sunkist Lemons

Source: Robinson, *100 Best Sales Promotions of 1976/7*, p. 50.

as a flour brand. It has generated increased interest in baking among both men and women, young and old, which can only help the entire Pillsbury line. It has helped generate new recipes that are often later used for promotions and advertising. Finally, it has generated millions of dollars worth of advertising and promotion for Pillsbury flour in the form of product publicity, free mentions, and photographs of the product in newspapers, magazines, and other media across the country. The "Bake-Off" is almost a category in itself. Overall, it's one of the best product publicity programs ever developed. And you can be sure that Pillsbury will continue to use it as long as it works. (See Figure 10-8.)

An idea that generated a great deal of product publicity on a local level was the "Sweetest Day" promotion developed by Fannie May candy in Chicago. Sales of candy, particularly packaged or loose chocolates, have been declining for several years. Was there a way to offset this decline with sales promotion? Fannie May tried with a program built

Figure 10-8   Creating Product Publicity: Pillsbury Flour

Source: Robinson, *100 Best Sales Promotions of 1976/7*, p. 28.

around the "Sweetest Day" idea (send candy to friends, lovers, or favorite people on this day). To tie in, the company built its sales promotion program around finding the "5 nicest people in Chicago." In addition to the contest results, it also got tremendous local publicity. Sales probably improved, too, since entrants had to visit the store in order to enter. This is an example of an excellent idea tied to a sound sales promotion program that generated product publicity and resulted in product sales.

While sports attendance has generally been growing, attendance at horse race tracks has been declining. Several things can be blamed, such as off-track betting and changes in life style, but the fact remains: people just aren't going to the track in the numbers they once were. The New York Racing Association (Belmont Park) had a five-year attendance decline. Even greater problems were on the horizon, since a competitive race track was opening in nearby New Jersey. To build attendance, Belmont developed a sales promotion program called the "World Series

Figure 10-9   Creating Product Publicity: Belmont Park Race Track

Source: Robinson, *100 Best Sales Promotions of 1977/8,* p. 13.

of Thoroughbred Racing" (Figure 10-9). While not designed specifically to generate track publicity, it was extremely successful in doing so. By developing several sales promotion activities and events within the overall framework of the program, Belmont generated media interest. The resulting publicity helped ensure the success of the overall promotion.

Often, a sales promotion program designed to generate product publicity does more than just that; it also helps build sales.

Figure 10-10   Changing the Package: Smucker's Products

Source: Courtesy of the J. M. Smucker Company.

Change the Package: Size, Shape, Design, Etc.

In a declining category, a change in the package can be used to develop an effective sales promotion program. As the category declines, consumer usage declines too. Sometimes, a change either to a·larger size, to keep consumers using your particular brand over a longer period of time, or to a smaller size, to encourage consumers to use up the product and make more frequent purchases of it, is in order. For example, sales of jams and jellies are generally declining. In an effort to combat this problem, Smucker's introduced a new larger-size product (Figure 10-10). The idea was to move volume at a lower cost per ounce by using the larger size.

As is clear by now, solving problems in a declining product category is probably one of the toughest jobs in sales promotion.

The examples we have given are merely a sampling of what can be done with sales promotion. The primary thing to remember is that the promotion must be unique and attention-getting. The category is obviously not as popular as it once was. It just doesn't have the appeal that a growing category has. Thus, you need exciting sales promotion ideas that have broad appeal and offer unusual or unique benefits. A sales promotion program for a product in a declining category is usually no place for a "standard" or "safe" promotion. It requires creativity and a willingness to try the unusual.

In the three following categories—declining share, static sales, and declining margins—we have not given any specific examples. While sales changes, particularly declines, in overall product categories are fairly common, the status of specific brand sales is considered proprietary information. Thus, to use specific illustrations of brands about which we have knowledge could be considered a breach of confidence. Therefore we will not use specific examples but will attempt to explain our ideas and recommendations in some detail.

Declining Share Problems

A common problem faced by many brands is a loss of share in the category. That simply means that other brands are increasing sales at the expense of your brand. These losses may be due to overpricing, lower comparative product value, insufficient media advertising, or poor or ineffective sales promotion programs. Again, we urge you to trace the problem to its source. Only by doing that can you hope to find the proper remedy.

Experience shows that there are eight sales promotion techniques that work best to help offset a brand share loss.

1. *Sampling.* Sometimes a share loss occurs simply because consumers have forgotten about the brand. It has become a "part of the scenery." A sample can often help remind consumers of the advantage of the product or how to use it more often or more widely. This works particularly well if the product has some new or improved feature that can be used as a new selling point.

2. *Couponing.* In a parity market, coupons are an excellent method of gaining product trial or retrial. Like a sample, the coupon gives consumers a reason to try the product or to retry it if they haven't done so in some time.

3. *Sweepstakes or contests.* Declining shares can often be reversed with a contest or sweepstakes that calls attention to the brand. In product

categories where there are multiple brands and none has a particularly outstanding feature, sweepstakes can be used to generate interest at a reasonable cost.

4. *Self-liquidators.* These offer an excellent method of calling attention to the brand. Since the major cost is in promoting the product and the liquidator, not in the premium, more advertising or sales promotion can be used. Tying the liquidator to a purchase helps overcome the trial problem.

5. *Premiums.* Like the self-liquidator, the premium is used primarily to gain attention for the brand. It can't and usually won't build long-term sales, particularly if a product defect is causing the decline. It can, however, generate renewed interest in the product.

6. *Distribution through new trade channels.* While not a sales promotion technique in itself, the use of new or previously little-used trade channels often helps to gain or regain share of the market. It works particularly well if the category has been stagnant and the new trade channels reach new triers or users for the brand.

7. *Holding devices.* Obviously, one of the best ways to maintain or gain shares in a competitive market is to hold your present customers. It is always easier to hold present customers than to gain new ones. Some of the more successful ways of holding customers are through refunds, continuity offers, and premiums.

8. *Post-facto techniques.* If the share loss has already occurred, the following steps should be taken. First, market research should be used to determine the cause of the loss. Second, having learned the cause and assuming it is a product problem as we have used the term, one of the above techniques, such as sampling, couponing, or sweepstakes or contests, can be used to regain trial. Third, if the problem is not the result of a product disadvantage, flaw, or other inadequacy, present customers can be held with loading techniques, such as price-packs, bonus packs, reduced prices on larger sizes, and continuity offers. More will be said about this in later chapters.

In all the above instances, with the exception of the seventh (holding devices), we have assumed the share loss was due to some outside influence or to the lack of promotion by the brand. If, indeed, the problem has been caused by competitive actions, or by lack of support from the sales force or the reseller, then you should study our suggestions in Chapters 11, 12, and 13.

Static Sales Problems

Often the problem facing the brand isn't quite so direct as a loss of share. It may be that sales of the product are flat or static in a category that is increasing. Over the long term, this will normally result in a loss of share. For example, assume that sales in the dry dog food category are increasing at a 6 percent annual rate. Your brand's sales, however, are increasing by only 1½ percent each year and you have a 30 percent share of market. In this case, your sales are relatively flat. Within two or three years, you will start to notice a share loss, because you're not keeping pace with the category. If the category continues to grow rapidly and your sales remain stagnant, your share loss could be substantial.

We have found five basic sales promotion techniques that seem to work well in solving the problem of static sales in growth markets. Again, we assume that research has been conducted and that the problem is not the result of a poor product or quality control. Instead, the problem appears to be that the product has failed to reach or hold its potential because of a lack either of advertising or sales promotion. The following strategies are usually successful.

1. *Continuity programs.* This is any type of sales promotion plan that encourages consumers to purchase the product on a continuing basis or over time. The goal is to generate more purchases than "normal," or several purchases in a row, by offering some sort of premium or saving. While sales promotion programs are usually designed as short-term incentives, continuity programs are based on the longer term.

2. *Coupons.* Often, the use of coupons can spur the trial or use of a product over a relatively short period of time. If the product is well known and simply suffers a lack of promotion, this technique can bring new customers in and old customers back.

3. *Price-offs.* Again, assuming a well-known or accepted product, a price-off is an effective way to generate trial or retrial by previous users. Usually, price-offs are done through a cents-off label or a trade deal with retailers. Although there are problems with implementation, price-offs seem to work very well in product categories in which there are few distinguishing characteristics among the various brands.

4. *Premiums.* Premiums, particularly in a growing category, seem to have great appeal. They are most effective when they are tied to the product in some way or designed to reinforce the advertising campaign.

5. *Bonus packs.* While this technique usually works best for package goods, bonus packs offer a verifiable value to the consumer. They seem to be particularly effective at the point-of-purchase, although they do require additional handling by the retailer.

As you can see from these suggestions, most of the ideas we recommend can be used effectively to call attention to the product or to differentiate it from others in the category. Where there are deep-rooted problems or the situation is such that a simple sales boosting technique is not the answer, we suggest you investigate the problem further and determine the exact cause. Based on that analysis, use the tools and techniques suggested in the relevant chapter.

Declining Margin Problems

Some of the most difficult problems with which to deal, particularly in inflationary times, involve declining margins. This problem is usually not the result of a lack of promotion. It often comes from rapidly rising ingredient costs that can't be passed along, pressure from competitors, an attempt to maintain a predetermined price in unfavorable circumstances, or similar situations. We suggest you research the problem thoroughly to determine the exact cause. If it is a problem in which sales promotion can be effective, you'll then know which tool to use.

We've found that many declining margin problems aren't really solvable with sales promotion techniques. Since sales promotion programs provide only temporary sales boosts, they may increase sales but not the long-term profits of the brand.

These techniques seem to work best with margin problems.

1. *Trade allowances.* Often, the cause of declining margins is simply the type of allowances made to the trade. Sometimes, it seems, trade allowances are developed on the basis of "what we did last year" or "what we've traditionally done" or "what competition is doing" rather than on what would make the best possible program. Take a close look at the allowances being made to the trade. Determine if they are correct. Is too much or too little being offered? One can be as bad as the other. See Chapter 4 for more details on trade promotions.

2. *Trade performance.* Trade allowances can be strengthened with sound trade performance agreements. These are simply plans whereby a retailer or wholesaler must do something—such as build a display, advertise a feature in the newspaper, or give a certain amount of shelf space to the product—to be entitled to the trade allowance. The trade allowance is not given unless the performance agreement is fulfilled by the dealer. These performance agreements help greatly in ensuring that deals and discounts to the trade are passed along to the consumer, where they can help achieve sales.

3. *Trade pricing.* While not specifically a form of sales promotion, trade pricing is a key ingredient in maintaining or achieving profitable margins. Unless there is sufficient margin in product price at the retail level, it is almost impossible to develop a strong sales pro-

motion program that will interest the trade. Unfortunately, the greater the margin to the trade, the lower the margin to the manufacturer, unless retail prices can be adjusted upward in some way.

4. *Packaging.* Again, although not specifically a sales promotion function, packaging can help to improve margins. For example, the product might be downsized; i.e., the amount of product can be ʳeduced slightly to allow a profitable margin on the new size. Or the package size might be increased, thus allowing a price adjustment and profit margin improvement. Finally, the type or method of packaging may be changed to provide more margin in the product itself. Since the packaging sometimes amounts to one-third or more of the total product cost, this can be an effective way to improve margins.

5. *Special consumer pricing.* Perhaps the best way to offset a poor margin is with special consumer pricing. By adjusting the price to the consumer, the manufacturer can then gain the needed margin. Increasing prices in an inflationary period is not too difficult. However, when prices are declining, that can be extremely hard to do.

One of the major difficulties in attacking margin problems with sales promotion techniques is that when margins are small, as they often are in these situations, the cost of a sales promotion program simply compounds the problem, unless price and margin adjustments are built into the sales promotion plan. Since sales promotion strategies are usually only incentives to purchase, unless the basic problem of the poor margin is solved, increased sales will only create more margin problems. We've found that in most pricing situations, sales promotion offers only temporary relief, at best.

Summary

When an otherwise good product isn't performing well, the sales promotion manager should pinpoint the precise nature of the problem. Is the product in a declining product category? Or is it suffering a specific share decline? Are sales static in a growing category? Or is margin declining in the face of static or rising category sales?

Each of these situations calls for solutions. Declining category sales, for example, may require industry-wide promotions, a search for new markets and uses, new publicity, or a change in packaging.

11

Competitive Problems and Opportunities

No area in marketing creates as many real or imagined problems as competition. Often, the threat is real. A competitor may do or has done something that is taking sales directly from the brand. In other instances, however, the threat is only expected, anticipated, or imagined. Then our job is to act before competition can either develop or implement its promotional program. Because competition is such a major threat to most brands' sales and profits, the proper use of sales promotion to meet real or expected competitive situations is vital to marketing success.

In this chapter, we identify the primary areas in which competitive actions create the greatest problems for consumer-goods marketers. Next, we identify various sales promotion techniques that work best in offsetting these problems. Wherever possible, we illustrate our suggestions with examples of what some marketers have done in these situations.

What Are Competitive Problems?

You'll recall that in Chapter 6 we identified seven specific problems that can be caused by competition. They are:

1. Product pricing problems
2. Competitive line extensions or new product introductions
3. Competitive product reformulations
4. Disruptive competitive activity
5. Revised levels of competitive advertising

6. Revised levels of competitive sales promotion

7. Improved competitive trade deals

We'll discuss each of these in more detail in the following pages.

Product Pricing Problems

These are situations in which competition has either increased or decreased the price of its product to the wholesaler, retailer, or consumer and thereby created a marketing problem for our brand. These pricing problems by competition usually result in losses of product distribution, declining sales or share of market, and/or unhappy distributors and retailers. Because price is one of the major elements in the marketing mix for all products, particularly consumer goods, the result of competitive pricing situations can dramatically affect sales.

These competition-originated pricing problems can be either short or long term. Short-term problems are usually caused by some sort of competitive product deal, feature, price-pack, bonus pack, or special that is available for a limited period of time. While the promotion is in effect, it can create serious marketing problems. Fortunately, however, not every price deal offered by competitors is effective. Some may be either overlooked or rejected by the trade. Also, the consumer may not react to a competitive price promotion. It is usually this uncertainty that makes competitive pricing problems so difficult to handle. If we react too quickly, we reduce margins unnecessarily. If we react too slowly, we may lose sales. Fortunately, competitive short-term pricing changes rarely have much long-term effect on sales or brand shares. They can, however, create havoc with sales and profit goals in the short run.

Long-term pricing problems are those created when the competition either increases or decreases the price of the product on a permanent basis. A competitive price decrease is usually more troublesome than a price increase, but either one can have a serious effect on sales and profits. Therefore, we normally attempt to deal with competitive price adjustments through pricing actions on our own part rather than with sales promotion programs.

In this chapter, we deal primarily with competitive price adjustments made at the consumer level. We also recognize that consumer price changes are often only part of a competitive plan and that most competitive price adjustments are accompanied by some sort of trade deal. We'll discuss these trade price adjustments in Chapter 12 when we deal with reseller and reselling problems.

Competitive Line Extensions or New Product Introductions

The market place over the past 30 or so years has been very dynamic.

We've seen a fantastic number of new products brought on by new technology, new manufacturing techniques and improvements, and new chemical discoveries. The result has been the development of new products and product line extensions at a phenomenal rate. For example, in 1980 it was estimated that more than 1,200 new food and drug products alone were introduced into test markets. All these products were promising enough to be manufactured, promoted, and tested. This doesn't include literally thousands of other new product ideas or concepts that never saw the light of day outside the laboratory.

As new products have been developed, old ones have been changed and improved. There are few brands that have been on the market any length of time that have not been improved in some way through new or different ingredients or improved performance. And there has also been a great number of line extensions. Almost every marketer with a successful product has considered or introduced a line extension, such as a new product size, a new flavor, or another product with the same name. The intent, of course, is to take advantage of the success of a product or to gain a larger percentage share of the total market.

While some of these line extensions and new products have been short-lived, others have survived long enough to cause the sales promotion manager real headaches.

Competitive Product Reformulations, Repackaging, or Added Ingredients

In this area we include problems that result from product improvements made by competition. Competitive reformulations or added ingredients can shift the product advantage to our competition, although formerly there may have been product parity or perhaps even an advantage for our brand.

The major problem in these situations is that usually product changes cannot be made quickly. Because of this, sales promotion is often used to offset or negate competitive product advantages until the manufacturer can develop the necessary product improvements. The same situation often occurs in packaging, with the same needs and results.

There is a big difference between new products and line extensions, as described above, and changes or improvements made in existing products. While the difference in the two may be slight to the uninitiated, it is very important when the sales promotion manager must choose a tactic to solve the problem. We'll cover the difference in detail later.

Disruptive Competitive Activity, Pressure on Present Dealers, or Invasion by Outside Brands

These problems will be covered in more detail in Chapter 12. Often, competition seeks to achieve sales simply by stealing away distribution, either at the wholesale or retail level. In most cases, these attempts include some form of trade price incentive. Often, other incentives, such as display or co-op allowances or introductory discounts, are used because they are designed to build retail sales. Whatever the activity, pressure is put on present distributors and/or distribution channels to either drop our line or to add the competitive line.

Another problem in this area is the invasion of our existing territories by a new competitor. For example, a regional brand may expand into our market, a national brand may enter or decide to place additional emphasis on certain of our markets, or a formerly small-share, non-promoting brand may suddenly become aggressive. Whatever the situation, a new competitor that had not previously existed must now be met. When this happens, dealers and distributors are pressured to stock new products or new brands. Often, they are offered very attractive financial incentives to do so.

Revised Levels of Competitive Advertising

A common competitive problem is the introduction of a major new advertising campaign. This can take the form of either increased competitive spending or a new advertising theme or appeal. It may also be a change in competition's media plan that puts particular pressure on our present customers. Whatever the situation, competition builds the pressure through media advertising rather than other forms of promotion.

In some cases, competitors may launch what is known as "investment advertising spending." In other words, competition is investing advertising money in excess of any results it expects to achieve during the time the advertising is appearing. It is spending now in hopes of gaining sales in the future. This is a most difficult problem to combat. For example, we don't usually know how much the competitor plans to invest, how long it might continue the tactic, or the results it might achieve. To meet this challenge, we can do investment advertising spending of our own or use a sales promotion technique. We believe that certain sales promotion activities are most effective in offsetting competitive investment advertising spending programs because they can be used to generate immediate sales when competition is concentrating its investments in longer-term media advertising.

Revised Levels of Competitive Sales Promotion

One of the most difficult competitive problems is combating an aggressive sales promotion program. Since both sides know the strengths and weaknesses of various sales promotion techniques, developing an effective offsetting sales promotion program at a reasonable cost is sometimes a near-impossible task. Another problem occurs when all brands in the market are using some form of sales promotion at the same time. When that occurs, the consumer may become totally confused and reject all attempts at persuasion. The consumer alternative in this situation is to "cherry pick" the best offer, which results in no real benefit to any brand. Although trying to offset a competitive sales promotion program is difficult, some techniques are better than others—and we will discuss them later.

One of the hazards of trying to meet a competitive sales promotion program is simply trying to get something into the market in a hurry. When this happens, the sales promotion device may be ill-conceived or ineffective. A sales promotion plan developed "overnight" simply to meet competition can often be more harmful than helpful. The best strategy is to investigate the competitive offer thoroughly. Determine its consumer strengths and weaknesses. Then, and only then, should you attempt to develop a sales program of your own. The best rule is, "Know what you are trying to do before you set about doing it."

Improved Competitive Trade Deals at the Wholesale or Retail Level

This problem is much like the one described above, under Disruptive Competitive Activity. Here, though, the problem is primarily competitive trade dealing through present distribution channels and with present wholesalers, distributors, and/or retailers. These "deals" need not always be based on price. They may include other forms of sales promotion, such as sales incentives, contests, and dealer loaders. Often, they are directed specifically at the dealer and not expected to be passed along to the consumer. Again, since this is technically a reseller problem, we will deal with it in more detail in the next chapter.

As you can see, each of the problems described above can be traced back to some specific competitive activity. Again, it is vital that you know the exact source of the problem before you try to solve it with a sales promotion program. If you don't, you may find that the supposed cure is worse than the disease.

All the problems we have described are actual, not anticipated ones. Too often, it appears that much sales promotion time and effort is spent trying to guess what competition is going to do rather than developing sound, aggressive, *offensive* sales promotion programs. It would be nice to believe that if we planned and used sales promotion properly, we might never have competitive problems. Being always on the offensive, we would never have to react to competition. They would always be reacting to us. We know, however, that such a situation simply isn't possible. Most marketers don't have the money, the market intelligence, or the people to carry out a sales promotion program of that magnitude. As a result, there will probably always be competitive problems. The real secret is to know how to handle them.

Solving Competitive Problems

In most of the situations we have described, a competitor has created some sort of problem for us. While sales promotion is not always the only solution to these problems, we will offer suggestions, ideas, and approaches that might be used. Often, the best solution is to combine sales promotion with other promotion techniques, such as advertising or personal selling. We'll look at some of those also.

While we always hope that a sales promotion program can solve or cure a competitive problem, often the best we can hope for is simply to negate the competitive threat—in other words, create a stand-off or maintain the status quo. But blunting the efforts of competition and holding present market shares and present customers is a very acceptable goal for a sales promotion program.

Assuming the situation you face is one of those listed above and you can trace the problem directly to competitive activity of some sort, we've found the following sales promotion tools are most effective. While it is often not possible to give specific examples of programs other marketers have used, we have included examples of the suggested solutions whenever possible.

Trade and Consumer Deals

We believe the most effective way to offset competitive trade deals is through some type of alternative sales promotion program. (Note: You'll find a more complete discussion of trade dealing in Chapter 12.) When you attempt to meet or beat trade deals on a dollar-for-dollar basis, it usually becomes a matter of who can make the highest bid. The use of an alternative sales promotion program, such as a dealer contest, a dealer loader, or exciting point-of-purchase material, is often as effective a way of competing and is usually far less expensive. The secret is in finding something that will excite the dealer in addition to offering him increased sales and profits. That's where the need for creativity in sales promotion becomes so apparent.

One example of a creative and complete sales promotion program is the L'Oréal trade offer shown in Figure 11-1. L'Oréal offered not just a trade deal of 20 percent off invoice but the potential of a retail sale of two products, a special promotion to the consumer, point-of-purchase dis-

Figure 11-1   Trade Deal: L'Oréal Preference Shampoo

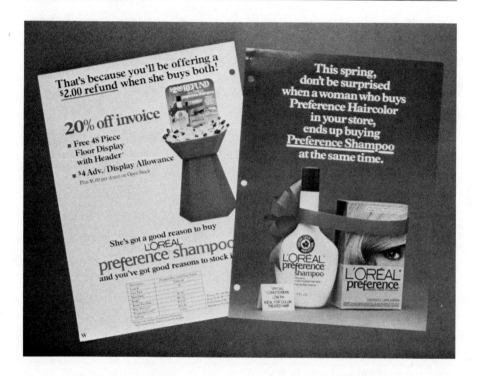

Source: William A. Robinson, *100 Best Sales Promotions of 1976/7* (Chicago: Crain Books, 1977), p. 39.

plays, and display allowances for the retailer. This is the type of total sales promotion program that gets action from the retailer in spite of heavy trade dealing by competition.

Consumer deals can take almost any form. They can include such activities as regular price-offs, price-packs, bonus packs, in- or on-pack coupons, or premiums, to mention a few. While "deals" are an excellent way to excite the trade, there is a major problem with some types of promotions, particularly when only a price reduction is involved. The offer or price reduction may be absorbed in the trade channel. The offer made to the wholesaler or retailer is expected to be passed along to the consumer but, unfortunately, it often isn't. For example, a $1 per case allowance on a case of 18 units should amount to a reduction in the shelf price of approximately 5¢-6¢ per unit. In some instances, however, this discount is not passed along. It is held by either the wholesaler or the

Figure 11-2   Consumer Deal: Tender Vittles Cat Food

Source: Printed with permission of Ralston Purina Company.

retailer as extra margin on the item, and the shelf price remains the same. What was supposed to be a "consumer deal" ends up being nothing more than a profit improvement for the trade.

One way to prevent this absorption of a planned consumer price reduction in the distribution channel is to require some sort of proof-of-performance from the wholesaler or retailer to qualify for the deal. That simply means the price reduction or discount is not paid to the trade unless the trade either reduces the shelf price to the consumer at retail or performs in some other way. The normal "performance" by the retailer may be either a price feature in media advertising, a special display in the store, or some other visible support to justify the price reduction.

Since proof-of-performance by the trade is often difficult and costly to police, many manufacturers use alternative types of consumer sales promotion tactics in which the actual sales promotion offer is made directly to the consumer. This ensures that the offer reaches the consumer at retail. For example, Tender Vittles cat food offered a 33 percent

Figure 11-3   Consumer Deal: Coca-Cola Bottlers

Source: William A. Robinson, *Best Sales Promotions of 1977/78* (Chicago: Crain Books, 1969), p. 152.

discount to the consumer on its packages, illustrated in Figure 11-2. Because the offer was printed right on the package there was no way it could get lost in the distribution channels. In addition, the offer was tied to a purchase—that is, to get the discount the consumer had first to purchase the product. While the 3-for-1 offer looked attractive, most likely the cost of the sales promotion program to Tender Vittles was much less than the cost of a 33 percent trade discount and probably just as effective.

Another example of an assured consumer price reduction was the offer made by the Denver Coca-Cola Bottlers of two quarts of Coca-Cola free when four quarts of Mr. Pibb or Sprite were purchased. Since the bottlers controlled the packaging and the offer, there was no way the offer could be absorbed in the trade channels. It's illustrated in Figure 11-3.

These are only a few examples of consumer "deals" that can be used to offset competitive actions. There are unlimited possibilities. The key is to make an offer the consumer wants in an easy-to-understand way and be sure it reaches beyond the retail level.

Point-of-Purchase Materials and Displays

Another effective method of solving competitive problems is through the use of point-of-purchase materials or displays in the retail store. The reason: when consumers are ready to buy, that's the time to tell the sales story. And what better time than when the decision is being made, right at the point-of-purchase in retail stores? While it is becoming increasingly difficult to get point-of-purchase material up in many stores, something that will help generate new or additional sales for the retailer will usually find a place. For example, in Figure 11-4 Campari met competition head-on and to the point with its display of "Campari Instead." Combined with the "game" appeal it was sure to get consumer action. This kind of display gets attention, tells the story quickly and clearly, and helps make sales. It's competitive and effective.

Everynight shampoo and conditioner faced tremendous competitive pressure from several new products in the market. To combat these entries, Everynight developed a free poster offer that it promoted strongly at the point-of-purchase. An example of just one of the point-of-purchase items it used is illustrated in Figure 11-5.

Point-of-purchase materials and displays are effective against many types of competitive pressure. For example, if competition is attempting to introduce a line extension or reformulation, point-of-purchase can be used to either call attention to the value of the product or take attention away from the new product. Point-of-purchase also seems to work well against increased competitive advertising. Even though the competitor is spending more money, you have a solid chance to make the sale if you can get the last word, right at the point-of-purchase.

Couponing

A very effective way of offsetting competitive activities is through a manufacturer-originated coupon. Media coupons usually ensure that the offer will get through to the consumer. Further, the use of a coupon guarantees that the offer will be exactly as you planned it in terms of length of time, value, and products. Since the marketer controls the coupon, it is highly flexible. For example, it can be sent into specific areas to meet regional and local competitive situations or varied in timing by market. Further, since you have control over the value, you can make rather dramatic offers. Often, your consumer offer can be much larger

Figure 11-4   Point-of-Purchase Displays: Campari

Source: "What's New in Packaging, Premiums, and P.O.P.," *Advertising Age*, May 24, 1976, p. 52.

Figure 11-5   Point-of-Purchase Materials: Everynight Hair Products

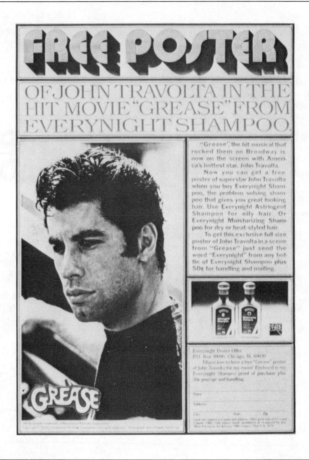

Source: William A. Robinson, *100 Best Sales Promotions*, (Chicago: Crain Books, 1980), p. 21.

than a discount to the trade. The reason is that you know the distribution of the coupon and thus the potential redemption. Since not every coupon will be redeemed, you can count on a large value at a relatively low redeemed cost. On the other hand, price reductions to the trade are at face value and can therefore be quite expensive.

One method some marketers use to deal with competitive coupons is to accept any competitive coupon as a reduction on the price of their product. While this is a highly risky venture, since the number that may be redeemed is not known, it is a dramatic and unusual twist. A few years

Figure 11-6   Coupon: Arby's Restaurants

Source: Robinson, *Best Sales Promotions of 1977/78*, p. 127.

ago, many retail food stores used this technique to take advantage of competitive coupons.

A more traditional couponing approach in competitive situations is shown by the "Break the Hamburger Habit" coupon offered by Arby's against its chief fast-food competition. This was a limited-area promotion, as you can see in Figure 11-6, but it helped meet the competitive challenge the hamburger chains had mounted.

Another way to use a coupon in a competitive environment is the device developed by Sun Giant raisins. Sun-Maid raisins has been the dominant brand in the market for years. Sun Giant was challenging it competitively. What better way than to offer a free sample of the product? (See Figure 11-7.) A coupon good for 100 percent off on the product is hard to top.

An interesting twist on ordinary couponing is to use the competitive product as a coupon form. Jewel Food Stores wanted to promote its

Figure 11-7   Coupon: Sun Giant Raisins

Source: Eugene Mahany, "'Price, Value' Are New Semantic Stars in Marketing Buzzword Sweeps," *Advertising Age*, Jan. 13, 1975, p. 32.

private label products. To do so, it offered 25¢ off the purchase price of any private label health or beauty-aid product. The consumer was to bring in not a coupon, however, but an empty container of the national brand—a clever twist that got the message across. (See Figure 11-8.)

The coupon can be an effective competitive sales promotion weapon, particularly for offsetting competitive pricing changes. Since the consumer has the coupon in hand, there is a good chance the brand will go on the shopping list. Coupons also work well in holding consumers against competitive product reformulations, line extensions, and even new prod-

Figure 11-8   Coupon: Jewel Food Stores

Source: Robinson, *100 Best Sales Promotions of 1976/7*, p. 126.

ucts. Couponing can be used effectively against increased competitive advertising pressure. A known saving through a coupon can often be more effective than a new advertising theme, particularly in the short run.

Sampling

Sampling, although not considered to be a primary tool in competitive situations, can also be used to offset competitive activity. When defending a market against competition, the manufacturer has a fairly good idea of who his customers are. In addition, these customers are usually familiar with the product. Under these conditions sampling works well. It reminds consumers of the product advantages and why they should buy or continue to buy.

Sampling can also be used to offset competitive sampling. That is, if competitors are sampling their product, an effective sales promotion tactic is to sample your brand. That can effectively negate the competitive sales promotion program, particularly if your product has a visible or distinct advantage.

Sampling can also be used as an offensive sales promotion tool to put the product in the hands of the competition's users. When competition is stressing line extensions, reformulations, or new packaging, sampling can be used to persuade their present customers to try your product. Since you can be highly selective with sample distribution plans, you can be very specific about whom and how you sample to improve your results.

Several new methods of sampling are now available. One is distribution through the media, such as newspaper or other print medium, for small, flexible products or pouches. McCormick/Shilling used a four-color insert with samples of its spaghetti sauce mix and Season All, plus coupons for other products, in this way. It's shown in Figure 11-9.

Excedrin used a free sample to help offset or take advantage of competition. Figure 11-10 shows its offer of a free sample of its product to any user of regular aspirin. While it doesn't always draw great numbers of redemptions, this form of sampling is a strong sales promotion technique and clearly targeted to the users of competitive products.

Used in the right way, sampling can shift the pressure from you back to competition and force them to either react or retrench. It is also a strong offensive weapon. The success of sampling by Agree conditioner was phenomenal. For example, in 1977, when it entered the market, S. C. Johnson & Company distributed more than 31,000,000 free samples of Agree conditioner and over 41,000,000 cents-off coupons. Competitors would be hard put to develop a more commanding sales promotion program than that.

In-Packs, On-Packs, and Near-Packs

In-packs, on-packs, and near-packs, all of which are actually premiums given with the product in some way, can also be used to offset competitive situations. For example, an in-pack premium of a given value can be used to either hold present customers or draw new ones in the face of competitive activity. In-packs are especially effective if they provide some additional or expanded use for the product. The same is true of on-pack premiums. They gain additional attention in the retail outlet and are often used to obtain off-shelf displays. A premium with the product can be one of the most effective ways to offset competitive activities. Since on-packs and near-packs can be used to generate retail displays, they

Figure 11-9   Sample: McCormick Products   **Figure 11-10   Sample: Excedrin**

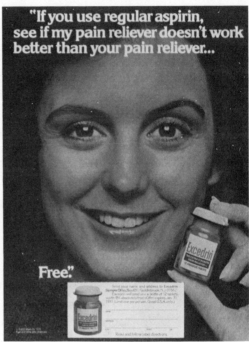

Source: Robinson, *100 Best Sales Promotions of 1976/7*, p. 126 and p. 131.

work quite well against many forms of competitive sales promotion plans.

Near-packs seem to be particularly effective in some competitive situations. Since they may be placed near the shelved product, they offer the advantage of getting a store display to generate excitement. Also, near-packs can be developed to offset a specific competitive offer.

In-packs and on-packs work well against competitive price incentives, particularly if they are strongly featured on the product package. Of course, the very nature of in-packs, on-packs, and near-packs means that many alternative types of offers can be made. Thus, most competitive situations can be either met or overcome with this sales promotion tool.

One example of an on-pack premium used to offset competition was the offer made by Gillette in Figure 11-11. The attachment of a free Trac II trial razor to the can of Trac II shave cream got attention and action. By

| Figure 11-11 | On-Pack Premium: Gillette Shave Cream | Figure 11-12 | In-Pack Premium: Mrs. Karl's Bread |

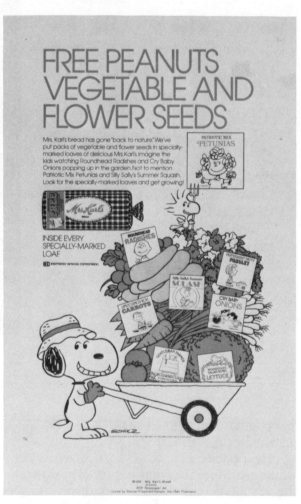

Source: Robinson, *100 Best Sales Promotions of 1967/7*, p. 133 (for Figure 11-11) and p. 132 (for Figure 11-12).

putting a free razor in the hands of the purchaser of Trac II shave cream, Gillette hoped to encourage use of its complete line of shaving products. It was trying to woo competitive users at the same time it was giving its present customers a reason to remain brand loyal.

Another sales promotion program designed to hold present cus-

Figure 11-13   Near-Pack Premium: Bounce Fabric Softener

Source: Courtesy of the Procter & Gamble Company.

tomers in the face of competition was the in-pack promotion by Mrs.
Karl's bread, illustrated in Figure 11-12. By including a package of
vegetable and flower seeds in specially marked loaves and by taking
advantage of the "Peanuts" characters, Mrs. Karl's offered a strong incentive to purchase to both current and competitive users. A feature of this
technique is the use of "specially marked loaves." With this approach,
Mrs. Karl's could increase or decrease the offer in the market, move it
from area to area, or adjust it in other ways. The promotion flexibility is a
big advantage of in-packs.

A near-pack that worked quite well in offsetting competitive pressure was the Bounce "Free Holder" promotion from Procter & Gamble.
(See Figure 11-13.) Bounce is a fabric softener/static cling remover used
in the laundry. While Bounce was the first product of this type, several
competitors had entered the field and there was much promotion.
Bounce offered the holder free with the purchase of a large roll of the

---

Figure 11-14   Bonus Pack: Heinz Ketchup

Source: Courtesy of Heinz, U.S.A.

---

product. The display unit was placed near the laundry products section in supermarkets.

Bonus Packs

The bonus pack is an effective method of meeting competition, particularly in pricing situations. Since the bonus pack offers an obvious value at the point-of-purchase, it can be used to overcome minor price promotions by competition. Additionally the bonus pack tends to hold current customers. Since they have more of your product, there is less likelihood that customers will switch to competition because of some sales promotion offer, such as a coupon, sample, or other device. Bonus packs also offer the flexibility often required in competitive situations. They can be sent in when needed and stopped when the problem has been solved. Bonus packs are usually a good alternative to a price-pack if there is retailer objection to that device. Finally, bonus packs provide the opportunity for off-shelf promotion in the store. That can overcome very extensive competitive sales promotion programs. For example, Heinz offered 38 ounces of ketchup for the price of 32 ounces in Figure 11-14.

Figure 11-15   Reusable Container: Heublein Products

Shaker gift.

Quite a gift—to keep for yourself or to give to someone else.
Instead of a quart-size bottle of Heublein's Gin Martinis or Vodka Martinis or
Manhattans or Daiquiris or Margaritas or Brass Monkeys,
you get a quart-size shakerful.
After the party is over and the drinks are all gone the shaker, of course, lives on.

Source: William A. Robinson, *100 Best Sales Promotions of 1975/6* (Chicago: Crain Books, 1976), p. 121.

Bonus packs offer strong advantages in many competitive situations. They have been used most effectively in the grocery and over-the-counter drug fields. Some product categories in which bonus packs are common are vitamins, coffee, bar soaps, and pet foods.

Reusable Containers

Reusable containers, which are usually a form of premium, can be used in many competitive situations. If they are unique or unusual, these containers can separate the product from competition at the point-of-purchase. They are also effective because they provide an "instant" reward to the purchaser. Buy the product, get the container premium. Many containers are directly tied to the use of the product, such as a refrigerator jar for a soft drink mix or a drinking mug for cocoa. Thus, they remind the purchaser of the brand each time they are used.

Heublein offered a reusable container with its line of premixed liquor drinks. Filled originally with the product, the reusable shaker was likely used over and over again. (See Figure 11-15.)

Figure 11-16   Reusable Container: Maxwell House Coffee

Source: Robinson, *100 Best Sales Promotions of 1976/7*, p. 137.

Another reusable container was the Maxwell House coffee offer in Figure 11-16. The storage jars differentiated Maxwell House from competition, and they also encouraged purchase continuity to get the whole set. Once customers started to collect them, they probably wanted them all. This illustrates how reusable containers can be used to hold present customers against competitive sales promotion tactics.

Refund Offers

A particularly strong sales promotion technique in meeting a competitive situation is the refund offer. On a refund, the marketer usually agrees to refund all or part of the product purchase price to the consumer. While similar to price-off promotions, refunds are a different way of rewarding the consumer for purchasing a particular product.

Refund promotions have one major advantage against competitive offers; i.e., the consumer must buy the product to obtain the refund. Because of this, competitive promotions are usually blunted. Additionally, refund offers can often be used to stimulate in-store displays and features since they normally represent fairly large values. They are also very flexible. They can be used or moved by the marketer at will to meet specific competitive situations. Refund offers also give the marketer a chance to key the refund to the need—that is, the refund can be made larger or smaller, depending on the competitive situation, the market, or the product category.

One example of a refund is the double offer from Purina Dog Chow. Consumers could get back $1 or $2, based on the size of the package they purchased. (See Figure 11-17.) That's a good way to trade the consumer up to a larger-size package by making the refund more attractive. It is also a way of blunting competitive offers, since the purchase of the larger size takes the consumer out of the market for a longer period of time.

While refund offers come in all shapes, sizes, and values, probably one of the most unusual ones was made by Playtex. The ad said, "Buy our new bra and mail in your old one and get a coupon for another one." That's not just one product in the consumer's hands, but two. It's sure to keep the purchaser loyal for a while and prevent any competitive inroads.

Premiums

A discussion of premiums has been held until last for several reasons. First, in most situations, we don't believe in getting into a premium race; i.e., seeing who can offer the largest assortment or the most unusual type. When this occurs, premiums tend to get further and further away from their original purpose, which should be to help sell merchandise or to gain or hold customers. Instead, as happened with banks and savings institutions in many markets, the sales promotion goal seems to have become having the largest or longest premium list, not the most effective one. If used correctly in a well-planned program, premiums not only hold customers and gain new ones, but also help offset many types of competitive sales promotion activities. Americans still want "something for nothing" whenever they can get it. When they can't, getting a "deal" on something is the next best thing. Today, almost anything can be a premium, as the offer made by Kool cigarettes a few years ago demonstrated: a sailboat for $700 and proofs-of-purchase.

To be successful, the premium must offer a solid value. It should also have some long-term potential for the marketer. We believe few marketers have done a better job of extending the brand image and holding off competition with premiums than Green Giant. The Green Giant

Figure 11-17   Refund Offer: Purina Dog Chow

Source: Eugene Mahany, "Package Goods Clients Agree: Promotion Importance Will Grow," *Advertising Age*, April 14, 1975, p. 48.

himself is a natural, and the company has made the most of him with giant footprint rugs, giant green kites, giant sleeping bags, and on and on. The "Sprout Inflatable" in Figure 11-18 is another extension of that general theme.

These are just a few examples of ways you can deal with competitive problems. Most of our suggestions have included some method of tying the brand to the sales promotion offer. We think that is extremely important in any competitive situation. Since the problem is that competition is trying to get your customers to buy their products, a key ingredient in

Figure 11-18   Premium: Green Giant Products

Free Sprout Inflatable
with 10 ingredient panels from
any Green Giant canned vegetables.

A lovable,
huggable,
inflatable
Sprout.

And he's yours free
with 10 ingredient
panels from any
Green Giant Brand
canned vegetables. Or for
$1.00 with 6 ingredient panels.
Or $1.50 with 2 ingredient panels.

*Order your inflatable Sprout
today. He's really a doll!*

Source: Robinson, *100 Best Sales Promotions of 1976/7*, p. 110.

any successful sales promotion program should be to continue to build
your brand. In our opinion, offers of unrelated premiums really have no
place in solving that kind of problem.

The well-organized sales promotion manager should have a list of
successful or planned sales promotion programs in his "war chest" ready
for any competitive situation. That's just good business planning. When
a competitive situation arises, the sooner you can get your own program
going, the more certain you can be that you can outmaneuver the compe-

tition. Often, the marketer who is able to meet competition head-on with a more effective sales promotion tool soon finds that he isn't challenged as often.

Summary

Competitive challenges are among the most serious problems that a sales promotion manager faces. But they are also the ones that can be most directly and effectively met with sales promotion weapons. You will be fighting on your own ground.

Competitors may strike in a number of ways: price changes, line extensions, new products or reformulations, disruption of trade channels, new advertising and sales promotion programs, or trade deals. Remember that the best defense is a good offense and examine your sales promotion armory. Among the best means of counterattack are your own trade deals, point-of-purchase attacks, couponing, sampling, in- and on-packs, bonus packs, reusable containers, and refunds. Pick the one best suited to blunt your competitor's attack and build your own brand.

12

Reseller and Reselling
Problems and Opportunities

A key ingredient in the marketing success of any organization is the distribution system. If the product is not available, no amount of promotion can either generate or influence a sale.

Distribution systems, which include the various sellers and resellers in the channel, may be either simple, complex, or somewhere in-between. For example, a McDonald's fast-food restaurant has a very simple distribution system, direct to the consumer. A McDonald's restaurant manufactures or processes hamburgers, French fries, soft drinks, and other products on the premises. These products are then distributed directly to consumers through the retail outlets. On the other hand, a television set manufacturer, such as Quasar, may have a very complex distribution system: the manufacturer sells to wholesalers, the wholesalers sell to distributors, and the distributors sell to retailers, and, finally, the retailers sell to the final consumer. Thus, before the television set actually reaches the final owner, it goes through at least three different types of distribution organizations or resellers. To see how simple and how complex distribution systems can be, look at Table 12-1. Starting with the producer of raw materials, there can be several intermediaries or none, depending on the type of product and the method of selling. Even within a single industry, such as the food business, distribution can also vary widely, as shown in Table 12-2. As you can see, there are four separate types of distribution systems that move the product from the manufacturer to the ultimate consumer.

In most cases, the distribution system a manufacturer employs depends on his marketing strategy. Generally, a marketer is said to use

257

Table 12-1   Channels of Distribution

Producers of raw materials (farms, mines, fisheries, etc.)

Wholesale enterprises

Manufacturing, processing, and service enterprises

Wholesale enterprises

Retail and service enterprises

Household customers	Government and other institutional customers

direct (labels on connecting lines)

Source: Dorothy Cohen, *Advertising* (New York: John Wiley & Sons, 1979), p. 80.

either a "push" or "pull" marketing strategy. In a "push" strategy, the manufacturer puts primary emphasis on pushing the product through the distribution channels. The incentives to purchase the product are directed toward the various wholesalers, distributors, and retailers rather than the final consumer, so that the reseller will then push the product to the consumer. This approach is particularly prevalent in

Table 12-2   Illustrative Channels of Distribution for Food Products

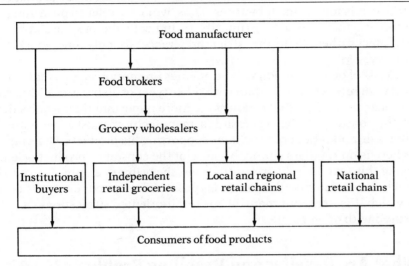

Source: David W. Cravens, Gerald E. Hills, and Robert B. Woodruff, *Marketing Decision Making: Concepts and Strategy* (Homewood, IL: Richard D. Irwin, 1976), p. 542.

product categories that require personal selling at the retail level, such as large appliances, automobiles, furniture, and clothing. Conversely, manufacturers of products sold primarily through self-service facilities, such as food, drug, variety, and discount stores, rely primarily on a "pull" marketing strategy. They are heavy users of media advertising, sales promotion, and other consumer purchasing incentives. The idea of the pull strategy is to build demand by the consumers, i.e., to get them to go to the store and either purchase or ask for the particular brand. The manufacturer hopes to pull the products through the distribution channels as a result of consumer demand brought about by his marketing efforts.

The type, form, and length of the distribution system used by a manufacturer greatly influences the type and number of resellers he uses. This distribution system also has a direct effect on the type of sales promotion activities used in the marketing mix.

Up to this point, much of our discussion of sales promotion has revolved around consumer-oriented activities or those that might be used primarily by marketers employing a "pull" marketing strategy. Here, we will investigate sales promotion tactics that can be used with wholesalers, distributors, and retailers in a "push" marketing strategy. A note of caution, though: Most consumer-product organizations employ some combination of both push and pull strategies. It is usually as important for the distributors and retailers to promote the products at retail as it is for the manufacturer. Thus, while we refer to push and pull strategies, they are used primarily to indicate the orientation of the marketer rather than the strict adherence to only one marketing strategy.

Most of our discussion will be on sales promotion tactics that can be used with retailers rather than with other types of distributors. This does not mean we believe that retailers are more important than wholesalers. On the contrary, to be successful, a manufacturer must have both the wholesale and retail organizations supporting his products. Our emphasis here is on retailers simply because of the consumer-product orientation of this text. In industrial situations, the primary emphasis would be on wholesalers or distributors. Sales promotion depends on the situation in which it is used, but many of our retail-oriented suggestions can also be used with other resellers.

What Are Reseller and Reselling Problems?

In Chapter 6 we identified the five most common reseller or reselling problems for marketers. They are:

1. A loss of distribution.
2. In-store sales promotion problems.
3. Entering new geographic areas.
4. Entering new trade categories.
5. Timing and frequency of sales promotion.

In the following pages we'll explain exactly what these problems are and how and when they usually arise.

A Loss of Distribution

Simply put, if there are fewer retailers stocking a consumer product, sales will usually decline. One reason is the high substitutability of consumer products. If their first brand choice is not available, most people will accept a second or third brand rather than go to another retailer to find their regular brand. This substitutability factor makes distribution a key ingredient in many consumer marketing mixes.

Distribution losses may occur for many reasons. Some of the most common ones are adverse competitive actions, faulty pricing, poor effort by the sales force, and negative environmental factors. Sometimes, retailers discontinue the line simply because there is no sound marketing program for the product. Of course, this includes the sales promotion program, which is often a major factor in a retailer's decision of whether or not to stock a particular product. Retailers usually look to the manufacturer to help presell the product to the consumer, usually with some form of advertising or sales promotion. They also expect the manufacturer to furnish the necessary materials to help them complete the sale, such as displays, features, and point-of-purchase materials for use in the store. Many have also come to expect trade deals, discounts, and promotion allowances that will enable them to promote the product in their own stores and through their own media. If these are not available or not offered, retailers can usually find a brand that offers this support. Thus, they tend to stock and promote products with sound, well-planned promotion programs.

With products at parity, most sales forces well trained, and many major media advertising programs equally effective, the retailer's decision on what products to stock and promote is based more and more on the sales promotion program being offered. It's often a major ingredient in whether distribution is held or lost.

In-Store Sales Promotion Problems

The second major reselling problem is the type or method of display of the product in the retail store. One common problem is incorrect or poor location of the product in retail outlets. For example, a product that sells best when displayed in the cosmetic department may have been placed in the drug section by the retailer. To maximize sales, the product needs to be relocated. Another problem is poor or inadequate shelf space. This could include not stocking enough of the product or not stocking all the sizes, all the flavors, and so on. This is a major problem for many manufacturers. It is illustrated in the chart developed by J. O. Peckham, Sr., based on A. C. Nielsen Company data. As you can see in Table 12-3, retailers do not always stock products according to their actual sales. In this example, while Brand B received 45.2 percent of the shelf facings, it generated only 34.4 percent of the sales. Brand A on the other hand had 65.6 percent of the sales but only 54.8 percent of the shelf facings. This example is certainly not unique in the retail field. And, as scanner data become available, we're learning more and more about the proper stocking and shelf allocation for products.

Another problem occurs when the product is out of stock on the shelf. Even if the retailer has allocated sufficient display space to the product, the sale is usually lost if the product is not physically on the shelf when the consumer is shopping. Finally, sales may suffer because display or promotional material is unused. Manufacturers spend large sums developing and shipping display and point-of-purchase materials to retailers. Often, however, these materials are either never used or not used in the best possible way to maximize sales.

Table 12-3   Leading Brands Generally Deficient on Share of Stocks and Shelf Facings

	Shelf facings	Retail stocks	Consumer sales
Brand B	45.2%	44.9%	34.4%
Brand A	54.8%	55.1%	65.6%

Source: J. O. Peckham, Sr., *The Wheel of Marketing* (Scarsdale, NY.: Privately printed, 1978), p. 32.

While these are four of the most common in-store promotion problems, there are doubtless others that may be more common in particular product areas. The problems discussed, however, seem to apply to most consumer goods. The increase in self-service retailing in many product categories has made in-store sales promotion an even more critical part of the manufacturer's promotional mix. If the product can't be found, it won't be bought. If it isn't properly promoted, sales will go to a competitive product. Therefore, display, stocking, and in-store promotion are critical to the success of most products. It's as simple as that.

Entering New Geographic Areas

Usually, this situation is more of a reseller and reselling opportunity than a problem. Many activities, plans, and techniques can be used to expand the distribution of a product into a new geographic area. As a regional brand expands into an adjacent area, a regional product expands its distribution to the national level, or a product that has been in test market is rolled out into the national market, new distribution is sought, new retailers must be convinced that the product should be stocked, and new consumers must be made aware of the product benefit.

Expanding an area is often a difficult task. Most retailers are relatively happy with the line of products they now have on hand. Indeed, many of them simply don't have room to stock any more new items. Therefore, simply obtaining distribution for a product in a new area may be a major undertaking. First, the wholesaler must be convinced that the product will sell—at a profit. Even if the manufacturer can do this, however, distribution may not be automatic. The retailer must be sold, even if the product is authorized by headquarters. Then, the retailer must decide what product to remove from the shelf to make room for the new item. With limited space, adding a new product often means discontinuing an old one. Finally, even if this is accomplished, advertising and sales promotion must generate consumer trial and, ultimately, continued use of the product to make it successful. All these steps require the use of sound, well-planned sales promotion programs to first convince the wholesaler and retailer to stock the product and then convince the consumer to buy it.

New distribution is difficult to obtain, and sometimes it is even more difficult to hold. Sales promotion plans are needed for both.

Entering New Trade Categories

Without expanded distribution, the opportunity for increased sales may be limited. Since more and more products are competing for the same or often less retail store space, one method of gaining additional sales is through distribution in either new or previously unused trade categories. For example, look at the way many food and drugstores have changed their product mixes in the last few years. Food stores now sell health and beauty aids, kitchen gadgets, hosiery, records, and even, in some places, clothing and furniture. Drugstores now stock food, hardware, outdoor equipment, sporting goods, and liquor. All types of manufacturers are attempting to expand the distribution of their products into these new or changing retail outlets. The goal is to make the product available to today's very mobile shoppers at the time and place it is most likely to be purchased.

The changing methods of distribution through retail outlets have created problems and opportunities for all types of marketers. When a marketer moves his product into a new retail category—for example, an automotive oil manufacturer starts distributing in food and drugstores in addition to automotive stores and service stations—there are serious questions about how and when to use various sales promotion techniques. Activities that have been quite successful in one type of retail outlet may not be suited at all to the new outlets. In addition, the typical retailing programs used in the new category may be totally foreign to the manufacturer. Thus, a program that has been successful in one category won't necessarily be successful in another.

To establish distribution in new retail categories, a sales promotion manager must be familiar with sales promotion plans and activities that will work in all types of retail outlets. The idea that there is one best form of sales promotion for any product simply isn't viable any longer.

Timing and Frequency

Another of the major problems in conducting a sound sales promotion program is determining the proper timing and frequency of promotional events. By scheduling promotions too closely together, much of the excitement may be lost. If promotions are scheduled too far apart, competition may have an opportunity to move in and undercut your program.

In addition, retailers like manufacturers to conduct promotions to fit their individual promotional schedules. Sometimes, these do not coincide with the needs of the manufacturer. To keep the retailer promoting the product, the marketer must therefore develop a sound, consistent sales promotion program that will appeal to the trade. And the timing can be as important to the success of the event as the sales device being used.

While there are undoubtedly other reseller and reselling problems, these five are the major ones. They are also the problems for which sales promotion can provide the most help.

Solving Reseller and Reselling Problems

Before suggesting specific sales promotion techniques that might be used to offset, overcome, or take advantage of the reseller problems and opportunities just discussed, let's first review several general points about sales promotion, the trade, and how the two work together.

First, we caution you to determine the exact cause of the reselling problem before deciding on a solution. Often, reselling problems are caused by other related factors, such as competitive activities or a poor effort on the part of the sales force. So, the first step is to determine as well as you can the root cause of the problem. Then, and only then, can you select the proper sales promotion tool to offset or overcome it.

To solve reseller problems, you must understand the difference between how the manufacturer and the retailer view sales promotion. The manufacturer looks on sales promotion as a method of increasing sales.

It's part of his marketing mix, with all elements designed primarily to move his specific brand of product from his plant to the retail store and then to the consumer.

Retailers, on the other hand, usually view a sales promotion program developed by the manufacturer on the basis of the time and cost required versus the amount of revenue they expect it to generate for them. The retailer's first concern is in making a sale at his store. Often, he doesn't really care what he sells as long as every customer who comes in buys something (assuming there are normal margins on products sold). Therefore, if the manufacturer's sales promotion plan requires a great deal of time to implement or doesn't generate store traffic, the retailer will not have much interest in it. The retailer is interested in sales through his store. If the manufacturer's program generates those sales, he'll cooperate. If it doesn't, or in his opinion won't, he will likely be unwilling to put much time or effort into supporting the promotion.

Before going on, we should also quickly review the manufacturer's objectives for sales promotion directed to the trade. According to the American Association of Advertising Agencies, sales promotion to the trade can help:

- Get or improve distribution.
- Increase shelf space in the stores.
- Build or flush warehouse inventories.
- Introduce product improvements, new sizes, new flavors, etc.
- Get retail activity.
- Counter competition.[1]

There may be others, but these are primary. The ultimate objective, of course, is to get additional consumer sales with the help and cooperation of the retailer.

There are several necessary ingredients in building a successful trade sales promotion program, regardless of its ultimate goal.

1. The sales promotion program must provide a financial incentive to the trade in the form of increased margins or increased profits or increased sales.
2. The timing must be correct. There are three primary times for sales promotion programs to the trade:
   a. A seasonal event to help build on a typically growing sales period.
   b. A trade sales promotion event designed to coincide with a consumer sales promotion program.

1. Sales Promotion Committee, American Association of Advertising Agencies, *Sales Promotion Techniques: A Basic Guidebook* (New York: American Association of Advertising Agencies, 1978), p. 49.

    c. A sales promotion event developed to offset or negate competitive activities.
3. The device proposed must require little additional work and minimal costs for the retailer.
4. It must generate additional sales immediately in the retail store, or it must generate additional store traffic.
5. It should help the dealers do a better selling job in the store or improve their method of retailing.

To simplify our discussion, we have divided trade sales promotion activities into two general groups: (1) internal activities, or techniques directed only to the trade, and (2) external activities, or techniques that go through the trade but whose ultimate objective is the consumer.

We have also divided our discussion here between sales promotion programs designed to be used with retailers and those to be used with wholesalers or distributors. Since the purposes of the two are often different, a separate discussion is necessary. More will be said about distributors and wholesalers in Chapter 13, which deals specifically with the sales forces, brokers, distributors, and sales representatives.

Internal Sales Promotion Techniques

The importance of internal sales promotion programs is growing rapidly. The increasing amount of self-service shopping and the declining importance of personal selling for many types of products require sales promotion programs to motivate not only the consumer but the reseller too. Remember, you might have the best product available, support it with the best advertising, and offer the best service. But if the retail salesperson says, "Yes, your brand is all right, but more of our customers like Brand Z and therefore, we're recommending it," your chances of generating adequate sales are poor indeed. That's why internal sales promotion is usually very important for any type of product.

Once the product leaves the manufacturer's plant, he usually loses control over it. He can't determine how it will be stocked, displayed, or sold in the retail store. In his media advertising he may show the product appropriately located and attractively displayed. But when the consumer comes to the retailer to buy, he or she may find the product tossed on the back of the shelf, placed in the wrong section of the store, or perhaps not even unpacked yet. Therefore, although media advertising may be necessary to presell the product, it is vital to get the retailer's cooperation in order to maximize the advertising investment. If retailers do not cooperate, all your advertising may go for nought.

Motivating the retailer is similar to motiving other resellers: that is, since the retailer has a wide choice of products to promote, the objective is to get him to promote yours. The problem with the retailer is much more severe, however. Whereas an independent wholesaler, distributor, or broker may represent and sell 20 to 30 brands, the retailer usually has a minimum of 5,000 brands in a supermarket and 7,000 in a drugstore. Many of these brands have developed or will develop some form of retailer motivation program, the objective of which is to encourage stocking and promoting a particular brand. With that many brands available, you can easily see how the sheer volume of materials and approaches presented to the retailer can be overwhelming. As a result, a program that is not carefully planned, not well promoted, and not filled with material of interest to the retailer usually falls on deaf ears.

We have identified seven specific areas of sales promotion that we consider effective internal activities, i.e., useful in influencing the trade: (1) contests, (2) incentives, (3) advertising, (4) trade shows and exhibits, (5) displays and point-of-purchase materials, (6) training materials, and (7) retailer services. The general objectives of these activities are to encourage retailers to stock the product, to show them how to improve sales and profits on the product, and to encourage them to feature and promote the product. We'll look at each area of sales promotion individually.

Before discussing these sales promotion techniques, however, we should point out that they cannot be used with some types of retailers. In most cases, major retail chains have instituted policies that prevent the store manager or personnel from participating individually in any sort of motivation program. Where this is a company policy, a program must usually be submitted to the headquarters office for approval prior to acceptance. This is a most important step. Trying to go around headquarters or doing something on the sly may only create additional problems for you and the store manager involved. When planning any sort of trade promotion program, check first to see who can and who cannot participate. If there are more who can't than can, perhaps an alternative device might be better. In spite of these difficulties, and they seem to be increasing, such programs can provide solid results.

Trade Contests

Contests are a popular method of motivating retailers to promote a particular line of products or a particular item. Generally, contests can be conducted in one of three ways: (1) based on an individual's accomplishment, (2) based on a team's accomplishment, or (3) based on competition among participants. They can be developed on anything from the amount of sales of a new line to just beating last year's sales totals. The type of contest usually depends on the objective, be it sales, profits, or number of items stocked. Contest prizes may range from a wide variety of relatively small prizes to fewer but more substantial prizes with a top award of a trip abroad or an automobile.

No matter who participates, what criteria are established, or what prizes are offered, one cardinal rule applies to all contests: There should be only one objective, and it should be clearly understood and carefully communicated. Since the contest description is not always presented in person but outlined in a brochure, it must be simple, direct, and (most of all) exciting. For example, the Gillette "Miss America" contest, based on the best display, made sure that every participant knew exactly what to do and what to expect (see Figure 12-1).

Trade Incentives

Often, when a contest isn't suitable, or the goal is not just increased sales but includes such objectives as obtaining displays, increased use of promotional material in the store, or expanded shelf space, a dealer incentive program is used. Normally, the incentive is offered for some specific task. The only requirement is that the retailer demonstrate in some way that the objective was achieved. For example, a company seeking off-shelf displays might offer a retail incentive for building a display. The retailer who builds it sends a photo of it to the manufacturer and then receives the award. Similarly, an incentive could be offered for increased product shelf space or the additional stocking of another product size or flavor. Incentives of this sort vary greatly.

Incentive programs to obtain distribution and stocking of a product are widely used. For example, a manufacturer may offer a substantial prize with the first order of the product. Additional incentives may be offered for other purchases, such as the total value of an order, ordering and shipping before a certain date, and ordering the full line. In these instances, the incentive is offered and paid to the retailer for simply complying with the terms of the offer.

Other incentive programs involve premiums for sales of certain products. For example, a manufacturer may set up a coupon program with a catalog of merchandise as incentives. For each unit or case sold, the retailer is awarded points. These points can then be applied against the number required to obtain merchandise from the catalog.

Retailers and their employees can also be rewarded for promoting a product line or brand with "spiffs," or "push money." This is simply an extra incentive, usually in the form of cash, given by a manufacturer to retail sales people to "push" particular models in the product line, certain extra accessories, or just the line itself. It is usually used when personal selling is required at the retail level. The amount of "spiff" needed to get a product promoted at the retail level is difficult to esti-

Figure 12-1   Trade Contest: Gillette Products

Source: William A. Robinson, *Best Sales Promotions of 1977/78* (Chicago: Crain Books, 1979), p. 53.

mate. It varies widely from product to product. For example, it might be only a dollar or so on a small item, such as an iron or hair dryer, but can range up to $20 or more on large appliances, such as washing machines, TVs, or dishwashers.

Dealer loaders are another method of providing resellers with an incentive to stock and promote a particular line or brand. Typically, a dealer loader is some form of display unit, such as a wagon, a wheelbarrow, or an outdoor grill that has been filled with the product and is to be used as a display in the retail store. The idea is that the display with the dealer loader will create interest at the retail level and generate extra sales. Once the promotion is over, the retailer gets to keep the unit in which the product was shipped and displayed.

To support a July 4th promotional period, Dr Pepper developed a sales promotion program tied to an outdoor barbecue event. The promotion combined a consumer coupon offer of $2 off on the purchase of steak for an outdoor barbecue and a reduced price on a grill. To generate in-store displays and merchandising for Dr Pepper, bottlers offered food store owners and managers a dealer loader in the form of the barbecue grill. (See Figure 12-2.) The grill was used as the focal point around which an in-store display could be built for the event. When the promotion period was over, the store owner or manager got to keep the grill as a reward for participating.

Dealer loaders can be quite effective, but they have some problems. Many chain stores have rules that prevent their store managers from accepting dealer loaders and prizes or even participating in contests. Before planning any sort of financial reward for dealers or retailers, be sure there is no rule against it by the chain or other dealer organization with which it is to be used.

Finally, retailer incentives often include gifts and premiums sent by the manufacturer simply to maintain the good will of the retailer. These are small inexpensive items mailed on a regular basis or distributed by the sales force. The most commonly used are personal items, such as pens, lighters, and desk sets. Called advertising specialties, these incentives are in widespread use throughout most forms of business.

Trade incentives can often be used to solve in-store sales promotion problems. They call attention to the product or product line and help generate both retailer and consumer interest. In addition, they seem to work well in opening up new geographic territories or new trade categories.

Trade Advertising

Another method of developing internal promotion support is through trade advertising. This is simply advertising developed by the manufacturer and placed in trade magazines read by resellers, such as *Supermarket News, Drug Topics,* and *Discount Merchandiser.* The advertising is used to advise the resellers of new or present advertising and promotional programs or simply to convince retailers to stock and sell the manufacturer's brand. An example of a trade ad is illustrated in Figure 12-3. As you can see, White Horse Scotch announced a new consumer contest to its dealers and sought reseller cooperation.

Trade advertising is commonly used to:

Figure 12-2   Trade Incentive: Dr Pepper

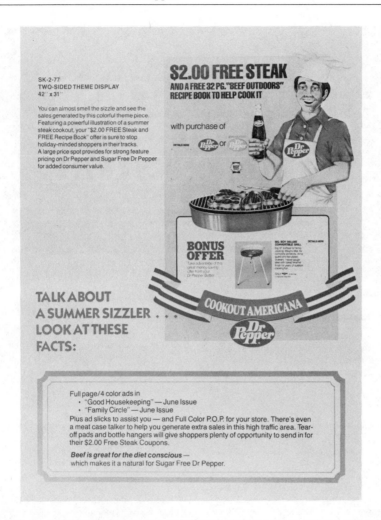

Source: Courtesy of Dr Pepper Co.

- Announce a new or improved product.
- Announce a special promotion, deal, or other event.
- Announce the availability of retail and merchandising selling aids, such as point-of-purchase material, advertising cooperative agreements, and training programs.
- Merchandise the consumer media advertising program to the

Figure 12-3 Trade Advertising: White Horse Scotch

WHITE HORSE BRINGS TRAFFIC TO YOUR STORE

Your customers **must** read a
White Horse back label to win one of these cars in the exciting
"Win A White Horse Of Your Own" Contest

Maverick.   Pinto   Mustang   Bronco

That's because the information needed to answer the contest questions can be found *only* on the back label of a bottle of White Horse Scotch.

36 million readers will see the advertisement announcing the contest this month in *Time, Newsweek, U.S. News & World Report, Esquire, New York Times Sunday Magazine* and *Ebony.* That means extra traffic in your store—and extra sales.

You're not legally eligible to win a car, but you can certainly win the extra business. There will be eye-catching counter cards and case cards, with entry blanks attached, to help you promote the contest—and to sell White Horse Scotch.

Don't get caught short. Stock up on White Horse now—and be sure to put it where people can see it. A lot of people will be looking for it.

BLENDED SCOTCH WHISKY • 86 PROOF • FOUR ROSES DISTILLERS CO., N.Y.C.

Source: William A. Robinson, *100 Best Sales Promotions of 1975/76* (Chicago: Crain Books, 1976), p. 28.

dealers. A common method is a list of where and when the consumer advertisements will appear, the amount being invested in the program, the theme of the advertising, and so on.

Trade advertising is often used to comply with laws requiring that resellers be advised of the available manufacturer's programs, such as discounts and special offers, to help them promote and merchandise their products.

Many manufacturers place little importance on trade advertising since they believe their sales force can do the entire selling job. While that may be true in some instances, it is not very common. And, therefore, trade advertising should be an integral part of any sales promotion program. Many manufacturers rely on wholesaler or distributor sales organizations to call on dealers and retailers. But when this is done, there is really no way of knowing whether these salespeople did a complete selling job. Trade advertising can help ensure that the sales message is delivered. It is a relatively inexpensive but usually effective way to sell dealers on your product and your sales promotion program.

While trade advertising can be used to overcome some of the reseller and reselling problems we have described, we believe it is usually better suited to help prevent the development of problems. With trade advertising, you can stay in touch with your resellers, telling them what you are doing to help them and illustrating more and better ways to profit from your products. If you can prevent the problem, you won't have to solve it later.

Trade Shows

In many industries, such as clothing, furniture, toys, and appliances, the trade show or exhibit is the main selling event for the manufacturer. Retailers travel to the trade show and place their orders for the coming season or the next several months. As a result, a manufacturer who does not sell his line at the trade show is often in for a rough year. In other product lines, trade shows and exhibits are not necessarily order-placing events but are an excellent opportunity to display and demonstrate the product line to prospective retailers or purchasers.

Some trade shows, such as the Food Marketing Institute's annual show for food retailers, involve specific industries. At the FMI show, food manufacturers exhibit their products, but equipment and service organizations catering to the food retailer do so as well. It is an excellent place to demonstrate and show related products to retailers.

There are more than 5,000 trade shows and exhibits each year in the U.S. and many international shows as well. The decision as to whether or not to attend or exhibit must be made on the basis of a cost-benefit analysis. For example, consider first how many of your customers or prospects are likely to attend the show. Next, relate this to the cost of attending. And be sure you have all costs, not just the display space. You must include the cost of building an exhibit and having someone attend to it and the incidental costs of participation, such as shipping the exhibit, travel for salespeople, and so forth. Then compare the cost to the number of prospects you might see and determine whether or not it is an economical sales method.

If you decide to enter a trade show or exhibit, we strongly urge you to enlist the aid of a professional display or exhibit builder. These people are experienced in developing displays that are attractive and easy to ship, store, and set up.

Trade show booths and exhibits may range in cost from a few hundred to several thousand dollars. The key ingredient in determining what to invest in a display is to determine what return it is expected to bring: How much in sales can you expect or how important is the display in your overall selling program?

Typically, the way to develop a display or exhibit is to have three or four exhibit manufacturers submit sketches and bids for units designed to suit your needs. On the basis of these bids and suggestions, you select the company that offers the most attractive unit at the most realistic price.

Trade shows and exhibits are often excellent ways to gain distribution in new trade categories. By demonstrating what can be done with your product, you can often obtain commitments on the spot. Since retailers are often on the lookout for new products or new lines that will help them improve sales and profits, trade shows can give excellent exposure. Trade shows also give you an opportunity to demonstrate to existing retailers how your product should be displayed and merchandised in the store. Seeing it in person is much stronger than simply seeing or hearing about it through printed sales materials. Finally, a trade show can be a good opportunity to present new or planned sales promotion events to both present and prospective resellers.

Displays and Point-of-Purchase Materials

Perhaps the single most important type of internal promotion to the trade is the offering of displays or point-of-purchase materials for use at retail. Usually, only 20 of some of the 9,000 to 10,000 items in a typical supermarket can be featured at any one time. To be one of those 20 requires a very effective sales promotion plan that the retailer believes will help increase sales. The product's sale is heavily dependent on the retailer's promotional activities. Point-of-purchase or display material furnished by the manufacturer can often help the retailer.

Figure 12-4   Off-the-Shelf Display: Florida Department of Citrus

Source: William A. Robinson, *100 Best Sales Promotions* (Chicago: Crain Books, 1980), p. 45.

A major method of increasing sales for many products is through off-the-shelf displays, i.e., displays or features in aisles or at the end of gondolas that are used in the store to increase or improve the sale of the product. They may or may not include manufacturer-originated p-o-p materials. For example, an off-the-shelf display built by one retailer for Florida canned orange and grapefruit juice is illustrated in Figure 12-4. Notice that it combined p-o-p material furnished by the Florida Department of Citrus and material the retailer developed on his own. The combination was most effective in helping move more Florida juice products.

In addition to the displays the retailer may build in the store, some manufacturers—such as cigarette companies, magazine distributors, and health and beauty-aids manufacturers—may actually rent space in retail stores for displays of their products. While this can be a costly method of distribution, it does guarantee that the product will be stocked and available. Often, this sort of approach is used with products that have difficulty getting regular floor or shelf space. A major problem with this technique is that, once started, it is almost impossible to stop. (In our opinion, when space is rented or floor space purchased on a long-term basis, it is not technically a sales promotion activity but simply a paid form of distribution.)

Point-of-purchase materials are items that the manufacturer makes available to the retailer for in-store display and promotional purposes. P-o-p materials may range from a shelf-strip to posters or banners to a counter self-merchandiser. An example of an integrated set of point-of-purchase materials developed by Borden, Inc., for its "Home for the Holidays" program is shown in Figure 12-5. Notice there are many types of materials. The idea is to provide in-store materials that will fit almost any type of food outlet and any size of display or feature the retailer may wish to develop.

Retailers use p-o-p materials to increase sales in the store, to encourage impulse sales, or to improve sales in self-service situations. This is increasingly important for food and drug stores, particularly, and increasingly so in other retail outlets, such as hardware, discount, and even appliance stores. A survey conducted by the Point-of-Purchase Advertising Institute and Dupont found that two out of three purchases made in supermarkets were "unplanned"; that is, shoppers did not have the item they eventually purchased on a shopping list when they went to the store. These are the growing "impulse" sales that p-o-p seeks to influence.

Also, in the Dupont study, the incidence of purchase and the presence of displays in the supermarket and advertising by the store were correlated. It was found that consumer purchases were greater when there was a display in the store than when there was not. Sales increased even more when the store had media advertising for the product, and they were the highest of all when advertising and displays were both used to influence shoppers. The net effect is that displays and point-of-purchase materials seem to have a definite effect on shoppers and encourage them to make either additional purchases or trigger the "impulse" purchase in a great number of food shopping situations.[2]

Point-of-purchase materials are offered and used more widely in

2. Louis J. Haugh, "Buying Habits Study Update—Average Purchase up 121%," *Advertising Age*, June 27, 1977, p. 56.

Figure 12-5 Point-of-Purchase Materials: Borden Foods

Source: William A. Robinson, *100 Best Sales Promotions of 1976/7* (Chicago: Crain Books, 1977), pp. 16-17.

some product categories than others. Table 12-4, developed by the Point-of-Purchase Advertising Institute, shows the very different percentages of advertising and sales promotion budgets spent on point-of-purchase materials by different industries.

Table 12-4 Percentage of Advertising/Sales Promotion Budget Spent on Point-of-Purchase Materials by Industry

Industry	Percent
Beer	21.7
Cosmetics	19.0
Liquor	17.2
Soft drinks	12.4
Petroleum products	10.0
Foods	7.9
Automobiles	5.0
Insurance	1.0

Source: Point-of-Purchase Advertising Institute.

Table 12-5 Methods of Distributing Point-of-Purchase Materials

Method of Distribution	Percent Using
P-o-p material distributed free	79.3
Small fee or nominal charge	5.2
Sold at full cost	5.7
Provided free with product purchase of a specified amount	8.6
Other methods	1.2
Total	100.0

Source: Point-of-Purchase Advertising Institute.

The average expenditure for all advertisers using point-of-purchase materials was 7.9 percent of their advertising and sales promotion budgets. In addition, it was found that manufacturers use varying methods of distributing point-of-purchase materials. (See Table 12-5.) As you can see, point-of-purchase materials are an important form of sales promotion for many types of industries, and, in most cases, these materials are given to the retailer free.[3]

The real questions that the sales promotion manager must answer about point-of-purchase materials are: (1) "What makes good point-of-purchase materials?" and (2) "How can I make sure they get used?" These are major problems, for, although you may design and ship what you consider to be an outstanding piece of point-of-purchase material, it is a waste of money unless it gets used. We estimate that only about 25 percent of all display materials sent out by manufacturers are ever used in the retail outlet. How can you make sure your material gets used? We suggest the following:

1. Design it for the outlet in which it will be used. In other words, know the size, shape, type, and construction of materials your retailers can and have used. Get into the store. Look at the available space. Make sure your material will fit in terms of both size and format.
2. Make sure the material fits the décor of the store. Don't use gaudy, day-glo materials with an expensive product. It will cheapen your image, and the retailer won't use it.

3. O. M. Stark, from a speech given at the "Tools of Promotion Workshop," meeting of Association on National Advertisers, New York, 1975.

3. P-o-p materials must be easy to set up and use. Retailers are in the labor business, too. If it takes too much time to erect, organize, or put up, your materials will stay in the storeroom.
4. Make it possible for the retailer to tie in. Go-togethers, combination offers, and the like give the retailer a chance to use one display for more than one product. And don't forget to leave a place for the store to insert the price. Lack of a price-spot may be the single biggest error in point-of-purchase materials shipped to retail stores.
5. Make the material exciting for the sales force. Give them things they like. If the salespeople don't like the p-o-p, they won't encourage the retailers to use it.
6. Design material the store manager will like. You must sell him too. If the manager doesn't like the material, it stays in the back room.
7. Finally, the material must sell consumers. You must give them a reason to buy. Trigger the impulse sale. Remember, more than half the sales in supermarkets are made on impulse.[4] Be sure your p-o-p materials help those sales.

A major factor to remember in developing point-of-purchase material is simply that the retailer is the "buyer" of p-o-p materials, not the seller. Give him something he wants and can use to improve all sales in his store, not just those for your brand. That's the key to getting the material used.

There are three major reasons that point-of-purchase materials are not used.

1. The p-o-p is poorly planned. There is no incentive for the retailer to use it. It is designed to impress the manufacturer, not the retailer.
2. The materials take up too much space for the amount of sales they will likely generate.
3. They are too unwieldy, too difficult to set up, too flimsy, or have other construction defects.

If you want your materials used in the store, avoid these problems.

Often, point-of-purchase materials fail because they are designed or developed by people who have little experience or background in the retail field. If you lack that experience, we suggest you contact display suppliers and have them help you develop sound, effective point-of-purchase materials. Most will submit designs and give you quotations for construction, including shipment. They can be especially helpful if you do not ship or distribute your own materials. The best way to work with a p-o-p suppliers is to invite two or three of them to hear your problem and then submit designs, suggestions, and estimates. Based on those quotes, you can then select a supplier and work directly with him.

---

4. Stark, "Tools of Promotion Workshop."

Point-of-purchase materials can vary widely in cost. Because each manufacturer's need is different, the best method of evaluating material cost is first to determine what it is to accomplish. Next, estimate how much of the selling job it should accomplish and the approximate dollar sales it should generate. Finally, relate this sales goal to the cost of the material. As a rule of thumb, the p-o-p materials should not cost more than 2 to 3 percent of the sales you estimate they will generate.

Finally, be sure the point-of-purchase materials are in the store when needed. That is a major problem for many sales promotion managers. The materials must be there in time to fit in with a planned event. For planning purposes, the following schedule seems to work for a major promotion:

- Plan the materials at least 24 weeks in advance.
- Have the materials designed 18 weeks ahead.
- Test the materials 15 weeks in advance.
- Produce the materials 10 weeks in advance of the date to be used.
- Distribute the materials four weeks ahead of the time they should be used.[5]

While this is only a rough estimate, it should give you an idea of the length of time needed to do a proper job.

Remember, point-of-purchase material must do one specific job: attract the attention of the consumer in the store. If it does not do that, it has failed to do the job either for you or the retailer.

Training Materials

Another way to combat or solve reseller problems is through sales training materials. If the retailer does not know how to merchandise, stock, or display your product properly, he cannot do the best job selling it. Sales training is more important in some product categories than others. For example, with products that require a high degree of personal selling, such as hi-fi sets, automobiles, and furniture, the knowledge of the salesperson on the retail floor can either make or break the sale. That is why it's important to develop sales training materials—and to get retailers to use them.

Sales training and sales training aids for retailers are often developed by the manufacturer and distributed to all retailers. These sales programs may be sent direct or distributed by the sales force or through meetings conducted by the sales force. Sales training usually consists of material or information that helps the retailer do a better product-selling job. That might include explanations of the product: how it is con-

---

5. Stark, "Tools of Promotion Workshop."

structed, how it works, or why it is better than competition. It may also consist of information and materials on how the product should be used by consumers or why a consumer would want it. Sales training devices may range from a simple brochure, shipped with the product or mailed to the retailer, to elaborate meetings, several days in length, held in a resort area, and paid for by the manufacturer. They might be detailed fact books or attachments, such as hang-tags, instructional booklets, competitive comparisons, and point-of-purchase and display materials. The amount of sales training depends on the importance of the retailer in the final sale of the product and the value of total business the individual retailer contributes to the manufacturer's sales.

The most common form of sales training is that conducted by the sales force as a part of their regular sales call. This might consist of reviewing a brochure with the retailer, showing a brief film clip, or perhaps running a filmstrip on a portable projector in the retailer's store. Sometimes, the salespeople may conduct full-scale sales training sessions with the retailers in a local meeting room or hotel. This is usually done when kicking off a new product or when introducing new models.

Since the actual sales training is usually the province of the sales department, there is no need to discuss it further. The primary responsibility of the sales promotion manager is usually in the preparation of sales training materials. In some instances, a request may be made for the sales promotion manager to write the sales training program itself. If you become involved in this area, we suggest you consult one of the several excellent books devoted entirely to this topic.

Training materials may be part of an overall promotion program or developed individually to support a single product. The Schick counter display in Figure 12-6, for example, was developed by the sales promotion department for use in retail stores to support the very successful promotion campaign.

If you are called upon to prepare training materials for retailers, be sure to consider the following points before you plunge headlong into an elaborate and costly project.

First, have a reason for providing sales training materials. Have a specific goal you want to accomplish. Don't just say, "Let's tell the retailer something." Sales training materials can be used to (1) explain the details of how a product works, operates, or differs from competition; (2) show a new or changed feature or improvement; (3) demonstrate how to sell more of the product or how to combine the product with other items to increase total store sales; (4) illustrate where and how to display the product; or (5) show how to build a display or how to conduct a special sale or simply how to sell more of the product itself. If you define your sales training goals, the job of developing the materials will be much easier.

Figure 12-6   Training Materials: Schick Shavers

Source: Robinson, *100 Best Sales Promotions of 1975/6*, p. 21.

Getting the sales training material used is a major problem, particularly with retailers, simply because they must take time away from their job or give up their free time. The best way to get sales materials used is to make them easy to use. For brochures, audio tapes, filmstrips, movies, and for very important events—such as new model introductions—a special meeting at a place away from the retail location usually works best. Whatever you choose, remember that the training material must be clear and comprehensible. Retailers simply will not spend time or effort to fight their way through long or involved explanations. Be simple and be direct.

Sales training materials costs can vary widely. Again, determine how important the training job is, what you expect it to do, and what sales increase you can expect if it works, and relate that to the anticipated cost. In that way you can see whether or not the cost is worth the benefit.

Retailer Services

While retailer services will not do the entire job, they can be used to help solve some reseller problems. These are general sales promotion materials or items that the manufacturer supplies to assist retailers in their overall sales efforts: ad-making materials, such as mats, cuts, and illustrations; or nonproduct posters, banners, flags, and other display materials, change mats, cash register signs, and the like. In general, retailer services are all those materials provided by the manufacturer that may not directly result in a sale of the product but can and will be used by the retailer in the operation of his business. Many times, these materials must be viewed as gifts or expenses since they don't directly generate sales, but the scheduling and handling of them is usually the responsibility of the sales promotion manager.

External Sales Promotion Techniques

We defined external sales promotion as those activities that may go through the trade but whose ultimate objective is to influence the consumer. We have found that there are six major types of external sales promotion activities that can help to overcome reseller or reselling problems: (1) cooperative advertising, (2) trade coupons, (3) trade deals, (4) demonstrations, (5) service programs, and (6) local and regional sales promotion programs. Usually these tactics are designed to help the retailer generate sales of the manufacturer's product directly to the consumer.

Cooperative Advertising

Cooperative advertising is often also called vertical cooperative advertising. This is to differentiate it from that form of advertising in which competitive firms join together to promote the common good. Here, we define cooperative advertising as an offer by a manufacturer or supplier to assist the retailer in promoting the manufacturer's products to the consumer in some form of media. The target of all cooperative advertising is the consumer. The goal is to create a consumer demand that will pull the goods out of the store.[6]

When we talk about cooperative advertising, we traditionally think of a newspaper ad placed by the retailer and partially paid for by the

---

6. Stark, "Tools of Promotion Workshop."

manufacturer. The truth is, cooperative advertising can be any cooperative effort by the manufacturer and the retailer to promote the product to the consumer, although it is usually an ad placed in some form of local media. Thus, it could include radio, TV, direct mail, flyers, and so on. An example of a cooperative advertisement is shown in Figure 12-7. The manufacturer is Glad trash bags and the retailers are the Centrella Stores listed in the ad. The advertisement ran in the *Chicago Tribune*, which covers the geographic area in which the stores are located.

The usual cooperative advertising agreement is an offer from the manufacturer to pay 50 percent of the cost of any approved local advertising placed by the retailer in support of the product. Normally, the advertising must meet certain specifications as to size, type of advertisement, and medium before the manufacturer will rebate his portion. For example, suppose a retailer and the manufacturer of Widgets set up a cooperative advertising agreement. The manufacturer agrees that he will pay 50 percent of any newspaper advertising placed by the retailer on behalf of Widgets. Thus if the retailer purchased an advertisement for $90, then the manufacturer would pay $45 on receiving proof that the advertisement appeared, such as a newspaper tearsheet. The rebate could be made either in cash or as a credit memo.

While the normal arrangement is 50/50 for the manufacturer and the retailer, many other types of cooperative agreements are possible. The retailer could pay 50 percent; the wholesaler, 25 percent; and the manufacturer, 25 percent; or the advertising cost could be shared equally among the three.

Manufacturers commonly use cooperative advertising for several reasons. First, cooperative advertising can be used when a manufacturer has limited distribution of the product in a market. That might be because of an exclusive retailer or a situation in which the product may be purchased in only a few locations. The idea in this case is to sell the brand, not the retailer, in the advertising, although the advertisement would identify the retailer as the place to buy the product. This is most common in the clothing, furniture, major appliance, and automobile categories. Second, if the retailer is not properly supporting the brand with retail advertising, the manufacturer might suggest a cooperative advertising agreement to get local support and representation. Manufacturers also develop cooperative advertising agreements to guarantee that the advertising is placed locally, to get some form of local price or retail feature advertising, and to take advantage of the difference in the local and national media advertising rates. Many newspapers and radio stations still charge retailers a lower rate than they do national advertisers, often as much as 50 percent less. In these cases, the manufacturer may institute a cooperative advertising plan simply to stretch his advertising dollars.

Figure 12-7   Cooperative Advertising: Glad Trash Bags

Source: Courtesy of *Chicago Tribune*.

J. O. Peckham, Sr., using data collected by A. C. Nielsen Company, suggests that cooperative advertising is most effective when it:

1. Is tied in with store display.
2. Is tied in with special feature price.
3. Reinforces the manufacturer's basic advertising story or consumer promotions.[7]

While the cooperative advertising agreement sounds like a great way to extend advertising funds, there are some problems as well as additional costs inherent in such plans.

1. The manufacturer usually supplies the retailer with the material necessary for the preparation of the advertisement. This cost is over and above the cost of the advertising space or time. With a large number of retailers participating in a cooperative advertising plan, production of advertising materials can become quite expensive.
2. There is always a mass of paperwork involved in a cooperative advertising program. The retailer must submit bills, tearsheets, etc., and the manufacturer must check, approve, and pay. In broadcast, the problem is even more complex since the proof of performance is an affidavit from the station that broadcast the commercials. In large cooperative advertising programs, several people are often required just to do the bookkeeping.
3. Unscrupulous retailers may "double bill" the manufacturer for the cost of cooperative advertising. That is, they may send the manufacturer false statements or statements from the media at higher rates than they acually paid. When the manufacturer rebates the agreed-upon percentage, he may be paying a great deal more than his share of the actual cost.
4. The retail advertising may have waste circulation. Since the retailer is usually not an advertising expert, the media buy may not be efficient or the media choice may be poor—at least from the manufacturer's point of view.
5. A cooperative advertising program can be quite costly and hard to control. Since, under the rules of the Robinson-Patman Act, the manufacturer must make the same cooperative advertising agreement available to all retailers on an equitable basis, once the program is started it can quickly get out of hand. While some strong retailers may use the program well, others may not. All must be paid on the same basis, however.

It is possible (but not likely) for all retailers to use all available

---

7. J. O. Peckham, Sr., *The Wheel of Marketing* (Scarsdale, N.Y.: Privately printed, 1978), p. 29.

cooperative advertising funds at the same time, in which case the manufacturer's budget would be quickly exhausted. Since normally the manufacturer assumes that only a portion of the retailers will use the available cooperative advertising, he normally doesn't budget for full use. Many times, the co-op budget is over- or underspent, which creates budgetary problems.

While the purpose of cooperative advertising agreements is to provide local support for the product, manufacturers sometimes use them as a competitive weapon. That is, a co-op program is started to prevent a competitor from obtaining support from the retailer. Although it is illegal under Federal Trade Commission regulations, some marketers attempt to use cooperative advertising as a method of gaining distribution. They do this by offering co-op advertising as an additional discount on the product, whether it actually appears or not. (See Chapter 15 for more details on the legal aspects of cooperative advertising.) Generally, though, most types of cooperative advertising programs are legal as long as they are offered to all retailers under the same conditions in a given marketing area. It is best, however, to have any program checked out by a qualified legal expert.

We believe cooperative advertising can be effectively used to help solve reseller problems. It can certainly help get support for the brand at the local level. Our major objection to this use of sales promotion money is the great amount of time and potential cost required to administer and monitor the program, and the lack of control manufacturers often have over what retailers do with the available funds.

Trade Coupons

Another form of trade promotion that can be used to solve reseller problems is the trade coupon, which often appears as an "in-ad" coupon. It is now estimated that about twice as many trade coupons are being used in the U.S. as are manufacturer coupons. This is a dramatic shift in emphasis in the past few years.

Trade coupons are usually manufacturer-supported coupons that either appear in the retailer's advertisements or are used in the retail store. In essence, they are a kind of cooperative venture between the manufacturer and a single retailer or retail chain. The usual basis is an agreement between the retailer and the manufacturer for some kind of advertising allowance. This permits the retailer to make some type of coupon offer, either as a price reduction or as a combination offer. An example of in-ad coupons is illustrated in Figure 12-8.

The most important advantage of trade coupons is that they usually generate great retailer enthusiasm for the product. Trade coupons give the retailer something his competitor may not have or may not be using

Figure 12-8   Trade Coupons: Walgreens Drug Stores

Source: Courtesy of Walgreen's Drug Stores.

at that exact time. (Note: Under the Robinson-Patman Act, the manufacturer must offer the same allowances to all retailers in a market area on a proportionate basis, but the promotions need not be scheduled at the same time.) Trade coupons also give the advantage of a reduced price or special offer, which retailers like and which also appeals to consumers.

When used to regain distribution, open up new areas, or move into new trade categories, the in-ad coupon has great appeal to both the manufacturer and the retailer. It makes sure the offer gets to the consumer and generates retail store traffic. It's a way of getting retailer cooperation in a sales promotion program. It also gives the manufacturer the opportunity to take advantage of retail strengths in the local market to build sales for the product.

Another major advantage of trade coupons is the fact that they seem to be much more effective in generating both short- and long-term sales than straight price reductions or other promotional devices, such as price-packs. J. O. Peckham, Sr., found that trade coupons had a greater effect long term in 83 specific case histories than did "in-store" special offers. This is illustrated in Table 12-6. As you can see, the trade coupons resulted in a higher level of sales after the promotion than was achieved through the "in-store" special.

In a trade coupon, retailers often offer the consumer more than the

Table 12-6   In-Store Special Offers vs. Trade Coupons

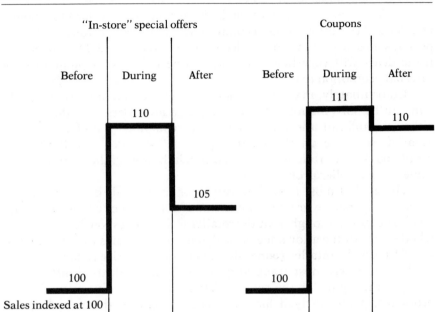

Source: Peckham, *The Wheel of Marketing,* p. 40.

discount the manufacturer has agreed upon. The retailer adds to the value of the coupon at his own expense to make it a "leader" or a "feature" item. When this happens, the value of the sales promotion device is quite attractive and usually generates substantial sales.

Trade and in-ad coupons are growing in popularity as manufacturers and retailers alike attempt to build sales through consumer incentives.

Trade Allowances or Trade Deals

Purely and simply, a trade allowance or a trade deal is nothing more than a temporary or periodic price reduction device used by the manufacturer to gain a short-term advantage with the retailer. In effect, it is a price reduction offered by the manufacturer to the retailer. It can take many forms, such as a buying allowance, a stocking allowance, free goods, or some other "deal." The key point is that the offer or price incentive is given by the manufacturer to the retailer. It may or may not reach the consumer, depending on whether or not the retailer decides to pass the reduction along. Although the sales promotion manager normally is not responsible for trade deals, he is often responsible for the development of materials to sell the "deal."

Probably no sales promotion device is more widely used for solving reseller and reselling problems than trade allowances or trade deals. And perhaps no sales promotion device is more often abused. In spite of this, trade deals will very likely continue to be the most popular form of internal promotion to the trade.

Unfortunately, many manufacturers believe that any reseller problem can be solved simply by offering a greater margin to the retailer either through an allowance or a price reduction. Therefore, there is great dependence on the technique as a "cure-all" for all types of problems. While trade deals can do much, however, they simply can't solve every reseller problem.

The goal of most trade allowances or trade deals by the manufacturer is to generate greater movement of the product at the consumer level. The fact is, though, that the retailer is the one responsible for seeing whether or not the allowance or deal actually generates increased retail sales. Unless the retailer cooperates and passes the price reduction along to the consumer, most trade allowances or trade deals result only in increased margins for the retailer. While this may solve some reseller problems, particularly if lack of margin is one of them, it does not necessarily result in increased consumer purchases.

Trade allowances or trade deals are almost always required on any new product or in any attempt to gain additional distribution, enter new areas, or gain distribution in new trade categories. The retailer usually has a sufficient supply of other products and brands on the shelf. To encourage him to either replace one of those with the new product or add a product to his inventory requires more than a normal profit margin. In addition, to prevent distribution losses, manufacturers often initiate trade allowances to load the retailer and also to make it unattractive for him to drop their product.

There are as many types of trade deals as there are manufacturers, each with its own particular advantages and disadvantages. In order to use the right trade incentive to solve reseller problems, it is vital to pinpoint exactly what the problem is and why it has occurred. Only by doing that can the sales manager know how to structure the price reduction.

Demonstrators

Although not a major factor in many product categories, the use of demonstrators as a sales promotion device has some specific advantages that can't be obtained in any other way.

A demonstration is simply an exhibition of how a product works or how a food is prepared or even how a product tastes. In most instances, the manufacturer hires a person (the demonstrator) to go to a retail store and show or demonstrate the product, its features, or its advantages. Typically, the manufacturer pays the cost of the demonstrator and the retailer's only obligation is to provide the space and have the product on hand. Usually, however, there is some cooperative agreement on how the demonstration will be publicized and advertised to the consumer and whether or not the demonstrator will pass out samples, coupons, or the like.

Almost any type of consumer product can be demonstrated in some way. For example, demonstrations have been held in department and appliance stores to show how vacuum cleaners work and how they operate. Demonstrators in hardware, department, and specialty stores have shown how certain pots and pans can be used to prepare special foods. Food companies have used demonstrators in supermarkets to hand out samples of their products, ranging from prepared frozen pizza to soft drinks. And even wine and liquor organizations have "demonstrated" the taste of their products with free samples in liquor stores. The primary purpose of the demonstration, of course, is to dramatize the product and illustrate how it works, tastes, or can be used and to attempt to generate an immediate sale.

In many instances, demonstrators can do what no other form of advertising or sales promotion can do—that is, put the product directly into the hands of the consumer and give a personal sales message. For that reason, they can be most helpful in generating in-store sales and interest. Often, demonstrators also pass out coupons good for a price reduction on the product for a limited period of time. Usually, this coupon is redeemable only in the location at which the demonstration is taking place.

Demonstrators can solve some types of reseller and reselling problems. They are particularly effective in introducing new products or introducing products into new trade categories. They can also be helpful in holding distribution in present locations by showing the retailer that the manufacturer is truly interested in seeing sales of the product increase in his store. Unfortunately, as helpful as demonstrators can be, there are disadvantages, the chief of which is cost. A minimum of $125 per day is usually required in urban areas to have a person demonstrate a food product in a supermarket. The use of demonstrators is also limited by agreement with the retailers, by restrictions on what can be demonstrated in some stores, and by laws about how food products must be prepared or served in a demonstration situation. Finally, a demonstrator is usually not a full-time employee of the manufacturer. As a result, quality varies widely, and while some demonstrators do excellent jobs, others may hurt sales more than help them.

Demonstrators should be used with great care. If you are not familiar with demonstrators, demonstrations, or in-store promotions of this type, you should do much experimenting to find the best mix for your individual product before launching an extensive program.

Service Promotions

Reseller problems may also be solved by use of a service promotion. By this we mean a sales promotion device that, although sponsored by a manufacturer, does not have the sale of the brand as its primary goal. One such example is the program Del Monte has used successfully for a number of years. In this event, Del Monte furnishes very general or "theme" in-store display material to the retail food stores. The retailers then build an in-store sales promotion program around that material. While Del Monte obviously wants the retailer to feature some Del Monte products in the retail sales promotion program, that is not the total goal of the event.

Service promotions are often hard to justify in a sales promotion budget. Since they are not specifically product oriented and are developed primarily as a service to the retailer, it is often difficult to know whether or not they have been successful. Normally, sales do not get a big boost from this type of promotion since the goal is to build a total sales promotion for the retail store and not just a branded one. There are long-term benefits that may accrue, such as increased awareness of the brand by consumers, but the chief gain is probably the good will of retailers who use the material successfully.

Local and Regional Sales Promotion Programs

Often, a sales promotion program is needed on the local or regional level to meet specific reseller situations. For example, there may be concern that a particularly important retailer is considering stocking a competitive brand or is evaluating alternative sales promotion programs for use at a particular time. In these instances, it is helpful to have available a few tested and proven sales promotion programs that can be initiated quickly. These can be left in the hands of the sales promotion manager or put into action by field personnel. A good example of this type of sales promotion program is the group of standing promotions maintained by the fast-food chains. If one chain starts a sales promotion or advertising program, competitors reach into their war chests and pull out promotions of their own.

Summary

There are many sales promotion techniques that can be used to solve reseller and reselling problems and take advantage of opportunities. The key, of course, is to use the proper tool. In this chapter, we have shown thirteen types of reseller or reselling sales promotion devices, including point-of-purchase materials, cooperative advertising, and trade deals. Some work better than others in specific situations. Sales promotion can solve reseller problems if you know the cause and know the techniques that work best.

13

Sales Organization Problems and Opportunities

So far, we have dealt with the major sales promotion problems and opportunities in relation to the economy, the consumer, the product, competition, and resellers. There is another area that is as important as any of these. It is a branch of "internal" sales promotion—i.e., trade promotion—that is directed to what we call the sales organization, which includes the manufacturer's sales force as well as wholesalers, distributors, and brokers. In short, it consists of all the middlemen between the manufacturer and the retailer.

For most products or services, the manufacturer uses his sales force to persuade the wholesaler, distributor, broker, and others to sell the retailer and thus move the product out of the plant and into the stores. These wholesalers, distributors, and brokers must also persuade the retailer to do more than just stock the product; they must be able to encourage him to promote it as well. The retailer must then properly display and promote the product to the consumer in order to complete the final sale. If there is a breakdown anywhere in this distribution chain, sales will usually suffer, and media advertising, sales promotion programs, public relations, and other marketing activities will be wasted.

More and more it appears that if the product is not available, is difficult to find, or is not properly promoted in the retail store, consumers simply won't search it out. They will purchase a substitute or make no purchase at all. That's why the sales organization is so vital to the overall success of the entire marketing program.

Most sales promotion activities directed to the sales organization consist of some form of motivation to encourage salespeople within the system to do a better selling job. Usually, the actual development and implementation of these motivational programs are the responsibility of the sales manager; however, the sales promotion department and the sales promotion manager are often directly involved too. How often, depends on the organization of the company and the extent to which sales promotion is involved in sales management operations. The involvement may range from simply developing and preparing motivation materials that have been planned and will be executed by the sales manager to helping set up and administer the entire sales motivation plan. In almost every instance, though, the sales promotion manager is called upon to help develop and provide materials for the motivation program.

We should stress that, while most of the motivation activities and programs we will discuss in this chapter are considered "add-ons" to the overall marketing and promotional program, without them the sales effort will certainly not be as successful as it could be. While it can't do the entire selling job, motivation does add the extra ingredient that can turn a "so-so" sales organization into a real winner. It can be as powerful a tool in moving additional product as a consumer promotion, a retail trade coupon, or a price reduction. It's the extra step that can make a big difference in marketing results.

For purposes of our discussion, we have divided the sales organization into two major groups, controlled and uncontrolled. The controlled sales organization is made up of salesmen who are directly employed by the manufacturer or marketer and whose activities are controlled by the company. The uncontrolled sales organization consists of groups and individuals who sell the manufacturer's product but over whom the manufacturer has limited control. Depending on the distribution channel, this could consist of wholesalers, distributors, brokers, and retailers. We include retailers in this group because they too must help sell the product to the ultimate consumer. See Chapter 12 for a discussion of how to motivate retailers.

What Are Sales Organization Problems?

Although they operate differently, because of the varying degree of control the manufacturer has over them, the problems and opportunities of the manufacturer-controlled organization (i.e., the manufacturer's sales force) and the uncontrolled sales organization (i.e., the wholesaler, the distributor, and the broker) are basically the same. Usually, the sales organization sells to resellers in some form of one-on-one situation—that is, a manufacturer's salesman calls on a broker or a broker calls on a chain store buyer or a wholesaler calls on an individual retailer. In all cases, the sales message is presented in person. The problems found in these situations are that the salesperson (1) is not achieving the desired sales goals, (2) is not adding to present distribution, or (3) is not obtaining the cooperation of the reseller to promote the product to the consumer. Generally, problems of this type can be traced to five basic causes, most of which can be corrected or eliminated by sales promotion or motivation efforts. They are: (1) poor attitude, (2) neglect of duties, (3) misallocation of time, (4) faulty incentive plans, and (5) inadequate training programs.

Poor Attitude

Studies have shown that many sales forces can be broken down into three production or performance categories: top, average, and marginal. Even those persons considered to be in the elite "top producer" category work only to about 75 percent of their potential capacity. The "average" salespeople work to about 55 percent of their potential, while the "marginal" work only to 35 percent of their true potential.[1] Many times, this inability to work to potential is simply a matter of attitude. For example, the salesperson may have no reason or has not been provided with a sufficiently good reason to encourage him to work or achieve beyond what he is doing now. This sort of situation can often be improved through the use of proper motivation techniques.

Neglect of Duties

Often, sales personnel neglect or do not follow through on what management considers important duties. Usually, this is the result of poor training or poor leadership. Sometimes, it is because the salespeople either do not enjoy doing the tasks or do not feel competent to do them.

All sales activities can be grouped into three basic areas or duties: (1) generating sales either from existing customers or new customers, (2) providing market information in the form of reports, and (3) servicing present customers. Often, the problem is simply that the salesperson has become confused over which of the three areas is most important to success. For example, if the sales manager is constantly stressing the importance of reports and having them in on time, the salesperson may well start to believe that the report is more important than generating new sales. While most sales managers believe their directions are clear, they often are not. The clear description of duties and the specific importance of each is vital in a motivation program.

---

1. O. N. Stark, from a speech given at the "Tools of Promotion Workshop," Association of National Advertisers, New York, 1975.

Misallocation of Time

Time allocation can be a problem in two ways. For the company sales-person, the problem may be the amount of time spent on each of the three sales duties listed above, or it may be the way time is allocated among various customers. For the uncontrolled sales force, time can be allocated to either the manufacturer's line or another noncompetitive line. In either case, the salesperson may not be devoting the proper amount of time to the brand or to the important duties connected with the brand.

Faulty Incentive Plans

Nothing can create more attitude or motivation problems with a sales force than the form, type, and method of remuneration. Although this is not usually the primary responsibility of the sales promotion manager, he is often involved.

The sales promotion manager may either develop or at least provide the materials for sales contests, bonus plans, and incentives for the sales force. These programs usually make up the "extra value" in a sales-person's compensation plan. If they are not well planned, executed, and promoted to the sales force, they can actually do more harm than good. A sales force that doesn't believe an incentive program is equitable, a sales contest goal achievable, or a bonus plan worthwhile will often do less work than if the motivation program had not been used.

The sales promotion manager has the responsibility in many cases of either setting up these plans or at least publicizing them to the sales force. If this is not done clearly and completely, the value and effect may be destroyed. Thus, the sales promotion manager does have a major responsibility in the area of salaries, incentives, and rewards.

Inadequate Training Programs

Many of the problems that occur with the sales force can be traced directly back to a poor sales training program. In most cases, selling today is not simply a matter of going from one reseller to another with the same "sales pitch." Selling at the wholesale and retail levels requires a highly sophisticated approach with total product knowledge, including how the product will perform and how it will fit into the retailer's promotion mix. Such areas as pricing, distribution, margin, and the general promotional program in support of the product are required to make a successful sales presentation. Thus, the sales force needs to be constantly updated on the latest selling techniques, the merits of the product, product information, and the market place. That comes through proper sales training.

In addition, the sales force is often responsible for training the retailers in how to sell or merchandise the product to the consumer. This might include the use of sales promotion programs, advertising schedules, display materials, product information, and so on. Here, unless the salesperson knows how to conduct a sales training program or what materials are available to him to train the retailer, the entire marketing effort may fail.

While the sales manager usually has primary responsibility for sales training, the sales promotion manager is often involved in the development and preparation of the sales training materials.

As you can see, although the sales promotion manager may not be directly responsible for many of the areas in which internal sales problems might occur, there is a strong indirect relationship between his job and that of the salespeople. Often the sales promotion manager is the one who provides the materials needed to help overcome both internal and external sales or selling problems.

Solving Sales Organization Problems

The problems a marketer faces with the sales organization can be many and varied. While the problems are somewhat different from those of the retailer, the primary question the sales promotion manager must answer for both is still: "How can we get them to sell more?"

Before giving suggestions on how to get a sales organization to sell more, let's review a bit. Generally, our efforts to motivate the sales organization (controlled and uncontrolled) will deal with "push" marketing strategy. You will recall that in Chapter 12 we said the "push" strategy is to concentrate the sales effort on the distribution system and the resellers in order to get them to push the product out of the store. That is opposed to a "pull" strategy in which primary promotion emphasis is placed on the consumer. There, the effort is to pull the product through the distribution channels and the retail stores with advertising and sales promotion. Whatever basic marketing strategy the manufacturer employs, the efforts in solving sales organization problems must be of the push variety. Therefore, all our motivation suggestions will revolve around ways to push the product through the distribution system and encourage the retailers to push it out of the store and into the hands of the consumer.

In discussing sales organization problems such as we have described, John C. FitzMaurice of Maritz, Inc., told the Association of National Advertisers Seventh Sales Promotion Management Seminar that he viewed the solution to these problems as an objective evaluation of each of the "means" available. While motivational techniques might

be the answer to the problem, the following questions all suggest promotion options open to the manager:

- Which enables management to organize strategies for accom-
  plishing many of its objectives into an overall marketing plan?
- Which offers the widest possible appeal (or incentive) to the greatest
  number of those subjected to the "push" strategy?
- Which is subject to the most appealing, effective communication?
- Which maximizes the involvement and support of the controlled or
  uncontrolled sales organizations?
- Which has the most favorable effect on cash flow?
- Which is most flexible in terms of its selective application to par-
  ticular accounts, or markets, or products/services, or to different
  levels of sales volume?
- Which provides the best marketing-information feedback? First, to
  assist in evaluating the results of using that particular marketing
  means and, second, to provide data for other management decisions.
- Which maximizes the effectiveness of people?
- How long can the options be used effectively? Are they best for short
  periods or longer periods of continuous use?
- What are the cost characteristics of the various options? Which have
  costs that are essentially fixed once the decision to use the option has
  been made? That is, costs that will be incurred whether the objectives are reached or not.
- Finally, what effect will the promotional alternative have, in a particular application, on some measure of profitability, such as the
  firm's return on investment?[2]

Using these general rules or "means" of FitzMaurice, we can now
look at the various alternatives that can be used to solve the problems
that may have been caused by or that may exist within the selling
organization.

We divide the solutions to problems with the uncontrolled sales
organization into two groups: (1) motivation programs and (2) sales
training and sales aids. Both can be used to overcome these problems.

Motivation Programs

Much of the responsibility for the development and implementation of
motivation programs does not lie directly with the sales promotion
department or the sales promotion manager. Usually, it is the responsibility of the sales manager. Even so, because the sales promotion

2. John C. FitzMaurice, from a speech given at the "Tools of Promotion Workshop," National Association of Advertisers, New York, 1975.

manager is often responsible for the materials and sometimes for the entire motivation program, it is worth discussing. We will deal only with areas pertinent to the sales promotion function and not with such questions as salaries, benefits, territories, sales goals, and the like.

The methods we have found most practical to motivate the sales organization are contests, incentives, and bonus plans.

Contests. Contests have long been a favorite method of generating enthusiasm for a particular sales task. Generally, contests are built around a definite sales goal, although they may also have other objectives, such as increasing new accounts, expanding distribution, and getting accounts to stock the full line. We will discuss the general approach to contests later in this chapter.

Incentives. Like contests, incentives are usually based on sales goals or on some particular achievement by the salesperson. Unlike contests, in which there is short-term competition for the prizes, incentives are usually of longer duration and there is no competition for prizes. If the salesperson achieves the set goal, the incentive is awarded. If not, he gets no reward. Any or all salespeople may win an incentive.

Incentives are set so that the salesperson has a chance of receiving some sort of award. For example, each new customer might be worth a certain prize or a number of points toward a larger prize. The salesperson could add to his or her awards by obtaining additional new customers.

Bonus plans. Bonus plans are similar to incentives, but the reward for achievement is typically increased pay or additional cash. For example, if a salesperson had a yearly sales goal of $1,000,000, he might be awarded a certain amount in the form of a "bonus" simply for achieving that goal. A bonus can be paid for almost any sort of sales activity. The usual objective of a bonus is to reward the meeting or exceeding of certain goals.

More information on these forms of sales force motivation will be found later in this chapter.

Sales Training Materials and Sales Aids

In addition to motivation programs directed toward the sales organization, two other kinds of assistance may be provided by the sales promotion department to help overcome sales organization problems: (1) sales training materials and (2) sales aids.

Sales training materials. The sales promotion manager may be called on to assist in the development of various sales training materials or sales training aids. Generally, there are two types: those used to train the sales organization in selling the product to wholesalers or retailers; and those developed for sales organization use in training their customers to sell the product, such as a sales training program for retailers.

Sales training programs may take many forms, the most common being folders, brochures, cassette tapes, slides and audio tapes, filmstrips, and sometimes even movies. The most common, of course, are printed materials, such as folders, booklets, flyers, and the like, which contain information about the product or how to sell the product.

Complete books have been written on the best way to prepare sales training materials. We won't attempt to cover the subject in detail here, but there are some key points you should keep in mind.

- Be brief but be complete.
- Be sure the story is clear. Remember, most people don't know as much about the product as you do.
- Wherever possible, demonstrate what you mean. Speak in the language your listeners use. Don't use big words. In other words, eschew polysyllabic verbiage.
- Keep it lively. Don't bore the listener.
- Tell why your suggestions work. Support your story.
- Use programmed learning. Tell them what you're going to tell them. Tell them. And then tell them what you've told them.
- Make the material easy to use. Don't require a lot of equipment or paraphernalia to make the program work. It may not be available.

Sales aids. It is usually the duty of the sales promotion department to prepare the sales promotion materials used in selling the product to other resellers or to the retailer. That means developing a package of sales promotion materials such as that illustrated in Figure 13-1 for the Stokely-Van Camp "Little Red Wagon" program. As you can see, this includes all types of sales promotion literature that can be used to explain the program to the sales force and then to sell the retailer.

Some of the more commonly used sales aids are:

1. *Sales manuals.* The sales manual is a descriptive book developed to assist the salespeople in making a complete sales presentation. It is usually designed for use in an office in a face-to-face selling situation. The manual may contain product information, background materials, price lists, models, and other information that will assist in presenting the product line to customers and prospects. The advertising campaign, advertising materials, and sales promotion program are usually an integral part of the sales manual.
2. *Sales portfolios.* These are usually developed as an external selling tool for the sales force. The portfolio may take any form, from loose-

Figure 13-1   Sales Aids: Stokely-Van Camp Products

Source: William A. Robinson, *100 Best Sales Promotions of 1975/6* (Chicago: Crain Books, 1976), p. 27.

leaf binders to booklets to brochures or flyers. They are often designed to be left with the prospect. The portfolio contains information on the product being promoted, price lists, the advertising
campaign, order blanks, and other selling materials. The importance of the promotional program, the type of market, and the needs
of the sales force dictate the type of sales portfolio to be created.
Often, the sales promotion manager is called upon to help develop
the sales portfolio because of his knowledge of the market, the advertising campaign, and the sales promotion program.

3. *Sales letters.* Sales letters are used to announce sales meetings and to
keep personnel enthusiastic during the course of a promotional program. They often contain information that can be used in follow-up
calls by the sales force on their prospects.

While these are certainly not all the materials or information the
sales promotion manager might be called upon to develop, they do give
an idea of the scope of the sales organization's needs. Later in this
chapter, you will find several types of additional materials illustrated
that might also be used by the sales organization.

Developing Incentive Plans

Incentive plans are often an important method of solving sales organization problems. Here are some suggestions on how to develop successful incentive plans for either the controlled or uncontrolled sales organization. Generally, incentive programs can:

1. Stimulate people to work at maximum efficiency and productivity.
2. Encourage people to sell harder, longer, more intelligently, and more enthusiastically in pursuit of increased sales and profits.
3. Gain employee interest, loyalty, and support to reinforce all other elements of a company's overall marketing program.[3]

In addition, John FitzMaurice of Maritz, Inc., suggests that motivation can supply a positive answer to these questions:

- Will your customers stock and promote your products or the products of other suppliers?
- Will uncontrolled organization salesmen promote your product/service or that of another supplier?
- Will salesmen present your featured product/service or one that is easier to sell?
- Will salesmen present your product/service now, at the start of the peak buying season, or after the order books are filled?
- Will uncontrolled sales organizations add your new products/services and train their men to sell them, or will they place their effort elsewhere?
- Will salesmen merely take customer orders without trying to accomplish the specific sale objectives of their employers or suppliers?[4]

Finally, a good incentive plan should follow these guidelines: (1) its results must be measurable; (2) its goals must be specific and realistic; (3) its rules must be clear; (4) its prizes must be attainable; (5) the prizes must be both effective and cost-effective; (6) the prize structure must be carefully designed; and (7) the program must be neither too short nor too long.

The Results Must Be Measurable

The incentive program must provide a measurable result for the manufacturer. Simply to say that "we want to increase sales" is not specific enough. What increase is needed in terms of dollars, units, or percentage?

---

3. FitzMaurice, "Tools of Promotion Workshop."
4. FitzMaurice, "Tools of Promotion Workshop."

Similarly, simply saying that the contest should produce an increase in the number of dealers for the product is also difficult to measure. The objective of the incentive program should be stated in measurable terms. For example: "The goal of the dealer contest is to increase the number of dealers stocking our product from the present 3,500 to 4,200 in the six-month period the contest will last." Only in this way can you determine at the end whether the incentive program succeeded or failed.

Further, if you set measurable goals, the cost of the incentive program can be put in perspective. For example, if we used the objectives above and knew that the cost of the incentive program would be approximately $15,000, our cost per dealer added would be $21.43 each. ($15,000 ÷ 700 new dealers). We could then determine if that amount was in line with the sales we would expect from these new dealers.

The Goals Must Be Specific and Realistic

As above, to be successful, the incentive program must have goals, and they must be specific and realistic. Setting a goal of every salesperson achieving a 100 percent sales increase, for example, is unrealistic.

The Rules Must Be Clear

While it is often exciting to create a complex contest or motivation program with awards, super awards, maximum awards, bonuses, and the like, the objective of the motivation program is to achieve sales goals, not to show how clever you are. Further, sales personnel may not have an opportunity to have you explain the program to them. Therefore, be sure the rules are simple and clear. How the prizes will be awarded must be fully explained, and special emphasis must be given to when the awards will be made.

The Prizes Must Be Attainable

The most discouraging thing to a salesperson or retailer who is involved in a motivation program is to know he has no chance of winning or obtaining a prize. That really defeats the purpose of the motivation program.

John FitzMaurice suggests three types of awards that should be included in a motivation program:

1. *Awards based on individual accomplishment.* Such awards should be the backbone of every motivation program. Accordingly, when all three types of awards are included, approximately 50-70 percent of the award budget should go for individual awards. The award sched-

ule should be set up so that, funds permitting, every participant who makes the necessary effort can earn an award(s) solely on the basis of individual effort. . . . And this award-earning potential should in no way be affected by the efforts and award earnings of any other participant.

2. *Awards based on team accomplishments.* Many people will work harder for a team than they will for their own benefit. . . . And whenever it can be done realistically, awards for team accomplishment should be included in motivation programs. By "realistically," we mean that the company's organizational structure should provide natural competition between branches, divisions, zones, or similar regional or area offices . . . or that, within the organization, the sales force can be readily separated into natural competitive groups or teams. When team awards are part of a program in which all three types of awards are offered . . . approximately 20-30 percent of the total budget should be allocated for such awards.

3. *Competitive awards.* These are top awards offered to individual participants whose performance in the program has been outstanding. Since many human beings thrive on competition, such awards add immeasurably to the effectiveness of motivation programs. When competitive awards are used in conjunction with individual and team awards, they should account for approximately 10-20 percent of the total award budget.

The problem involved in offering competitive awards lies in the fact that it is difficult to make competition fair and equitable in most sales organizations. The reasons for this are self-evident. Unless the participants feel that competition is fair and equitable, sometimes offering such awards can actually have a negative effect.[5]

Prizes Must Be Large Enough to Be Effective but Small Enough to Be Cost-Effective

There are many schools of thought on what it takes to develop a good award base. Generally, though, the "rule of thumb" is that the award must be large and attractive enough to get the participants to accomplish the goals, yet affordable to the company or brand.

One of the best ways of deciding on the size of the prizes is to relate them to the regular income of the participants. The more money the participant makes, the larger the award must be. As general rules, Fitz-Maurice suggests the following:

1. When the program duration is 90 days or less, the average partici-

---

5. FitzMaurice, "Tools of Promotion Workshop."

pant should be able to earn 5 to 10 percent of his regular compensation for the program period. For example, in a 90-day program, a salesman who earns $800 per month or $2,400 for the period should be able to earn from $120 to $240 in awards, preferably on the high side.

2. When the program is of longer duration than three months, the percentage can be reduced to 3 to 5 percent—3 percent for year long programs and 5 percent for four- or five-month programs.[6]

The Prize Structure Must Be Carefully Designed

There are three basic forms of awards in a motivation program: merchandise, travel, and honor or recognition. The major advantage of merchandise or travel over cash is that often the salesperson might start to consider a cash award as part of his regular compensation. It becomes expected, in which case it loses its value.

Merchandise awards are considered to be the most motivating. Experts suggest they should make up 75 percent of the awards budget. Travel is an exciting award, but it can be expensive, particularly if it is to a place that will generate high enthusiasm. Usually, travel is considered the top award. No matter what it is, however, the top award should represent no more than 20 percent of the total budget. Honor and recognition awards should make up the balance. Don't underestimate them. They can add the extra punch a contest needs. Recognition goes on long after the merchandise and travel awards have been forgotten.

The Program Must Be Neither Too Short Nor Too Long

While they may vary, depending on the objectives of the motivation program, most motivation contests should not last longer than three to six months. In fact, if possible, shorter contests are better. Interest fades after a period of time and it is hard to keep enthusiasm up.

Keep one fact in mind: The contest must be long enough so that your sales goals can be achieved and the participants have time to earn the awards. Don't expect to add 1,000 new dealers to your distribution in just 30 days. It doesn't work that way.

Although these rules are quite general, they should be helpful to you in planning motivation programs. If you are planning a very complicated program or one that will include retailers, you should contact one of the many experienced incentive and motivation organizations available to you. They have the background and experience to help you plan and execute a successful program.

---

6. FitzMaurice, "Tools of Promotion Workshop."

Some Examples of Motivation Programs

On the following pages, you will find some examples of motivation programs that have been used successfully by other marketers. While they certainly don't cover the full range of motivation approaches, they are indicative of the various types that can be used.

Contest for Sales Organization—Controlled

To help back up its "Heinz Ketchup Giveaway" consumer promotion (Figure 13-2), Heinz also developed a contest for its sales force on a regional basis. Points were awarded for volume of cases sold, displays generated among retailers, feature prices obtained from retailers, size of consumer ads, and the use of p-o-p materials on display. Video tape decks were awarded as prizes at all levels of the sales force.

Contest for Sales Organization—Uncontrolled

To involve the retail salespeople and encourage them to promote the promotion, Timex gave "Rub Off" cards with each Timex Quartz watch they sold. When they rubbed off the spots, they won from 50¢ to $25. Obviously, the more watches they sold, the better their chances to win the $25 prizes. In addition, wholesale salespeople and wholesale sales managers were given an opportunity to win in their own contest. Wholesale sales managers, for example (Figure 13-3), had the opportunity to win up to 10 percent of the amount won by their salespeople during the time of the promotion. By integrating its sales organization promotions with the consumer activity, Timex got double duty in terms of motivating all salespeople at all levels in the distribution system.

Contest for Retailers

The retail display contest in Figure 13-4 is an example of developing a contest around an activity that benefits both the retailer and the manufacturer. The manufacturer gets his product displayed and probably generates more sales, while the retailer has a chance to win a substantial prize in Green Giant products.

Incentive Program for Sales Organization—Controlled

When Northern tissue introduced new packaging, it used a "Northern Girl Sweepstakes" at the consumer level. This was backed up with a regional display contest for the field sales force and was related to the number of displays obtained, size of display, use of Northern p-o-p

Figure 13-2   Contest: Heinz Ketchup   Figure 13-3   Contest: Timex Quartz Watches

Source: William A. Robinson, *100 Best Sales Promotions* (Chicago: Crain Books, 1980), p. 17 and p. 15.

materials, and the like. Based on the points accumulated by the sales force, an award fund was established in the form of a "pot" that was used at the local sales manager's discretion.

Bonus Plan for Sales Organization—Controlled

Banks and savings institutions are some of the most common users of internal sales force bonus plans. While we don't normally think of banks as being in the "sales" business, there are many opportunities for employees to help build business through suggestions of additional bank services, new account development, and savings plan selling. E. F. Mac-Donald Company, one of the leading incentive development organiza-

Figure 13-4   Contest: Green Giant Products

tions in the world, developed a program for the New York Bank for Savings titled "Spotlight on You." The objective was to generate $32,000,000 in new business for the bank.

This program was tremendously successful. In fact, it generated $137,000,000 or 430 percent of the objective that had been set. Eighty-three percent participation of employees in new business referrals was achieved. And the goals were accomplished at a cost of less than 1 percent of the volume of the four-month program.

Sales Training Program for Sales Organization—Controlled

As part of a continuing training program for its dairy products driver-salespeople, Borden, Inc., developed a series of training films, merchandising aids, and sales room posters. All the material was designed to help the sales force do a better job of selling, merchandising, and collecting from their customers. (See Figure 13-5.)

Incentive Program for Retailers

To generate restaurant usage of the American Express card, American Express developed the "Winning Menu" promotion. Included was a sweepstakes for restaurant owners/managers based on the applications for American Express cards generated in the restaurant. In addition, an "Entree" sweepstakes was conducted for owners, managers, and employees, using each American Express "Record of Charge" over $5 during the contest period. (See Figure 13-6.) With over $40,000 in prizes in these two incentive programs, there was great restaurant owner/employee interest.

Sales Aid for Retailers

The Nikon "Owner's Course," in Figure 13-7, is an outstanding example of a retailer's sales aid developed by a manufacturer. By offering clinics to show how to use the camera, Nikon not only built sales but also made sure the retailer knew the product. Here's a way to make sure retailers cooperate in a sales promotion event.

As you can see, there are many ways to use sales promotion with sales forces. Usually, the secret in any good program is motivation, either to do a better job or to earn some form of reward. And, with any motivation program, success is achieved if the people involved know the goals of the program and understand how they can help to achieve them.

Figure 13-5   Sales Training Program: Borden Foods

TP-1

TP-4

TP-2

TP-5

TP-3

TP-6

Source: Courtesy of Borden, Inc.

Summary

When a sales organization is not up to snuff, the sales promotion manager can help the sales manager in restoring an effective selling force.

Figure 13-6   Incentive Program: American Express

Source: Robinson, *100 Best Sales Promotions*, p. 49.

Figure 13-7   Sales Aid: Nikon Cameras

Source: William A. Robinson, *100 Best Sales Promotions of 1976/7* (Chicago: Crain Books, 1977), pp. 24-25.

First, identify the cause of the inadequacy—poor motivation, faulty incentive plan, inadequate training, or other lack. Then develop the proper incentive plan, remembering that any such plan must have specific goals, clear rules, attractive prizes, and measurable results. Examples of motivation programs include contests and bonus plans.

14

New Product Problems
and Opportunities

One of the most exciting tasks for the sales promotion manager is the introduction of a new product. One reason is that the effect of sales promotion activities is often more quickly visible with a new product than with an established one. With the new product, things happen immediately, i.e., trial, repeat purchase, and establishment of a market share. Some of these factors are more difficult to pinpoint with an established product simply because success cannot always be related directly to the sales promotion program.

While new product introductions are very exciting, they are also very difficult. The difficulty comes not just in terms of the amount of work involved but in the success rate of introductory programs as well. The failure rate of new products is high. Some experts estimate that as many as 70 percent of all new products never make it as a successful brand.

Using data collected by A. C. Nielsen Company, J. O. Peckham, Sr., made a study of 49 new brands in seven product categories, that had been introduced since 1955. He found that merely introducing a new brand is not an automatic road to marketing success. As indicated in the chart in Table 14-1, 33 percent of the brands studied failed and another 33 percent were only marginally successful. He also found that only 22 percent, or 1 out of 5 nationally introduced brands, developed a market share sufficient to establish them as brand leaders.

Many new products fail simply because there isn't a place in the market for them. The marketer did not have or did not develop a point of

Table 14-1 Long-Term Market Share Performance of 49 New Brands in 7 Product Categories Introduced Since 1955

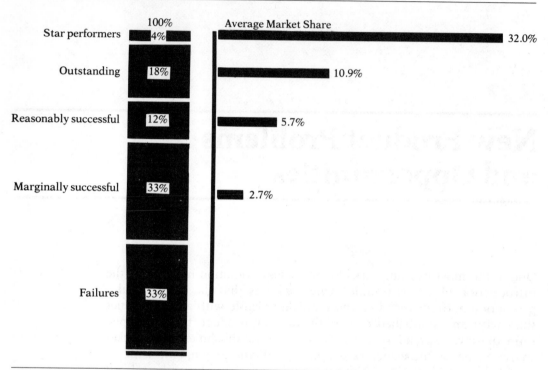

	100%	Average Market Share
Star performers	4%	32.0%
Outstanding	18%	10.9%
Reasonably successful	12%	5.7%
Marginally successful	33%	2.7%
Failures	33%	

Source: J. O. Peckham, Sr., *The Wheel of Marketing* (Scarsdale, NY: Privately printed, 1978), p. 53. 2.

difference between the new product and all the established brands already on the market. Thus, there was really little or no reason for the consumer to notice, much less try, the product to see if it filled a need. Without trial, of course, the product failed.

In our opinion, most new products that fail are not really product failures. Rather, they are marketing failures. The marketers did not find a point of difference in their product or did not communicate a point of difference the product might have had to prospective consumers. When this happens, we can only blame the marketing plan and the promotional program, not the product.

If the promotion idea or the promotion mix is usually the cause of the product failure, what then is the best way to prepare a sound and successful new product introduction? That is what we will discuss in this chapter. First, however, we need to take a general look at new product introductions and the role of sales promotion in them.

Sales Promotion and New Product Introductions

We must assume that the necessary background work was done on the product prior to developing a sales promotion plan: that basic market research was conducted; that it indicated a market for the product; and that the product itself was tested and found suitable for the purposes proposed. Also, we assume that the fundamental marketing approach for the product—the advertising theme or the sales message to be communicated—was developed. Until all these preliminary activities have been performed, a sound sales promotion plan can't really be developed as an ingredient in the marketing mix. To be most effective, sales promotion must be keyed to the theme of the overall promotion program. Obviously, that must be established prior to the time the sales promotion manager starts to outline his objectives for the sales promotion program.

Two Key Concepts

To understand the success of a new product introduction, you must understand two key marketing concepts. The first is the use of "market segmentation." This simply means that most new products will appeal primarily to a certain segment of the entire market or category. An example will illustrate the point.

In the detergent section of almost any major supermarket, you can probably find most of the following brands on display. You'll notice that each has a different selling message, usually called "creative strategy." For example:

Dreft	"The Detergent for Baby's Laundry"
Ivory Snow	"Softens as it Cleans"
Gain	"A Clean You See, a Fresh You Smell"
Cheer	"The All-Temperature Detergent"
Bold	"Cleans Even Tough-to-Clean Modern Fabrics"
Tide	"Tide's In—Dirt's Out—America's Favorite"
Dash	"The Low Suds Concentrate"
Oxydol	"Bleaches as it Washes"

All detergents are designed to do basically the same thing: help remove dirt from clothing when used in an automatic washer. So why all the different products? Why all the different brands? Why all the different claims? Why all the different slogans? The reason is simple. Each brand was developed to fill a different consumer need or to appeal to a different segment of the market. Some consumers want the advantages of a detergent that can be used in all water temperatures. Others prefer detergents with bleach. Still others want one that creates low suds. In other words, the detergent market has been highly segmented. Each segment wants something different from its detergent. To serve these various markets, detergent manufacturers have developed a number of different product formulations. Each is designed to appeal to one of these market segments. To communicate the benefits that the brand offers, each has a different advertising or creative strategy. Each product is attempting to carve out a niche for itself among the many competitors in the market place. To gain a share, the brand must promise a different benefit or propose to solve a different problem for the consumer. That's known as market segmentation through advertising or creative strategy. And smart marketers, such as Procter & Gamble, have been segmenting markets for years. In fact, the example we have just given proves that—since all the brands named are marketed by P & G.

Market segmentation is often influenced by another marketing idea, the "heavy-user" concept. Market research studies have shown that in most product categories, a small percentage of the population accounts for the consumption of a very large portion of the total. For example, approximately 20 percent of the beer drinkers consume approximately 75 percent of all the beer drunk in the U.S. The same is true for other product categories such as those illustrated in Table 14-2.

Thus, marketers attempt to develop products that will appeal to specific market segments. Also, they hope to develop a product that will appeal to the heavy user. These two points are also vital in the development of sales promotion programs for new products.

These two ideas, market segmentation and heavy users, can be most important planning tools for the sales promotion manager. They often play an extremely important role in determining the type of sales promotion program that should be developed for a new product.

The Role of Sales Promotion in New Product Introduction

New products need a formal, planned sales promotion program just as much as existing products do. In looking at how sales promotion can help launch a new product, the chart shown in Table 14-3, developed by Bud Frankel of Abelson-Frankel, will be helpful.

The chart in Table 14-3 shows a series of integrated steps in the introduction of a new product. Step 1 is to inspire and excite the sales force, whether controlled or uncontrolled. This means you must make sure the salespeople have all the information and motivation needed to sell the new product. They must know what the product is, what it does, what the test market results have been, and so on. They must know the market segment at which the product will appeal. They must know what advertising and sales promotion is planned to appeal to that market. And they must know what the product can mean to them as a new source of

Table 14-2   Percent of Total Product Usage Accounted for by the Heavy Users of Specific Products

	Heavy users % of population group	Heavy users % of total usage		Heavy users % of population group	Heavy users % of total usage
Car rentals in past year (men)	3.6	89.6	Laxatives	28.2	92.8
Liquid dietary products	4.1	98.0	Rice	28.8	82.7
Air trips in past year (men)	7.8	87.3	Peanut butter	29.6	82.4
Automatic dishwasher detergents	9.0	100.0	Cake mix	34.1	84.4
			R.T.E. cereal	37.2	80.2
Hair coloring rinse or tint (women)	11.3	88.1	Upset stomach remedies	37.3	89.2
Scotch whiskey	12.6	98.6	Shaving cream in pressurized		
Cigar smoking (men)	17.1	98.6	cans (men)	38.7	98.0
Rye or blended whiskey	18.4	98.5	Frozen orange juice	41.0	92.1
Bourbon	18.8	98.7	Soft drinks	4.18	84.9
Canned type dog food	19.3	99.2	Paper napkins	42.9	83.2
Dry dog food	20.7	99.2	Bleach	43.7	81.6
Canned ham	22.8	83.0	Tomato sauce	44.9	90.7
Instant coffee	26.1	80.6	Cleansing or facial tissues	45.2	82.9
Cold or allergy tablets	27.0	84.3	Frozen vegetables	49.9	92.1
Cigarettes (all adults)	27.2	84.1	Regular ground coffee	50.5	92.7
Hair tonic (men)	27.8	76.8	H.H. laundry detergents	50.8	81.4
			Headache remedies	52.6	93.1

Source: Norton Garfinkle, "The Marketing Value of Media Audiences—How to Pinpoint Your Prime Prospects," a speech given at the Association of National Advertisers Workshop on Advertising Planning and Evaluation, New York, 1965.

Note: The total population group is based on total households except for those products specifically designated otherwise.

income or a new method of doing their job better. The next step is for the sales force to make the trade aware of the new product (Step 2). Usually, this is done through a retailer presentation (Step 3), which must include information about what benefit the new product offers the retailer. That is usually determined by the sales potential, margins, what the product will replace on the shelf, the promotion to support the product, and so on (Step 4). Step 5 is that the product must be available in the proper quantities to fill retailer's needs.

The sales force must next get the order from retailers. To do this, it may be necessary to develop forms of trade promotion for the retailers, such as dating; incentives to buy early, such as stocking; and other allowances (Steps 6 and 7).

With orders from the retailers in hand, the product must then be

Table 14-3   The Role of Sales Promotion in New Products

```
                        ┌──────────────────┐
                        │   New product    │
                        └──────────────────┘
                                  │
        ┌─────────────────────────┤
        │                         │
        │          ┌──────────────────────┐         ┌─────────────────┐
        │          │ (1) Motivate re-     │─────────│ (2) Trade       │
┌───────────────┐  │ talier sales force   │         │ awareness       │
│ (14) Advertise│  └──────────────────────┘         └─────────────────┘
└───────────────┘             │
        │          ┌──────────────────────┐
        │          │ (3) Retailer         │
        │          │ presentation         │
        │          └──────────────────────┘
        │                     │
        │    ┌───────────────┐│  ┌─────────────────┐
        │    │ (5) Proper    │──│ (4) What's in it │
┌───────────────┐ quantities │  │ for retailer    │
│ (15) Sample   │ └───────────┘  └─────────────────┘
└───────────────┘            │
        │    ┌───────────────┐  ┌─────────────────┐
        │    │ (7) Early buy │──│ (6) Dating      │
        │    └───────────────┘  └─────────────────┘
        │                     │
        │          ┌──────────────┐  ┌─────────────────┐
        │          │ (8) Ship to  │──│ (9) Create retail│
        │          │ retailer     │  │ excitement      │
        │          └──────────────┘  └─────────────────┘
        │                     │
┌───────────────┐ ┌───────────────┐ ┌──────────────┐ ┌─────────────┐
│ (16) Coupon   │ │ (12) Local ads│─│ (10) Store   │─│ (13) Refund │
└───────────────┘ └───────────────┘ │ display      │ │ offer       │
        │                           └──────────────┘ └─────────────┘
        │                                   │
        │                        ┌─────────────────┐
        │                        │ (11) Price      │
        │                        │ reduction       │
        │                        └─────────────────┘
        │                                   │
        │          ┌────────────────────────┐
        └──────────│   Consumer purchase    │
                   └────────────────────────┘
```

Source: Louis J. Haugh, "A Sales Promo Plan Can Mean Success for Your New Product," *Advertising Age,* February 20, 1978, p. 41.

shipped to the stores (Step 8). Once the product is in the stores, the next logical step is to use sales promotion to create some excitement at the retail level (Step 9). This may consist of the merchandising displays in the stores (Step 10) and may or may not include price reductions at the retail level (Step 11). Often, price reductions or other sales promotion activities are featured in the local newspaper ads of the retailer (Step 12), or perhaps a refund offer is made at the shelf (Step 13).

While all these retail activities are taking place, the manufacturer will probably be in the process of advertising the product to the consumer in the media (Step 14). At the same time, the product may be sampled either through the mail, through the media, or door-to-door (Step 15). Coupons may also be used, either to accompany the sampling program or run in the media. In either case, the coupons must be directed to the market segment at which the product is aimed (Step 16). Assuming all the steps work, the ultimate result of these activities should be a consumer purchase.

This integrated advertising and sales promotion plan clearly points up the importance of sales promotion to both retailers and consumers. If the sales promotion plan breaks down in any of these areas, the new product introduction may not be successful.[1]

This type of sales promotion program would be needed whether the new product introduction was carried out on a roll-out or crash basis. A roll-out new product introduction means simply starting with a small test area and moving the introduction of the new product from market to market across the country. The roll-out can be either fast or slow, depending on the financial resources of the manufacturer, the acceptance of the product, the need to beat competitors to the punch, and so on. The alternative approach to a roll-out is the crash introduction. This simply means that after test, the product is introduced as quickly as possible in as many markets as possible. Often, a crash introduction is done when the product is of the fad variety or has questionable long-term potential. It is most often used when there is fear that competition can or will introduce a similar product or when the manufacturer wants to take advantage of an obviously successful new product as quickly as possible.

No matter what the new product introductory plan, the problems in new product introduction are similar. We look at them next.

What Are New Product Problems?

Whether the new product introduction is simply a market test to determine the viability of the product for a more widespread introduction or a full-scale introduction of the product after the test, there are three general objectives of all new product marketing efforts that include sales promotion activities.

1. Getting distribution of the new product.
2. Getting trial of the new product.
3. Getting repeat purchases after initial trial.

We will deal with each of them separately.

1. Louis J. Haugh, "A Sales Promo Plan Can Mean Success for Your New Product," *Advertising Age*, Feb. 20, 1978, pp. 40-41.

Getting Product Distribution

Often, the toughest job in introducing a new product is simply to get distribution in retail stores. The average supermarket stocks over 10,000 separate items. The average drugstore stocks more than 15,000. With that sort of inventory, one would think it would be quite simple to squeeze another product or another brand into the store. Unfortunately, it doesn't work that way. Here's the reason. Think of the retail store as a large box in which items are kept—for in fact that's exactly what it is. As with a box, once it is full, the only way to put something else in is to take something out. To place a new product in the store, you must take an existing product out of the store. The question is, then, what product can be taken out so your new product can be put in? Why should the retailer accept your product in place of one he already has? Retail stores operate on the basis of movement and margin. To get your product to replace something else, you have to promise better movement, better margins, or both. There is really no other way. If you can't make that promise, the retailer has no real reason to make room for your product.

To make the problem more difficult, many other manufacturers are trying to get their new products on the shelf at the same time. They have new flavors, new packages, line extensions, and the like. They also want more shelf space for their existing products. In short, you are usually just one of many voices trying to get retailers to listen to a new product sales story in order to get shelf space for the product. The important thing that you as the sales promotion manager must provide is the plan and program that will prove your product provides the best margin and movement for the retailer among the new product alternatives or even among existing products.

Finally, remember the brand you are trying to replace is going to fight just as hard to hold the space as you will in trying to gain it. That is why the sales promotion program must be as strong as possible. You must get into the retail store. You must get distribution or the product will never get off the ground. You must get on the shelf to make sure the consumer can find the product. Only in that way can you hope to get product trial.

Getting Product Trial

As important as gaining distribution is, the next step is just as vital. You must get the consumer to try the product. Gaining distribution only to have the product sit on the shelf invites disaster. You must get movement, which means product trial by the consumer. In the next section, we will suggest several ways this can be accomplished. But first, let us look at how product trial normally comes about.

Table 14-4   Distribution of New Product Adopters

Source: Reprinted with permission from Everett M. Rogers, *Diffusion of Innovations* (New York: Free Press, 1962), p. 162.

One way of understanding how people try new products is to understand how people go about adopting new ideas. Everett M. Rogers did much work with what he called "the diffusion of innovation" or the adoption process. Using several studies, Rogers separated the entire population, or at least those who finally adopt a new idea, into five groups. He called them the "Innovators, Early Adopters, Early Majority, Late Majority, and Laggards." This idea is illustrated in Table 14-4. It shows the speed with which various groups accept new ideas over time and the approximate percentage in each group.

In Rogers' view, those who first accept a new idea are called "Innovators." These people make up only a small number, although they are very important since they are the first ones to try a new idea. The next group to accept the idea are the "Early Adopters," a much larger group. This group is followed by the "Early Majority." As you can see, these three groups make up over half the people who will eventually accept or adopt the new idea. The "Late Majority" and the "Laggards" are the last to accept the new idea and become users. The important point here is not the names of the groups but the general concept that all persons do not rush out and accept a new idea when they first hear about it. They move slowly into the market, as shown by the fact that "Innovators" usually make up only about 2½ to 3 percent of all those who will ever accept the idea. This same adoption process seems to occur with the introduction of a new product. This should give you a better idea of why trial of a new product is such a difficult task to accomplish.

If new products are accepted in the same manner as new ideas are, you can see the importance of sales promotion. To encourage the "Early Adopters" and the "Early Majority" to act and try the new product, short-term incentives to purchase are needed. Most retailers will not continue to stock nor can most manufacturers survive just on the purchases of the "Innovators" alone. The group is just too small. Thus, it is vital that sales promotion programs be developed that will encourage trial by as many people as possible. Since we have already suggested that much media advertising, as such, is not action-oriented, the importance of sales promotion in the introduction of a new product is vital to success.

Another reason the trial of new products may be slow in coming is simply the crowded situation in the market place. Opportunities to market truly revolutionary new products, such as the Polaroid camera, the handheld calculator, and the L.E.D. watch, are few and far between. In most cases, the new products we attempt to market are usually only imitations of or improvements on products that are already available. Thus, one of the major problems in new product introduction is simply to sell the benefit of the new product. The second is to convince the consumer that this benefit really is either necessary or desirable. Finally, prospects must be convinced that they should try the product. Usually, that means a change of purchasing habits, and that is one of the most difficult things sales promotion can be called on to influence.

A major obstacle to getting new product trial is the consumer's prior commitment to a product that satisfies his needs or desires. When this is the case, the manufacturer must wait until the present product is used up, because most consumers will not throw away a half-used pack of one product just to try another. Of course, there are other problems in getting trial, but these are the primary ones. In spite of all the trial-achieving problems, however, trial must be accomplished if the new product is to succeed.

Getting Repeat Purchases

The third step in a new product introduction is getting customers who may have tried the product to repurchase it or to become regular users. It might seem that once we have achieved distribution and trial, new users would quickly become regular users, but, unfortunately, that simply isn't so. There are several reasons why this is the case, but the most important one to sales promotion managers is: Competitors do not simply lie down once you have achieved trial with their customers. In fact, they usually fight that much harder to get their customers back. And many of these battles are conducted as sales promotion programs in the stores and in the media. Thus, sales promotion programs for new products should not, in our opinion, be conducted as "one-shot" plans that seek only to obtain trial. While trial is vital, a successful new product introduction must be a complete program that also includes the use of follow-up advertising and sales promotion programs to get repeat purchase of the product.

Solving New Product Problems

Several sales promotion techniques are quite effective in solving or overcoming the new product problems we have described. Although sales promotion is obviously not the solution to all new product problems, it should be an integral part of any new product plan.

While we described three problems with a new product (getting distribution, obtaining trial, and ensuring repurchase), they really break down into two separate promotion needs. First, getting distribution consists almost entirely of events, activities, and plans directed toward the trade. The second two, getting trial and repeat purchase, are more directly related to consumer programs. Although you must have the support of the trade and retailers, to get trial and repeat purchases, we've found that sales promotion activities directed toward the consumer are most important.

Getting Distribution

Several sales promotion techniques are normally used to encourage the trade and retailers to stock a new product. In fact, sales promotion is probably *the* most important method of achieving that goal.

To stock an item, the retailer must be convinced that the new product will offer him greater sales or greater margins than other products he presently handles. Usually, this proof is developed in a test market in which the product is actually merchandised and sold. In a test market, several approaches to both advertising and sales promotion may be tried, including different advertising claims, different sales promotion devices, and different consumer incentives. Based on the results of the test market, the best possible promotion plan is then developed and implemented. The sales force then uses the previously tested advertising and sales promotion program, plus the results of the test market, in their sales calls to the trade and retailer. The new product introduction package given to the sales force usually consists of at least the following materials.

Sales brochures. These often contain information on the test market, how the new product was received, and the expected sales in the new markets where it will be introduced, along with all the advertising and sales promotion materials to be used in the introduction in that market.

Figure 14-1   Sales Brochure: Velamints

We've just captured all this freshness and put it in a new sugar free mint! Know how?

Source: Courtesy of Ragold, Inc. and Don Tennant Company, Inc.

While we discussed sales brochures in some detail in Chapter 13, the example of the new product introductory brochure used by Velamints illustrates the various items required for an effective sales brochure. (See Figure 14-1.) This particular brochure contained product information, illustrations, display units, the television commercial storyboard, deal sheets, product illustrations, and display allowance information.

Product samples. The trade and the retailers are always given samples of the new product. They are usually presented by the salesperson, but they may also be mailed or shipped to the home or office of the prospective buyer. A common technique in the food business is the "cutting" of the product with the buyer, the new product committee, or the retailer. This simply means that the new product is tasted, or demon-

Figure 14-2   Product Sample: Velamints

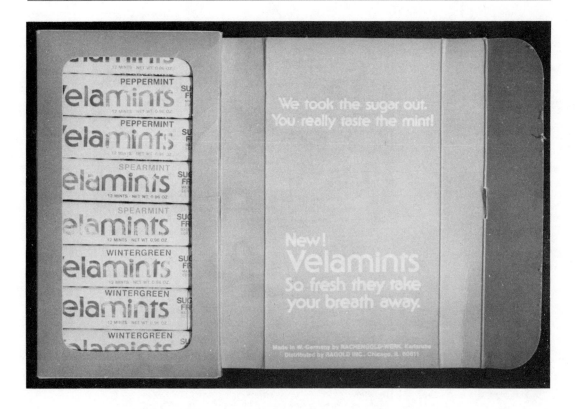

Source: Courtesy of Ragold, Inc. and Don Tennant Company, Inc.

strated in some other way, against the competitive products on the shelf. These "cuttings" can be conducted in either an informal or quite elaborate way, depending on the particular customer and the particular product.

An example of a trade sample is illustrated in Figure 14-2. Notice how Velamints sampled its product with the trade. As you can see, the trade sample consisted of a special pack of the product containing two each of the three flavors, with the advertising theme featured on the box.

Trade allowances or deals. These are the promotional allowances given to the trade or the retailer for buying and stocking the new product. (See Chapter 12.) This may consist of a stocking allowance, dating, display allowance, proposed trade coupon, or a multitude of other plans

Figure 14-3   Trade Deal: Velamints

Source: Courtesy of Ragold, Inc. and Don Tennant Company, Inc.

that are designed to appeal to the retailer. The specific plan will, of course, depend to a great extent on the product margin and the overall sales plan that has been developed.

A typical trade deal to introduce a new product is shown in the example in Figure 14-3 from the Velamints introduction. As you can see, there was a special offer to retailers to encourage them to stock and display the product.

In-store promotional materials. The sales force usually also presents any in-store merchandising and point-of-purchase materials that have been developed to help introduce the new product. These include

Figure 14-4   P-O-P Materials: Velamints

Source: Courtesy of Ragold, Inc. and Don Tennant Company, Inc.

any dealer loaders that can be used as displays and any tie-ins with the advertising campaign that can be used in the store. Sample point-of-purchase materials should always be included because the retailer wants to see them. He must understand how they can be used in his store. If possible, pictures or illustrations of how these materials were used in the test market are helpful.

While there are many kinds of in-store promotional materials, those used by Velamints were very effective. Samples are illustrated in Figure 14-4.

Details on contests or incentives. The sales force must be supplied with the details and materials on any retailer contests or incentives offered in connection with the introduction of the new product.

An example of a strong dealer contest for the introduction of the new Timex Quartz watch is illustrated in Figure 14-5. The contest was actually built around the same idea as the consumer contest in which prizes were awarded based on a "Rub-Off" watch face prize card. Whole-

Figure 14-5   Contest Details: Timex Quartz Watches

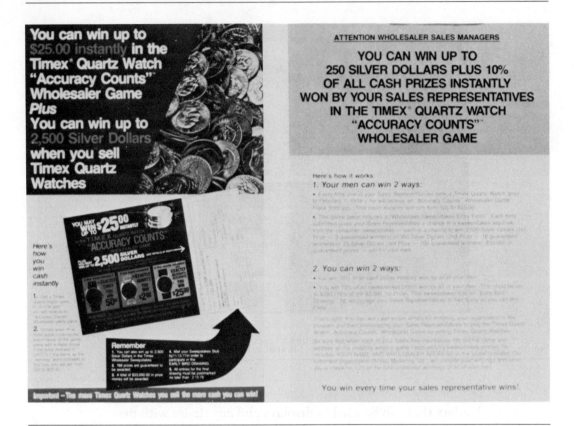

Source: William A. Robinson, *100 Best Sales Promotions* (Chicago: Crain Books, 1980), p. 15.

sale salesmen were given one game card worth from 50¢ to $25 for each watch sold, and all entries were placed in a sweepstakes drawing with $33,000 in total prizes. In addition, prizes matching those of the consumer contest were also awarded to the dealers. The contest is credited with not only increasing consumer sales but with reducing dealer inventories as well.

The sales promotion brochure to support a new product introduction can also contain other materials that might help gain distribution for the new product. In short, any and all things that might either help get distribution or display of the product are used.

Manufacturers of new products sometimes offer samples of the product that can be sold in the retail stores or suggest that demonstrators be used in the retail outlets. Special events can be held with the retailer's cooperation—a store-wide promotion to tie in with the new product or a similar activity. All these sales promotion incentives and more are used in an attempt to gain product distribution in the retail outlets. Later in this chapter you'll find illustrations of successful trade and retail introductory sales promotion programs.

Getting Trial and Repeat Purchases

The second major area of new product introduction is usually carried on with the consumer. While new product sales promotion devices require the cooperation of the retailer and trade in many cases, the true thrust of the program is toward the consumer. You may want to refer back to Chapters 8 and 9 for details on some of the techniques we discuss below.

While getting product trial and getting repeat purchases for a new product may be totally different problems, the same sales promotion techniques may be used for both. The secret is the way in which the sales promotion program is conducted or the manner in which the offer is presented. We'll discuss that here and hold the discussion of the creative approach until we show examples in the next section, since the major difference is in the creative approach used and not necessarily the technique.

The most important sales promotion techniques used to obtain trial of a new product are sampling, price-offs, refund offers, in-pack coupons, cross ruffs, and third-party sampling. Examples of each are discussed in the following pages.

Sampling. Obviously, the best way to demonstrate a product's superiority is to get the prospect to try it. That's done with a sample. The sample can be either a full-size package or carton of the product or simply a small amount of it. There are many forms of sampling and many ways of getting the sample to the consumer. No matter how it is done, however, sampling is usually the key to most successful new product introductions.

One of the most extensive sampling programs for a new product ever conducted was by S. C. Johnson & Sons in 1977. To introduce Agree cream rinse to prospective customers, the company distributed more than 31,000,000 free samples of the product. Most of these were distributed through the mail in either solo or cooperative mailings. The samples used are illustrated in Figure 14-6.

An alternative method of distributing free samples is the one used by Nestlé a few years ago to introduce its new cookie mix. Nestlé ran a full-page newspaper advertisement that had a coupon good for a free

Figure 14-6   Sampling: Agree Shampoo

Source: William A. Robinson, *Best Sales Promotions of 1977/78* (Chicago: Crain Books, 1978), p. 23.

full-size sample of the product. (See Figure 14-7.) The consumer simply took the coupon to the store and got the product free.

Price-offs. Often, a price-off or price reduction is used to introduce a new product and to generate trial. A reduced-price offer can also be used after the first trial to help build repurchase. The most common method of making this consumer offer is through the retailer. For example, the manufacturer may use a trade coupon or a specially reduced product price in the retail stores. These price reductions are often made through some sort of retail deal, such as a trade proof-of-performance allowance program, as described in Chapter 12. While reduced prices may be offered directly to the consumer, many marketers believe that going through the retail trade is a stronger, more effective approach. The offer not only gets made at the local level in stores with which the consumer is familiar; it also serves to convince the retailer that the product will sell and thus should continue to be stocked. If the retailer moves great numbers of the new product with the reduced-price offer, he is usually more willing to promote the product himself. That helps ensure repeat purchases, along with guaranteeing the product shelf space in the store.

The initial offer can be a strong incentive to action for the consumer, if used properly. Figure 14-8 illustrates the offer Bic made to consumers through the retailer in the form of a half-price trial pack in a display unit.

Figure 14-7   Sample: Nestlé Cookie Mix

Source: William A. Robinson, *100 Best Sales Promotions of 1976/7* (Chicago: Crain Books, 1977), pp. 22-23.

Figure 14-8   Price-Off: Bic Shavers

Source: Robinson, *Best Sales Promotions of 1977/78*, p. 34.

Refund offers. To help remove some of the consumer reluctance to invest in a new or unknown product, the manufacturer often makes a refund offer during the introductory period. This guarantees that the consumer will be taking no risk or at least a reduced risk in trying the product. The usual offer is a refund of the entire purchase price, although sometimes other amounts are used.

The refund offer can also be used to gain repeat purchases of the new product. Since the consumer has tried and is satisfied with the new

Figure 14-9   Refund Offer: Bob Evans Farm Sausage

Source: Courtesy of Bob Evans Farms.

product, a refund offer can be used to help continue usage or to attempt to build brand loyalty.

An excellent example of a refund offer to introduce a new product is the 50¢ refund made by Bob Evans Farms sausage on its new Savory Sage product. An advertisement is illustrated in Figure 14-9.

Figure 14-10   In-Pack Coupon: Lemon Tree Drink Mix Display

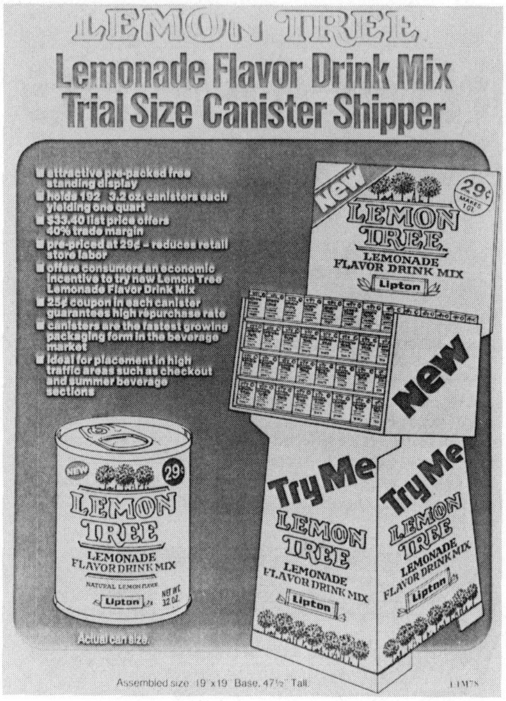

Source: Courtesy of Thomas J. Lipton, Inc. Lipton and Lemon Tree are trademarks of Thomas J. Lipton, Inc. Englewood Cliffs, N.J.

In-pack coupons. In-pack coupons may help in generating trial of the new product although they seem to be more effective in obtaining repeat purchases. Usually the coupon included is for cents-off on the product being introduced, for example, a coupon good for cents-off on the next purchase. It can, however, be used with other products in an effort to induce trial. For example, the manufacturer may load the new product with coupons good for cents-off on other, established products. The consumer, it is hoped, will buy the new product simply to get the savings offered on the other products.

In-pack coupons can take many forms. For example Lemon Tree lemonade flavor drink mix had a 25¢ coupon included in a trial package that was sold in the store. The idea was to generate trial with the smaller sample and then a full-size purchase facilitated by the coupon. Figure 14-10 shows the in-store display and the trial can.

Figure 14-11   Cross Ruff: Flintstone Vitamins and Cheerios Cereal

Source: A Cross-Ruff Clearing House Promotion.

Cross ruffs. Cross ruffs are sales promotion devices by which one product carries coupons good on another noncompetitive product. For example, a shampoo may carry coupons good for a reduced price on a rinse or conditioner, or a flour may carry a coupon good on sugar. This technique is often used to help introduce a new product in the line. It is also a way to enable a popular, established product to help introduce a new product.

For example, when Miles Laboratories introduced its Flintstone vitamins with extra C, Flintstone's management wanted to locate a cross-ruff carrier brand that would create awareness/trial among households with children aged 1 to 12. General Mills' Cheerios was one of the vehicles identified that could accomplish the Miles Labs goal. A total of 10,000,000 Flintstone 25¢ coupons were distributed through this cross-ruff promotion during the fall, 1980, introduction. (See Figure 14-11.)

This was timed to coincide with the advertising and other coupon events that had started in September.

Third-party sampling. Third-party sampling is simply having a sample of your new product distributed by another company. For example, a sample of a new blend of coffee might be given free with the purchase of a new coffeemaker, a new detergent might be included with the purchase of a new washing machine, or a new spaghetti sauce might be sampled with the purchase of the pasta. Usually, third-party sampling is carried out by noncompetitive, complementary products. It works two ways. The carrier uses the sample as an incentive to purchase the brand and the new or existing product uses it as a sampling device.

The obvious advantage of this third-party sampling technique is the low cost of distribution. Unfortunately, most of these methods give only limited control over where the samples or the coupons will be distributed. They can, however, provide a unique method of distributing new products.

Another form of third-party sampling is shown in Figure 14-12. The S.A.V.E., or Shoppers Association for Value and Economy, is an organization that distributes product samples to a list of members. About four times a year, S.A.V.E. sends out a package of new and established product samples. The members pay for these samples and the companies doing the sampling pay to have them distributed. In many cases, the samples are full size rather than trial size. The association is similar to other third-party groups that do the same sort of sampling job with college students, brides, new mothers, and others.

Obviously, other sales promotion techniques can be used in a sales promotion program for a new product. Those discussed above, however, are the most popular and successful methods and have proven themselves over the years.

When planning a sales promotion program for a new product, we strongly suggest that you review the various sales promotion techniques that are available to you. Decide which can or cannot be used to help get distribution, encourage trial, or build repeat purchases for your product. It's very important that your sales promotion program build all three of these new product introductory steps into the overall plan. If not, you may find that although you might accomplish one or two, all three are needed to ensure a successful introduction of the product. New product introductions are quite different from sales promotion programs for established products. Keep that in mind when doing your planning.

Is There One Best Way to Introduce a New Product?

J. O. Peckham, Sr., seems to have found one answer to that question, although perhaps not the definitive one. Using A. C. Nielsen Company

Figure 14-12   Third-Party Sampling: S.A.V.E.

Source: Courtesy of S.A.V.E.

data, he tracked a new brand as it was introduced. Here's what he found.

A new brand was introduced in about half the country with price-off merchandise as shown in the upper portion of the chart [Table 14-5], and in the other half with a home sample and coupon having the same face value as the "price-off" merchandise shown in the lower portion. By the end of Period 5 (10 months), the brand had reached what appears to be its introductory market share level of 5.3 percent [in the home sample area] while the area with "price-off" merchandise had reached only 3.1 percent of the market, and did not reach the 5.3-5.5 percent level until Period 13—some 16 months later.

Table 14-5   New Product Introduction: Share of Market

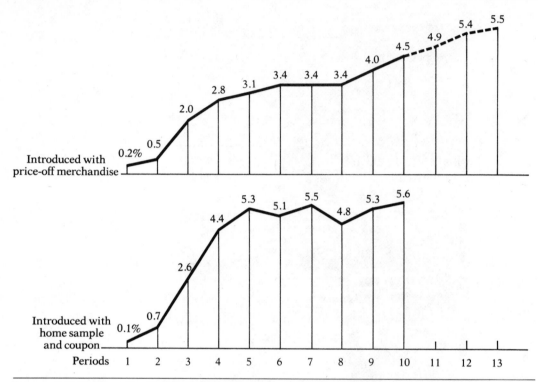

Source: J. O. Peckham, Sr., *The Wheel of Marketing* (Scarsdale, NY: Privately printed, 1978), p. 43.

Thus the sampling/coupon device seems to reach consumers more quickly, even though the two areas may ultimately arrive at the same approximate share of market. This means that a manufacturer using sampling/couponing—relatively a much more expensive proposition—can enjoy a higher case volume earlier and minimize the risk that a competitor might preempt his position with a new brand of his own before the original brand could establish itself on the market place.[2]

Granted, Peckham's examples may not apply to all products at all times. In spite of this, we believe that it verifies a point we have been making throughout this text. A combination of sales promotion devices used together usually achieves more than any single one technique alone. That's synergism and it works, particularly in sales promotion and especially with new products.

2. Peckham, *The Wheel of Marketing*, p. 43

Figure 14-13   Media Advertising: Timex Quartz Watches

Source: Robinson, *100 Best Sales Promotions*, p. 13.

Some Examples of New Product Introductions

On the following pages, we have illustrated two new product introductory programs. We have included as much of the introductory material as possible, particularly that which is directly related to sales promotion. We believe you will see from these examples why we consider sales promotion to be such an important factor in the overall success of a new product.

The Timex Quartz Watch Introduction

The first example of a sound new product introduction is the program for the Timex Quartz watch. The use of quartz was a major innovation in a series of technological improvements in the watch market. Timex, although the sales leader in the total watch category, was late in introducing a product into the category and faced entrenched competition from Seiko and Bulova. To make the introduction successful, Timex developed a total advertising and sales promotion program built around the idea of an "Accuracy Counts" game. It was introduced through full-page media advertisements such as that shown in Figure 14-13.

Figure 14-14   Game Piece   **Figure 14-15   Display Materials**

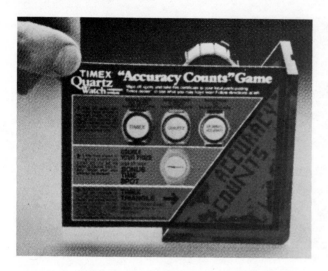

Source: Robinson, *100 Best Sales Promotions*, p. 14.

A consumer game piece was distributed through national magazines. Winning certificates were determined by matching the word on a "rub-off" watch face with a scrambled word on the watch package at the retail display. If the unscrambled word matched the word on the "rub-off" watch face, the holder was an instant winner. If the "bonus spot" showed 6:00, the prize was doubled. A "Second Chance" sweepstakes for unclaimed prizes was also held. The consumer game is illustrated in Figure 14-14. The promotion was supported at retail by counter cards and "Second Chance" entry blanks available only at the point-of-purchase. The dealer was encouraged to display the material since consumers would want to try their winning entries. (See Figure 14-15.)

The consumer promotion was backed up with a wholesaler and dealer contest to build enthusiasm at the retail level. For example, wholesaler salesmen could win from 50¢ to $25 for each watch sold, plus the opportunity to compete in an additional sweepstakes for over 700 prizes, as illustrated in Figure 14-16. And wholesaler sales managers could also win prizes equal to 10 percent of that won by their sales force. (See Figure 14-17.) Thus, there was incentive from top to bottom to merchandise and sell the new Timex Quartz watch.

The total promotion package for Timex worked beautifully. Factory shipments of the Timex Quartz watch were up 12.6 percent and distribu-

Figure 14-16	Wholesale Salesmen's Sweepstakes	Figure 14-17	Wholesale Managers' Sweepstakes

Source: Robinson, *100 Best Sales Promotions*, p. 15.

tion increased 80.1 percent in terms of number of stores in which the watches were stocked. Consumer sales increased 53.9 percent and 100 percent of the wholesalers participated in the event. You really can't expect much more from a sales promotion program than that.

Diners Club International's New Services, "Double Card," and New Corporate Identification Program

The program to "reintroduce" the Diners Club card to the market and to introduce a host of new services, plus the "Double Card," is an excellent

Figure 14-18 Trade Brochure

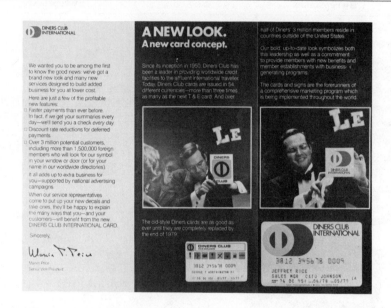

Source: Courtesy of Diners Club International.

example of a well-organized, well-integrated advertising and sales promotion package. It included a combination of several sales promotion tools, both internal and external.

The objectives of the Diners Club program, which took 10½ months to develop and implement, were quite clear. During the mid-1970s, Diners Club had fallen on hard times. The company itself had been sold, management had changed, and the marketing program had been less than aggressive. Competition, particularly in the form of American Express, had made giant strides while Diners Club had maintained an almost flat growth rate. In 1977 the decision was made to initiate a new corporate design program, introduce several new card features built around the "Double Card" idea, and revitalize the internal and external sales forces for Diners Club with a new marketing program. Specifically, the tasks broke down into 10 specific areas, each directed at a separate target market. While it is impossible to give the total scope of the program here, in the following pages you'll find representative materials and items from each of the 10 programs.

To give you an idea of the scope and depth of the Diners Club program, in Table 14-6 you'll find the flow chart of the various specific items and materials that were integrated into the promotional program.

Figure 14-19   Trade Advertisement

Source: Courtesy of Diners Club International.

Introduction of the new program to internal management, field sales, and other employees. Much of this material consisted of multimedia presentations made in various locations around the country. These were considered the key to building enthusiasm and morale among Diners Club personnel. In addition, a series of interest- and enthusiasm-building letters and reminders were sent to all personnel who attended the multimedia shows.

Brochures, advertising, mailing pieces, and point-of-sale devices for the trade. Since Diners Club was going through a complete redesign of materials and logotype, it was important that the trade be not only advised of the program, but inspired as well. Figure 14-18 illustrates a brochure designed to advise the trade of the change. Figure 14-19 illustrates a trade advertisement that was developed.

Table 14-6   Flow Chart

	January					February				March				April				May					June			
Establishment program	2	9	16	23	30	6	13	20	27	6	13	20	27	3	10	17	24	1	8	15	22	29	5	12	19	26
1. Sales blitz—new m/e's										▬	▬	▬	▬	▬	▬	▬	▬	▬	▬	▬	▬	▬	▬	▬	▬	
2. Decal and sign placement														▬	▬	▬	▬	▬	▬	▬	▬	▬	▬	▬	▬	
3. New graphic education																										
existing m/e's																										
most wanted																										
key chain execs																										
trade ads																				■						
sn 10—all m/e's																										
4. Take one apps and boxes								Design and approve						▬	▬	▬	▬	▬	▬	▬	▬	▬	▬	▬	▬	
5. Support advertising																										
radio test																										
6. POS materials																							▬	▬	▬	
Member/Consumer Program																										
1. Pre renewal mailing																										
2. Resolicit cancellations																										
3. Graphics education																										
4. Publicity	▬	▬	▬	Media interviews			▬	▬	▬									Thomas Cook					Walter Cavanagh			
5. Consumer advertising																										
signature																		TC's insurance program								
newspaper announcement																										
print schedule																										
spot television																										
outdoor display																							▬	▬	▬	
6. Direct mail acquisition						Old program 750 M				400 M				300 M				500 M								
New Cards Valid																										
New members																										
Renewals																										

Source: Courtesy of Diners Club International.

July					August				September				October					November				December				
3	10	17	24	31	7	14	21	28	4	11	18	25	2	9	16	23	30	6	13	20	27	4	11	18	25

Mail and sales calls

Direct mail   Check stuffer   Check stuffer

Incl. comp. card offer

Print   Placement blitz   Normal distribution   Where mag. 22 top mkts.

Test 3 mkts.

Review designs   Produce and distribute

OCT NOV DEC JAN FEB MAR OCT APR OCT NOV

Remittance "nester"

N.Y. press conference   Media interviews

| TC's insurance program | Announcement two page | Doublecard two page | New TC page Cash adv. page | International travel 2 pages | Insurance program |

New program
1,260 M   1,500 M   1,100 M   615 M   420 M

Figure 14-20   Salesman's Presentation Kit

Source: Courtesy of Diners Club International.

A complete training and sales promotion program for the field sales staff. This program included selling kits plus merchandising materials explaining the entire communications effort. Figure 14-20 illustrates some of the pages from a salesman's presentation kit that was used with retailers. Figure 14-21 illustrates a field sales package that was filled with information and material for use by the sales force in their calls on retailers.

Figure 14-21   Salesman's Sales Package

Source: Courtesy of Diners Club International.

Revision and redesign of existing materials directed to present Diners Club members. All Diners Club members had to be advised of the new program and services being offered. This information included a prerenewal mailing piece, billing insert announcements, insurance mailings, and follow-up advertising in *Signature*, the Diners Club magazine. The prerenewal mailing is illustrated in Figure 14-22.

Figure 14-22   Prerenewal Mailing

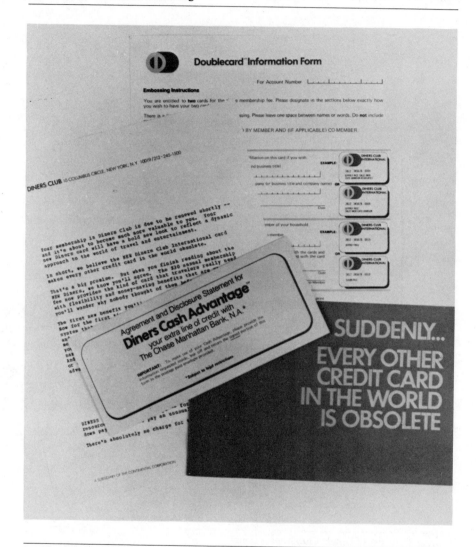

Source: Courtesy of Diners Club International.

Redesign of necessary forms and development of introductory material to be used with the new "Double Card." The simple replacement of the logotype on the many forms and materials used daily is a massive task. In addition, materials to support the new products had to be developed. A new form was designed to be sent with the "Double Cards" to new members.

Figure 14-23   Application Folder and Take-One Box

Source: Courtesy of Diners Club International.

Development of a complete new member acquisition package. This package included materials necessary to introduce and explain the new services and facilities of Diners Club. It took several forms. For example, a new take-one box and application folder for use in member retail establishments was developed. (See Figure 14-23.)

An introductory press kit to help obtain media publicity. As you can see in Figure 14-24, this kit consisted of a mass of materials that were distributed to editors to serve as background and informational material on what Diners Club was doing. In addition, a press party was held in New York to help kick off the program.

Figure 14-24   Press Kit

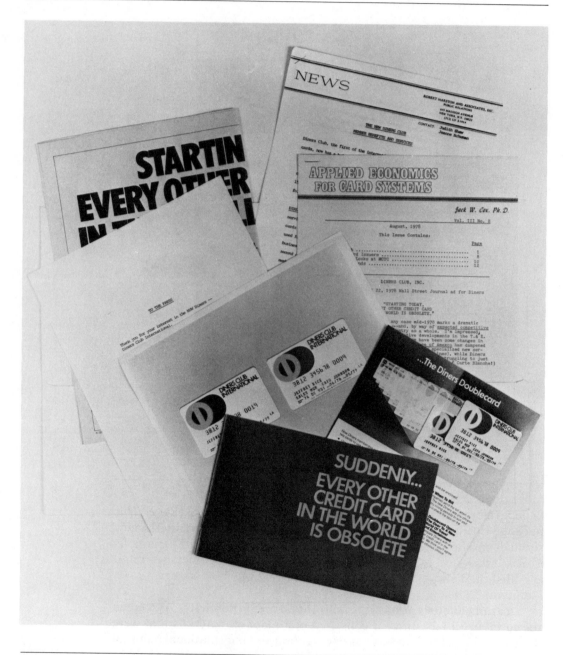

Source: Courtesy of Diners Club International.

Figure 14-25   Public Relations Campaign

Source: Courtesy of Diners Club International.

A complete public relations campaign to support the advertising and sales promotion effort. This campaign was integrated into the other aspects of the marketing program to provide a total communications package. In Figure 14-25 you'll find a few samples of the press coverage that Diners Club obtained.

Redesign and redevelopment of the U.S. directory of business establishments that accepted the Diners Club card. With the heavy emphasis on obtaining new retailers, this was a major step in the reintroduction of the card.

The development of a consumer advertising program. To get the total message across, a complete consumer media advertising program

Figure 14-26   Magazine Advertisement

Source: Courtesy of Diners Club International.

was developed. This included magazine and newspaper advertisements, plus television. Illustrated in Figure 14-26 is just one of the series of magazine advertisements introducing the "Double Card." Others in the series dealt with the other new services introduced at the same time. Shown in Figure 14-27 is the storyboard for the introductory television commercial for the "Double Card."

What we have illustrated in the Diners Club program is just a sampling of all the advertising, sales promotion, public relations, and publicity materials developed and implemented to "reintroduce" Diners Club to the market. It worked beautifully, simply because it was well planned, well organized, and well executed.

Figure 14-27   TV Commercial

Source: Courtesy of Diners Club International.

Summary

Distribution, trial, and repeat usage are the three major hurdles in introducing a new product. As a sales promotion manager, you must first understand the concepts of market segmentation and the importance of "heavy users" and how to attract them in order to bring your new product to success. Then, in a series of marketing steps, you must excite and influence the sales force, the trade, and finally the consumer, as you move the product into distribution, to trial usage and, at last, to repeat usage and respectable market share. At each step of the way, there are specific sales promotion techniques that work.

PART III

AVOIDING PROBLEMS WITH SALES PROMOTION

15

Sales Promotion and the Law

One area of growing concern to the sales promotion manager (and all business management as well) is the increasing complexity of federal, state, and local legal restrictions and controls on advertising and sales promotion. These controls apply not only to what sales promotion activities may be conducted but also to the wording and content of the promotional material. In addition to the legal controls, many industries and trade organizations have developed voluntary promotional regulations that apply to their members. From a practical point of view, these regulations can have the same effect as laws. As a result, in many situations the only persons who can truly determine "what you can and can't do and say in advertising and sales promotion" are lawyers. It appears, unfortunately, that the problem will become worse instead of better in the future.

Because of the complexity of the legal requirements for advertising and sales promotion, we can offer only the broadest guidelines. We have, however, found some common problems that seem to apply to all products and activities, particularly those that fall under federal regulations. To avoid these problems, we present some general ground rules that will help most sales promotion managers regardless of the area or category in which their product may be marketed. However, we strongly urge you to seek qualified legal counsel in any area in which the rules are not clear-cut. We will also discuss how to do that in this chapter.

Our best advice on all legal questions is: "If you're in doubt or don't know, ask." The small amount of time and money required to obtain qualified legal counsel is well worth it when compared with the cost of a legal defense for you or your company because of sales promotion activities.

The Names of the Players and What They Do

The easiest way to begin a discussion of the legal aspects of advertising and sales promotion is to identify the participants, i.e., the regulatory agencies. In most cases, they consist of various federal, state, and local bureaus, agencies, and departments, which have the responsibility of developing, implementing, and/or enforcing the various controls, regulations, and standards that apply to all aspects of advertising and sales promotion.

Federal Regulatory Bodies

The major federal regulatory bodies are the FTC, the FDA, the U.S. Postal Service, the Bureau of Alcohol, Tobacco, and Firearms, and the FCC. More specialized agencies include the SEC and the FAA. Their jurisdictions are defined in the following pages.

The Federal Trade Commission. The FTC is the agency most involved in and concerned with advertising and sales promotion activities. The FTC's primary charge under the Federal Trade Commission Act of 1914 and subsequent acts and laws was to prevent, control, or rectify deceptive acts or practices in interstate commerce. It was felt that such acts or practices could result in unfair competition, which was specifically prohibited by law. The FTC was organized to enforce these regulations, but over the years its activities have been expanded to deal more specifically with advertising and sales promotion.

The FTC is empowered to act against individual companies, groups, or even entire industries to seek relief from what the Commission considers to be unfair trade practices. As a part of this activity, the FTC has determined that false or misleading advertising as such is unlawful. In addition to enforcing the law, the FTC has formulated trade regulations in various product categories, including Advertising Guides and Trade Practice Rules. So far, Advertising Guides have been developed on deceptive pricing in advertising for tires and tubes, television sets, products made of gold, correspondence schools, and luggage, to mention a few. The real effect of these guides and rules is uncertain. If you have products in these areas, however, you should obtain copies of the relevant FTC documents. The FTC has also developed special statutes for some product categories or industries, including oleomargarine, wool products, fur products, and textile fiber products. Again, if you are involved in any of these categories, you should obtain copies of these FTC statutes and follow them *carefully*.[1]

The FTC derives its power to issue broad rules that have the effect of law from the Magnuson-Moss Act. Its most common redress against violators is to obtain a Consent Order. This simply means that the advertiser agrees to comply with or accept the decision of the FTC in regard to advertising that the Commission has found objectionable. If an advertiser refuses to enter into a Consent Order, the FTC may proceed with a hearing and ultimately secure a Cease and Desist Order. In some cases the FTC may obtain a Corrective Advertising Order. The Commission also has the power to seek injunctions or other remedies, such as restitution, for violations.

Since most products are in interstate commerce (that is, they are sold in more than one state, or advertising is placed in publications that cross state lines), most manufacturers are subject to the rules and regulations of the Federal Trade Commission. The FTC has been very active in recent years and has vigorously pursued companies and organizations that the Commission has reason to suspect of wrongdoing, at least in areas in which it believes redress is possible.

The Food and Drug Administration. The Food and Drug Administration is a unit of the Department of Health and Human Services. Under the Food and Drugs Act of 1906 and the Food, Drug, and Cosmetic Act of 1938, the FDA is empowered to rule on the accuracy of the labeling of products that come under its jurisdiction. This includes ingredients, nutritive claims, use directions, etc. The FDA can move against companies for failing to label at all or for failing to label completely, just as it can against those whose labeling is false or incorrect.

If you are in the food or drug field and your product is under the labeling restrictions of the FDA, we urge you to check the regulations that might apply to your products.

The U.S. Postal Service. The Postal Service has three areas of control over advertising and sales promotion. First, it can control obscene material and refuse to handle it if the person to whom it is directed considers it obscene. Second, it also has control over delivery of materials or advertising connected with lotteries, which are illegal, both by federal law and in all states. If sales promotion material contains the elements of a lottery, i.e., a prize, consideration, and chance, the Postal Service may refuse to handle or deliver it. Finally, the Postal Service has an implied, but seldom exercised, authority over advertising through the

---

1. Philip Ward Burton, *Advertising Copywriting*, 4th ed. (Columbus, O.: Grid, Inc., 1978), pp. 259-77.

second-class mailing privilege used by most publications. In effect, the Postal Service can withhold or deny the reduced-rate delivery service (second-class mail) to publications that carry false or misleading advertising. Since the action would be against the publication and not the actual advertiser, this capability has been little used by postal officials.

The Bureau of Alcohol, Tobacco, and Firearms. This Bureau is part of the Treasury Department. Its primary activity in advertising and sales promotion is control over the liquor, beer, and wine industries. It not only may take action against false and deceptive advertising; it also controls the type of information that may or may not appear on alcoholic product labels.

The liquor industry is one of the most regulated in the country. In addition to the elaborate rules and regulations administered by BATF, nearly every state has its own liquor advertising laws and regulations. In some states you can't show a drinking scene, in others you can only picture the bottle, and in still others you may not list retail prices.

Because the laws are so strict and so varied, we strongly urge you to obtain qualified legal counsel if you are dealing with a product in this category.

The Federal Communications Commission. The FCC exerts a limited amount of control over broadcast advertising through its authority to license radio and television stations. The FCC's primary area of decision is in license renewal, which is based on whether or not the station is acting or has acted in the "public interest, necessity, and convenience." Because the law is somewhat vague, the FCC's authority over advertising is somewhat indirect, and it has therefore been lax in using its powers. The Commission prefers to control through the licensing of the individual broadcast stations.

Other government organizations. The Securities and Exchange Commission is responsible for the control of advertising of stocks, bonds, and other securities sold in interstate commerce. The Federal Aviation Agency has control over advertising by airlines.

While these are not all the federal agencies involved in advertising and sales promotion regulation, they represent the most important ones. There are numerous statutes, laws, and regulations covering various individual products and product categories. In addition, new laws are coming into being every year, and new powers are being given to various agencies. While it is a difficult task, you must keep up with the laws and regulations that apply to your products or services. Often, the best way is through your trade or professional organizations, in addition to legal counsel.

One important point we should make is the overlap of jurisdictions among federal agencies. For example, the FTC has jurisdiction over liquor advertising, as does the BATF. Various other governmental agencies, such as the Environmental Protection Agency, overlap the jurisdiction of the Agriculture Department and the FTC. In short, don't overlook any of the agencies or rule-making bodies that may have authority, control, or jurisdiction over your sales promotion activities.

State and Local Laws

In addition to the federal regulations, there are also numerous laws enacted by the various states to regulate or control specific aspects of advertising and sales promotion. In some cases, even local governments have set up their own regulatory groups that have established rules. Generally, state laws pertain to products sold in intrastate commerce— that is, within the confines of that state. Some examples of state laws are those that control lotteries, cosmetics, securities, and bait-and-switch advertising. By far the greatest number of regulations at the state level are over the advertising and sales promotion of liquor, beer, and wine.

In addition, some state regulations have a direct effect on advertising and sales promotion programs carried in the national media, such as network television, radio, and national magazines. While the Federal Trade Commission has rules on the use of the word "free," the state of Florida and several other states have additional regulations. Each state has regulations on the subject of contests and sweepstakes and different states have different approaches. For instance, the definition of what constitutes "consideration" in defining a lottery varies among the states. In some states, it is "consideration" to have to go to a store to pick up an entry blank or to leave it there. In other states, almost anything that requires any kind of an effort may be consideration. The state of Washington controls some promotional offers, and some localities, such as New York City, even regulate the type of sales promotion programs that can be used and the way in which promotional activities can be conducted. As you can see, you have to be familiar not only with federal regulations but with state regulations as well when you develop a broad-based sales promotion program.

From this very brief review, you can see that federal, state, and local legal requirements are quite complex. That is why we recommend that you seek qualified legal counsel for any advertising or sales promotion program that is out of the ordinary or that might appear in areas with which you are not totally familiar.

Self-Regulation

In an effort to prevent or forestall further legal controls on advertising and sales promotion, several groups, particularly trade organizations, have developed and promoted self-regulatory programs in various product categories and industries. Although these self-regulations are not laws, because of the strength of the trade organization or the arousal of public opinion, they often have the same effect in terms of what individual marketers can and cannot do in their advertising and sales promotion programs. Some of the better-known self-regulatory organizations or programs are described in the following pages.

The Better Business Bureau. Better Business Bureaus, local organizations operating in most cities, attempt to control false or misleading advertising. Initially, the BBB was formed by local business people to control unfair trade practices. Since advertising and sales promotion were considered to be trade practices, the BBB naturally became involved.

Most BBB activities are conducted on the local level. The Bureau is primarily involved in such areas as bait-and-switch, false or misleading advertising, and false solicitations. Normally, the BBB attempts to control unfair or misleading advertising and sales promotion practices through the use of publicity in the local media. Sometimes, however, it may resort to legal action.

The National Advertising Review Board. The National Advertising Division of the National Council of Better Business Bureaus and local Better Business Bureaus acts as the initial investigatory arm of the Council. If the NAD cannot settle or adjudicate a matter, it may send the case to a self-regulatory body called the National Advertising Review Board. Most NARB actions deal with adjudication of "comparative" advertising, although it will hear any type of complaint. The complaints may come from the public, competition, or interested third parties. The NARB action consists of a series of hearings before a group of peers who attempt to arbitrate the disagreement or clarify the complaint.

The NARB has no real powers other than that of releasing information to the press and thereby publicizing its actions. It has no legal power but can call the FTC's attention to specific problems.

The National Association of Broadcasters. The National Association of Broadcasters has developed a rather specific group of guidelines for the advertising and sales promotion activities and materials that may appear on member radio and television stations. Since most broadcast stations abide by the NAB codes, you should be familiar with the rules and regulations pertaining to broadcast advertising generally and to your products in particular. Some areas of interest are those that prohibit the advertising of liquor and contraceptives, forbid the impersonation of doctors, establish rules on method, and control advertising aimed at children.

Individual media regulations. Some media exercise great control over the type and content of the advertising they carry. For example, each television commercial scheduled for network use must be approved in advance by the network. Typically, advertisers submit storyboards of planned commercials to the networks in advance of production to obtain their approval. Print media may also exercise the right of censorship over advertising that appears in their pages, although this is the exception rather than the rule. Technically, any publication may accept, reject, or ask for modification of any planned advertising, as they desire or see fit. Generally, individual media base their judgments on whether or not the advertising or sales promotion is false, misleading, in bad taste, or obscene. Since there is no recourse against these individual media, you should check questionable copy with each medium before planning your program.

Throughout this chapter, we have discussed false or misleading advertising as if it were clearly determinable. It isn't. In many cases, whether something is false or misleading is a subjective matter, and honorable people can disagree. For instance, whether or not a particular clinical test for a product justifies a specific product claim can be subject to *bona fide* disagreement among well-meaning people. Quite often, even lawyers disagree on whether a claim is properly supported or whether an advertisement is false or deceptive. For these reasons, we strongly urge you to seek qualified legal counsel on all sales promotion activities prior to use of the material to avoid any problems.

Individual industries. Through their trade associations, affiliations, or other organizations, many industries have developed a set of suggested advertising and sales promotion guidelines to aid their members. These are peculiar to each industry and usually contain the best thinking of the members of that group. They are not binding on any of the members. For example, the Distilled Spirits Institute, a liquor trade organization, has developed a quite complete list of suggestions on what members can do in their advertising and sales promotion programs. Similar guidelines can be found in many other product categories, such as meat packing and banking. You should contact the trade association or organization that represents your product category to determine what advertising and sales promotion suggestions have been offered.

As you can see, the number of organizations, bureaus, and groups with legal authority or nonlegal influence over what can and cannot be said in advertising and sales promotion is quite large. The safest way to avoid trouble is to know the law generally as it applies to advertising and sales promotion and to know the specific laws and regulations pertaining to your particular product or industry. Then check your copy, plans, and program with legal counsel. Only in that way can you be assured you are complying with all the regulations and guidelines related to your sales promotion program.

Most of our discussion so far has been primarily concerned with advertising regulation. For legal purposes, advertising and sales promotion are not separated since sales promotion is considered to be part of the broad category of advertising. Because most organizations and most regulatory bureaus do not discriminate between advertising and sales promotion, read "sales promotion" whenever you see the term "advertising regulations." That's the safe way.

The Important Acts and Laws

In addition to the rules and regulations imposed on advertising and sales promotion, there are a number of laws, acts, and other legal requirements relating specifically to the field of sales promotion. Space permits us only to review them briefly. Again, we urge you to seek qualified legal counsel to clarify any points that may arise or answer any questions you may have about how these particular laws or regulations pertain to your specific product or brand.

The Sherman Antitrust Act of 1890 was an attempt to break up or prevent the establishment of monopolies, cartels, and trusts that result in restraint of trade. This act is the basis for most current advertising and sales promotion regulation in force today.

The Clayton Antitrust Act of 1914 was designed to clarify the Sherman Act, particularly in the area of price discrimination. The act states that there can be no price or other discrimination against purchasers by a manufacturer. All buyers must be treated on a proportionately equal basis. The Federal Trade Commission Act of 1914 set up the FTC and empowered it to prevent restraint of trade through deceptive acts or practices resulting in unfair competition.

The Robinson-Patman Act of 1936 was a further attempt to guarantee equal treatment by manufacturers of all who buy from them. Under this act, equal terms and conditions must be given to all purchasers by manufacturers. They must also give proportionately equal assistance to those reselling the product, in such areas as advertising allowances and p-o-p materials. Interpretation of the Robinson-Patman Act has been strongly influenced by one important court decision. In *FTC* v. *Fred Meyer* the court ruled that a small retailer who buys from a wholesaler is entitled to the same price structure and the same advertising and promotion assistance from the manufacturer as large, direct purchasers. This case extended the coverage of Robinson-Patman to retailers.

The federal Food, Drug, and Cosmetic Act of 1938 empowered the FDA to control the labeling of all foods, drugs, and cosmetics that come under its jurisdiction. The Wheeler Act of the same year regulates false advertising in foods, drugs, cosmetics, and therapeutic devices. The Lanham Act of 1946 protects trademarks and trade symbols from infringement and misuse. The Magnuson-Moss Warranty Act of 1975 deals with the clarification of manufacturer warranties and guarantees on products and how they must be communicated.

In addition, miscellaneous specific acts directly relate to advertising, sales promotion, and labeling or packaging of products in interstate commerce: the Wool Products Labeling Act, 1938; the Fur Products Labeling Act, 1951; the Flammable Fabrics Act, 1953; and the Textile Fiber Identification Act, 1958. You are urged to follow up on these specific laws and acts if they apply to your products or services.

Common Legal Problems in Sales Promotion

As we have stressed throughout this chapter, our comments are not intended as legal information or legal guidance. Our primary purpose has been to point out regulatory problems that have caused trouble for sales promotion managers in the past. By understanding these problems now, you should be able to avoid them in the future.

To that end, in the following pages we discuss some general problems in the area of regulation. In our treatment of each problem we attempt to give the gist of the legal situation as it now stands. Obviously, we cannot relate each one to your particular product or brand. However, the discussion should prove helpful in enabling you to determine the areas in which you might want to seek legal advice.

Illegal Acts

In each of the areas below, there are specific laws or court decisions defining what can or cannot be said or done.

Puffery. The general category of "puffery" or "puffing" has generated a great deal of comment and controversy. Legally, the manufacturer has a right to expound on the value or merit of his product as long as it is an expression of opinion rather than a specific product claim or is taken as a characteristic of the product. For example, subjective claims of "the most beautiful" or "the finest" or "the best value" are considered harmless exaggerations. It is assumed that most buyers will understand these claims and not consider them to be literally true.

Puffery becomes false or misleading advertising when it makes an implied or stated claim for product quality that might induce a purchase. For example, the statement that "this is the most beautiful two-carat diamond ring in the world" could be considered puffery in terms of the seller's impression of beauty. But it could not be considered puffery in terms of the two-carat size or weight of the diamond. In other words, the seller can claim that the diamond is "the most beautiful in the world" in his opinion. But he cannot say that in his opinion it is "a two-carat diamond" or that it appeared to him that it was two carats in size and weight.

However, there are some people in the FTC and other areas of government who do not consider puffery to be a defense against charges of deceiving the public. They contend that when you say "the most beautiful" you are deceiving the public, unless you have a market survey showing that a significant number of people consider it to be "the most beautiful."

In spite of this disagreement, the usual basis for distinguishing between puffery and a product misrepresentation is whether there is a reference to a clearly definable, objectively ascertainable product quality or performance capacity in the advertising. Thus, Burt Reynolds can lead a customer into a purchase with a smile and the statement, "I think it is beautiful."

Generally, puffery has been allowed when the claim is immaterial and when the exaggeration is insubstantial and immeasurable. Puffery is widespread in advertising and sales promotion. Indeed, without puffery, most sales promotion material would be quite dull. The sales promotion manager must be able to distinguish, however, between those claims that are merely puffery and those that might tend to mislead or deceive. The first are legal. The latter are not.

False and misleading advertising. Unfortunately, it is not easy to define what is "false and misleading" in advertising or sales promotion. Everyone has his or her own ideas. In the following paragraphs are some very general guidelines that may help you. Of course, if the claim is false, it is false no matter how many or how few see or believe the sales promotion claim. There is no question on this point.

There is a somewhat different problem with misleading advertising or sales promotion. The courts have decided that if the advertising or sales promotion is misleading to a reasonable proportion of the population, it is misleading to all. Thus, even though a statement may be technically true and could be understood by a college graduate, if it is not readily understood by the man on the street or by a substantial portion of the population, it is considered misleading. Thus, even utter truth cannot be supported if it can be misunderstood.

As a general rule, a claim should be considered false and deceptive if it is not supported by scientific evidence or clinical experience, if it misrepresents the quality or performance of the product, if it is ambiguous, or if the *net impression* created in the reader or listener is deceptive and misleading, even though the actual words used are accurate. The principal areas of deception are lack of proper disclosure and lack of support for product claims.

This area of misleading claims is a very tricky one. Generally, the best approach is to avoid any attempt to hide or disguise facts about the product or the promotion. Clearly state the benefit of your product in your sales promotion program and avoid the problem.

Incomplete disclosure. Full disclosure is generally taken to mean that the manufacturer should provide sufficient information about the product or service so that the consumer can make an informed buying decision. For example, while a credit card company may talk about the convenience of credit purchases and the opportunity to pay purchases up over time, it must also advise the customer that finance charges will be made on the unpaid balance if the payments are extended, if and when talking about the way the bills are rendered or charges are incurred.

The manufacturer must list the primary positive and negative facts about the product that might influence purchasing, particularly facts relating to the specific claim being made.

Deceptive pricing. Deceptive pricing and bait-and-switch advertising can create major problems since both are illegal and the restrictions are clearly defined.

Deceptive pricing is an attempt to mislead or misinform the prospective consumer about the true price of the product. For example, it is a form of deceptive pricing to illustrate an offer with a complete unit—such as a camera—while actually offering only the shell of the camera for a low price but not advising the consumer that the offer does not include the lens and other extras shown in the illustration. The same is true for products that must be purchased in sets or paid for over time with finance charges. The failure to inform the consumer of such buying and paying requirements is strictly illegal.

Of particular interest in the area of deceptive pricing are claims of special savings, extra discounts, and reductions from ticketed prices. In all instances, savings must be calculated on the basis of normal and usual prices.

In addition, such words and phrases as "clearance," "special purchase," "manufacturer's close-out," and the like, cannot legally be used unless the claim is true. Thus, a manufacturer or retailer may not advertise a saving for a particular reason unless that is truly the reason for the saving. The same is true of a "two-for-the-price-of-one" sale or a "1¢ sale." Both are illegal unless the two products are actually sold at either the normal retail selling price of the single product or 1¢ more. These are not difficult rules to follow since they relate to truthful statements about price and pricing.

Bait-and-switch advertising. The same general requirements apply to bait-and-switch advertising. This occurs when a retailer advertises or promotes a low-priced article without intending to sell it, not having the article available or attempting to sell the purchaser a more expensive article by using the low-priced product as bait to lure him or her to the store. An example would be to advertise a particular sewing machine model at a very low price and then have only one or two machines available or none at all. The bait-and-switch plan would be to tell customers who came in to take advantage of the bargain that the advertised machine was sold out or that it was not a good value. The sales people would then attempt to sell those customers a more expensive machine that was in stock. In other words, the seller used the low-priced product as "bait" to bring the customers in. Then he attempted to "switch" them to a higher-priced product. Bait-and-switch advertising is patently illegal.

Trademark infringements. Trademarks are usually well protected. Thus, it is vital that you observe two major rules. First, always use another's trademark correctly. This is especially important in the use of trademarks in promotional material for other brands or when products are used as premiums. Second, before using a new trade name or a trademark, make a thorough check of the possible prior use of the mark. This includes checking the Trademark Register, obtaining legal counsel, and initiating a formal trademark search. The primary purpose is to ensure that you are not infringing on a mark already in use or a name currently in use by another company.

Copyright violations. A copyright does not protect the basic idea of the author. It does, however, protect the actual language or the close paraphrasing by another party. Thus, while you may use the general idea of copyrighted material, you may not use it as it was written, without the permission of the copyright holder. To do so is an infringement. This refers to copying or using a large amount of the material. There is a doctrine called "Fair Use," under which you can use excerpts from copyrighted material. For example, you may use a quotation from a work without permission of the author. You cannot, however, use a full chapter from a book or a similarly large portion of the work without obtaining permission.

Copyrighted music follows the same rule. You may not use the words or melody of a song without the express permission of the copyright holder. Some songs that have been in use for many years are now in the "public domain." This means that there is no single copyright holder, and the words and/or music can be used by anyone. Before using any published material, be sure to have your legal counsel check with the copyright holder.

Libel

It is possible to libel a person, a company, or a product, for libel simply means to injure the reputation by writing something that you know to be untrue. In advertising and sales promotion, we are much more concerned about the libel of a company or a product. Libeling a product means that you are making a false statement about the product. If, for instance, you were to say that Borden milk is made of chemicals and not of cow's milk, that would be trade libel.

Invasion of privacy. The use of the name or picture of a person without permission is a violation of his or her right to privacy. That means you must have a written release form for each and every person whose name or picture appears in any form of advertising or sales promotion materials. Infants' releases must be signed by the parents. This rule applies to models as well as the general public. For example, if you photograph a crowd scene and plan to use it in a sales promotion piece, you must have the release of every person in the picture. No exceptions. While this requirement is a burden, a lawsuit later can be an even greater burden.

Problem Areas

Besides the illegal acts mentioned above, the sales promotion manager should also be aware of certain areas in advertising and sales promotion in which legal requirements are quite specific and violations of which are also illegal.

Labeling. While proper labeling is required by the FDA and varies by product and product category, nutritional claims by a manufacturer may be quite another matter. There are standard formats and measurements required for discussions of the nutritional content of some product categories. These must be followed closely. In cases in which there are no such regulations and the manufacturers determine their own nutritional claims, there must be substantial proof that the claims are true and correct. They must be established on the basis of properly conducted research and acceptable as scientific facts.

Guarantees and warranties. The words "guarantee" and "warranty" have caused considerable confusion. Usually they are considered to mean the same thing, but a "warranty" is attached to or printed on the product, the package, or the label, while a "guarantee" is usually used in advertising. Warranties and guarantees can carry any conditions manufacturers choose to set forth, such as "guaranteed for one year" or "guaranteed not to break." The key element in both is that the conditions, if any, must be disclosed clearly and completely. That is, there should be no doubt about what the manufacturer is willing to do as part of the guarantee, or what, if anything, the customer has to do to obtain the benefits of the guarantee. For example, if the guarantee is that either the unit will be replaced or the purchaser's money will be refunded, then the choice is up to the consumer either to take the refund of the purchase price or to accept a new unit. The choice is not up to the manufacturer as to which can be done. The Magnuson-Moss Warranty Act requires that warranties attached to the product be labeled either "full warranty" or "limited warranty." Very few warranties are "full"; there is almost always some kind of limitation.

The legal requirements for warranties and guarantees are about the same. Limitations in either must be clearly spelled out. Any "ifs, ands, or buts" must be conspicuously and clearly identified. Since there is a legal obligation with warranties and guarantees, a qualified legal counsel should be consulted not only for help in writing them, but also for advice on the manner in which they may be used in advertising and sales promotion materials.

Free offers. The word "free" can cause many problems for the sales promotion manager. The misuse of the word has brought forth a list of rules on how the term can and cannot be used. For example, in its Standard "Free" Rule, the FTC prohibits the use of the word "free" under circumstances where there has been some change in the price, quality, or quantity of the regular merchandise that is offered as "free." In other words, when the free offer is tied in with something else, the seller may not mislead consumers into thinking that they are going to get the free article, plus something they are accustomed to getting, if that article has been changed. For example, if a furniture retailer had previously sold a bedroom set consisting of a bed, a chest, and two night stands at $750, it would be considered misleading for him to advertise that same bedroom set at the $750 price and say it consisted of a bed, chest, and one night stand and that he was offering the second night stand "free." Because the second night stand was originally a part of the set, the retailer would be misleading the consumer by stating it was now "free."

You may make a free offer of any sort, if it is legitimately free. If the "free" product is not truly free, however, the stipulations must be spelled out clearly and completely.

Testimonials and endorsements. The key ingredient in a testimonial or endorsement is that it must be the truth. While an advertiser may hire a person to give an endorsement and not disclose the fact that the person is being paid, the testimonial given must be true and correct. A testimonial cannot be taken out of context, and if only a portion is used it must contain the elements of the entire statement.

One of the important requirements for selecting an endorser of a product or someone to give testimony is that he or she must be qualified to pass judgment on the product or service. In other words, if the person is presented as an expert, he must be an expert in fact. For example, a movie starlet with an opinion about how a shampoo cleans her hair is qualified to discuss the product on that level. But to have her discuss the relative merits of the pH values of the shampoo would not be acceptable unless she is also an expert—a chemist or a cosmetologist.

There are several other regulations on testimonials and endorsements. Check them thoroughly before you use this technique.

Premiums. The most common problem in the use of premiums is the misstatement of the value of the premium. The stated value of the premium must be the actual value at which the premium has normally been sold or the estimated price if the product were to be sold on its own. In addition, in order to protect against state and local laws, most premium offers should carry the line, "This offer void where prohibited, taxed, or otherwise restricted."

Contests and sweepstakes. A contest is a perfectly legal sales promotion device in most areas. Problems with a contest usually arise when it is not truly a contest but becomes a lottery, which is illegal in all states. The second problem comes about when the advertiser does not give full details of the contest requirements or when the contest is conducted fraudulently or deceptively.

A contest is a game of skill in which there may be participation costs or some consideration required to win a prize. The key ingredient in a contest is that the winner be determined and selected strictly on the basis of skill or ability, not chance or luck. If chance or luck is involved, then the contest is not a contest but a lottery, which is defined as a game or event in which three components are present: the element of chance, a consideration, and a prize. A sweepstakes may offer a prize and the winner may be selected by luck or chance, and yet the event may not be considered a lottery. The difference is in the consideration element. In other words, if no consideration is required from the sweepstakes entrants, then chance or luck in selecting the winner may be legally used. However, we should caution you here, again, that various state laws differ on what is considered "consideration." In some states it is "consideration" to have to go to a store to pick up an entry blank or leave it there. In other states, almost anything that requires any kind of an effort is felt to be "consideration." We strongly urge you to check with qualified legal counsel or a professional contest and sweepstakes organization to determine what can and cannot be done in this area. It is quite complex and the rules vary widely.

A second area of legal concern is in sweepstakes conducted by some retailers or in retail games. In these events the marketers are required to calculate the odds of winning, state them, and advise the entrants of them. (The calculation is based on the estimated number of entries, the prize structure, the number of winners, etc.)

The rules of the sweepstakes or contest must clearly state how the prizes will be awarded. For example, if it is a lucky number sweepstakes and the lucky numbers for all prizes are not claimed, the sweepstakes sponsor must have an alternate method of awarding the prizes or must clearly state that the awards will not be made. This will change the value of the contest and the method by which it can be advertised and promoted. The usual method of awarding prizes in sweepstakes in which consumers do not claim their prizes is through a random drawing of all entries at the close of the sweepstakes.

Finally, there are state and local regulations for contests, sweepstakes, and similar sales promotion devices, not only in how but also under what conditions they may be conducted. These regulations vary greatly. You are best advised to obtain the services of a qualified legal counsel to investigate them for the areas in which your program will appear. Because of the complexity of contests and sweepstakes, the use of a qualified contest service organization for any but the simplest local contest is usually well worth the cost involved.

Language. There are some words and phrases that can create problems for the sales promotion manager if not used correctly. Philip Ward Burton has called them "red flag" words since they often signal an improper claim for the product. Some of the more common ones are:

- *Banish, rid, stop, end.* Each of these words implies finality—that is, if you use this product, the problem will be solved forever. If the product will not do that, don't use words that suggest that it will.

- *Cure, remedy, therapeutic, curative.* Unless the product will actually cure the disease, these words cannot be used. In most cases, medications treat only the symptoms, not the cause. Be sure the product will actually "cure" the disease before you use any of these words.
- *Safe, harmless.* These words are to be taken literally. Safe means safe under any conditions. Harmless means that no harm will come, regardless of whether the product is used correctly or incorrectly. If the product is not totally safe or not totally harmless, avoid these words or qualify them; i.e., say, "Safe when taken as directed."
- *Science, scientific, test, evidence, proof, research.* These words must be used cautiously. Scientific proof must be arrived at scientifically. Tests must be scientific tests. Proof must be substantiated. Because these words can create such misleading impressions, they should be used sparingly unless there is sound, scientific proof for your claim.
- *Doctor, laboratory.* The NAB Codes preclude the use of anyone pretending to be a doctor or representing a person in any way so as to indicate professionalism, such as by wearing a white coat. The same is true of the words *doctor* and *laboratory*. If you plan to call a person a doctor, or if he or she is to represent a doctor, they must be licensed to practice medicine if they are to appear in broadcast. In print, you could show a laboratory set or perhaps casually show an actor in a white coat, as long as the representations in the advertisement don't mislead.

There are numerous other restrictions that apply to medical proof or approval. Check with your legal counsel to make sure that what you have in mind can be done without risk.[2]

These are some of the more common areas that cause sales promotion managers problems. No doubt there are others. We have found the best solution to legal problems is: When in doubt, ask your legal counsel.

Getting Advice on Legal Problems

Generally, there are four sources of legal counsel available to most sales promotion managers. They are: (1) your own legal staff, (2) the legal staffs of your associated agencies, (3) your trade organization, and (4) legal specialists.

Internal sources. Most larger companies have their own legal staff, either in-house or on retainer. In such cases, it is a simple matter to contact the legal department either personally or through a memo whenever a legal question arises. Certainly you should have major promotion

---

2. Burton, *Advertising Copywriting*, pp. 259-277.

programs reviewed prior to the time they are printed and distributed. It is much easier to solve a problem before production than to try to retrieve the promotional materials from all over the country after they have been distributed.

External sources. If internal legal advice is not available, you will have to go to outside sources: law firms, the legal counsel for your advertising or sales promotion agency, or the legal counsel for your vendors, such as fulfillment organizations. Because they are experienced with sales promotion practices, these groups are often of more help with specific sales promotion questions than internal legal advisors simply because they work with the problems every day. If these people are available to you, use them.

A couple of notes of caution: If you plan to use an outside law firm, be sure it has had experience in advertising, sales promotion, or promotion in general. The area is quite complex, and legal counselors who are not experienced or have not practiced in the area regularly may require much more time to reach a decision than those more familiar with the advertising and sales promotion field.

Ask your advertising agency or your sales promotion agency to have all work cleared through their legal counsel prior to submission to you. There is no reason for you to review work that cannot pass legal muster. Then, get the opinion of your own legal counsel if you have a question.

We have found that while it may be troublesome, the routine approval of all sales promotion copy by qualified legal counsel can save more than it costs. We suggest that you have everything cleared through legal. If you can't, be sure you cover the most sensitive areas.

Trade organizations. Often, if you are with a member company or there is a question that pertains to a specific category or product group, you can ask the legal advice of the trade association or organization. Since most trade associations are responsible for the legal questions on their products, they are up to date on the latest information and legal opinions.

Legal specialists. In addition, you may find it necessary to call on more specialized legal counselors, such as copyright lawyers and patent attorneys. Usually, if your regular legal counsel cannot provide a ready answer to your question, he will recommend a specialist in the field. Although a specialist's fees may be higher initially, you usually will save time and money in the long run.

Summary

There are many governmental bodies, at federal, state, and local levels, whose regulations may affect your sales promotion plans. In addition, there are a number of product-category self-regulation groups that you should know about. A good sales promotion manager should also be familiar with the body of basic law that governs advertising and sales promotion.

Specific areas to watch out for include false and misleading advertising, deceptive pricing, and bait-and-switch advertising. Copyright infringements and other copyright violations, and the possibility of libel and invasion of privacy should also concern sales promotion managers. In addition, specific sales promotion techniques, such as premiums, free offers, and contests may raise legal questions and require legal advice.

In all these areas, there is no substitute for qualified legal advice, whether it comes from your in-house legal department or outside counsel. The comments and suggestions we have made in this chapter are based on our own experience in the sales promotion field. Your problems may be different. We urge you to take full advantage of legal counsel on all questions concerning the legality of your promotions and the manner in which they are presented. In this case, the old saying "Better safe than sorry" is absolutely correct.

16

Sales Promotion and the Budget

The budgeting of funds, time, and effort is one of the most important and difficult areas of sales promotion management. Usually, the problem comes about not because there is no need or interest in the subject; rather, the greatest difficulty is simply finding an acceptable method of controlling the funds and the effort. A Marketing Science Institute study by P. J. Robinson and J. J. Luck in 1964 revealed that some of the deterrents to systematic decision making in sales promotion were high personnel turnover, shortage of information about past promotions, lack of understanding of corporate goals by the planners, lack of pertinent information to make decisions, poor attitudes among senior executives, lack of communication between line and staff members, lack of assistance from new product managers, failure to define promotion objectives, and uncoordinated revision of marketing plans.[1] No doubt many marketing companies suffer from at least one of these problems. Unfortunately, the problems found in 1964 still cause the most trouble today in sales promotion budgeting.

In spite of these problems, however, a budget must be set and followed. The obvious question is, "What is the best method of budgeting?" We will look at several ways to budget in this chapter and make some suggestions that should help the novice and experienced budgeter alike. In addition, we will discuss two budgeting problems all managers face:

---

1. P. J. Robinson and J. J. Luck, *Promotional Decision Making: Practice and Theory* (New York: McGraw Hill, 1964), Chapter 8.

how to allocate funds between advertising and sales promotion and how to control costs.

Before discussing specific methods of budgeting, we need an overview of the relationship between the advertising and sales promotion budget. As a general rule, many companies never get more deeply involved in sales promotion budgeting than simply allocating or determining the ratio between what funds are to be spent on advertising and what are given to sales promotion. Less thought is given to determining an overall promotion budget than to the allocation of the budget between advertising and sales promotion spending. No doubt, part of this is caused by the still-unresolved question among many marketing executives about the relationship between the two. While we believe they work in combination and that the combined effect of both is greater than the individual effect of either, other managers are still not quite sure. They question whether advertising and sales promotion are complementary, work independently of each other, or are, in fact, interchangeable—i. e., you can simply substitute sales promotion for advertising and achieve the same effects. This uncertainty exists partly because some marketing executives have a natural preference for advertising over sales promotion. Advertising is felt to be somehow less "commercial" and perhaps more "professional" than sales promotion. Therefore, the advertising budget is often determined first. Then the funds for sales promotion are determined by the "leftovers"; that is, what is not used for advertising is "left over" for sales promotion. We believe this is poor planning, particularly because it can actually harm the overall marketing program.

The Components of the Sales Promotion Budget

A major problem in establishing a sound promotion budget for the company, particularly an advertising and sales promotion budget, is an apparent lack of understanding by some executives of exactly how promotion dollars are generated. The people who are establishing the budget do not really know how or why marketing budgets work. To put the sales promotion budget in focus, we will look first at how overall budgets are established.

Where Do Advertising and Sales Promotion Dollars Come from?

A primary problem in establishing an advertising and sales promotion budget is the continuing inability of some managers to explain or quantify the effects of advertising and sales promotion in terms of what contributes to actual sales or profits for the firm. The basic problems are (1) the effects of intervening variables that may distort the direct cause-and-effect relationship that makes evaluation possible, and (2) the time

Table 16-1   Hypothetical Operating Statement for a Consumer Package-Good Product

(A)	Retail price 69¢ per can/12 per case		$8.28	
(B)	Retailer's margin @ 20%		1.66	
(C)	Gross price to retailer		6.62	
(D)	Less trade promotions/deals @ 2%		0.13	
(E)	Net price to retailers		6.49	
(F)	Wholesale/broker commission @ 7%		0.45	
(G)	Net sales price		6.04	(100%)
(H)	Cost of goods		3.32	(55%)
(J)	Fixed costs 20%	$0.66		
(K)	Variable costs 80%	2.66		
(L)	Gross margin		2.72	(45%)
(M)	Distribution expense		0.12	(2%)
(N)	Contribution margin		2.60	(43%)
(P)	Direct expenses			
(Q)	Advertising	0.36		(6%)
(R)	Sales promotion	0.24		(4%)
(S)	Management and sales expense	0.92		(15%)
(T)	Research and development	0.06		(1%)
(U)	Total direct expenses		1.58	(26%)
(V)	Product margin		1.02	(17%)

Source: Don E. Schultz and Dennis G. Martin, *Strategic Advertising Campaigns* (Chicago: Crain Books, 1980), p. 49.

lag of promotion results—i.e., promotion funds spent today may not result in sales or profits until several days, weeks, or even months later. Without specific evidence of promotional results, managers are hard-put to justify requests to management for funds or even to establish a relationship between increased results based on increased spending. In spite of this, there must be some method of establishing a promotion budget. Knowing and understanding the operation of a typical consumer brand (Table 16-1) will be of help.

Assume you are the brand manager for Ajax Company. Your primary brand responsibility is Eastern-Style chili. The chili is packed in 14-ounce cans and shipped 12 cans to the case. The normal (out-of-store) retail price of the chili is 69¢ per can.

Line (A) illustrates the retail price of a case of 12 cans of chili at 69¢ each. From the retail price of 69¢, the retailer usually takes a gross margin of 20 percent. Thus, on a per-case basis, the retailer's gross profit is $1.66, Line (B), leaving a Gross Price to the Retailer on a case of chili of $6.62, Line (C).

From the Gross Trade Price, a deduction for trade promotions or deals must be made, Line (D). Since chili is not usually responsive to trade promotion, Ajax Company plans to offer trade promotions amounting to only 2 percent of Gross Sales to the Retailer during the year. This trade deal will be offered only once, as an advertising allowance, to tie in with Western Week, the Ajax Company's umbrella promotion for all brands. The cost of the proposed trade promotion is deducted from the Gross Price to the Retailer to give the Net Price to the Retailer, Line (E). Thus, the Net Price per case to the Retailer is $6.49, Line (E).

Since Eastern-Style chili is not sold directly to the retailer, but through a broker or wholesaler, that commission must be deducted. The average commission to a broker or the margin required by a wholesaler is 7 percent of the Gross Price, Line (F), in this case, 45¢. This amount is deducted from the Net Price to the Retailer, leaving a Net Sales Price for the chili of $6.04 per case, Line (G). This is what Ajax Company will receive for the sale of every case of Eastern-Style chili.

The cost of manufacturing and packaging the chili must be deducted from the Net Sales Price. The total Cost-of-Goods, as determined by the production and accounting departments, amounts to $3.32 per case, or 55 percent of the Net Sales Price. The Fixed Cost, Line (J), the chili's share of the company's general overhead, is calculated at 20 percent of the Cost-of-Goods, 66¢ per case. The Variable Costs, Line (K), are calculated at 80 percent of the Cost-of-Goods of the product, or $2.66 per case. The Variable Costs include such items as raw materials, cost of manufacturing, filling, and packaging the chili, and some storage and handling until it is put into the distribution stream. Thus, by deducting Cost-of-Goods, Line (H), from the Net Sales Price, the Gross Margin on the product, Line (L), is obtained. The Gross Margin is the amount available for transportation and marketing expenses and any profit to Ajax Company on the sale of each case of chili.

Using the Gross Margin available, Line (L), of $2.72 per case, Distribution Expense, Line (M), is first deducted. This is the actual cost of physically moving the product from the manufacturing plant to the wholesale warehouse or the retail store. Here, the Distribution Expense is calculated to be 2 percent of Net Sales, or 12¢ per case. Subtracting this Distribution Expense from the Gross Margin leaves a Contribution Margin of $2.60 per case, Line (N). If there were no selling or other expenses, this Contribution Margin would be the amount each case of chili could contribute to the profit of the company. Realistically, however, there are promotional expenses that are referred to as Direct Expenses, Lines (P) and (U).

Direct Expenses include all promotional costs, such as Advertising, Line (Q), Sales Promotion, Line (R), Management and Sales Expense, Line (S), and an allocation for Research and Development of new or improved chili, Line (T). These costs are combined as Total Direct Expenses, Line (U).

While the final profit on each case of chili is shown as Product Margin, Line (V), and appears to be what is left after all costs and expenses have been deducted, the format is somewhat misleading.

Usually, management of Ajax Company, after reviewing sales and expense forecasts for all company products and brands, assigns a profit margin percentage or a total dollar figure to the chili brand as a goal for the coming year. This goal is determined on the basis of an adequate return on the company's investment in the chili brand and as a proper contribution to the overall financial income and profit of the company. Thus, in actuality, using the profit goals established by management for the brand, the available amount of money for marketing, including advertising, sales promotion, sales, and R&D, is the difference between the Contribution Margin, Line (N), and the Product Margin, Line (V), or in this case, $1.02 per case of chili sold. It is from this Total Direct Expenses amount, Line (U), that brand management makes the allocation for any advertising campaign or consumer sales promotion activities. Quite often, these two are combined simply as "promotion," with the allocation made after the overall plan has been approved.

There are, of course, circumstances that could help to increase or decrease the funds available for Total Direct Expenses, Line (U). Such things as increased sales might reduce the Variable Costs of the product, Line (K), as manufacturing economies of scale are realized. With larger sales, the fixed cost per case would also be reduced. The possibility exists also of reducing or completely deleting all Trade Promotions/Deals, Line (D), and concentrating efforts on the consumer, although this is not too realistic. If sales could be concentrated closer to the manufacturing plant, Distribution Expenses, Line (M), might be lowered. A change in any of these costs would directly affect the number of dollars available to the product manager for Total Direct Expenses, Line (U). For purposes of this illustration, however, the assumption is made that the sales forecast is fairly firm, the trade promotions and deals are already established, and distribution expenses will not vary. It is within this framework that the brand manager with the advertising or sales promotion agency must determine how best to allocate the available marketing funds to generate the best return on the investment.

In most instances, Management and Sales Expenses, Line (S), and Research and Development costs, Line (T), are most difficult to manipulate. For example, Management and Sales Expenses, Line (S), consist of the salaries and expenses of the sales force who call on the trade. In a multi-product company, this expense is usually allocated to individual brands on the basis of total sales volume, or brand management determines how much of the sales force's time they would like devoted to the brand. The cost to the brand is then determined as a percentage of overall sales costs. In addition, the salaries of the product manager, any assistants, and the clerical staff, are included in this figure. As a result, reduction of Management and Sales Expense is a difficult task, although some alternatives are available.

The same is true of Research and Development costs, Line (T). In this instance, because Ajax Company manufactures many food products, a general Research and Development program for the entire company is operated under an R&D Unit. Because this group works on behalf of all brands, costs of their efforts are allocated on an equalized basis. The chili brand pays a prorated share of all costs of Research and Development, with the understanding that the group is working on behalf of the chili brand a proportionate share of the time. R&D expenses charged to the chili brand are allocated by top management and difficult to reduce.

It quickly becomes evident that the actual funds available for advertising and sales promotion, using the illustration of the chili brand, are greatly constrained. The available funds are the result of a build-up or breakdown of sales and expense forecasts made by brand or top management. Any increases in funds available for advertising or sales promotion must be a direct result of increased sales or reduced costs.

In some cases, it appears, there is little understanding of how and where the promotion funds are generated within a company or by a brand. The usual result of this misunderstanding is an unrealistic sales promotion proposal or a request for additional advertising or sales promotion dollars that are not available. Hopefully, this simplifed explanation clarifies how advertising and sales promotion dollars are generated within a company and what must be done to justify proposed campaigns or to request additional funds. It also indicates why so much emphasis is placed on the division of advertising and sales promotion dollars. With limited funds available, it may seem more important to properly allocate what is available rather than to generate additional funds.

There are, of course, other approaches to promotion budgeting. Sometimes the sales promotion manager may not be privy to the complete operating statement of a particular brand or company. Top management may prefer not to release specific profit-or-loss margins on products or even the whole company for analysis. In these cases, the sales promotion manager and any sales promotion agency's prime task is allocation of an approved promotion budget and execution of the approved promotion plan for the brand. Unfortunately, this is the usual approach. Certainly, it is more common than the system we have just described.[2]

Thus, all charges directly related to the use of measured media should be directly charged to advertising. This would also include production of materials used, talent, media costs, and the like. A question arises, however, when media is used solely to promote sales promotion events, such as a sweepstakes or a direct mail program. Although the case is not so

---

2. Don Schultz and Dennis Martin, *Strategic Advertising Campaigns* (Chicago: Crain Books, 1980), pp. 49-51.

clear, we believe that charges of this type should go against the sales promotion budget.

It is quite clear that charges for activities that are specifically considered sales promotion are legitimate. That would include, for example, all charges associated with a couponing program, from the printing of the coupons through the redemption costs. The same would be true for other common sales promotion programs, such as sampling, premiums, cents-off, and reusable containers.

What Goes into the Sales Promotion Budget?

As the harassed sales promotion manager at budget time often says, "When there is no place else to put the expense or when no one else wants it, it gets charged to sales promotion." Unfortunately, that is often true. There seems to be no standard way to determine what can and cannot be charged to the sales promotion budget. It varies widely from company to company and from product to product. Sometimes, it is even based on the perceived strength of the sales promotion manager—especially his clout with management. In spite of these problems, there are some standard areas of expense that legitimately should be charged to sales promotion.

If we use the standard definitions of advertising and sales promotion, we can begin to distinguish between actual sales promotion expenses and non-sales promotion expenses. Using Roger Strang's definitions, advertising and sales promotion are defined in the following ways.

> Advertising—All nonpersonal communication in measured media under clear sponsorship. This includes TV, radio, print and outdoor media but does not include direct mail.

> Sales Promotion—All other forms of sponsored communication apart from activities associated with personal selling. It thus includes trade shows and exhibits, couponing, sampling premiums, trade allowances, sales and dealer incentives, cents-off packs, consumer education and demonstration activities, rebates, bonus packs, point-of-purchase material and direct mail.[3]

While the following list is not complete, it includes some of the charges that belong in the sales promotion budget.

- Sales promotion consultants or agencies
- Sales promotion pretesting services
- Costs for consumer contests, premiums, and sampling promotions
- Sales promotion department travel and entertainment expenses
- Sales promotion department salaries

---

3. Roger A. Strang, "Sales Promotion—Fast Growth, Faulty Management," *Harvard Business Review*, July/August, 1976, p. 120.

- Association dues
- Cost of refund promotions
- Subscriptions to periodicals and services for department
- Storage of sales promotion materials
- Cost of trade coupons
- Catalogs for consumers
- Cost of price-off promotions including packaging changes
- Advertising and sales promotion aids for salespeople
- Cost of stamp or continuity programs
- Dealer help literature
- Direct mail to dealers, wholesalers, jobbers, and retailers
- Sales promotion department office supplies
- Point-of-purchase materials
- Catalogs for dealers
- Costs of exhibits
- Sales promotion department share of overhead
- House organs for customers and dealers
- Cost of cash value for sampling coupons
- Cost of contest entry blanks
- Cross-advertising enclosures
- Contest judging and handling fees
- Mobile exhibits
- Consumer contest awards
- Premium handling charges
- House-to-house sample distribution
- Packaging charges for premium promotions
- Cost of merchandise for tie-in promotions
- Product tags
- Cost of non-self-liquidating premiums
- Consumer education programs
- Packaging costs for reusable containers
- Product publicity
- Instruction enclosures
- Samples for middlemen
- Coupon redemption costs
- Gifts of company products
- Cost of deal merchandise
- Cost of guarantee refunds

While some may argue with this list, in our opinion most of these charges
fall in the area of sales promotion.

Who Sets the Sales Promotion Budget?

Again, this depends on the company and the operating philosophy it has adopted. In most cases, where the brand management system is used, the brand manager is responsible for determining the total amount to be invested in sales promotion. This amount is usually developed as part of the overall marketing plan for the brand.

The general approach is for the brand manager to develop a marketing plan for the year, with forecasts of both income and expenses. Under expenses is the general category of promotion expenses, which usually include anticipated advertising, sales promotion, personal selling, and public relations expenses. Although this budget is not always broken down further, advertising and sales promotion are usually separated into individual totals. This marketing plan is then approved by the marketing management of the company and, in some cases, by top management as well.

When the brand management system is not used, the sales promotion manager usually develops a total sales promotion budget for the department that includes all expected expenses. This budget may be broken down into either products or areas of operation. Usually, however, salaries, sales promotion activities, department expenses, ongoing costs, and similar charges are individually budgeted.

Whatever the system, we strongly recommend that an internal accounting system be developed for each specific brand or for each specific sales promotion program. Only in this way is budget control possible. We'll suggest methods of doing this later in this chapter.

In some instances, the promotion budget is generated by top management or at a level above the sales promotion manager. In these situations, the actual job of the sales promotion manager does not include developing a sales promotion budget but rather concerns allocating the available funds to various brands or activities. This is usually done by the sales promotion manager or in combination with or in consultation with an advertising or sales manager. This is a fairly common approach in many small, single-line, or one-product companies.

Regardless of who sets the budget, the method of allocation is vital to the success of the program. We'll say more about this later.

Typical Methods of Sales Promotion Budgeting

Over the years, a number of methods of estimating, budgeting, and allocating promotion expenditures have been developed. M. A. McNiven conducted a national survey of advertisers for the National Industrial Conference Board to determine how promotion budgets were established. Based on that survey, he classified the responses into three general categories.

1. *Guidelines.* Methods that use historical data on which to develop an allocation.
2. *Theoretical.* Methods that use econometric or marketing models based on historical data to determine the most profitable budget level.
3. *Empirical.* Techniques built on experimental feedback from the marketplace rather than on historical data.[4]

Guideline Approaches

There are three primary approaches to guideline budgeting: fixed guidelines, arbitrary appropriations, and the Objective and Task Method.

Fixed guideline approaches. In fixed guideline approaches the budget is based on a fixed ratio or percentage of sales dollars, gross margins, units of product sold, retail outlets, or competitive expenditure. Each method has its particular advantages and disadvantages.

1. *Percentage of sales.* The most widely used method of guideline budgeting is a percentage of past or estimated future sales of the product or brand. The ratio used is often determined by either past experience or industry or category guidelines. The computation is fairly simple. A given percentage of past or future sales is used to determine the allocation. For example, if sales totaled $100,000 last year, and 2 percent is the arbitrary figure selected as appropriate for the budget, $2,000 would be budgeted for sales promotion for the coming year ($100,000 × .02 = $2,000).

   While the percentage of sales method is quick, easy, and widely used, it has an inherent weakness. When sales are good, the promotion budget increases. When sales are bad, promotion is reduced. The basic principle at work is that promotion is a result of sales. However, this is contrary to our basic understanding of promotion— that is, promotion should help increase sales, and not the other way around. Another problem with the percentage-of-sales budgeting approach is the lag-effect in planning. For example, a 1983 marketing plan would be developed in 1982. The promotion budget would be based on the last full year sales, in this case, 1981. As a result, the promotion budget for 1983 would actually be based on 1981 sales figures, or figures that would be two years old by the time the budget was implemented.
2. *Percentage of gross margin.* Another popular method of promotion

---

4. M. A. McNiven, *How Much to Spend for Advertising* (New York: Association of National Advertisers, 1969).

budgeting is using a percentage of the gross margin (net sales less cost-of-goods) of the company or brand. The calculation is the same as percentage-of-sales except that percentage of past or anticipated gross margin is used as the base. For example, if a company had a gross profit margin on a product of $1,000,000 and invested 5 percent in promotion, the budget would be $50,000.

3. *Fixed sum per units sold.* Similar to but not quite the same as percentage of sales is the allocation of promotion dollars on a per unit basis. For example, an affordable promotion cost per unit is determined by the marketer. By estimating the number of units that will be sold, the promotion budget is established. The automobile industry usually uses this type of promotion budgeting. For example, if a promotion investment of $25 per automobile was established and 50,000 units were expected to be sold, the budget would then be $1,250,000 (50,000 units × $25 = $1,250,000). This method has the advantage of tying the promotion appropriation directly to the unit of sale but again raises the question of whether promotion creates sales dollars or sales dollars create the promotion budget. In this case, the budget is not actually generated until the unit is sold. Since promotion investments must usually be made in advance of the sale, the marketer never really quite has control of the budget until the last forecast unit is sold.

4. *Fixed sum per retail outlet.* Many durable goods manufacturers and other firms that rely heavily on the retailer for a personal selling effort set promotional budgets on the basis of the number of outlets through which the product will be sold. For example, suppose a consumer finance organization determined that the company could invest $100 per loan office per year to generate personal loan applications. Assuming there are 5,000 loan offices across the country, the advertising budget would then be $500,000 (5,000 loan offices × $100 = $500,000).

This per outlet approach is easily calculated. However, it overlooks the fact that all loan offices are not alike. Some offices may need considerably more than $100 per year in promotion support and others less. In effect, the approach suggests that the cost of supporting an office in New York City is the same as supporting one in Seminole, Oklahoma. There is a major difference, if only in actual media costs, which makes the technique somewhat suspect.

5. *Percentage of competitive expenditures.* Some marketers base their budget on what their competitors are spending, either on a dollar matching basis or as a percentage of what is spent in the entire category. For example, a marketer may determine from some source that his major competitor in the field is allocating $450,000 for promotion during a certain period of time. The marketer would then

appropriate the same amount to achieve a competitive parity or allocate a percentage amount that equalizes market share. Thus, if the competitor against whom the plan were developed had a 20 percent share of the overall market and our marketer had only a 10 percent share, the appropriation would be $225,000 (20 percent share vs. 10 percent share = .5 ratio. $450,000 × .5 = $225,000).

Another budget technique using the competitive parity approach is to budget a percentage of the total promotion investment by all competitors in the same category. In most instances, this percentage is related to perceived market share or sales in the category. For example, if all promotion in the silver polish category amounted to $200,000 and Sparkling Company had a 10 percent share of sales in that market, the promotion budget would then be established at $20,000 ($200,000 all promotion × .10 share = $20,000 budget). In some instances, marketers set their budgets at a figure above or below their market share in hopes of either capturing a larger portion of the market or achieving promotion effectiveness at a slightly lower cost.

The competitive approach has the advantage of keeping the budget in line with competition so that promotion "wars" are usually avoided. Further, the ability to tie the expenditure directly to the market share is appealing to many marketers. On the minus side, the competitive parity approach assumes that competition knows the best level for expenditures in the category, whether they actually do or not. Another problem is that competitive or total promotion expenditures in the category may be difficult to determine. This is particularly true with sales promotion since it is generally very difficult to estimate what even a particular competitive program might cost. The chief disadvantage is that the promotion budget is determined outside the company by competition whose problems and opportunities may be entirely different.

Arbitrary appropriation approaches. Arbitrary allocations of promotion budgets are made by many companies. By some formula or estimation, management determines the amount to be invested in promotion (or advertising and sales promotion) on the basis of the financial situation of the entire company rather than the situation of an individual brand.

Because these arbitrary appropriations are so widespread, we will briefly review the basic methods used.

1. *Management decision.* The total appropriation is established by top management and simply allocated as the amount available to be spent. The appropriation may be tied to either the needs of the brand or the needs of the company. The sales promotion manager is in-

volved only in the allocation of the budget, not its determination.

2. *What can be afforded.* Top management allocates the promotion budget on the basis of what it feels can be afforded by either the brand or the company. The overriding factor in this management decision is usually the total profit desired as a return on investment. In other cases, the need may be to revitalize an existing brand or to attempt to halt declining sales of a product or brand by investing promotional funds. Since each case is individual, there may be many rationales for the decision of what can be afforded. Here, too, the sales promotion manager is involved only in allocation of an already determined sum.

3. *Go-for-broke.* In rare instances, management makes a decision that promotion may be used to either capture a market or attempt to save a dying brand. Promotion funds are then allocated with no relationship to sales, profits, or even return on investment. The basic plan is simply to overwhelm consumers or competition in the marketplace with advertising and sales promotion. Although unusual, this approach is sometimes successful. Top management is usually responsible for the budget allocation since the plan has a direct bearing on the overall financial stability of the company.

The objective and task method. To develop a more scientific approach to budgeting, particularly advertising, the Association of National Advertisers commissioned a study by Russell Colley.[5] Published as a text, *Defining Advertising Goals for Measured Advertising Results* (DAGMAR) proposed that advertising should be budgeted to accomplish specific predetermined advertising goals. (Note: While Colley's work does not deal specifically with sales promotion, the general concepts can be applied to the field. The method is commonly called the Objective and Task Method). The approach is by far the most practical and scientific of the guideline methods. Yet, in spite of its appeal and soundness, the DAGMAR budgeting plan is apparently not widely used.

The DAGMAR approach suggests that a specific promotional campaign objective be set in advance. Whether the objective is product awareness, brand trial, or some other result, the amount of promotion necessary to accomplish it is then determined. The budget is based on a predetermined goal rather than on past or future results. The DAGMAR approach offers the opportunity to measure whether the goal set for the promotion campaign is achieved, something other guideline approaches often ignore. This approach may be used with any type of sales promotion program since the objective can be determined on the same basis.

5. Russell Colley, *Defining Advertising Goals for Measured Advertising Results* (New York: Association of National Advertisers, 1961).

The major problem in using the DAGMAR budgeting method is that although promotion goals and objectives are set in advance, it is very difficult to determine how much money is needed to achieve those goals. For example, the objective of achieving 20 percent awareness of an advertising campaign theme is easily set by the planner. It is quite another task, however, to determine how much media reach and frequency will be needed to achieve that level of awareness among consumers. While the Objective and Task Method of promotional budgeting is more scientific and solidly based than other guideline methods, the chief advantage may be determining whether or not the money was well spent after the fact rather than in setting the original budget. The lack of data again hinders what seems to be a solid approach to budgeting.

Theoretical Approaches

Theoretical approaches to promotion budgeting are usually based on some form of mathematical model using historical data as input. The model may include market share, pricing, competitive activity, and variations from year to year. Most models are proprietary or require information not easily obtainable for most companies. While these methods are not practical for many companies at this time, they may have a bright future, with the growth of computers and more available data.

The primary quantitative methods are:

1. *Sales model.* Promotion is considered the only variable affecting sales so that an optimization approach may be used to determine the ideal budget.
2. *Dynamic model.* This model attempts to account for the effects of promotion on sales over time. A typical approach is to incorporate the carry-over effects of present activities into the future through some model.
3. *Competitive model.* Modeling the activities of competition is another method. The common base is some form of game theory. This approach assumes that all players are interdependent and that uncertainty results from not knowing what the others will do. A strategy is then developed to reduce and/or control this uncertainty, and predictions are made based on the model.
4. *Stochastic model.* Two major approaches using the laws of probability have been developed. One is based on Markov Chains and the other on the Stochastic Learning Model. Again, both attempt to predict the ideal budget based on the model developed.
5. *Simulation.* Several computer models that simulate consumer behavior from stored data have been developed. Through experimental

approaches, various levels of budget allocations are tested to determine the most effective return based on investment.

Quantitative methods are not widely used at this time because of three basic problems: (1) necessary information is not available at a reasonable cost; (2) most models assume that promotion is the only variable in the marketing mix; and (3) many assumptions in the various models appear to be quite arbitrary.

One of the most successful commercial theoretical budgeting techniques is the Hendry model. While details of how it works are, unfortunately, secret, it is said to be based on a mathematical model containing the "fundamental laws of consumer behavior which have been deductively derived." Developed in 1962, the Hendry model correlates the relationship between varying levels of promotion expenditure and the resulting share of market and contribution to profit. Since inputs (the direct manufacturing margin, the promotion expenditure level, and the share of market) are easily obtained, the system has a number of enthusiastic followers.

Empirical Approaches

The empirical method of budgeting is quite different from others since it is built on experimental feedback rather than historical data. This budgeting approach is sensitive to specific characteristics of a given product class and to the marketing factors acting on the product at the time the concept is set. Because experimentation requires trial and evaluation over time, it can be used only for specific brands and cannot be projected to other product classes or even to other brands in the same category. Most empirical approaches to budgeting are highly proprietary, and little information is available on them.

A typical example of an empirical approach is one based on a series of test markets. Assume that the product for which the budget is being determined is a brand of frozen orange juice. Initially, several frozen orange juice test markets of equal population size, usage, and brand share would be selected and matched as closely as possible. Using these markets, varying budget expenditure levels would be set. For example, Market A might be budgeted at the current national program for that particular brand. Market B might be set at 50 percent of that amount and Market C at 150 percent. Results in terms of both brand and total frozen orange juice category sales would be measured in each market. In addition, communications effects and sales promotion results would be tracked. By comparing the results obtained over time, estimates of how the varying budget levels might perform on a broad-scale basis could be made. As a result of these experimentations, budget levels for the frozen orange juice brand could be established with more precision than with other, less sophisticated approaches.[6]

Problems and Solutions in Budgeting for Sales Promotion

On the previous pages, we have described many of the methods that have and are being used to establish promotion and ultimately sales promotion budgets. While in many cases the sales promotion manager has little or no say in the method being used, since this is typically the realm of top management, we believe there is one approach that offers solutions to many of the problems in other budgeting methods. We offer it now as an illustration of what we consider to be a sound approach to sales promotion budgeting.

The following approach works very well for companies employing the product manager system. In fact, it works well for any sales promotion manager who is responsible for developing a budget for his department.

The Profit Planning Approach

This budgeting method consists of four basic steps:

1. The accurate forecasting of predicted sales for the coming budget period. This assumes that the budgeter has a fairly firm estimate of fixed and variable product manufacturing costs.
2. The conversion of the sales forecast into a Contribution Margin for the product or brand. (See Table 16-1.)
3. A knowledge of the desired profit margin for the product, company, or brand, either in total dollars or as a percentage of Net Sales Price or Gross Margin.
4. The allocation of the available Direct Expense funds for marketing into advertising, sales promotion, selling expense, and research and development budgets.

This method approaches promotion budgeting with a managerial view. It emphasizes achieving the desired profit margin for the firm based on adjustments of the sales forecasts or the direct expenses as necessary to achieve those goals. Each step of the profit planning approach is now outlined in theory and practice.

Accurate forecasting. Profit planning promotion budgeting places

---

6. Schultz and Martin, *Strategic Advertising Campaigns*, pp. 47-60.

primary emphasis on the ability of the manager to know three basic things:

1. The fixed and variable manufacturing costs for the product at all levels of sales.
2. The specific percentage or dollar amount desired as a profit margin for the company product or brand.
3. The competitive market situation and consumer attitudes, so that an accurate sales forecast can be made.

Any capable manager has or can obtain this information about the product line.

As Table 16-1 shows, there are few variables the manager can manipulate in developing the budget. Once the desired profit margin has been established, assuming a competitive pricing situation, the only true variables are the number of units forecast to be sold, the variable product cost, and the direct expenses to be allocated. With a top line established by the sales forecast and a bottom line dictated by the desired profit margin, the manager's manipulative control over the costs in the middle are limited. Thus, primary emphasis in the profit planning approach to budgeting is on development of the sales forecast.

Initially, the sales forecast should be done in units rather than dollars. This unit forecast can then be converted into dollars, based on the selling price less the necessary discounts, leading to the second step.

Estimating the contribution margin. Once the net sales price of the product has been determined, the Cost-of-Goods on the forecast sales are deducted. This gives the Gross Margin. Distribution Expense is then deducted, leaving the Contribution Margin (see Table 16-1). This Contribution Margin truly defines the funds available for all marketing including sales promotion.

Deducting the desired product margin. Once the Product Margin has been established, either as a lump sum or as a percentage of Net Sales Price, it is then deducted from the Contribution Margin of the product. The result is the total amount available for marketing activities (Direct Expenses).

Allocation of the marketing funds. The total available marketing funds (Direct Expenses in Table 16-1) are now established. Based on that amount, the manager then allocates the available funds among sales expense, advertising and sales promotion investments, and research and development to achieve the best return. This is the point at which the budgeter knows the true alternatives available. It is also the point at which the effects of various expenditures for sales promotion versus advertising or sales promotion versus personal selling can be estimated with some accuracy.

The major difference between the profit planning method and more traditional budgeting approaches is its establishment of the promotion budget within the framework of the entire product operating sheet rather than as a separate entity. Sales promotion is a function directly related to the profit margin and a part of the total mix of product income and expense. Promotion is no longer theoretical; it is a practical item to be used by the manager.

In the profit planning approach, since sales promotion is directly related to the sales forecast, effective promotion results in increased budgetary dollars. Sales promotion and actual sales are inextricably intertwined. Also, the sales promotion budget is in the hands of the person responsible for the sale and profit of the product. By developing the sales forecast, estimating sales and costs, and knowing other expenses charged against the product, the manager can justify the sales promotion investment to management.

The profit planning approach may not be feasible for some budgeters due to the lack of information on costs, profit margins desired, etc. It is strongly recommended, however, as a sound, realistic approach to establishing a promotion budget and ultimately a sales promotion budget.[7]

Some Important Concepts in Sales Promotion Budgeting

In the past few years, several concepts have been offered and widely accepted as methods of improving the effectiveness and efficiency of sales promotion budgeting. Since these concepts can be used in almost any type of sales promotion management situation, we will describe each of them briefly. You will likely find ways in which each of these approaches can assist you in budgeting.

Lost revenue analysis. In many instances, the budgeting of a sales promotion event is based on the break-even point of the promotion event. In other words, it depends on how many units must be sold to cover the cost of the sales promotion program. Based on that, a simple break-even calculation is made. For example, assume that you are the sales promotion manager for a line of canned green beans. In an effort to generate additional sales and to clear the warehouse stock to make room for the new crop to be canned, a special $1 per case allowance is planned for retailers to encourage them to develop in-store support and features. Packed 24 to a case, your price to the retailer for the green beans is

7. Schultz and Martin, *Strategic Advertising Campaigns,* pp. 60-67.

currently $20. You are presently selling approximately 2,000 cases per week. At your price of $20 per case, this generates gross revenue of $40,000 per week. Your margin on the green beans is approximately 50 percent on wholesale or $10 per case. Therefore, your gross margin on the brand is about $20,000 per week.

In addition to the trade deal of $1 per case, to assure consumer activity, you also decide to offer a 15¢ in-store trade coupon. You estimate your cost of this coupon to be the 15¢ consumer reduction, plus 7¢ for retailer handling and 3¢ for clearing house charges. Thus, your net cost per coupon will be 25¢ each. The question is, how many cases of green beans will you have to sell to break even?

Assuming 100 percent redemption of the trade deal, with a sales promotion cost of 25¢ for each can sold and packed 24 to the case, your sales promotion cost per case would be $6.00 (24 units @ 25¢ each). Since your margin per case is $9 (selling price of $19, your regular $20 less the $1 trade deal, less $10 cost-of-goods), you would have to increase your sales by 77.8 percent. At first glance, it would appear that you might only need to increase sales by 66 percent on the cost of the consumer couponing program. That's where lost revenue comes in. Here's why. In calculating your margin, you arbitrarily assumed that you would accept the cost of the trade deal of $1 per case and reduce your margin to $19 per case from the original $20. In other words, you have an actual promotion cost of an additional $1 for the trade deal in addition to the consumer offer. Your sales promotion cost is then not $6 per case but $7 per case. Therefore, your actual sales increase needed to break even is 77.8 percent ($7 per case ÷ $9 per case margin = 77.8 percent increase needed).

The $1 trade deal is called "lost revenue" since without the sales promotion event the additional $1 margin would have been obtained. In many cases, this "lost revenue" figure is never calculated, although it is a true sales promotion cost. To be accurate, the cost of the promotion must include all costs, including the cost of "lost revenue."

Cost per incremental case increase. Directly related to the concept of "lost revenue" is the idea of the cost per incremental case. This is a calculation that indicates the cost required to obtain additional business and hold it. This concept is particularly important in sales promotion since sales promotion activities may often generate a short-term increase but lose that increase when the sales promotion event is over. The idea of cost per incremental case is a method of determining exactly what the cost was to obtain a sales increase with a sales promotion technique over a period of time.

The cost per incremental calculation is usually determined on the basis of a pre-post promotion measure. This simply means that sales prior to the event are measured for a period of time, say 12 weeks. An example will help explain the idea. Let's assume that a cost per incremental case increase for the green beans discussed above is to be obtained. In Market Alpha, the sales of our green beans were found to be 50 cases per week prior to the sales promotion event or a total of 1,200 units (50 cases × 24 units per case = 1,200 units). During the time of the trade deal and the consumer promotion, our sales increased to 65 cases per week, or an increase of 30 percent for the period (65 cases − 50 cases = 15 cases, 15 cases ÷ 50 cases = 30 percent). Further assume that the sales promotion event ran a total of four weeks. Thus, since our break-even was a 77.8 percent increase (from #1) and we achieve only a 30 percent increase, we can say the promotion was not successful. We didn't break even. For example, our costs for the promotion event amounted to $1,820 for the period ($7 per case × 65 cases per week × 4 weeks = $1,820) while our gross margin on the brand was only $2,340)$9 per case × 65 cases × 4 weeks = $2,340) or a net income of only $520.

You might wonder why we say the promotion was not successful. We increased our sales for the period and made a net profit. But, our gross margin for the four weeks actually declined over what we would have made without the promotion. Our income for the 4-week promotion period was $520 (sales income $2,340 less cost of promotion $1,820 = $520). The fact is, however, during a regular period without the promotion, our income would have been $2,000 (50 cases per week × $10 margin × 4 weeks). In other words, the promotion actually cost us $1,480 in lost revenue. Thus, the sales increase of 60 cases (65 during the promotion less 50 normally sold = 15 case increase per week × 4 weeks) resulted in a net loss of approximately $5.69 per case ($1,480 lost revenue ÷ 260 cases = $5.69 in total sales). That's not a very profitable promotion.

There is, however, another way of looking at the cost of promotion: the cost per incremental case. Let's assume that instead of dropping back to sales of 50 cases per week after the four-week price reduction, we measured the sales for the eight weeks following the sales promotion event and found sales were now averaging 60 cases per week. Using this information, we can now calculate the cost per incremental case for the sales promotion event just concluded.

With the promotion, sales of 60 cases per week gave us an average weekly increase of 10 cases. During the eight-week post-test period we therefore sold 480 cases of green beans @ $20 per case (at our normal margin of $10 per case, $20 wholesale price − $10 cost-of-goods) for income of $9,600 and a gross profit of $4,800. Without the promotion, we would have anticipated sales of only $8,000 (50 cases per week @ $20 per case × 8 weeks) and a gross margin of only $4,000. In other words, our promotional activity during the four-week period actually had a carry-over effect on sales. In this case, we spent $1,820 during the promotion period to build sales. That investment has now resulted in $1,600 in additional sales in the 8 week post-test period. Our actual cost per incremental case for the sales promotion event is thus only $2.75 ($1,820 cost of the promotion less $1,600 increased gross margin or $220 net cost. $220 ÷ 80 cases—10 cases per week × 8 weeks—resulted in a cost of $2.75 per case).

As you can see, the true cost of a promotion must be calculated on the basis of the amount expended in the actual promotion, but allowance must also be made for a long-term sales increase. In our example above, if sales had fallen back to the previous 50-case-per-week level after the promotion, he event could not have been considered successful.

The payout analysis. A primary calculation in budgeting, which every sales promotion manager should know, is the "break-even analysis" discussed above. It is simply a calculation of the cost of the sales promotion event compared to the results to determine how much must be sold to recoup costs. As we demonstrated above, this is quite a simple and straightforward mathematical calculation. Another calculation that can be most helpful is called a "payout analysis," which is used to compare various promotional alternatives. Louis Haugh explains it this way.

> One of the strengths of the sales promotion part of marketing is that, because of its tactical nature, it affects sales quickly and measurably. When preparing a promotion budget, many brand managers use a payout analysis to evaluate the upside potential and the downside risk of a promotional event.
>
> A payout analysis can be constructed to evaluate the feasibility of a couponing event or other price promotion; for other promotions such as sampling or a premium offer (where the takeaway may not be as dramatic) such analysis is also often possible.
>
> The mathematics of a payout analysis are relatively straightforward and typically are a part of the planning for any promotion event. For a cents-off coupon program, the payout analysis will show the net profit for the brand as well as the break-even point.
>
> As an example, let us construct an analysis for a product that sells for $1 per unit to the trade with a gross profit of 40 percent per unit. The first step is to determine the distribution cost for the coupons. To distribute 15,000,000 coupons at a cost per thousand of $5, the total distribution cost would be $75,000.
>
> Assuming a 10 percent redemption rate and a 10¢ face value and 5¢ handling charge, the redemption cost would be $225,000.
>
> The gross profit for the brand in this event would be $600,000, i.e., the total number of units redeemed (1,500,000 times 40¢); the net profit would be $300,000, i.e., net profit less distribution and redemption costs.
>
> For a sampling event, it may be necessary to add the cost of goods for the sample size. There are, of course, additional calculations that can be made in a more sophisticated payout analysis, such as the additional revenues generated by gaining new users, less those current users rewarded with the

coupon or those taken out of the market with the sample. Or the cost of gaining a new user and the net profit of converting that customer to part of the brand's core user group.

Perhaps the most important part of a payout analysis is the estimate of a brand's downside risk in a promotion event.

Again, by using the same assumptions as for our $1 product above, a break-even redemption rate for a coupon event would be 2 percent. A 15,000,000 drop would move 300,000 units. The distribution cost of $75,000 plus the redemption costs of $45,000 puts the total cost of the event at $120,000.

Gross profit for the brand, having moved 300,000 units, is also $120,000; hence the program would be a wash. In both of these payout calculations, it is important to note that no misredemption has been included.

An important benefit of a payout analysis is its ability to help a brand manager judge the efficiencies of different couponing programs, say a newspaper program as compared with a magazine program. The analysis can also illustrate the bottom line results of two different promotion events, such as a coupon event vs. a premium program.[8]

Allocating Funds between Sales Promotion and Advertising

With the above sales promotion budgeting concepts in mind, we now move to one of the most difficult of all decisions for the sales promotion manager or indeed any marketing executive, the allocation of available funds between sales promotion and advertising. While every person involved with sales promotion seems to have a pet theory or method of making this allocation, none is better developed or better supported than the concept of "Consumer Franchise Building" by Robert M. Prentice. Rather than risk a translation, with a necessary loss of content, we have reprinted the explanation of this important concept from *Advertising Age* as Prentice wrote it:

> Why does one brand succeed in the marketplace while another brand of comparable quality and price fails? Why does one brand build a consumer franchise that grows stronger every year while similar brands, marketed by similar companies spending about the same dollars for marketing support, find their franchise dwindling and sales declining? Why does one brand continue to generate increasing profit year after year—long after its so-called "life cycle" should be ending—while another brand of equal worth and promise becomes less and less profitable?
>
> Certainly product quality, advertising creativity and effectiveness, good salesmanship in the field, and skillful execution of marketing strategies are

8. Louis Haugh, "Payout Analysis Can Help Assess Promo's Strengths," *Advertising Age*, June 19, 1978, p. 52ff.

factors vital to marketing success. But if two brands are more or less equal in all these respects—and if one is successful and the other is not—there must be another factor at work.

This other factor, in my opinion, is the way each brand has allocated its marketing funds between advertising and [sales] promotion. I have found persuasive evidence that the mix of advertising and [sales] promotion has a more significant effect on brand sales—and particularly on brand profits—than most marketing people realize.

The advocates of heavier promotion appear to be winning the argument against advertising agencies that push media advertising: A study by Marketing Science Institute, Cambridge, Mass., indicates that promotion expenditures now represent an estimated 60 percent of total marketing expenditures—and the percentage is steadily increasing. The study shows that this growing promotion emphasis often is based on short-term considerations, assumptions, and personal opinions—some of doubtful validity.

A better way is evident in a study I made of two major brands through ten years in a rapidly-growing grocery-store product category. These two brands were so closely matched that they will delight even the most meticulous researcher. In three of the first five years they had identical dollar sales volumes. They were priced identically (except for one brief period in Year 2 when Brand B delayed meeting a price reduction by Brand A). They spent almost the same amount of money for advertising and promotion during the first five years, and their profits (before indirect charges and taxes) were almost the same.

Throughout the ten years, the two brands were more or less equal in product quality and performance; whatever advantage one brand might gain one year was washed out the next as the other brand made its own improvements. Likewise, because both brands were marketed by important companies with similar resources and agency talent, any qualitative differences in advertising copy and creative work evened out over time. Each brand had its share of advertising successes and bombs.

Yet at the end of ten years, these two brands that were so nearly equal during the earlier years were not even in the same league. Brand A's annual sales in Year 10 were up 94 percent over Year 1, but Brand B's were down 12 percent. More importantly, Brand A's annual profit had increased by 120 percent, while Brand B's had fallen a disastrous 40 percent.

Funds Must Build Consumer Franchise
Why? The major reason for these differences lies in the way these two brands apportioned their marketing funds between advertising and certain types of promotion. When we analyze each brand's expenditures—using a new "Consumer Franchise Building" (or CFB) approach—we find significant differences in the way these brands spent their money. We can also see how these different expenditure patterns affected brand sales and profits.

The CFB approach is not a research technique, for I am a marketing man, not a researcher. I wouldn't know a Latin square from a standard deviation. No, the CFB approach involves a very practical concept that lends itself to simple marketing-management analysis. The concept grew out of many years' experience in trying—often without much success—to relate brand expenditures on advertising and promotion to sales and market share. It was further developed and investigated during my work with Marketing Science Institute on the study of the advertising/promotion mix—a study, by the way, that indentifies serious weaknesses in the way that many package goods companies plan their promotions and incorporate them into their marketing programs.

The CFB concept first took form when I began to realize that the traditional advertising-versus-promotion analyses might not be producing conclusive results because the arbitrary definitions of "advertising" and "promotion" do not accurately reflect what actually goes on in the marketplace. The real need was to consider what goes on in the consumer's mind and how each type of marketing activity works to build long-term brand preference and to influence short-term decisions to buy.

Establish a Good Value-Price Image

Accordingly, the following CFB rationale developed:

1. To generate profit over an extended period, a brand must build a strong consumer franchise. It must establish a significant, lasting value in the minds of an important segment of consumers.
2. But value isn't enough. Consumers must believe that the brand's value is worth the price. If they don't, the marketer will have to reduce the price or increase the value to the point where they are willing to buy it—to the point where consumers believe that value and price are in balance. (But the marketer must realize that if he hasn't established a high value in the consumer's mind, a price reduction will generally cut into his profit.)
3. A brand's share of market at any given time reflects how consumers perceive the brand's price/value relationship in comparison with other brands.
4. How does the consumer arrive at his or her perception of brand value? Obviously, a lot depends on experience with the product and on its unique performance and the satisfaction it provides. But a lot also depends on the ideas the consumer gets about the brand which make the brand uniquely different—in important respects—from competitive brands. These ideas arise from the brand's name, its positioning, the package, and the various marketing activities that implant unique and important ideas about the brand in the mind.
5. What kinds of marketing activities do this? I call them Consumer Franchise Building (or CFB) activities. They include:

    Advertising—perhaps the most common way to register such ideas (although some advertising, we have to admit, does a fairly poor job in this respect).

    Certain types of promotion—if they register unique and important selling ideas about the brand, such as:

    Sampling—because the package highlights the product's advantages. Because the proof of the pudding is in the eating and because a descriptive folder with a strong selling message usually accompanies the sample—an ad, if you will.

Cents-off coupons—distributed by the manufacturer by mail, or in print ads, or in or on a package. These coupons can also register unique and important ideas about the brand—provided that an effective selling message accompanies the coupon or appears on it. This distinction is important, for it excludes most coupons that appear in retailers' own ads, which usually say "Brand X, 10¢ off with this coupon. Good only in this store for this week only." There is no selling message with these trade coupons, nothing about the brand's unique attributes or advantages—they are simply a means of cutting the price. Therefore, trade in-ad coupons are not considered a CFB activity.

Demonstrations, either in-store or before home economics classes or other groups of consumers, are CFB activities.

Service material, recipes, etc., which enhance the image of a brand and register ideas of its unique superiority and value, are also CFB activities. All of these CFB activities perform two functions: (1) they build long-term brand preference, and (2) they generate immediate sales (often more effectively than many people realize).

6. All other activities I classify as non-CFB activities. Their job is to accelerate the buying decision, to generate immediate sales, but they generally do not implant unique and important ideas about the brand in the consumer's mind. Instead, they simply reduce the price, or add temporary, extraneous value (as in the case of most premiums and contests), or help obtain retail distribution or cooperation. These are important and necessary functions—but they do not register important and unique ideas about a brand in the mind.

Using the CFB concept outlined above, I have analyzed some 20 different package goods brands and have made some startling, highly practical discoveries.

How CFB Differs from Other Programs

Before describing the ten-year case history mentioned earlier, let me clarify the differences between the CFB analytical approach and the usual kinds of marketing analyses and research studies that most companies undertake:

1. This analysis introduces a new way to classify marketing expenditures. Instead of looking at advertising versus promotion, we are looking at CFB versus the traditional share of market or sales non-CFB expenditures; we are looking at expenditures for activities that implant unique and important ideas in consumers' minds versus those activities that do not.

2. The CFB analysis covers an extended period—ten years in the excerpt that I am about to describe. Most marketing analyses cover only a few months, or at most a year or two. The CFB analyses that I have made cover anywhere from four to ten years—a long-range view.

3. It covers all the major brands in the category—not just one or two brands in a vacuum. (Although I show only two brands in the ten-year case study, I have data on six other brands in the category which I do not show for the sake of simplicity.)

Table 16-2   Two Brands: Sales, Advertising, and Promotion Expenditures and Profit (millions of dollars)

	Year 1	Year 2	Year 3*	Year 4	Year 5*	Year 6	Year 7	Year 8*	Year 9	Year 10	% Change (10 Years)
Sales $											
Brand A	28	30	26**	28	29	34	40	45	43	54	+ 94%
Brand B	28	30	32	31	29	28	29	27	25	25	− 12
Total advertising and promotion $											
Brand A	7.0	6.8	7.1	8.1	8.6	8.5	9.4	10.0	11.0	12.8	+ 83
Brand B	6.7	7.4	7.3	6.9	7.0	6.9	6.3	7.6	6.3	6.2	− 7
Profit $											
Brand A	7.3	8.2	5.2	4.6	7.3	8.8	12.0	13.6	14.3	16.1	+120
Brand B	7.0	7.7	8.9	8.1	7.2	6.9	8.1	5.2	4.4	4.2	− 40

Source: Robert M. Prentice, "How to Split Your Marketing Funds Between Advertising and Promotion," *Advertising Age,* Jan. 10, 1977, p. 41.

  * Years when competitive new brands were introduced.
**Price decline by Brand A (not immediately met by Brand B).

4. It covers the overall marketing mix—advertising plus promotion. CFB plus non-CFB—not just a single element.
5. It focuses on profit, rather than on volume, as the only meaningful measure of marketing success. After all, you can't deposit market share in the bank, or pay dividends with it.
6. The analysis is simple. The complete CFB analysis involves only five simple graphs for each brand—for our purposes here, three are shown in tabular form. These graphs stress two fundamental questions:

- What did you spend (and how did you spend it)?
- What did you get (in terms of dollar sales and dollar profits)?

So let's get back to the two brands that started out so much alike, but were so different ten years later in sales and profit. Let's look first at the dollar total for these two brands [Table 16-2] for sales, for advertising and promotion combined, and for profit. (In the tables all data have been multiplied by a constant factor to protect confidentiality. All profit figures are before indirect charges and taxes.) The figures in [Table 16-2] show that for the first five years both brands were closely matched in sales revenue. They were also closely matched in dollar expenditures for advertising and sales promotion, although in Year 4, Brand A increased its investment sharply—but at the cost of a further reduction in profit. The short-term loss in profit, however, seems to have paid off; sales, advertising/promotion expenditures, and profits began a steady increase the next year.

Brand B's sales, on the other hand, began a steady decline in Year 5. Nevertheless, total expenditures were maintained at a fairly stable level, despite the decrease in sales revenue—but only at the expense of profit, which fell drastically.

Table 16-3   Two Brands: Expenditures, CFB, and non-CFB (millions of dollars)

	Year 1	Year 2	Year 3	Year 4	Year 5	Year 6	Year 7	Year 8	Year 9	Year 10
Total advertising and promotion $										
Brand A	7.0	6.8	7.1	8.1	8.6	8.5	9.4	10.0	11.6	12.8
Brand B	6.7	7.4	7.3	6.9	7.0	6.9	6.3	7.6	6.3	6.2
Total CFB $										
Brand A	5.4	5.4	5.1	6.6	6.8	6.2	5.9	6.2	7.1	7.2
Brand B	4.8	5.1	4.5	4.7	4.4	4.5	3.2	3.7	2.5	2.1
Total non-CFB $ (consumer and trade)										
Brand A	1.6	1.4	2.0	1.5	1.9	2.3	3.5	3.8	4.5	5.6
Brand B	1.9	2.3	2.8	2.2	2.6	2.4	3.1	3.9	3.8	4.1
Total promotion portion of non-CFB total										
Brand A	0	0.2	0.1	0.1	0	0.1	0.4	0.3	1.2	2.0
Brand B	0.3	0.2	0.1	0.3	0.3	0.3	0.6	1.8	1.5	2.3

Source: Prentice, "How to Split Your Marketing Funds," p. 42.

By the tenth year these two brands, so similar in every respect in Year 1, were quite different—not only in sales, but more importantly in profit. Brand A was at the peak of success and continuing to grow. Brand B was out of the race, losing more sales and profits every year.

Why did Brand A succeed while B was failing rapidly? The figures in [Table 16-2] don't really tell us the answer. So let's look more closely at [Table 16-3] to see how each brand apportioned its expenditures between CFB and non-CFB activities.

Now we begin to see some significant differences. For example:

- Brand A has consistently outspent Brand B on CFB activities—by an average of about $500,000 per year for the first three years, and almost $2,000,000 per year in Years 4 and 5.
- Brand B, on the other hand, in every one of the first six years spent more on non-CFB activities than Brand A did.
- As sales and profits began to slip, Brand B further reduced its CFB expenditures—so much so that in Year 7, Brand B's non-CFB expenditures began to match and eventually exceed its CFB expenditures. This is something that successful Brand A never did, despite the increase in later years in its non-CFB activities.
- Both brands increased expenditures for trade promotion (a non-CFB activity) during the last three or four years. The significant difference, however, is that Brand B used trade promotion much more heavily than did Brand A. As a matter of fact, Brand B spent more on trade promotion in Year 10 than it did for CFB activities.

In a nutshell, Brand B has put much less emphasis than Brand A on activities that implanted unique and important ideas about the brand in

Table 16-4   Two Brands: CFB Ratio and Profit

	Year 1	Year 2	Year 3	Year 4	Year 5	Year 6	Year 7	Year 8	Year 9	Year 10
CFB ratio (%)										
Brand A	77	79	72	81	79	73	63	62	61	56
Brand B	72	69	62	68	63	65	51	49	40	34
Profit ($ millions)										
Brand A	7.3	8.2	5.2	4.6	7.3	8.8	12.0	13.6	14.3	16.1
Brand B	7.0	7.7	8.9	8.1	7.2	6.9	8.1	5.2	4.4	4.2

Source: Prentice, "How to Split Your Marketing Funds," p. 42.

consumers' minds. Conversely, it put more emphasis on price-off packs, on trade allowances, trade couponing and other non-CFB efforts—none of which reflected anything unique about the brand.

Non-CFB Spending Starts Sales Drop
The differences in the way these two brands spent approximately equal sums of money during the first five years may well have determined what happened later. Here is a comparison covering the first five years:

- Brand A spent only 7 percent more than Brand B in total (advertising/ promotion combined).
- But Brand A spent 14 percent more than Brand B on advertising.
- And Brand A spent 23 percent more than Brand B on CFB activities.
- Conversely, Brand B spent 40 percent more than Brand A on non-CFB activities.

These differences were the start of Brand B's decline in sales and profits. By Year 10, Brand A's profits were 283 percent higher than Brand B's profits.

Further analysis provides additional evidence that these differences in expenditure patterns had a direct influence on brand profitability. For this purpose, I have computed what I call the CFB ratio, which states CFB expenditure as a percentage of total advertising/promotion expenditures (the total of CFB and non-CFB expenditures, in other words). [Table 16-4] shows the differences between these two brands over the 10-year period in terms of CFB ratios and profits.

Brand B has consistently had a lower CFB ratio than Brand A, ranging from 5 to 16 points lower during the first six years and dropping to only 34 percent in Year 10—22 points below Brand A's ratio. Furthermore, as shown in [Table 16-3] Brand B's CFB dollar expenditures have declined by more than 50 percent since Year 1 to only $2,100,000 in Year 10. It is clear that Brand B's consumer franchise is declining because the brand is paying less attention to implanting unique and important ideas in consumers' minds.

Don't Let CFB Drop Below 50 Percent
There is another very significant relationship. In Year 7, Brand B's CFB ratio

dropped from 65 percent to 51 percent. Profit declined sharply the next year and every year thereafter as the CFB ratio declined even further. In looking at more than 20 brands, I have generally found this same eye-opening relationship. This has led me to the general conclusion that:

When a brand's CFB ratio drops below the 50 percent to 55 percent level, profits will almost always decline, either immediately or within the next year or two.

I believe this is one of the most useful tools that marketing and corporate managements can use to improve brand profit performance over the long term. It gives marketers and their advertising agencies a practical, easy-to-use guideline to help decide how to split funds between advertising and certain types of promotion, to build strong brand franchises and improve profit growth—provided, of course, that the brand is not deficient in product quality, copy effectiveness, and the other basics.

This new Consumer Franchise Building approach, which I believe can be applied by almost any company selling a product or service to the consumer, demonstrates at least three things:

1. The CFB approach helps greatly in understanding the roles of advertising and various types of sales promotion activities in building strong brand franchises and generating increasing profits over many years.
2. Brands that put more emphasis on CFB activities—other things being more or less equal over an extended period—are significantly more successful and profitable than brands that emphasize non-CFB activities.
3. If a brand's CFB ratio falls below 50 percent to 55 percent, profit will almost always drop, either immediately or within the next year or two.

Although the CFB concept has been tested on only a limited number of brands, I am confident that the insights and the practical guidelines it provides will encourage marketers and agencies to analyze their own data. I believe that if it does nothing else, it will focus attention on how well each brand or service is implanting its unique and important ideas in the minds of consumers. And that will be a net gain for marketing people, corporate financial officers, and chief executives alike.[9]

Budgeting Expenses, Time, and Work

Budgeting in sales promotion deals with much more than simply allocating dollars to various promotional activities. To be a successful sales promotion manager, you must also know how to control the budget that has been allocated and, further, how to budget the time and effort that go into a sales promotion program. We look at these areas in this section.

Sales promotion is the one area in which costs can escalate so rapidly

---

9. Robert M. Prentice, "How to Split Your Marketing Funds Between Advertising and Promotion," *Advertising Age*, Jan. 10, 1977, pp. 41-42.

Table 16-5 Project Estimating Form

Job No. _____   Date _____
Budget Control _____   Brand/Description _____
Prepared by _____

1. Copy/Planning

Hours	Rate	Amount

Total copy/planning $ _____

2. Art Direction/Design

Hours	Rate	Amount

Total art direction/design $ _____

3. Premiums/Refunds/Coupons

Number	Cost	Supplier

Total premiums/refunds/coupons $ _____

4. Printing

Material	Units	Cost $

Total printing $ _____

5. Media Support

Type	Cost $

Total media support $ _____

6. Internal Promotion

Incentive	To whom	Amount $

Total internal promotion $ _____

7. Art & Mechanicals

Illustration . . . . $ _____
Photography . . . . $
Dye transfer . . . . $
Retouching . . . . $
Mechanicals . . . . $
Mock-ups . . . . $
Composition . . . . $
Model fees . . . . $
Miscellaneous . . . . $
Total art & mechanicals $

8. Trade deals

Type	Est. units	Amount $

Offer _____

9. Shipping

Number units	Per unit	Total $

Total copy/planning . . $
Total art direction/design . . . . $
Total premiums/refunds/coupons $
Total printing . . . . . . $
Total media support . . $
Total internal promotion . . . . . . $
Total art/mechanicals $
Total trade deals . . . . . $
Total shipping . . . . $
Out-of-pocket expenses . . . . . $
Total job . . . . . . $

Approved by: _____

and control be lost so quickly that it is imperative to establish some form of control. The same is true of time. Unless all elements of the sales promotion program come together at a central location at a predetermined time, all the investment may be wasted. Part of the reason for this difficulty in budgeting time and money in sales promotion is simply that we are dealing with such small individual elements we often don't look at the overall effect. For example, an in-pack premium costing only ¾¢ doesn't seem like much until we multiply it by 8,000,000 packages. Likewise, a delay of one-half day doesn't seem critical until we understand that the delay may force other suppliers to change their plans so that not a half-day is lost but very quickly a full day and then a week and then more. For these reasons, it is vital that we have some control over the sales promotion program, which means control over the expense and the time involved.

A Budget Control System for Expenses

The best method we have found for controlling budgeted expenses is through a form of estimating system. An illustration of a suggested form is shown in Table 16-5.

As you can see, we have attempted to cover most of the costs that occur in the development of a sales promotion program. While there may be others peculiar to your particular job or product category, the form in Table 16-5 provides for most of the necessities.

We recommend you use this form in two ways. First, use the form as a control sheet; that is, estimate what you think the various charges for each of the items to be used might be. That will give you a "ball-park" estimate of the overall cost of the sales promotion program. Second, use another form to keep track of actual costs. By comparing the two, you can see if and when one estimate is too high or too low. That gives you an idea of what is happening in the promotion as it occurs so that it is possible to make adjustments. Waiting until the job is done and then totaling up the costs does nothing to help you control costs.

We also recommend that you develop some form of cost control. If, for example, you use purchase orders, set up a file or control sheet similar to the one shown in Table 16-6 so you will know what you have authorized on that particular job. That way, you can check purchase orders against actual costs. In addition, you will know what is still to be billed against any one particular program.

A Time Control System

Perhaps as important as a monetary control system is one in which time is allocated. Unless the sales promotion manager knows where each

---

Table 16-6   Purchase Order Control Sheet

Purchase orders on Job # _____

P.O. # _____   Dated _____   Issued to _____   For $ _____

P.O. # _____   Dated _____   Issued to _____   For $ _____

P.O. # _____   Dated _____   Issued to _____   For $ _____

P.O. # _____   Dated _____   Issued to _____   For $ _____

---

piece of a sales promotion program is at any given time, he is helpless to control the outcome. Usually, sales promotion success is simply a matter of having all the parts arrive at the proper time and place.

The best method we have found for budgeting time and effort is through a flow chart system. In Table 16-7, you'll find the flow chart Diners Club International used when it introduced its new company logotype and new "Double Card" system. As you can see, each element is listed and blocked out on a calendar on a weekly basis.

Your flow charts may not be this elaborate, but the idea is the same. You have a visual picture of where everything is and when it is supposed to be done. In the case of Diners Club, separate flow charts were also developed for each individual piece in the promotion. This would include such things as time for writing, art, printing, and delivery. In some instances, some sales promotion managers have found that a weekly sales promotion flow chart is even better. That way they can follow each task on a daily basis. Whichever form you choose, we've found the flow chart is a sound idea to help you better control your sales promotion program.

Control is one of the major problems that must be solved in most sales promotion departments. If you haven't set budgets, you have no way of allocating your funds. If you don't have an idea of how to calculate the costs of various promotional programs, you have no way of determining if sales promotion is making a profit or losing money for the brand. If you have no financial controls, costs can quickly get out of hand. If you have no time controls, you are helpless to determine if and when a program will come together as planned. Controls are vital, but one word of caution: Don't let the controls run your business. Use them to help you manage. Don't use them as a crutch to explain why something didn't work.

Table 16-7   Time Flow Chart

	January					February			
Establishment program	2	9	16	23	30	6	13	20	27
1. Sales blitz—new m/e's									
2. Decal and sign placement									
3. New graphic education									
existing m/e's									

Source: Courtesy of Diners Club International.

Summary

Budgeting for sales promotion is, in many companies, a murky proposition. Where do the dollars come from? In what proportion should advertising and sales promotion share the available funds? How can budgets be established to control sales promotion expenditures? There are no easy, and perhaps no totally correct, answers.

However, budgeting must be done and it is possible to do it effectively. There are a number of methods to develop good workable budgets. Some use *guidelines* from past experience; others are based on *theoretical* econometric and marketing models. Still others develop *empirical* practices from marketplace experiments. The methods should be considered in detail.

Once a budget is set, you must maintain control over expenditures in money and time so that you can keep within the budget and still get the job done. It is a never-ending task and one of the sales promotion manager's most important ones.

17

Sales Promotion and Evaluation

While it might seem a bit odd to discuss pretesting and evaluation of sales promotion programs in the same chapter, there is a reason. Probably no two areas of the field have had more lip service and less action than these. Yet, the testing and evaluation of a sales promotion plan are vital to the successful management of the entire sales promotion program. If you don't know what you want to achieve, you really have no way of knowing whether or not your program will be successful. If you're not sure you're doing the right things, you have no way of even projecting a result. And if you don't evaluate your program, you have no way of knowing whether it was worth the cost.

If you mention testing among a group of sales promotion managers, you'll probably get a nod of agreement and a comment something like "We know we need to do it but we don't have the time, money, people, or (you fill in the blank) to do it." Perhaps that is so. But, the more basic question is, can you afford not to test? With costs constantly increasing, competition more fierce than ever, and retailers more difficult to deal with, can you really afford not to spend a few dollars in advance to help ensure the success of a program on which you may be spending thousands of dollars later? We think you must test in some form or fashion simply as good business practice.

Unfortunately, lack of testing and research isn't confined to smaller companies. It happens with the larger ones too. For example, Roger Strang of the University of Southern California conducted a study among 55 of the largest manufacturers of packaged goods marketers. He asked

Table 17-1   Research Budgets

% sales budgeted for research in:	Sales promotion	Advertising
None	20%	4%
0 to ¼ of 1%	56	27
¼ of 1% to 1%	13	50
More than 1%	11	18

Source: Roger A. Strang, from a speech given at the "Promotion Testing/Evaluation Workshop," Association of National Advertisers, New York, 1977.

them, "How much money is being spent on advertising and sales promotion research and evaluation?" The answer is shown in Table 17-1. As you can see, one fifth of the respondents budgeted no money at all for sales promotion research, and the average expenditure was a small fraction of one percent of sales. These figures are for companies whose sales promotion expenditures range up to 40 percent to 50 percent of total company promotional expenses. This is a sad situation indeed.

The same is true of evaluation. There is no way you can accurately budget unless you evaluate the results of a program. If you don't know whether or not the sales promotion program worked, what will you do the next time a problem rolls around? Also, how can you relate your expenditures to the sales and profits of the company if you don't evaluate your program? Remember, in Chapter 7 we suggested that you formulate specific sales promotion objectives. The question we suggested you ask of any sales promotion program is, did it or didn't it achieve your predetermined objectives? You can only know by evaluating the results.

Our answer to the question of pretesting and evaluation is a simple "Yes, you must test" and "Yes, you must evaluate" to be an effective sales promotion manager. The problem is, how is it done? That's what we will cover in this chapter.

What Should Be Tested?

This question can't be answered with a list or formula. Quite simply, you should test or pretest any major promotion in which substantial dollars will be invested. Obviously, you can't test every piece of point-of-purchase material in a salesman's brochure. You can, however, test those events, activities, and materials in which you plan to make a major investment.

Before we continue, a word about terminology. Often the terms testing and pretesting are used interchangeably. We do not use them in that fashion. When we say "pretest" we refer to activities that take place prior to the actual implementation of the sales promotion program or any part of it. Pretesting means showing the idea or material to a limited number of people and asking their opinion, comparing various ideas, making internal evaluations, and the like. In short, pretesting means obtaining information, but not in a market or competitive situation. Testing, on the other hand, means measuring the actual results of a sales promotion technique in the marketplace. This takes place under normal selling conditions, such as competition, pricing, and the like.

The real key to determining what should be tested is simply a matter of dollars and sense. First, find out what it will cost you to test the sales promotion program. Next, relate that to the amount you plan to invest in the promotion. Generally, this should be in a ratio not to exceed 1 to 50. In other words, if the expenditure for sales promotion material or a sales promotion program will be about $25,000, testing costs should be $500 or less. If you're relating testing cost to product sales, then a ratio of 500 to 1 is a good rule of thumb. By that, we mean if product sales for the promotion period will be approximately $250,000, you should be able to budget approximately $500 for testing the sales promotion prior to use. That is about 1/5 of 1 percent of sales. Strang's study in Table 17-1 shows how few companies invest even the minimum in testing and pretesting.

We'd suggest that all premiums be pretested, whether they are in-pack, on-pack, near-pack, free-in-the-mail, or self-liquidating. Further, all major sales promotion programs, particularly those directed to the consumer, should be pretested in some way. When we say "major" we simply mean those sales promotion programs that will affect the sales of the brand in all areas—couponing programs, direct mail plans, or refund offers. Additionally, where possible, trade promotions should be evaluated in some way. That means looking at and testing point-of-purchase materials, trade deals, trade coupons, and the like.

How to Pretest Sales Promotion Materials and Programs

The most common reasons given by sales promotion managers for not pretesting a sales promotion program or device are: (1) "We've got experience with that. We know it works," and (2) "We don't know how to pretest that sort of thing." We'll discuss the first reason here and follow that up with examples of how to pretest.

While experience is an excellent teacher, it is also somewhat limited in scope. For example, just because a sales promotion program worked once doesn't mean that it will work again. Experience simply means that you know what a particular device will do under a certain set of conditions. It is not necessarily the best possible technique you could have used then or could use under different circumstances. What you really need is experience with several devices so you can select the proper one. That's the idea of pretesting.

Everyone values experience. And no one knows better than you what has worked with your products and brands. It may be, however, that you need to expand your horizons. Get new ideas. Try new approaches. That's the benefit of pretesting as we see it.

In pretesting, we'll deal with two specific areas, the pretesting of premiums and the pretesting of other sales promotion devices and sales promotion programs. Since they are so different, they will be handled separately.

Pretesting the Premium

The idea of pretesting is to select the best possible alternative to use in your sales promotion program. In premium pretesting, the idea is to select the best possible premium for your particular product, promotion, or plan. There are several ways to go about it. First, we must emphasize that several of the pretesting methods we recommend are not really feasible for you to do alone. These are best handled through a commercial market research organization. Since such organizations have existing facilities and the experience to handle these pretesting programs, you should investigate using one of them.

Premiums may be pretested in one of two ways: (1) through consumer reactions in a pretesting situation and (2) in an actual market test. We'll discuss each approach separately.

Consumer Pretests

Consumer reaction premium pretests consist of showing consumers two or more premiums and asking their opinion as to which they would select and why. In this type of pretesting procedure several premium ideas under consideration are shown so that the best one can be determined. To aid in the evaluation the consumer is usually told the approximate cost of each premium. The pretesting may be done in one of several ways.

The focus group. A focus group is conducted by gathering at a central location 8 to 10 people who are logical prospects for the brand or product. At this meeting, which normally lasts 1½ to 2½ hours, a panel moderator shows the group several premiums that are being considered. The group may or may not be told what brand or product is considering their use. The group is then told to freely discuss the premiums—what they think of them, which ones are good, which ones aren't, and so on. The primary objective is to get the group to discuss the various alternatives in detail and to dig into the subject. In other words, interest is "focused" on the premium alternatives—thus the name of the technique. The idea is to attempt to come to a group consensus or choice of one premium from the group.

While many people believe they can conduct focus groups, only experienced people can do so correctly. The role of the moderator is to be completely impartial, keep the discussion on track, and to probe into the true feelings of the participants, not gather just surface comments. It's a tough job and an inexperienced person often has trouble with it.

To get qualitative information, a focus group is excellent. However, it doesn't provide any quantitative data, and focus group opinions may be either supported or contradicted by more comprehensive research.

Consumer groups. Often, panels of consumers are set up to evaluate premiums. The first step is to obtain permission from garden clubs, church groups, civic organizations, PTA's, and the like to have their members evaluate potential premiums. This is usually done at a regular meeting of the group, but it may also be done at a special meeting. The pretesting takes place by asking members of the group to look at the premiums being considered and then give their opinions. While this method does provide a larger group of people, the answers are not usually as detailed as those that a focus group can provide. The information is often limited to the group's preference(s) and does not include other qualitative data. A consumer group is therefore a good, inexpensive method of getting top-of-mind reaction to premium choices.

Ballots. Another method of obtaining information is through a consumer mail ballot. Usually, this consists of mailing a printed ballot to a list of consumers or to a special panel. The premiums to be judged are illustrated and some additional information is given about each one. The respondents are then asked to select the premiums they like best or to rank them in some fashion. They then return the ballot to the research organization by mail. Ballots are tabulated and the winner determined.

Ballot testing is a relatively inexpensive method of obtaining a limited amount of research information. It has the advantage of representing the premium as it might appear in advertising or promotional material. The disadvantage is that the respondents may not be typical prospects for the item. It is the pretesting method most often used by marketers.

Portfolio tests. A system similar to the ballot method is to design a portfolio of premium illustrations with brief descriptions or to develop the actual offer as it would be made. This portfolio is then shown to consumers who are asked to select their favorite.

In the portfolio test the best possible premium among those shown is determined by elimination rather than voting, simply by matching all choices against each other. Usually, portfolio tests must be conducted in person. This means that a panel must be selected or a group organized for the pretest. While it is more expensive than the ballot, the information obtained is considered more accurate.

The jury method. The jury method is actually a combination of the ballot and portfolio techniques. It simply means that a group of consumers vote on the premium they like best when presented with several choices. Juries are usually groups who evaluate the various ideas for some sort of remuneration.

The jury method can be conducted through a personal interview, by direct mail similar to a ballot, or as a direct mailing test. Since we have discussed the personal interview method and the ballot system, only the direct mail pretest will be covered.

The direct mail pretest consists of sending a postal card, brochure, or other material on a premium to be tested to a group of people. Another permium is sent to another group of consumers, and so on. Each of the premiums is offered for sale at a reduced price or at the price anticipated in the premium offer. Then, based on the number of orders received for each premium, the winner is selected. The advantage of this method is that the choice is made in a way that reflects the interest in the premium; in other words, consumers don't normally order something they don't want. Thus, their investment in a particular premium is considered a strong vote for it—much stronger than a mere choice on a ballot.

Mall intercepts. Another method of getting consumer reaction to premiums is through mall intercepts. This is done by stopping people at a shopping mall and asking them to evaluate the premiums under consideration. The test can be made in any of several ways. For example, the people might be shown the actual premiums, given a paper ballot, or handed a mock-up of the offer. Some research companies have facilities for showing film clips of the premiums as they might appear on television. In this way, both print and broadcast offers can be evaluated.

The mall intercept gives an opportunity to reach people when they are in a shopping mood and to get a wide variety of consumers. A pretest of this sort, however, is quite expensive to set up and conduct.

Market Tests

The market test is simply a test of the premium offer in the marketplace to determine consumer reaction. In other words, after the premiums are selected they are put into the same sort of retail situation they will face if they are actually used. The best one is then selected on the basis of test results.

The direct mail test listed above might be considered a market test since it asks consumers to order the premium. We do not consider it so, however. In a direct mail test, the premium is not subjected to all the various marketplace conditions of a retail test, and, often, it is not actually identified as a premium offer. In a market test, the premium is identified as a premium, used on or with the product and subjected to all the market variables.

The primary advantage of the market test is that it is realistic and usually projectable, because the test indicates how the premium will actually perform. It also gives the sales promotion manager an idea of what to expect if and when the premium is put into actual use. The major disadvantage is that it is an expensive method of testing since the complete art work, packaging, and promotional materials must be done in order to make the test. The cost of doing that for the losing premiums is obviously wasted. Further, in most market tests, the number of usable premiums is usually limited to a maximum of three. Some of the more common methods of market testing premiums are discussed below.

Store tests. Store tests are those in which the premiums are put in retail stores and the response to the offer is then measured. The premium offer is made in exactly the same way it is planned to be used. It can be an in-pack, on-pack, or near-pack offer. The key is to test exactly what you plan to do and then evaluate the results.

There are two methods of testing in stores: (1) side by side, where two or more offers are made on in-packs, on-packs, or the like and are put side by side on the shelf. The test is then to see which premium produces better product sales or which premium gets better response if it is a mail-in. Often, the premiums themselves are put on sale in the stores without any other offer. In this case, the test is based on which premium sells better out of the store. (2) The alternative method is to use a matched panel of stores with individual premiums in each. In these situations, if the stores are matched, it can be assumed that the results of the product sales are due in large part to the premium. Therefore, one premium can be selected based on the store sales achieved.

A third method is to sell the premiums in a matched panel of stores. In other words, one premium would be sold in one store, another premium in a second store, and so on. If the stores are matched evenly, the assumption is made that the premium with the greatest sales is the winner. Thus, the pulling power of the premium can be determined from these sales tests.

Newspaper or magazine split-runs. Another method that is quite accurate and highly projectable is made through a split-run offer in a publication. In this test, the premium offers are developed completely, just as they might appear. They are then inserted in a newspaper or magazine, but each offer is run in only part of the circulation of the publication. For example, if three premiums were being tested, the first third of the publication's circulation would carry premium offer #1; the second third, premium offer #2; and so on. Since all things are equal except the premium offer, the one that pulls best in terms of sales, response, or other measure is the winner.

The obvious advantage of this method is that it is measured from results in the actual marketplace. The cost, however, is quite high, since you must prepare a minimum of two premium offers and only one will likely be used.

As you can see from these alternatives, there are many ways to pretest or test premiums. The choice of method, of course, is based on what you are trying to learn. If you simply want to see which premium the consumer prefers, consumer tests are probably best. If you want to learn how the premium performs with the product and what actual product sales might result from the use of the premium alternatives, then a market test is probably a better choice. The key point is that no matter which test you use, you will have a basis for judgment and an indication of what might happen. You won't simply be shooting in the dark and saying, "I think we have a hot idea here. Let's guarantee 200,000 premiums."

In the world of premiums, since they can actually reduce sales of a product if chosen incorrectly, it seems to make a great deal of sense to test or pretest. This is particularly necessary if there is some sort of agreement that commits a large sum of money to purchase premiums in advance. We believe the cost of a pretest or test procedure is a sound investment.

Testing the Program

In addition to testing premiums, we strongly urge that you also test major sales promotional programs. By that, we mean any activity in which you will invest as much as 20 percent of your sales promotion budget, including programs directed to the trade, the consumer, or even the sales force.

Generally, the same types of pretesting and testing procedures can be used with complete promotional programs as can be used with premiums. In addition, there is a new area of promotional testing, called trade testing. We'll discuss them individually, since there are some differences.

Consumer Pretests

As with premiums, there are three basic methods for pretesting a sales promotion program or technique: focus group tests, consumer group tests, and mall intercepts.

Focus groups. The difference between using focus groups to pretest a promotion or a promotion technique and using them to pretest premiums is simply the orientation of the group. Your primary purpose in pretesting a promotion program is to see if it will generate additional sales at retail. Therefore, the key question is not whether the focus group participants like the idea but whether or not it will make them act. This is where a skilled focus group discussion leader is vital. As a marketer, you must learn the true value of your sales promotion idea and not just get the answers the participants think you want to hear. Usually the best way to do this is to have two or three ideas to present and let the group make suggestions on each. That seems to take some of the pressure off group decision making.

Consumer groups. The method previously described can be used with consumer groups. That is, groups of consumers can be used to evaluate sales promotion ideas and techniques prior to a market test. Here the information you get won't be as detailed, but you will have an opportunity to get quantitative information, which isn't available from focus groups.

The best way is to have the sales promotion idea developed along with some sample pieces of promotion material. Ask the consumers why they like it or don't like it. If you find several of them saying the same thing, chances are you're onto a solid idea.

Mall intercepts. Mall intercepts are an excellent method of pretesting a sales promotion program. The consumers are in a shopping environment and probably attuned to other sales promotion ideas they have been seeing. The intercepted consumer can particpate in a portfolio test, a jury test, or simply a concept test, in which the idea is presented with little or no back-up material. In this case, you can get quantitative but not qualitative information.

There are, of course, other methods for testing sales promotions. However, those discussed above seem to represent the most useful and most successful types.

Market Tests

After the pretest, the next step is an actual market test. That is, the promotional materials are first prepared and then tested on a small scale prior to widespread use. For major promotions, consumer pretests are usually done first. Based on the pretests, two ideas or approaches are selected for a market test. This enables the marketer to learn in the field which sales promotion approach or device will produce the best results. In addition, market tests are often used to test various levels of sales promotion spending, types of offers, coupon values, and the like.

Usually market tests consist of testing either two separate markets against each other or matching several stores in the same market against one other. In either case, the sales promotion device or program being tested is the only variable. All else is kept constant.

Test markets and test stores are used to show what can be expected from the sales promotion program or device. For example, a sales promotion manager may want to know how much more response can be expected from a coupon compared to a price reduction of the same amount. Does a trade coupon pull better than a price-pack? Will consumers respond in the same way to sampling plus a coupon as they will to a sample plus a price feature? The goal is to find out what will actually happen in the marketplace with all the extraneous variables at work.

Market testing methods for sales promotion programs are approximately the same as those used to market test premiums. They are matched store tests and matched market tests.

Matched store tests. These tests use two matched stores, or 20 or 100, depending on the needs of the sales promotion manager. The goal is to try one approach in one store or set of stores and another in another store or set of stores. Everything else should be as similar as possible; only the sales promotion technique or program is varied. Then, sales from each store or stores are measured and the results determined.

The secret to this method is to use stores that are as closely matched as possible. If they aren't and there is a big discrepancy between them, the results could be very misleading.

Matched store tests are most successful when they are used to test on-shelf or off-shelf promotion, point-of-purchase materials, pricing strategies, in-packs, on-packs, near-packs, and reusable containers. They aren't usually successful when you're trying to test various sales promotion devices that require the use of media.

The split-run technique is most effective for evaluating offers made in the media. But it doesn't work well if the offers require additional support at the store, for pricing tests and the like. You must be able to hold all things constant and vary only the media offer. The split-run test can be expensive and is not available in all markets. Thus, you may have to test in areas you don't consider ideal simply to have the facilities available.

Matched market tests. The most extensive testing procedure is to use matched markets against each other. For example, one sales promotion program might be run in Albany, New York, and another in Jacksonville, Florida. The programs could be entirely different in each of the markets or they could be similar, with only one or two items varied. For example, a couponing and sampling program might be used in Albany and a refund and trade coupon in Jacksonville. The idea is to see which delivers the best results.

In addition, varying levels of trade allowances might be used in the two markets to test that part of the program. Sometimes even the product is varied to see if a large size moves better than a smaller size. In short, matched market tests can be used to evaluate almost any type of sales promotion program or device.

Test markets are commonly used with new products. The idea is to see if the product will be successful prior to spending large sums of money to introduce it either regionally or nationally. The same can be done with sales promotion programs.

While test markets can be very successful, there are two major factors that must be recognized. (1) You must not vary so many things in a market that you can't tell what is creating the difference. For example, you should be testing only one or a maximum of two major differences in each test market. If you go beyond this, you really can't attribute the difference you may find in the markets to any one factor. (2) When you test-market, you may reveal your plans to your competition. They too can see what you are testing and how you are varying your approach. They can usually also read your test market as well as you can. While there are some simulated market tests available, there is really no successful way to overcome this problem. In spite of this, test-marketing is the only sure way to learn in advance what a sales promotion program might achieve.

Test markets are usually expensive to conduct. They also take a long time to get results. A meaningful test usually takes three to six months; 9 to 12 months is the ideal. When you include the planning and implementation time prior to the actual test and the amount of time required to gather the test results, one to two years may be required for a complete new product market test. One major manufacturer tests sales promotions the first of every year. Based on those tests, the successful programs are then used the following year. Thus, there is a two-year cycle of new sales promotion programs.

Testing of the sales promotion program in the field is vital for major programs and desirable for others. The primary questions the sales promotion manager must ask himself are: (1) What is it we want to know? and (2) What is the most effective and least expensive method of gathering that information? Usually, a test market can provide those answers.

Trade Testing

Often, sales promotion managers plan, test, and implement very exciting sales promotion events for the consumer, only to find that the trade won't accept the idea or the product or only gives partial support. This can occur for any number of reasons. The timing or pricing may be wrong, there may not be sufficient margin in the program for what the trade is being asked to do, and so on. In such cases, no one took the time to find out what the trade could or would do with the promotion. Too often, the trade is a forgotten factor until the sales promotion program is already committed. Always remember, in most sales promotion programs the cooperation of the trade can either make a so-so program highly successful or make a potentially great program a miserable failure.

It is possible to pretest and test some aspects of sales promotion programs with the trade—particularly materials that are used in-store or that rely on the retailer's cooperation to make them work. The easiest way to pretest a sales promotion program is simply to go to several key retailers or buyers and discuss the plan with them. You get immediate feedback and if you select the buyers and retailers correctly, they will give you honest answers that will help both of you. Often, they can point out ways in which you can actually strengthen the program you are planning. One way to do this is through a Feedback Council or similar group, which was discussed in Chapter 7.

An alternative to contacting the retailer directly is to use a third party. There are marketing service organizations who have strong contacts with the retail trade. They may be hired to anonymously present your ideas, approaches, or programs to the trade for their reaction. Since you are not identified, you can get a truer picture of what will actually happen than if you presented the idea yourself.

Since the trade is such an important part of sales promotion, it only makes sense to pretest your program with them prior to implementation. And it can make your job as sales promotion manager a great deal easier.

Summary: Pretesting and Testing

With all the tests and methods we have just reviewed, the question naturally arises: "Is there one best way to test or pretest sales promotion tools?" The answer is probably no. But there are some techniques that have proven successful. Charles J. Allessi made the following suggestions to an Association of National Advertisers' workshop.

> It is important to understand that there are many ways to test and evaluate promotion, and it is our job to choose the method that will give us the required information at the lowest cost.
>
> Here are some of the more basic approaches.

The objective: To build the overall business or increase volume and share. I believe that this requires full-scale test marketing to achieve a meaningful measurement of results. We need to know trade reaction, changes in distribution, actual increases in Nielsen share, changes in inventory levels and so forth, and a comparison of volume and share versus a base period and versus a control area.

Another objective: Trading consumers up to larger sizes. In this case controlled, matched panel in-store testing would be the route to go. This allows exact measurement of movement by size, avoids disruptive trade activity, for example, featuring the smaller sizes, tracks not only performance of our brand but of all competitors in the category, and, finally, gives us a very clear and precise measurement of whether or not we actually traded people up to a larger size.

Another objective: Measurement of the pure consumer appeal of a premium item. The route I would follow here is ballot testing with randomly selected direct mail lists. In most cases, this kind of testing should include a control item of known appeal for comparison. Ballot testing can, on a relatively inexpensive basis, provide us with exact information on the relative appeal of premiums, and this device is the one to use when that is our objective.

Another objective: To determine the effect of a major change in promotion strategy. Here again a full-scale test market is in order. In addition, however, I believe that detailed market research needs to be undertaken, perhaps in the form of a diary study. The reason is that we need to track the results of a change in basic promotion strategy over a period of time. Through a diary study we can isolate the change and usage habits by consumers in the category in which we are interested.

The alternative would be a series of individual research studies done at certain intervals of time after the strategy was implemented.

Next, the choice of measurement boils down to the importance of the event, previous experience, potential risks, cost alternatives, and so forth.[1]

On the preceding pages, we have briefly outlined some of the methods that can be used to pretest premiums and/or sales promotion programs. There are two primary reasons why a sales promotion program should be pretested. First, you want to select a program that has every chance of working. You want all the bugs out. Second, you pretest or test a sales promotion program to get an idea of how well it will succeed. That means you want to know approximately how many coupons will be redeemed, how many premiums will be ordered, how large a discount is required, and so on, so that you can make an accurate forecast of the results and budget accordingly.

The forecast of results leads us directly to the next stage, evaluation. As we said in Chapter 7, you must know what you think will happen with

---

1. Charles J. Allessi, from a speech given at the "Promotion Testing/Evaluation Workshop," Association of National Advertisers, New York, 1977.

a sales promotion program in order to set objectives. You must also have a method of measuring what you did in order to see if it worked. You pretest to set objectives. You evaluate to determine results and relate them to your costs. Only in that way can you maximize your sales promotion investment.

Evaluating the Sales Promotion Program

We consider the evaluation of a sales promotion program to be as important as testing. Only by knowing what a sales promotion program has accomplished can you hope to justify the time and/or expense invested. When you don't evaluate, you simply have no way of knowing whether you should spend more or less on similar programs or whether what you spent was right. Unfortunately, it seems that sales promotion is one of the few areas of marketing in which evaluation is done on a "seat-of-the-pants" basis, if at all. While some companies do measure the results of their sales promotion programs in very sophisticated ways, the great majority seem to take the "Well, we think it worked" approach.

Only a few manufacturers allocate funds for testing or evaluation research. No doubt, this is one of the major problems the sales promotion manager faces. Perhaps, in some cases, it is the first thing that should be changed.

On the following pages, we'll suggest some specific methods of measuring sales promotion results. You'll find that most of the suggestions are quite easy to set up and follow.

What to Measure

The first step in setting up an evaluation plan for sales promotion is to determine exactly what you are going to measure. Most companies evaluate on the basis of consumer response or participation: the number of premiums liquidated, the number of coupons received, or the number of samples distributed. We believe quite strongly, however, that such data are not an adequate basis for sales promotion evaluation. Here's why.

Sales promotion is, after all, a short-term incentive to *buy*. Its objective is sales—only sales. Therefore, the only valid basis for determining its failure or success is sales. And when sales promotion managers evaluate their sales promotion programs by measuring nonsales data, they are simply misevaluating. The issue is not the number of participants in the program but the actual short- and long-term benefits for the brand. As we said in Chapters 5 and 6, objectives should be measurable. More specifically, they should be measurable primarily in terms of sales in the broadest sense: units sold, dollars earned, share of market gained, and so

Table 17-2   Sales Promotion Evaluation

Measures used	% respondents
Sales units	74%
Market share	72
Sales dollars	63
Distribution level	63
Executive judgment	51
Profitability	51
Consumer panel data	28

The table shows that sales measures are most important, with profitability well down the list and consumer panels used regularly by only a minority of the respondents. A comparison with advertising evaluation measures reveals that sales promotion is very much the junior partner in the promotional program.

Source: Strang, "Promotion Testing/Evaluation Workshop."

on. Although sales can't be measured in every case, as we'll explain later, they should be the main basis for evaluation when they can be measured.

Table 17-2 shows that the leading consumer packaged goods companies tend to prefer sales and sales-related data for evaluating their sales promotion programs. Professor Roger A. Strang surveyed fifty-five of the major organizations and asked them which measures they favored. As you can see, sales and market share lead by a wide margin. Participatory data do not even appear on the list.

Nonsales data should be used as a basis for evaluation only when consumer response or participation is expected to be long-term and when sales results are hard to determine. In a continuing special event, for example, it is difficult to measure specific sales promotion results in terms of increased sales or shares. Furthermore, one of the goals of this kind of event is continuing—that is, long-term—consumer involvement. The number of people participating in the event and the amount of free publicity it receives are therefore valuable for two reasons. First, they may be the only hard information available. And, second, they are better indicators of the success of the promotion than similar data would be for more short-term programs, such as sampling and couponing.

Sources of Evaluation

Regardless of what you are measuring or what technique you are using, there are two sources of evaluation: internal and external.

Internal sources. Internal evaluation sources are records ordinarily kept by the company or organization: on sales, shipments, dealers, displays, distributors, and the like. Anything on which data is recorded and which might be affected by the sales promotion program can be used in its evaluation.

In addition, evaluations may be based on special records kept just for the sales promotion event. For example, assume that you are developing a sales promotion program to attempt to offset competitive inroads in one of your dealer territories. Although you do not gather such information on a regular basis, you might ask the sales force to survey all the dealers in their territory—first, to see how many are stocking the competitive product prior to the sales promotion program and then to see how many are stocking it after the program. Technically, the results of the survey would be internal records since they were gathered by the sales force and not by an outside contractor or organization.

External sources. External sources might include audits made by research organizations; trade or industry records; sales or share data gathered by other organizations; estimates of changes in sales or share data gathered by research groups; or estimates of changes in sales or share, stocking, distribution, etc. by companies hired for this purpose.

In many instances, companies simply don't have the manpower to gather sales promotion data. They therefore rely on outside organizations, either on a regular basis or in connection with specific promotions. Such groups can also be used to measure special products or geographic areas. We'll say more about them later in this chapter.

In addition to measuring sales, shares, and the like, external organizations are commonly used to measure the success of a sales promotion device by tabulating the number of premiums distributed, coupons returned, or sweepstakes entries submitted. This is usually done by premium fulfillment companies, coupon clearing houses, and contest and sweepstakes judging organizations. We strongly believe that all evaluation should be related as closely to actual sales as possible. In some instances, however, these organizations offer the best method of evaluating a sales promotion program.

Methods of Evaluation

Setting up an evaluation plan is quite simple if the necessary advance planning is done. Usually, any difficulty in evaluation comes about because the necessary data isn't collected before the sales promotion program is instituted. Consequently, estimates of results are not based on complete information.

Two types of sales promotion evaluations are usually done: (1) comparing sales during the promotion to sales from a previous period, and (2) comparing sales after the promotion to sales before.

Monitoring sales. The simplest but least accurate method of measuring a sales promotion is to measure the sales results during the period of the sales promotion event. For example, if an in-store display contest is being conducted from June 1 until August 1, sales results would be measured during that time and either compared to the same period the previous year, the previous two months, or average sales for that period over the past few years. Since this data is easy to measure, the evaluation can be quickly done. However, the monitoring method assumes that all sales results are from the sales promotion event, which may or may not be the case. Furthermore, it tells you nothing about what happens after the sales promotion program is over.

Malcolm A. McNiven has suggested four types of sales monitoring techniques. As you can see, each has specific advantages, and some are more effective than others.

A. *Monitoring Sales Data by Time Periods*
It's generally of little value to look at the bare sales figures and try to estimate the effects of a promotion. It does help to be able to pin down the sales data to the exact time periods that the promotion ran, so that if you can study week by week sales prior to the promotion and after the promotion and compare those changes, you can often detect the specific effect of the promotion.

B. *Monitoring Sales Data by Matched Markets*
A second way, which is a little more helpful, is to use matched cities and compare some cities where the promotion ran and some where it didn't run. This allows you to identify the effects of the promotion when most other things were comparable. Some companies have found it useful to identify sets of matched cities and to use these on a regular basis to compare the effects of promotions and other activities. In fact, this is very similar to the development of an experimental design, which we will talk more about later.

C. *Comparison of Sales Forecasts with Results*
A third method of monitoring is to compare the sales of your promoted products in a market or area to a forecast previously developed. The difference between actual and forecast is the effect of the promotion, maybe. It is possible to use statistical methods for developing quite accurate forecasts for short time periods in a specific market, based on historical data. If a specific promotional activity is over and above normal types of marketing activities that have occurred historically, then it is often possible to develop a forecast that will give you a sales level that would occur without promotional effort. If these comparisons are done for several markets or areas, one can often see a clear pattern of the effects of the promotion.

D. *Comparison of Data by Retail Chains/Stores*
A fourth method of monitoring is to use store or chain data rather than

market or area data. This is generally much more precise and allows you to detect the effects of a promotion easier.[2]

Pre-post measurement. A method of evaluation we greatly favor is the pre-post test. It takes into account not only what occurred during the actual promotion event but also the longer-term results that the sales promotion event may have generated.

Typically, the pre-post test requires that sales, shares, distribution, or whatever the criterion may be, be measured for a period of 12 weeks or so prior to the start of the same promotion event. Then, the measure is made during the actual event itself, just as we described above. Finally, a measure is made again during the 12 or so weeks after the event has been completed.

This method provides several advantages. Most important, you can determine not only what happened during the time of the sales promotion but also the changes in sales, shares, or other measures attributable to the event on a longer-term basis. For example, sales during the actual promotion period may have increased only slightly, say 2-3 percent. But they may continue at that level after the sales promotion is over. This is an important measure. It may be even more important than just the actual sales during the promotion period.

No matter what type of evaluation plan you use, it will require cooperation from several groups. For example, if you are measuring sales, you will need the help of the sales department and possibly accounting. If you plan to measure the number of displays, you will need the help of the sales force and perhaps the retailers. If you are measuring the increase in shelf-facings, you will need the assistance of the sales force to give you an accurate count. Often, all these measures are better made by outside research organizations, since they are unbiased and therefore unlikely to misreport. In any case, make sure that what you are measuring is exactly clear. State what you want to measure and how you want it measured. That always simplifies the evaluation for those who are to conduct it.

Measuring Consumer Response

When it is not possible to measure sales, shares, units, displays, and the like, another measure is often used: the measurement of consumer awareness and attitudes. While not as precise as the measurement of actual sales or other quantitative changes, it can often give you informa-

---

2. Malcolm A. McNiven, "Setting Sales Promotion Strategy," a speech given to the Association of National Advertisers West Coast Conference, Los Angeles and San Francisco, 1973.

tion on the longer-term results of sales promotion programs. While many of the measurement techniques used in measuring consumer response are only available through commercial research organizations, we will discuss them here briefly simply to acquaint you with the terms and methods.

The most common methods for measuring consumer response are telephone calls, mailed questionnaires, and personal interviews. Telephone interviews are used when the data to be gathered is rather simple, a large number of persons must be reached, and speed is required. Mailed questionnaires are used when longer questions or more information is needed and when large numbers of people have to be polled. Personal interviews are used when a face-to-face encounter is required or when the interviewer needs to ask or show something to the person in order to obtain the information. Direct mail is the least expensive method and personal interviews by far the most expensive. Most sales promotion consumer research uses telephone calls or personal interviews.

Usually, the information sought is related to changes in consumer awareness, attitude, or actions in reference to a specific company or a specific sales promotion event. For example, research may be conducted about a person's awareness of a sales promotion program. Checks might also be made to see whether or not the person has taken or plans to take advantage of the event. Measures of any changes in attitudes about the company or the product as a result of the sales promotion event can also be made. One of the common measures used is the brand bought last and the brand planned for at the next purchase.

While tests of consumer awareness and participation in sales promotion programs are not widely done, they do give a better view of the market effects of the sales promotion program than just measuring the sales results. One must always remember that even though sales promotion programs are designed to provide a short-term sales stimulus, not everyone is in the market for a given product at a given time, nor are they even likely to be reached with the sales promotion message—regardless of the media used. In spite of this, consumers may be influenced by the sales promotion program and be motivated to purchase at some time in the future. That, too, is a key measure of sales promotion success.

Outside Evaluation Organizations

Up to this point, our discussion of evaluation has dealt primarily with internal methods of measurement. It may be more important, however, particularly in the consumer products field, to consider the organizations that conduct continuing audits of sales, movement, distribution, shelvings, out-of-stocks, and other measures that indicate the situation in the marketplace. While we cannot give a complete outline of all these firms, some of the major organizations and a summary of their services follows.

Acker Retail Audits, Inc.
1200 Wall Street West
Lyndhurst, New Jersey 07071

Acker Retail Audits, Inc., specializes in all phases of in-store research with particular emphasis on trend and projectable sales audits, controlled sales experiments, distribution studies, inventory studies, product age studies, retail product purchases services, and in-store consumer intercepts.

Burgoyne Research Services
309 Vine Street
Cincinnati, Ohio 45202

Burgoyne Research Services offers five major services. (1) The Burgoyne Store Test is a completely controlled, real-world performance forecast for new products or merchandising/promotion ideas. (2) The Burgoyne Check is an in-store observation and reporting system that provides accurate, ongoing information on the retail conditions of the product or competition. (3) The Burgoyne Product Pickup is a product purchase service that delivers samples of any product, including competition, from any market, in any amount, from any type of store or warehouse. (4) The Burgoyne Store Audit is a custom retail sales study for any market, coverage area, for any length of time, which delivers product movement data. (5) Burgoyne Consumer Research provides personal or telephone consumer studies.[3]

NPD Research
9801 West Higgins Road
Rosemont, Illinois 60018

NPD Research offers four syndicated research services. (1) The CREST Report (Consumer Reports on Eating Share Trends) provides data on consumer buying habits in restaurants. (2) The Gasoline Market Index provides a continuing measurement of both the national and regional gasoline and allied products markets. (3) Textile Apparel Market Index provides a continuing measurement of the household textile, apparel, and home sewing markets. (4) The Toy Market Index provides continuing measurement of the national toy market.[4]

---

3. From folders and sales materials furnished by Burgoyne, Inc., Research for Marketing.
4. From folders and sales materials furnished by NPD Research.

A. C. Nielsen Company
Nielsen Plaza
Northbrook, Illinois 60062

Nielsen provides a wide variety of research, audit, and tracking services. They break down into six basic groups with several services in each. (1) Nielsen Retail Index System, through an auditing system, provides data on distribution, movement, pricing, inventories, out-of-stocks, advertising, competition, etc. on products sold through food, drug, and mass merchandise stores in the U.S. (2) Supplementing the Retail Index are several other services, such as the Nielsen Early Intelligence System, which provides information on potential new product areas; and Market Appraisals, which provides information on planning new market entries. (3) Test Marketing Services include: Data Market Service, real-world testing of new products; Major Market Service, direct service to any or all of 38 diversified marketing areas; and Custom Audit Service, a customized panel of test stores. (4) Nielsen Store Observation Service provides product distribution, pricing, and display information. (5) Nielsen Product Pickup Service locates, purchases, and ships retail product samples. (6) Scanning Services provides supermarket scanner information in selected local markets.[5]

Selling Areas-Marketing, Inc. (SAMI)
Time & Life Building
Rockefeller Center
New York, New York 10020

SAMI provides three major services to marketers. (1) SAMI is a report of warehouse withdrawals which shows movement of all dry grocery and household supplies, frozen food, health and beauty aids, and certain warehoused refrigerated items in 39 major markets making up 77 percent of national food sales. (2) SARDI (SAMI Retail Distribution Index) reports the retail availability of grocery products in the 39 major markets served by SAMI. (3) SAMI Scanner Services provides a complete facility for test marketing, including store and panel data.[6]

Universal Product Code Scanners

A major new research technique is now being used in many retail outlets. It is based on research information collected through the use of Universal

---

5. From folders and sales materials furnished by A. C. Nielsen Company, Northbrook, Illinois.
6. From folders and sales materials furnished by SAMI, New York, NY.

Figure 17-1   UPC Code

Product Codes and scanning devices in food and drug stores. While the information being gathered is not yet within the financial reach of many marketers, preliminary results are quite exciting.

The data come from scanners in food and drug stores, which capture and record individual sales of products by brand, size, flavor, color, and price. They also show whether any coupon or reduced price was given. All this information is recorded by a computer using the 10-number UPC code. An example is shown in Figure 17-1.

By using this code, a sales promotion manager can measure the actual effects of sales promotion activities in individual stores and chains on a day-to-day basis. For example, assume the Jones supermarket built a display for Smith products. The UPC information on sales of the product the week prior to the display and the week of the display can be compared. Assuming other things were equal, this comparison gives an accurate appraisal of the effect that the specific sales promotion device had. The same can be done for all other types of sales promotion techniques, including price-offs, in-packs, coupons, and even differing shelf prices.

As we mentioned in Chapter 4, the use of the UPC scanner will provide a mass of new information in the very near future. It will make sales promotion a much easier device to measure and evaluate and help solve many of our present problems.

A System for Evaluating Sales Promotion Ideas

The final step in managing a sales promotion program is acquiring the ability to evaluate sales promotion ideas that you generate yourself, receive from your associates, or acquire from a sales promotion or advertising agency. If you have followed the suggestions we have made in the previous chapters, you have an idea of how to identify sales promotion problems, you have a general knowledge of the various techniques with which to solve those problems, and you have some understanding of how the sales promotion function can be managed. What we haven't discussed yet is what makes a good sales promotion program and how you can distinguish good ideas from bad ones. In other words, how do you tell if a sales promotion idea is even worth testing?

Over the years, we've developed a three-step sales promotion evaluation system that seems to work quite well. While it won't guarantee the success of every sales promotion event you use it on, it is a sound, consistent, logical method of determining which sales promotion ideas and approaches have the best chance of working. At least, your chances of implementing a sure loser will be greatly reduced. We've found the system works in almost any marketing situation and for almost any type of product or service. Best of all, it's inexpensive and you can do it yourself with a pencil and paper.

Here's how it works.

Step 1

Write the objectives of the sales promotion program on paper. In other words, what is the sales promotion plan supposed to achieve? Setting down objectives may seem like a very simple step, but it's absolutely necessary. Objectives are made, not born—if you don't develop them you won't have them. And if you don't write them down you may forget them or misremember them. You need to know exactly what they are in order to plan correctly and evaluate accurately.

Therefore, the first step in the evaluation system is to write down the sales promotion objectives; i.e., to generate trial, hold current customers, fend off competition, or get distribution. Also, include the target market for the promotion—current customers, new customers, the trade.

At this point, you should also be able to state in rather specific and measurable terms exactly what the ideal sales promotion program should achieve. You should be able to say, "This promotion is designed to move 25 percent more cases than were moved in the nonpromotion period last year." Or, "We'd like to have 10,000 prospects try our product in the next six weeks." Unless you can do this, there's really no way for you to evaluate one plan against another.

Step 2

Make sure everyone involved with the product's marketing agrees with the objectives developed—that is, what the sales promotion is supposed to do. Too often, people working on the same project have totally different ideas of what the program objectives are. Sometimes, even the people developing the sales promotion plan don't have the same goals. Such a problem usually occurs when you give the sales promotion agency or even one of your assistants vague directions on what the promotion is supposed to achieve. For example, asking the agency, "Can you give us a few promotion ideas we can use with Brand X next quarter?" will usually result in a presentation of useless programs. The reason? The agency really doesn't know what you want to accomplish or why. Had you given more specific promotion objectives with the assignment, you would have greatly improved your chances of receiving usable ideas to evaluate in the beginning. It is always easier to evaluate a sales promotion suggestion against a specific set of predetermined promotion objectives than against some broad, general ideas of what either you or the person who developed the promotion program thinks the event might do.

Step 3

Once the objectives are set, the evaluation system can be implemented. This consists of a five-point checklist that can be used to evaluate any or all sales promotion plans, programs, or ideas. You may assign points to each of the five checkpoints as a means of judging promotion plans overall. For our purposes, we will assign two points to each one.

The five checkpoints in the evaluation system are as follows.

1. How good is the general idea? There are some rather basic facts about what various sales promotion techniques can and can't do, what type of response the techniques generate from consumers, and under what circumstances or market conditions each is most effective.

   For example, sampling, although often expensive, is one of the most effective ways to generate product trial. Further, experience has shown that when a coupon is added to a sample, trial often doubles or triples.

   Sweepstakes are an excellent way to build interest and get customers talking about products or services. In-pack or on-pack coupons are usually a more effective means of rewarding current users than new ones.

   Each of the 12 basic sales promotion techniques has its own advantages and disadvantages. By knowing the strengths and weaknesses of each, a sound basis for judging a promotion's effectiveness can be developed. (See Chapter 2.)

   Here's an example. AMF has used the promotional theme, "We make weekends" for several years. It literally took AMF out of the sporting goods category and into the broader category of leisure time equipment. (See Figure 17-2.)

   To build on that theme, to generate interest in the AMF line, and to make AMF synonymous with leisure sports activities, AMF chose a sweepstakes as its sales promotion technique. AMF's "Superstakes" gave the winner a chance to spend a week with a favorite sports hero. Combining a sweepstakes with a tie-in to the TV superstars competition and then building the use of AMF leisure equipment around it, draw points on our rating system. It's a great idea that was well executed.

2. How well will the sales promotion idea appeal to the target market? When the objectives for the sales promotion are established, the target market should also be described.

   For example, will the promotion be directed to consumers or the trade? Is it designed to influence current or prospective customers? Is the target market men, women, children, or all of them?

Figure 17-2   AMF Sweepstakes

Source: Don E. Schultz and William A. Robinson, "Rating Sales Promos as Easy as One, Two, Three," *Advertising Age*, Nov. 17, 1980, p. 64.

Since the target market is defined in the objectives for the promotion, it is now a simple task to look at the proposed promotion and ask, "Will this appeal to or get action from the target market?" If it won't, throw it out and begin anew. It's that simple.

If you know the target market, speak its language. Understanding how the market thinks and feels will help eliminate problems in developing sound promotional programs.

For example, Levi Strauss & Co. wanted to generate store traffic for its line, which was facing increased competition. The company's promotion technique was a sweeps that required the entrant to visit a Levi's retailer to obtain an entry blank. (See Figure 17-3.) That sounds like a fairly straightforward approach, doesn't it? The theme and structure of the sweeps is where the idea really took off, however.

"Ten chances for you to win the world at its best" was the sweeps that directly targeted the market Levi Strauss wanted to reach.

Figure 17-3   Levi Strauss Sweepstakes

Source: Schultz and Robinson, "Rating Sales Promos."

Among the 10 prizes: "The best tan—two weeks on the beaches of the Pacific. The purest white sands to highlight a perfectly bronzed body. Basted in Bali, medium rare in Maui, toasted in Tahiti, grilled on the Great Barrier Reef in Australia." Another prize: "The best bike paths—Over 200 miles of the prettiest [and flattest] cycling terrain in the world. Through the lowlands of Holland along the Rhine River in Germany. Stay at medieval castles, eat at country inns. And, ride your own new ten speed bike."

3. Does it have competitive uniqueness? That's simply developing an approach, an idea, a technique, or a concept that hasn't been used to death in the promotion arena, particularly by a major, direct competitor.

   Look what happened to the airline industry. United was the first to offer the half-price coupon to travelers and got most of the credit. But it wasn't long before American, TWA, and others jumped on the

Figure 17-4   Cracker Jack Sweepstakes

Source: Schultz and Robinson, "Rating Sales Promos."

bandwagon. Therefore, the second and third (and so on) airlines that offered coupons came off as "me too" promotion planners, not leaders.

In most cases, it seems that once a brand or product uses a specific promotion or promotional technique or offer, all the competitors duplicate or improve the offer. And often with much less success.

A good example of developing competitive uniqueness is the Cracker Jack program for its "Instant winner super surprise sweep." Cracker Jack took a standard idea, an in-pack premium that they originally helped introduce, and gave it a twist to set the pattern for other categories. Cracker Jack, known for its toy surprises, increased the value of its prizes by including Mattel toys and Mazda automobiles. This set it apart from other confectionary items. Now, that's competitive uniqueness that really stands out.

If we could, we would give Cracker Jack's more than a two rating for its competitive uniqueness with the "Instant winner sweeps" idea.

4. Presentation of the sales promotion idea. After reviewing many sales promotion programs, it's amazing how many are almost undecipherable. That is, it's difficult, if not downright impossible, to learn what the promotion is, what offer is made, or how the consumer can participate.

Most of the time, the culprit is either the "artsy craftsy" layout, the "too cute" headline, or the really oblique artwork. But sometimes it's the idea itself. It simply isn't clear, practical, or worthwhile. Sometimes it seems the artists, writers, and sales promotion people forget to communicate ideas or offers or propositions clearly and completely. Consumers shouldn't have to work to learn about the offer. In fact, they won't. There are simply too many other things to do or too many other competing messages or too little time.

A better way to judge the presentation of the promotion idea is to look at it as a consumer. Would you be able to tell what the offer is by glancing over the magazine or newspaper page? Could you understand the promotion offer if you saw it once on TV or heard it once on the radio? If you can't, then it's almost a certainty your customers can't. Remember, you already know what the offer is—you've worked with it. The consumer doesn't have that background. So, make the presentation clean, clear, and easy to understand. In this area, General Foods and Maxim, specifically, have done a fine job of getting promotional messages across clearly and completely. Maxim's offer of a free decorator jar and a 40¢ coupon is a good example. (See Figure 17-5).

The consumer knows quickly and clearly what the offer is and how to respond to it. Compare this with some of the "deco art" layouts found in many newspapers and magazines.

Maxim gets two points on our rating scale for a clear and complete presentation.

5. Cost efficiency of the sales promotion idea. The final point in sales promotion evaluation is the expected or anticipated cost efficiency of the promotion. In other words, will the promotion meet the objectives at a cost that is affordable? With today's promotion costs, this may be the most important consideration of all.

For example, there's little doubt product trial can be obtained at some price. The real question is, can it be done efficiently? You can probably get a trial for a packaged goods product at $8, but can you

Figure 17-5   Maxim Reusable Container

Source: Schultz and Robinson, "Rating Sales Promos."

do it for 80¢, 8¢ or 8/10¢? That is really the bottom line in sales promotion evaluation. What will you get for the money you invest? And will you achieve the objectives you set for the promotion?

Achieving objectives assumes that you set measurable objectives for the promotion from the beginning. If you use very loose parameters such as "improve sales" or "appeal to competitive users" as your objective, then there will be trouble in measuring results.

If you're still measuring sales promotions results on the activity of the promotion vehicle itself, such as number of sweepstakes

Figure 17-6   Johnson & Johnson Self-Liquidating Premium

Source: Schultz and Robinson, "Rating Sales Promos."

entries, number of refund coupons redeemed, or the number of premiums liquidated, you may not have a very good grip on cost efficiency.

Sales promotion is defined as "a short-term incentive to purchase a particular product or service." That definition says absolutely nothing about how many contest entries you receive, how many free premiums you distribute, or how much money you give away. It implies, "How much product did you sell, and how much return did you receive on your investment?" Brand image is fine if that's the objective, but don't trade it for sales if it doesn't meet objectives.

It is not easy to get accurate numbers or accurate sales contribution. However, an attempt should be made to evaluate every sales promotion program on the basis of the established objectives. When you are judging a promotion, ask, "What will I get back based on what I'm spending?"

Johnson & Johnson baby products developed a real knack for sales promotion programs that are not only cost efficient but sales efficient as well. Its self-liquidating offer of "The First Wonderful Year" baby book for $4.95 and proofs of purchase, tied to couponing and based on the full J&J baby product line, had to be a very cost efficient sales promotion idea. (See Figure 17-6.)

That's the rating system we use and one we believe will work for you. If you will follow the first three steps, which are vital to properly establishing the objectives for the promotion, the five-point checklist is simple and easy to implement. Does it work? Try it for yourself and see.

Summary

Testing and pretesting at one end of the sales promotion program, and evaluation at the other, are essential but often neglected elements of successful sales promotion. Testing and pretesting help assure you that you have picked the right tools to do a specific sales promotion job. Depending on your time and money budgets and the nature of the promotion, you may try any of a great variety of specific testing schemes.

In evaluating a sales promotion, you may use external research organizations or internal sales monitoring. With the advent of Universal Product Code Scanners, such monitoring is likely to become more and more efficient and useful to sales promotion managers.

A good sales promotion manager must develop some method for evaluating sales promotion ideas before they are put into use. A three-step program of setting objectives, reaching consensus with others involved, and systematically measuring the value of the idea against specific questions works well.

Appendix   I

Special Events

The special event is a special sales promotion program that usually employs a number of sales promotion techniques. That's why many sales promotion people like to run and hide when the subject comes up. Special events require careful planning and coordination. So, if you've been in the sales promotion business any length of time, you've no doubt been associated with your share of "special event disasters" or at least "flubs." The Grand Opening when the door wouldn't open. The carload sale when the carload didn't arrive. The personality who took the wrong plane and ended up 1,000 miles away from the autograph session. The 24-inch snowfall on the "day" you had been planning for six months. All these and more "horror stories" can be told about special events. In spite of these problems, however, special events are the backbone of many promotion calendars, particularly at the retail level. They're the events that continue to generate sales year after year. They're the activities that, in some cases, have become so much a part of the sales promotion planning program they aren't even considered special events any longer. They're simply methods of boosting sales and profits for the company.

We have found that, from the sales promotion management view, the real secret of a special event is simply to identify and plan for it. If the event is well conceived, has a reason for being, and is well planned, most of the headaches never occur. Usually, it's the last-minute special event that causes the real problems—for example, the decision to try to build a major sales promotion for 500 stores with only a week's notice or to slap together a Labor Day event starting on the first of August. With that sort of timing, things are certain to go wrong.

The event itself, however, is just as important as the timing. Usually, the successful sales promotion manager is the one who can spot a tie-in opportunity, develop a sales promotion program from a random suggestion, or recognize the sales promotion opportunity in a normal, everyday event. If you can do that and you know how to plan a sales promotion program, you should be successful with special events.

On the following pages, we'll take a look at special events and the sales promotion opportunities they offer. We'll also look at some successful sales promotion programs and analyze why they worked or didn't work.

Special Note: Again, we look at the sales promotion field from the view of a manager of a consumer-goods manufacturing organization. We confine our remarks to those special events that might be appropriate to his or her area of responsibility. We do not discuss retail events as such. For information on how to conduct retail special event promotions, we suggest you refer to any of the excellent retailing textbooks.

Types of Special Events

While special events may be categorized in any number of ways, we recommend the following division: (1) manufactured events, (2) seasonal events, (3) annual or continuity events, and (4) special continuity events. In each instance, there are certain inherent opportunities for sales promotion programs. Using one of these basic four types, the aggressive sales promotion manager can probably develop many new or alternative events from one basic idea. The key to success with special events is to be able to take the same situations that are available to all marketers and develop sound sales promotion programs from them. This doesn't take luck, it takes skill and talent. It takes looking beneath the surface of an anniversary, a holiday, or an event, such as a Presidential election campaign, and finding the hook on which a strong sales promotion program can be hung. We'll demonstrate what we mean.

Manufactured Events

Manufactured events are simply those everyday occurrences that sales promotion experts have turned into sales promotion special events. The basis is neither a season nor a holiday; the event is developed specifically as a sales promotion opportunity. Many of the manufactured events, such as birthday sales, anniversary sales, carload sales, and back-to-school promotions, you will recognize immediately. The secret of their success, however, is that the sales promotion manager has built the event into a selling situation or a reason to ask the consumer either to buy more of the product or to buy it at a particular time. Thus the event has the excitement, fun, and appeal that gets consumers interested and buying. Perhaps some illustrations will show what we mean.

Extravaganzas. Although this is not a text for retailers, nobody does it better than Neiman-Marcus when it comes to extravaganzas. For more than twenty years it has been staging its "Fortnights"; a recent one was "A Celebration of Britain," shown in Figure I-1, which was the 23rd in the series. This is an excellent example of a well-integrated, well-organized sales promotion event that is totally manufactured by Neiman-Marcus. There is no reason for it other than to generate excitement, publicity, and additional sales. Because it is so well planned, so well organized, and so well executed, consumers really don't look at the event as a Neiman-Marcus sales promotion to build store traffic and sales. They think only of the excitement and the new ideas the event generates. While our discussion is about manufacturer-originated events, we can learn much from retailers like Neiman-Marcus.

Traditional events. Traditional events have a reason for being or at least some historical or consumer-accepted basis for being. They include such things as grand openings, anniversaries, birthdays, historical dates, and the like. Unfortunately, many of these traditional events come across to the consumer as obvious sales promotions. They seem to shout: "We made this event up so we could try to sell you some merchandise!" But that's really not the way to do it. Traditional events and promotions of this sort can succeed, if they are done well. Part of the secret is turning the event into something the consumer rather than just the manufacturer can benefit from. In other words, slant the promotion from the consumers' side so they can say, "Here's a good reason to buy that product." That's a much more effective approach than one in which the manufacturer comes across as saying, "Here's a chance for me to sell something."

How can you stage a traditional event in a memorable way? Here are a couple of examples.

Arctic Cat wanted prospects to come to its dealers' stores at the start of the snowmobile selling season. How to get them there? An open house, of course. But not just any open house. This one had "Six Reasons to Come to Our Open House." (See Figure I-2.) And the reasons were sound ones.

Everybody has an anniversary but not everyone made it as successful as Miss Clairol haircolor. For its 25th Anniversary, Miss Clairol tied together a real "Silver Anniversary" and gave customers a reason to try Miss Clairol haircoloring. An example of the print ad they used is shown in Figure I-3.

Again, a traditional event can be successful if there's a reason for the customer to buy, not just for you to sell.

Figure I-1   Extravaganza: The Neiman-Marcus "Fortnight" Promotion

Source: Courtesy of Neiman-Marcus, Inc.

Figure I-2   Traditional Event: Arctic Cat   **Figure I-3   Traditional Event: Clairol**

Source: William A. Robinson, *100 Best Sales Promotions of 1976/7* (Chicago: Crain Books, 1977), p. 66 and p. 52.

Advertising-oriented events.   A sales promotion program that can be integrated into an advertising campaign has an extra measure of value going for it. Here, we don't simply mean that you take the sales promotion event and run a few media ads in support of it. We mean that the sales promotion plan is totally integrated into the entire promotional campaign.

Some manufacturers have had excellent success with advertising-oriented events. Unfortunately, others have had real "bombs." The key to a successful advertising-oriented event is to make it seem a natural extension of what you are or have been doing in your advertising campaign. That way, it comes across as just another extension of your overall

Figure I-4   Advertising-Oriented Event: Muriel

Source: Robinson, *100 Best Sales Promotions of 1976/7*, pp. 20-21.

theme. For example, Muriel cigars took what could have been a real problem, the selection of a new spokesperson for the brand, and turned it into a true sales promotion success when the company selected a new Miss Muriel. (See Figure I-4.) It had consumer involvement, it had excitement, and it had interest. But, most of all, it was a continuation of the Miss Muriel theme the company had been using in its advertising and sales promotion campaign for several years. It was a natural extension of this program, and it worked.

Invented holidays. Although you might think we already have more special days and holidays than work days, there always seems to be room for one more. Here, we're not considering the manufactured holidays, such as Mother's Day and Father's Day, since they already have wide acceptance. What we mean by invented holidays are Washington's birthday, Millard Fillmore's wedding anniversary, and Columbus Day, among others. These are events that, while they may have some basis in fact, have been developed by companies or organizations to give them a reason for a sales promotion event. One of the soundest ones was the Sweetest Day program developed by Fannie May Candy Shops. It had all the elements of a sound sales promotion event, including the potential to get extensive free publicity, which it did. It called attention to the product, it created consumer excitement, and it got consumer interest. It was an invented holiday that worked.

As you can see from these examples, sales promotion events can be manufactured by the marketer. But, if they are well conceived and well planned, they don't seem as manufactured as they really are. In most cases, the sales success of the activity usually goes back to the basic idea of the sales promotion event. If it's a consumer-oriented promotion and not a manufacturer-oriented event, it's usually more successful.

Natural and Seasonal Events

Natural or seasonal events are those that can be tied to established holidays or changes in the seasons. For example, there are numerous holidays, either religious or secular, that offer great sales promotion opportunities. Memorial Day and Labor Day have traditionally been big promotional times for auto tires, batteries, and liquor companies. Each company has built its own promotion around this seasonal event and made the holiday a reason to buy its product. Others are even more well recognized, such as New Year's, Thanksgiving, and July 4th.

Special days. While all manufacturers have the same opportunity with these natural or seasonal events, the most successful are those that show the greatest amount of creativity or at least create the widest possible selling opportunity for their brand. The success of a natural or seasonal sales promotion event does not depend on the event that triggers the promotion but on what you do with it. For example, almost any manufacturer can stage a Father's Day promotion. Few, however, have ever done it with the flair and imagination that Johnny Walker Black Label scotch whisky showed in its 1978 promotion. The company took a traditional event (and one that was a natural selling time for its product anyway) and turned it into one of the soundest sales promotion programs in years. The secret: taking a well-known event, an attractive premium, and consumer-oriented advertising and pulling it all together into a sound sales promotion event.

Seasonal events. Seasonal events have been done—and overdone. That's true, but it's probably the poorly planned or poorly executed sales promotion events you recall. The good ones seem to continue to make sales year after year, in spite of being repeated. They work because they have a sound selling idea behind them, not just the season.

For example, the Coca-Cola Bottlers' "Play Ball" promotion was

Figure I-5   Seasonal Event: Coca-Cola

Source: Robinson, *100 Best Sales Promotions of 1976/7*, p. 78.

more than just a summer sales promotion gimmick. It had a reason for being and a well-organized program for promoting the product. A tie-in to eight different sports guaranteed that there would be plenty of interest from all types of consumers. (See Figure I-5.) The offer of balls for games has wide appeal, and it's a natural event of the season.

Annual or Continuity Events

Many manufacturers have developed special events that take place year after year. They may be either manufactured, seasonal, or natural. But we put them in another category because they have been built up over time. We also include in this group events that occur regularly but not annually, such as Presidential elections, the Olympics, and centennials, sesquicentennials, and bicentennials.

In our opinion, the success of these annual or continuity events can again be traced back to two reasons: (1) taking a rather mundane idea and turning it into a sound sales promotion event through creativity in planning and execution, or (2) turning the event from a manufacturer's selling event into a consumer's purchasing opportunity. Some examples will illustrate what we mean.

The U.S. Bicentennial was one of the biggest national birthday anniversaries ever. There were literally thousands of promotions. Unfortunately, a great number of them were rather bad. Campbell's Soup, however, took its basic promotional program, using the Campbell's Kids, and turned it into a sound sales promotion device. Why did it work? Because Campbell's brought the Bicentennial into the promotion as a way to celebrate and remember the event rather than as an opportunity to just sell soup. That's usually the difference between a successful and an unsuccessful special event. Take a look at how Campbell's presented the idea in Figure I-6. No hoopla. No gimmicks. Just a sound premium tied to the Bicentennial idea.

In terms of annual events, probably nothing has worked like the American Dairy Association's annual promotion of "June is Dairy Month." (See Figure I-7.) From what started simply as a promotion to help reverse the decline in consumption of dairy products during the warmer months, this program has become one of the best-known and most accepted food store promotions of the entire year.

While it is not specifically an annual or continuity event, another area of sales promotion deserves mention. It's a special event directed to the trade. While most of our comments have been about consumer-type promotions, special events developed for or directed to the trade can be quite successful in achieving sales promotion goals. One that illustrates this point is the Super Bowl program developed by Eveready batteries.

Figure I-6   Continuity Event: Campbell

In this case, the company offered the same prizes to the trade as were being offered to the consumer: a trip to the Super Bowl (Figure I-8). That's the part of promotion follow-through that can make a special event a real success. Don't forget the trade when it comes to special events. They're often as important to you as the consumer. In some product categories they may be even more important.

Continuing Special Events

The final category of special events is what we call continuing special events. These are simply programs that don't fall into any of the above

Figure I-7   Annual Event: American Dairy Association

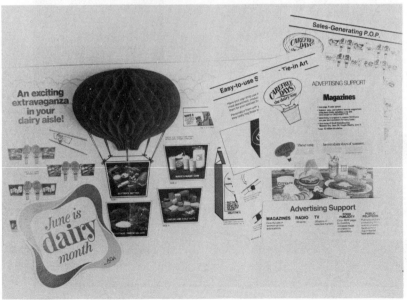

Source: Courtesy of American Dairy Association.

Figure I-8   Trade-Oriented Special Event: Eveready

Source: William A. Robinson, *100 Best Sales Promotions of 1975/6* (Chicago: Crain Books, 1976), p. 48.

categories but continue on a regular basis either annually or throughout the year. They are usually sponsored events, like Ford's "Punt, Pass, and Kick Competition" and the Avon Tennis Tournament. These are special events not specifically tied to a single selling situation or to specific in-store product activity or consumer promotion.

More and more of these continuing special events are being developed by manufacturers to build brand awareness, provide a tighter focus on the consumer target market, and create trade excitement. Here are two examples of what we call continuing special events.

The first year for the "Pitch, Hit, and Run" promotion sponsored by Thom McAn shoes in cooperation with Major League Baseball, Inc. was 1978. It had all the elements of a successful continuing special event. It involved both parents and children in an activity that was fun and exciting. It had prizes on local, regional, and national levels. It required the entrants to visit a Thom McAn outlet for an entry, it was a natural tie-in with Thom McAn Jox athletic shoes, and it was targeted to a group that is traditionally hard to reach with regular promotions, kids 9 to 12. The promotion was obviously a selling event for Thom McAn; the company wanted to sell more Jox shoes. But to the kids and their parents, the program gave them a way to show their skill and ability and the chance to win prizes. That's what we mean by consumer orientation rather than manufacturer orientation in a promotion.

Probably the most successful single sales promotion event in the history of the country, if it can truly be called a sales promotion event, is the Jerry Lewis Labor Day Telethon on behalf of the Muscular Dystrophy Association. The 1979 Labor Day event raised more than $20,000,000 for MDA research. The major question in any activity of this sort is how to take advantage of the event without turning a charitable activity into a commercial venture. 7-Eleven Stores found the answer with the "Let Jerry Keep the Change for His Kids" theme. (See Figure I-9.) It helped promote the MDA event and it got 7-Eleven Stores the publicity and public awareness they wanted without the appearance of commercialism.

As you can tell from these illustrations, special events can be used successfully as sales promotion tools. We know they can work, if they are planned and executed properly. One of the secrets is, of course, creativity in the sales promotion planning—being able to take a rather mundane event and turn it into something special. Another is the ability to turn a sales promotion program into a consumer buying event rather than a manufacturer's selling event. That's really very simple with a bit of effort. Look at the promotion from the consumer's view as a buyer rather than from your view as a seller. Finally, it takes a great deal of planning to make a special event work. When you combine these three elements,

Figure I-9   Continuing Special Event: 7-Eleven

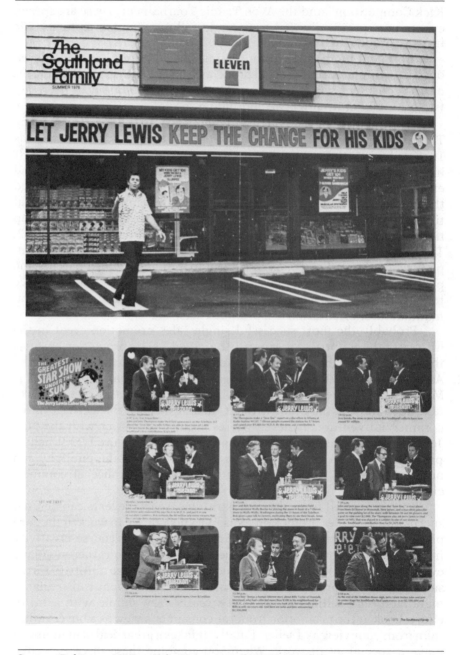

Source: Robinson, *100 Best Sales Promotions of 1976/7*, pp. 32-33.

anyone can build a successful sales promotion program around a special event. The next step is how.

Making Special Events Work

The key to successful sales promotion programs is often simply knowing the proper tools to use. On the following pages, you'll find some of the tools we've found most helpful in special events. Not all will fit the event you are planning, but they should help.

Integrating the Parts

Successful promotional programs are usually the result of a combination of advertising and sales promotion efforts. They work synergistically, as one helps the other. To do this, though, they must have the same theme and selling idea. While this might seem an obvious point, you would be surprised at the number of major advertisers who are using one theme in their advertising and another in their sales promotion program. The best they can hope to accomplish is to confuse the consumer. And the consumer probably ends up neither looking at nor responding to either of them.

Take another look at the integrated advertising and sales promotion programs for Muriel cigars, and 7-Eleven Stores that we discussed earlier in this chapter. These are excellent examples of how to tie all the special event activities together into one cohesive program. That's one of the reasons they worked.

Sales Promotion

Often it just isn't practical to tie advertising and sales promotion together to support the special event. Or, it may be that advertising isn't necessary to make the idea work. While this is a disadvantage, special events can be successfully conducted using sales promotion and very little media support. As an example, the Gillette Company's "Miss America Sweepstakes" budget was $2,600,000 for trade promotion, $725,000 for sales promotion, and only $325,000 for media, since this was primarily an in-store retail purchasing event. The emphasis was on the promotional event itself. The advertising was used only to support the "Miss America Sweepstakes" idea.

Publicity and Press Releases

While the public relations department is usually responsible for publicity and press releases, the sales promotion manager is often called on

462 Sales Promotion Management

to assist or complete the program. That's an advantage because publicity and press releases can stretch the sales promotion budget many times over, if used correctly. For example, the Borden "Home for the Holidays" promotion included recipes and information sent to food editors of major newspapers across the country. This resulted in a 206 percent increase in free publicity and food linage using the Borden name during the promotion. The same sort of publicity and media coverage was obtained by Muriel on a tour of the country to help publicize the "Election Sweepstakes." Jox shoes from Thom McAn, by planning in advance, generated widespread publicity and free mentions with the "Pitch, Hit, and Run" local and regional winners.

Don't overlook the value of free media publicity for your sales promotion event. If the promotion truly has news value, you'll usually have little difficulty getting the media to use it. The major problem often comes when you have a blatantly biased story that obviously should be paid advertising. Remember, news sources are looking for news that is of interest to their readers. But they aren't looking for ways to help you sell products. The orientation of the sales promotion program can be one way to get publicity. If your promotion is designed to help consumers buy, it stands a much better chance of being successful than if you are just trying to sell.

Personalities

Often, personalities such as movie stars, musicians, television personalities, authors, and the like can give your special event a boost. A key word of caution here, however: Make sure the personality has a reason for being involved. The mere fact that you have a famous person at an event may draw the curious, but it won't necessarily draw the buyers. Just attracting attention really isn't enough any more. You need to have the attention related to what you are trying to accomplish.

The right way to use a personality is the way Jerry Lewis is used in the 7-Eleven MDA promotion material. He has a reason for being in the promotion and he's closely tied to the MDA. That works. While not a special event, the use of A. J. Foyt, the racing driver, by Valvoline motor oil makes sense. (See Figure I-10.) He knows cars and he knows oil. What he says, people believe. He's an expert. He is a personality who fits and adds to the promotion.

Unlike Valvoline, some advertisers try to use celebrities or personalities simply because they are well known or well liked, though they have no relationship to the product. For example, John Wayne was one of the best-loved Americans of recent times, yet he proved to be a terrible spokesman for Datril. He simply didn't fit.

Figure I-10   Personalities: Valvoline

"With this free booklet and
Valvoline, you can save up to $7
on every oil and filter change.
Maybe
more!"

Valvoline

DEALER NAME & ADDRESS

Source: Robinson, *100 Best Sales Promotions of 1976/7*, p. 19.

Personalities: Use them if they fit. Avoid them if they don't. It's that simple.

Gifts and Give-Aways

A problem for every sales promotion manager is the gift or give-away. Should you or shouldn't you? Nobody seems to know for sure. Again, our position is, if the gift or giveaway fits, use it. If it doesn't, forget it. Don't feel you have to give everyone an ashtray simply because they showed up at a grand opening or a news conference. That's more a bribe than a sound use of sales promotion dollars. The Arctic Cat "Open House," described earlier in this chapter, had reduced-price gifts for people attending, but the gifts were all tied to the product in one way or another. That's the way gift-giving should be done.

Trade Sampling, Trade Shows, Exhibits, and Traveling Groups

Trade promotion is one of the most important aspects of sales promotion programs built around a special event. As we stressed in Chapter 12

(Reseller and Reselling), the trade can either make or break most sales promotion programs. Often, however, sales promotion programs are directed only at the consumer. The trade is ignored. In our opinion that's a serious mistake.

For any special event, you should build in a program for the trade. If you can use the consumer program with a few minor adjustments, fine. If not, it's worth the time, effort, and investment to presell the trade on what you plan to do. For example, Borden designed a separate brochure for retailers to show them how to use display materials. Johnny Walker Black Label had a complete program for the trade to demonstrate how its Father's Day program could help them. Involve the trade to ensure success for your sales promotion program.

Whether the program you plan calls for trade sampling, trade shows, exhibits, traveling programs, brochures, or other material, don't overlook the retailer. If your sales promotion material doesn't get put up in the stores, all your planning may have gone for naught.

Continuing Special Events

An area that is growing quite rapidly in sales promotion is what we call continuing special events. While the majority of these events have been sponsored by major corporations in the past, we see increasing opportunities for all types of marketers in this area.

We define continuing special events as programs in which marketers sponsor sports, cultural, charitable, and other events as specific marketing opportunities. These are usually a combination of sales promotion and public relations events that can get exposure for the brand's selling message, positioning, and name more efficiently than conventional paid advertising media can. These continuing special events can be used to focus in more tightly on demographic targets, create consumer good will, and stimulate trade excitement.

Right now, the biggest and fastest growing area of continuing special events is sports sponsorship. This can range from cosponsorship of a racing car to a classic national golf tournament. For example, Colgate-Palmolive has been a leader in sports sponsorship, having invested over $7 million in 1979 in golf, tennis, racquetball, and track events, excluding the cost of TV commercials. Several of these events ended in nationally televised finals, generating exposure for the brand name and products far in excess of what could have been generated by an equal amount spent on paid commercial time. Two areas in which Colgate has been particularly interested are women's sports and community youth programs. Figure I-11 illustrates the type of program the company supports: the Colgate

Figure I-11   Continuing Special Event: Colgate-Palmolive

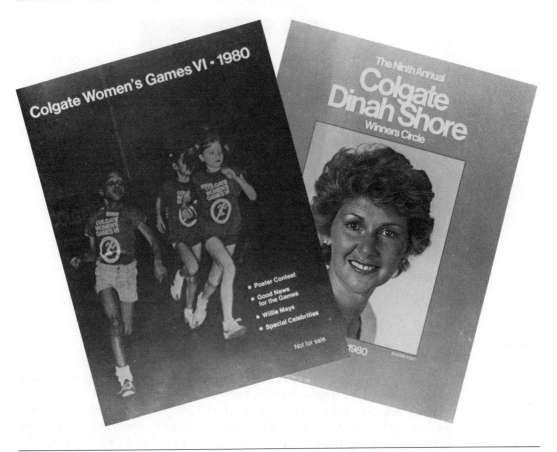

Source: Courtesy of Colgate-Palmolive Company.

Women's Games VI and the Colgate Dinah Shore Winners Circle Golf Classic.

Michelob Light's tennis program is a good example of how Anheuser-Busch has used sports sponsorships in conjunction with a wide number of marketing activities. It sponsors eight professional tennis players during the tournament season. (See Figure I-12.) Along with providing extensive publicity for the product during the tennis season, the pros also support wholesalers with personal appearances during the off-season. They sponsor collegiate tennis tournaments that reach a prime young audience as well as allow for a number of retail tie-in promotions.

Figure I-12   Continuing Special Event: Michelob

Source: Courtesy of Anheuser-Busch, Inc.

The second largest area of continuing special events is cultural. Bell Telephone, for example, has sponsored symphony orchestra tours for years. Under its American Orchestras on Tour program, AT&T provided an estimated $10,000,000 to help support tours by seven major American orchestras across the United States from 1979 to 1983. (See Figure I-13.) The program included nearly 100 concerts in 1979.

Kool cigarettes has developed a growing program of popular music festivals across the country. The Kool Super Nights, Jazz Festival, and Country on Tour were held in various cities in which the music was targeted to a particular segment of the market Kool wanted to expand, i.e., youth, Black, or rural.

In the area of charities, the top activity in the country is the Muscular Dystrophy Association's Telethon, with Jerry Lewis. 7-Eleven (discussed earlier), Brunswick Corporation, and McDonald's are also sponsors. In addition to participating in the MDA Telethon, McDonald's also sponsors Ronald McDonald Houses, places for parents to stay while their children are in the hospital. (See Figure I-14.) A number of these are operating across the U.S., located near large pediatric hospitals.

Figure I-13   Continuing Special Event: Bell Telephone

Source: Courtesy of American Telephone & Telegraph and the Bell System Orchestras on Tour.

In addition, McDonald's is starting a program in the U.S. that was quite successful in Canada, called McHappy day. Franchisees set aside one day's profits for a donation to a favorite charity.

All of these continuing special events have worked successfully and they can be adapted to your own markets. You don't have to sponsor a national event—local or regional activities can be just as profitable. There are some critical areas that you should investigate, however, before you make any decision on any sort of special event, whether it is a continuing program or not.

- Compare the cost efficiencies of the special event versus those of advertising, sales promotion, and even the sales programs you have now.

Figure I-14   Continuing Special Event: McDonald's

Source: Courtesy of Children's Oncology Service, Inc.

- Make sure the activity matches your marketing objectives.
- Make sure all possible publicity, advertising, sales promotion, and trade opportunities are explored in the special event.
- Make sure the activity matches the demographics of the brand's target market.
- Make sure you have expert administration. It takes a great deal of experience to make these special events pay off.

Special events are one of the most challenging areas for the sales promotion manager. By following our suggestions, we hope you can make special events more of a pleasure and less of a pain.

Appendix **II**

Balancing Advertising and Sales Promotion: Case Studies

Throughout this book, and especially in this chapter, we have stressed the importance of synergism in marketing. These effects, almost everyone agrees, are especially apparent in the relationship between sales promotion and advertising. One of the most important studies was conducted by Roger Strang. Strang set out to articulate what most people knew—or thought they knew—instinctively. His studies of the long-term effects of increases in brand sales promotion spending in relation to advertising are reprinted in the following pages.[1] By examining the relationship Strang has developed and analyzed, you should have a much better understanding of how advertising and sales promotion interact. You should also be able to relate that information to your own product category and brand.

Strang based his findings on five experimental studies of (1) the effect of a premium announcement in a television advertisement, (2) the relationship between advertising and point-of-purchase display, (3) the comparative effects of sampling and advertising, and (4 and 5) the inter-active effects of advertising and sales promotion for both food and non-food products. There appears to be little doubt that advertising and sales promotion together generate more results than either one used alone. The questions are, what are the conditions and what are the effects?

The first two cases deal with brands that dominated their markets.

1. Roger A. Strang, with contributions by Robert M. Prentice and Alder G. Clayton, *The Relationship Between Advertising and Promotion and Brand Strategy* (Cambridge, Mass.: Marketing Science Institute, 1975), pp. 58-74.

The final case involves a comparison of several brands that used different strategies in the same market.

The Relationship Between Advertising and Promotion and Brand Strategy

Data have been published (Darby, 1972) on two brands that completely dominate their markets, a situation where the effect of other marketing factors (e.g., competitive strategy) might be expected to be substantially reduced. [Table II-1] charts advertising, promotion, and sales histories for Lucozade (an energy drink) and Ribena (a black currant drink). Both of these brands are marketed by the Beecham Group in the United Kingdom. Neither of them have any national brand competitors, although in a very broad sense they compete against other soft drinks or against other forms of vitamin supplements. Only Ribena faces private label competition. Both brands have a long history of national advertising support.

. . . [Table II-1] shows that increases in promotion relative to advertising are accompanied by a decline in sales. On the other hand, increases in advertising relative to promotion are accompanied by an increase in sales. There are many unanswered questions relating to these data, but the relationship between sales and advertising/promotion appears to exist and to operate in both directions.

Multibrand Studies

Weber study. R. J. Weber documented the fortunes of three brands as they changed their advertising/promotion strategy over a four-year period. The market is not identified but appears to be for a frequently-purchased consumer good. The three brands are the largest selling ones, with over 55 percent of the total market. Private labels account for 18.3 percent of the market and six other national brands account for the remainder, so the three brands under study dominate the market. The data were provided by each of the companies concerned.

In 1970, the new product manager for the smallest of the three brands began a strategy of cutting back on television advertising and increasing promotion activities. His strategy was followed in varying degrees by executives in the other two companies. [Table II-2] shows the effects of this strategy change on the sales and share of the three brands. Total advertising and promotion expenditure almost doubled during the period, the proportion of this total devoted to advertising dropped from 63 percent to 22 percent, and sales barely increased. This market had previously been growing at twice the population rate.

Table II-1   Comparison of Advertising and Promotion Expenditures and Sales for Two Dominant Brands

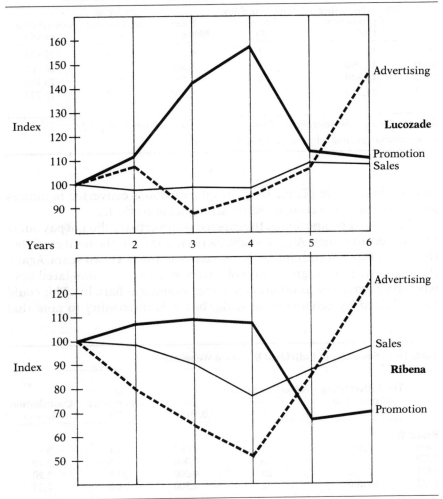

Source: Strang, *The Relationship Between Advertising and Promotion*, p. 61.

[Table II-3] gives details of the advertising/promotion expenditure patterns for each of the three brands. The largest brand maintained the highest A/P (advertising/promotion) ratio and increased both sales and market share. The smallest brand had the lowest A/P ratio and, after a short burst, lost both sales and share. In this market, increasing promotion at the expense of advertising did not provide any real long-term

Table II-2   Summary of Three-Brand Weber Market

	Total advertising and promotion ($000)	Advertising share of total (%)	Sales (000 cases)	Share of total market (%)	Contribution* ($000)
1969	12,855	63	8,200	55.5	25,851
1970	13,790	43	8,200	54.5	26,360
1971	18,640	24	8,750	56.6	23,192
1972	23,015	22	8,500	54.1	16,773

Source: Strang, *The Relationship Between Advertising and Promotion*, p. 62.
*Contribution available for net profit and overhead.

increase in sales. In [Table II-4] the information is converted to indices and ratios for easier comparison of strategies and effects.

Increasing promotion at the expense of advertising did not pay out in terms of profit either. After a slight increase one year, the total contribution of the three brands fell by 36 percent over the next two years. Again, the brand with the highest ratio of advertising to promotion fared best, while the aggressive, promotion-oriented brand was hard hit. This could be explained by economies of scale, but it is interesting to note that

Table II-3   Summary of Individual Brands in Weber Market

	Total advertising and promotion ($000)	Advertising share of total (%)	Sales (000 cases)	Share of total market (%)	Contribution ($/case)
Brand W					
1969	5,560	64	4,000	27.1	3.36
1970	5,840	60	4,000	26.5	3.70
1971	7,800	26	4,200	27.2	3.20
1972	10,800	32	4,500	28.6	2.33
Brand H					
1969	3,775	57	2,500	16.8	3.21
1970	3,750	49	2,300	15.3	3.06
1971	5,500	21	2,550	16.5	2.35
1972	6,840	16	2,600	16.4	2.02
Brand T					
1969	3,520	68	1,700	11.6	2.58
1970	4,200	29	1,900	12.7	2.38
1971	5,340	23	2,000	12.9	1.88
1972	5,375	9	1,400	9.1	0.74

Source: Strang, *The Relationship Between Advertising and Promotion*, p. 63.

Table II-4   Weber Market Brand Comparison

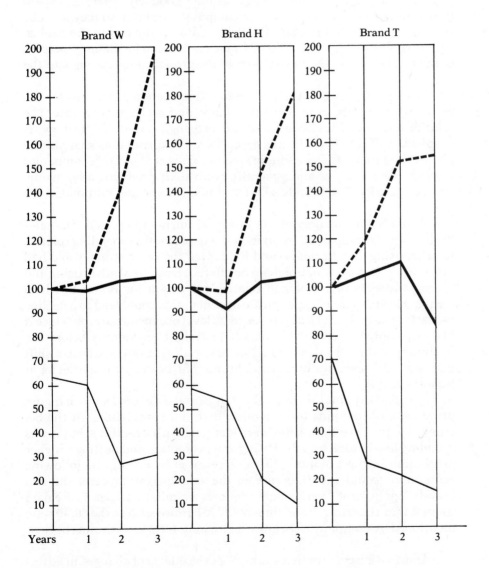

Source: Strang, *The Relationship Between Advertising and Promotion*, p. 64.

although the contribution rates of the two larger brands were relatively close at the beginning of the period, the gap widened over the following three years.

Market Alpha. A more extensive collection of unpublished data for another market ("Alpha") was made available for this study. Again, the product is a frequently purchased consumer good. However, the expenditure and profit data are based on company estimates, so they must be considered less reliable than the Weber data. At the end of the twelve-year period studied, eight national brands accounted for about 90 percent of the total market. The market was in the growth stage throughout the period.

[Table II-5] gives advertising/promotion spending patterns for the four largest brands, as well as sales, share, and profit performance. The relationship between sales and advertising/promotion strategy is graphed in [Table II-6]. In this case, share is expressed as share of the eight-brand market. These four brands are marketed by large companies with ample resources and generally equivalent products, advertising, and sales skills. The brands sold for similar prices and dominated the market.

Brand S was the only one to lose sales during the period. The sales decline was accompanied by an increase in promotion spending relative to advertising, but Brands Q and R adopted the same strategy and had sales gains. Two explanations can be offered. First, total advertising and promotion spending remained relatively constant for Brand S, which means that its share of expenditure declined; this could lead to a decline in market share. Brand P also reduced its level of expenditure, but since it had been introduced to the market just eighteen months before the beginning of the period, its reduction in spending could be seen as a shift to a "normal" level (the other three brands had been on the market for at least six years).

A second explanation might be that Brand S devoted a much higher percentage of its funds to promotion than did competitors. At the beginning of the period, its sales were identical with Brand R's, but it was spending less in total for advertising and promotion and putting a higher proportion into promotion. This difference grew during the following years, and so did the difference in the sales performance of the two brands. Again, profit performance follows a similar pattern. These data suggest that there may be a "threshold" A/P ratio (such as the 60/40 ratio mentioned by Company D) below which a long-term sales decline begins.

Andrex-Delsey. Another example of the effects of changes in advertising/promotion strategy comes from the United Kingdom. Stephen King of the J. Walter Thompson Company has described the history of

Table II-5   Summary of Individual Brands in Market Alpha

Years	Total advertising and promotion ($mm)	Advertising share of total (%)	Sales (mm cases)	Share of total market (%)	Contribution ($/case)
Brand P					
1	12.0	40	4.1	17	0.51
2	15.3	33	4.7	18	
3	14.6	38	5.3	19	
4	9.4	56	5.9	20	
5	9.7	56	5.9	19	
6	8.0	59	6.7	18	1.88
Brand Q					
1	11.4	68	6.1	25	1.68
2	9.7	70	6.8	26	
3	10.2	68	7.5	27	
4	12.0	65	8.2	28	
5	12.0	63	8.4	27	
6	15.1	59	9.4	28	2.07
Brand R					
1	8.6	66	4.3	18	1.69
2	8.5	68	5.0	19	
3	9.4	52	5.8	21	
4	10.0	62	6.4	22	
5	11.6	61	6.8	22	
6	12.8	56	7.7	23	2.09
Brand S					
1	7.0	58	4.3	18	1.67
2	6.9	65	4.3	17	
3	6.3	51	4.2	15	
4	7.6	43	4.1	14	
5	6.3	40	3.7	12	
6	6.2	34	3.6	11	1.16

Source: Strang, *The Relationship Between Advertising and Promotion*, p. 66.

two brands of toilet tissue: Andrex, marketed by Bowater-Scott, and Delsey, marketed by Kimberly-Clark. [Table II-7] shows market share and advertising expenditures for the two brands for the twelve years from 1958 through 1969. The two brands were the first to introduce soft toilet tissue, and their success attracted other manufacturers with national and private-label brands. This competition led to an increase in promotion activity directed both to the trade and to the consumer.

The data show that the two brands adopted different strategies in response to the increased competition. The Delsey strategy after 1962 was to pay for the increased promotion by cutting advertising. Andrex, on the other hand, maintained its advertising at a relatively high level and also maintained a balance with its promotion activities. The results

Table II-6   Alpha Market Brand Comparison

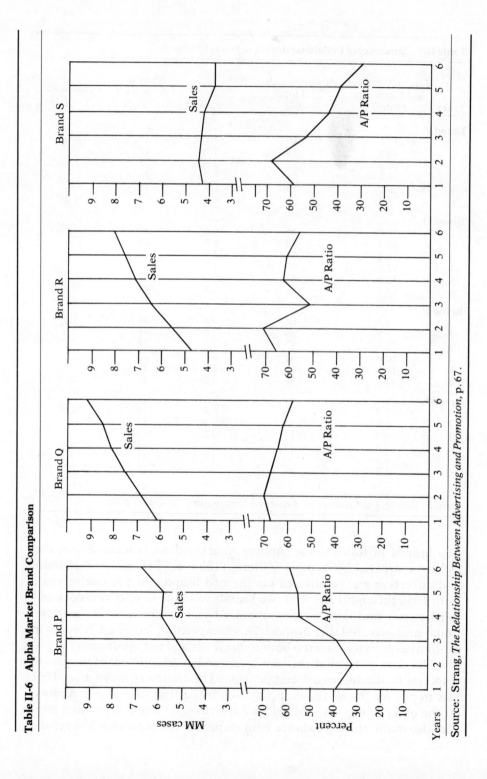

Source: Strang, *The Relationship Between Advertising and Promotion,* p. 67.

Table II-7   Advertising Expenditure and Market Share for Andrex and Delsey

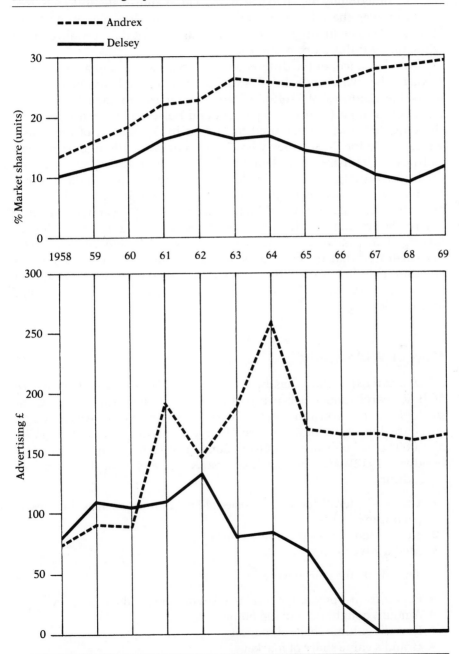

Source: Strang, *The Relationship Between Advertising and Sales Promotion*, p. 69.

of these strategies are reflected in the market shares of the two brands. Delsey immediately began to lose share, while Andrex steadily increased its share over the following years, to dominate this market. Andrex's strategy of concentrating on advertising also meant that it could expand while maintaining a premium price.

Another effect of the difference in strategy was a change in attitude towards the two brands. In 1964, the percentages of housewives attributing the qualities of "softness" and "strength" to each brand were relatively similar (Andrex, 40 percent and Delsey, 33 percent). By 1969, these qualities were attributed to Andrex by 55 percent of the housewives, while for Delsey they were 29 percent (strength) and 36 percent (softness). The increase in the favorable associations with Andrex is no doubt due both to Andrex's high level of expenditure and to the fact that it was steadily increasing its share of advertising in the total market. Nevertheless, this trend highlights another area (consumer attitudes) where the impact of advertising is believed to be greater and longer lasting than that of promotion. One study (Tuck and Harvey, 1972) demonstrated that in some cases, money-off and premium promotions can diminish the image of the brand, although another study (Hamm et al., 1969) has shown that a free sample can have a positive effect on image and attitude. . . .

Market-Wide Study

. . . One extensive study has been done in the United Kingdom, where AGB Research undertook a broad analysis of the effects of different strategies in five consumer goods markets. Their analysis was based on purchase diaries maintained over a four-year period, from 1967 to 1970, by 1,000 households in a Television Consumer Audit panel (described by Goodwin, 1972). AGB Research compared the effects of three types of expenditure:

1. Offers—generally consumer-oriented promotion, such as coupons or premiums
2. Deals—temporary price reductions
3. Media advertising

The effects measured were:

- Penetration—percent of total market buying product category
- Amount bought per buying home
- Brand's volume share of market
- Brand's value share of market

The analysis covered five different product categories: fruit squash

Table II-8   Response to Marketing Activity for Liquid Detergents

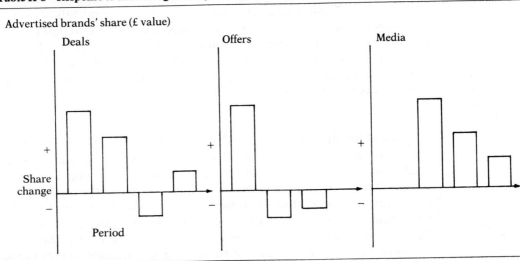

Source: Strang, *The Relationship Between Advertising and Promotion*, p. 74.

(sweetened drink), dentifrice, heavy-duty detergents, instant coffee, and liquid detergents. They found that the effects of the three types of expenditures differed from market to market, thus supporting some of the comments made by respondents in our study. Some of their other findings are described below.

Market size. In the instant coffee market, neither offer nor deal activity increased the total size of the market. Any increase in penetration or amount purchased per buyer was offset by reductions in the ensuing periods. This finding supports Peckham's analysis of Nielsen data in the U.S.A. for mature markets. In the fruit squash market, it was found that heavy price promotions actually contracted the total market. A similar effect is suggested in the Weber market, where the heavy increase in trade promotion increased sales of the three brands in the first year, but a similar increase the following year was actually accompanied by a sales decline.

Relative effect. In another mature market, liquid detergents, none of the three types of expenditures had any short-term effect on penetration or amount bought per buying household. However, they did have some effect on market share for the sponsoring brand. These effects are diagrammed in [Table II-8], which shows that both deal and offer activity increased share in the initial period but had diminishing and/or negative effects in later periods. Media expenditures had no immediate effect on share but had greater positive effect in following periods.

A similar finding was reported by Montgomery and Silk (1972) in their study of sales of a pharmaceutical product. They found that journal advertising had a more substantial and longer-lasting effect on sales than sampling by detail men or direct mail promotion. Their recommendation was that the company use the relative impact of the three approaches as a basis for allocating funds.

Brand loyalty. Analysis of the data revealed that brand loyalty to the major brands was supported by media advertising and actually eroded by promotional expenditures, particularly among the heavy buyers. Again, this supports the observations made by the executives in our study. The AGB study also found that the development of private label brands was restricted by media advertising but not by promotion. . . . In order to preserve the dynamics in marketing that favor the manufacturer, it is important for there to be an adequate level of media expenditure which is significant in relation to that below the line, i.e., promotion.

Index